y's *War Front to Store Front* is a very personal portrayal of his
itment to supporting U.S. efforts to bring peace and stability
fghanistan. Through his leadership at the Defense Department,
to improve the lives of countless Iraqis and Afghans, providing
stability, employment, and economic security, along with the
eir lives would improve. Paul's account provides solutions for
Washington's bureaucratic obstacles, and moving postwar
ward more effective reconstruction."

—Howard G. Buffett, Chairman and CEO,
Howard G. Buffett Foundation

y captures America's experience in Afghanistan and Iraq beyond
His fascinating narrative describes a Gordian knot of politics,
culture, and economic realities that confronted, and often
the best of intentions. A must-read for engagement in the
l."

cChrystal, GEN, USA (retired), Commander, International
Security Assistance Force–Afghanistan, 2009–2010

o Store Front is two intertwined tales: one, a fascinating
ow U.S. businesses can play a new and crucial role in stabi-
a's overseas conflict zones, and another, a rollicking yarn about
m of young Americans dodging bullets and bomb blasts to
eir unique mission from the Tigris River to the Hindu Kush.
"

rden, former CIA Station Chief, author of *The Black Tulip*,
and coauthor with James Risen of *The Main Enemy*

roach to foreign assistance should take a page out of *War Front*
For every culture and every country, it's about jobs and the
at this book demonstrates is that peace and prosperity need
egy. People want the dignity and stability that comes with
perity. Paul Brinkley's Task Force created economic strategies
provinces and then supported the local implementation of

those strategies. The Task Force made major contributions to the stabilization of Iraq. We need to understand the lessons learned and incorporate them into our approach to foreign assistance."

—Tom Pritzker, Chairman, Hyatt Hotels Corporation

"This is an important book. Not only does Paul Brinkley capture the bureaucratic impediments to effective civil-military efforts in conflict zones, he also demonstrates how we can become more effective in development and stability missions. The lessons are not theoretical—they are practical and the author and his team demonstrated how to apply an entrepreneurial approach to difficult problems."

—H. R. McMaster, MG, USA, author of *Dereliction of Duty: Lyndon Johnson, Robert McNamara, the Joint Chiefs of Staff, and the Lies that Led to Vietnam*

"Paul Brinkley weaves a fascinating yarn that is not one but 'five years of living dangerously' in which the real enemy was not Iraqi insurgents, Afghan Taliban, or Al Qaeda, but the U.S. government and its often inane policies that prevented us from winning the conflicts in Afghanistan and Iraq. This is a must-read, whether for those who crave a good tale of true adventure or policy wonks wishing to understand the vagaries of American decision making."

—Harlan Ullman, Chairman of the Killowen Group, Senior Adviser at the Atlantic Council, principal creator of the military strategy of "shock and awe"

"Paul Brinkley's commonsense approach to rebuilding Iraqi business and industry to provide jobs, incomes, and goods to meet the country's needs, and to drain insurgencies of manpower and motive, is one of the most significant civilian efforts ever undertaken during warfare. Mr. Brinkley's brave and relentless engagement of U.S. military and civilian leaders and of Iraqis and Afghans at every level of government and industry—from farms, villages, and the front lines of battle to the U.S. Capitol, give him a breadth of knowledge and perspective like no leader in Operation Iraqi Freedom or Enduring Freedom/Afghanistan. His is an essential record to be read, debated, and relied upon by military and development specialists for decades to come."

—Edwin Price, Professor of Agriculture and Founding Director, Norman Borlaug Institute for International Agriculture, Texas A&M University

"Paul Brinkley provides a compelling and highly readable assessment of Afghanistan from an economic and a political perspective, and America's shortcomings in trying to build a stable Afghan state, based on his experiences throughout the country. I highly recommend this to policymakers as the transition of Afghanistan from military engagement to long-term development takes place in the next several years."

—Daud Saba, Ph.D, Governor, Herat Province, Afghanistan

"*War Front to Store Front* is a reflective documentation from a unique prospective on a seminal era of American foreign policy that will or should influence all military interventions in the future."

—Graham Head, President and Vice Chairman, ABC Carpet & Home, New York

WAR FRONT TO STORE FRONT

Bill –

Thank you for all
of your service &
support to our country!

[signature] Feb 2014

PAUL BRINKLEY

WAR FRONT TO STORE FRONT

AMERICANS REBUILDING
TRUST AND HOPE IN
NATIONS UNDER FIRE

WILEY

Turner Publishing Company / Wiley General Trade

424 Church Street • Suite 2240 • Nashville, Tennessee 37219

445 Park Avenue • 9th Floor • New York, NY 10022

www.turnerpublishing.com

War Front to Store Front: Americans Rebuilding Trust and Hope in Nations Under Fire

Cover design: Doug Stern

Book design: Glen Edelstein

Photographs: Tina Hager

Library of Congress Cataloging-in-Publication Data

Brinkley, Paul.
  War front to store front : Americans rebuilding trust and hope in nations under fire / Paul Brinkley.
      pages cm
  ISBN 978-1-118-23922-3 (hardback)
  1. Economic assistance, American--Middle East. 2. Economic assistance, American--Africa.
  3. Economic development--Middle East. 4. Economic development--Africa. I. Title.
  HC415.B75 2014
  338.91'73056--dc23
                                        2013040724

Printed in the United States of America

14 15 16 17 18 0 9 8 7 6 5 4 3 2 1

Dedicated with love to Cindy, Jack, and Lindsey

*In memory of Sgt. Michael C. O'Neill, 3rd Battalion,
75th Ranger Regiment, 21 November 2004*

CONTENTS

	PROLOGUE	1
1.	NEW RECRUIT	9
2.	A GENERAL'S CALL	31
3.	STATE OF CONFUSION	61
4.	PRESSURIZATION	81
5.	BUILDING MOMENTUM	107
6.	DARK DAYS	125
7.	THE BUSINESS OF DIPLOMACY	147
8.	OUR BEST YEAR YET	171
9.	OUT OF AFRICA	201
10.	INTO AFGHANISTAN	207
11.	LAND OF THE PURE	231
12.	BLACK HORROR	241
13.	UPON FURTHER REVIEW	253

14. CHECKMATE   281

15. FIXING THE SYSTEM   307

     EPILOGUE   327

     ACKNOWLEDGMENTS   335

     APPENDIX A: PRINCIPLE CONTRIBUTORS, 2006–2011   339

     APPENDIX B: MAJOR PROJECT DESCRIPTIONS: IRAQ AND

        AFGHANISTAN, 2006–2011   345

     NOTES   367

     INDEX   369

PROLOGUE

As a nation, we take great pride in our military. The stirring advertisements that blanket our weekend sports broadcasts, recruiting young men and women to join our all-volunteer force, reinforce the honor and respect we convey to our military personnel. Movies, television programs, and popular literature reflect the position of the military as the one element of our government capable of excellent performance in its mission.

This unique position held by the military extends to nontraditional challenges. From hurricanes to earthquakes to oil spills, we are only certain a disaster is being taken seriously when a senior military commander is placed in charge—only then do we breathe easier with confidence that somebody competent is on the job.

Our civilian institutions are, too often, another story entirely.

"The best minds are not in government. If any were, business would steal them away."

President Ronald Reagan's sentiment as expressed in the 1980s is widely held today. Since the 1970s, every administration, Republican and Democratic, has at some point berated the federal bureaucracy as at best inefficient, and at worst incompetent.

As civilian government institutions have fallen in both performance and in public esteem, the word bureaucrat has too often become an epithet. This negative view of government service generates a self-fulfilling spiral of continual decline in government capabilities. Given the grim reputation of the federal bureaucracy, our government workforce does not generally attract our best and brightest citizens, and so it continues to fall further and further behind our private institutions in its ability to execute its tasks. In this continual decline lies the foundation of a problem that threatens every aspect of our national well-being, including our foreign policy and our foreign assistance programs.

To most Americans, foreign assistance—money donated to relieve suffering in poor countries—receives little attention. Once in a while, at times of budgetary conflict in Washington, politicians will attack overseas aid spending as a waste of money in comparison to pressing needs here at home, generating a few headlines but not much else in terms of debate. The structure and purpose of our foreign assistance system receives minimal attention outside of the halls of power in Washington.

The system was developed during the Cold War, with a focus on humanitarian aid—the provision of clean water, food, electricity, and medical care—to impoverished peoples as a sign of American goodwill. While these basic needs remain challenges in many parts of the world, in other nations that receive U.S. assistance, populations have developed higher expectations. Humanitarian aid is not necessarily what is wanted, or needed. In an era of satellite televisions, where even mud huts in impoverished areas often have a satellite dish, the poor are demanding access to economic opportunity—something they see once-impoverished nations across Asia and Africa achieving.

Ironically, the United States—the nation that developed and champions the very economic principles that create prosperity in so many once-troubled countries, has limited ability to extend its most important element of power—its economic dynamism—to the troubled nations of the world. Our foreign assistance system is incapable of delivering economic-development support to populations seeking to move up on the hierarchy of needs from subsistence to prosperity. Foreign assistance should seek to enable nations to provide for their own needs rather than continually depending upon foreign charity.

"You are going to be the proud owner of 25 million people. You will own all their hopes, aspirations, and problems. You'll own it all."

In stating his now-famous "Pottery Barn Rule"—*you break it you own it*—on the eve of the launch of the U.S. invasion of Iraq, Secretary of State Colin Powell seemed to see what too few civilian appointees in the early George W. Bush administration understood—that once the shooting stopped, our government would be responsible for rebuilding a nation brutalized by decades of war and economic sanctions. But Iraqis didn't expect just new roads and schools, they expected help achieving a version of the so-called "American Dream." Iraqis wanted economic prosperity—a foundation upon which stable institutions could be built. Who did we send in to help them? Well-intentioned government bureaucrats and young volunteers lacking experience and knowledge in building a vibrant private-sector economy.

That the United States, a nation with so little public confidence in its federal institutions' basic competence, could believe that this same government has the ability to restore shattered Middle Eastern societies has proven a remarkable, and ill-advised, leap of faith.

From North Africa to Afghanistan, from large countries like Egypt and Pakistan to small nations such as Yemen, unemployment and lack of prospects for a better life define daily existence for millions of restive young people, in spite of massive amounts of aid funding channeled from U.S. taxpayers, and endless promises from traveling U.S. politicians that Americans would help them create a better life.

While we may hold our civilian bureaucracy in relatively low regard here at home, we have had no problem continually channeling billions of dollars to civilian agencies working overseas to provide postconflict economic development. Those institutions have too little to show for their efforts—leaving military force as our only effective tool of foreign policy, with an outcome of lost American lives, broken societies with disaffected embittered populations, and untold financial debt here at home that will burden future generations for years to come.

✳ ✳

It doesn't have to be this way.

The greatest element of American power, our private-sector economic dynamism, has largely remained untapped during the past decade of conflict following September 11, 2001. Yet this economic dynamism can be a powerful instrument of foreign policy, if institutions capable of leveraging this capability to create opportunity in the developing world are established.

This book is the unlikely story of a group of business leaders who encountered the civilian federal bureaucracy at war, when they were asked to step in and reverse a failing American postcombat economic policy in Iraq. While first focused on restoring employment to Iraq's workforce, and reducing the sympathies of everyday Iraqis with a growing insurgency and ever-increasing violence, we encountered the federal bureaucracy at its most intransigent, in a journey that would go on for five long years, and expand to encompass efforts in Afghanistan, Pakistan, Sudan, and Rwanda.

Eventually reporting directly to Secretary of Defense Robert Gates, this unorthodox team would grow to include hundreds of men and women operating outside of the restrictive security imposed on other American civilian organizations, embedded with our military forces in areas of open armed conflict, and eventually independently working in conflict zones.

Before our work would be complete, we would witness the horror of war, and the courage of our armed forces struggling to restore stability to communities falling into open conflict among religious sects and tribes in the absence of hope for a better future.

We would personally experience violence and the continual direct threat of violence, and the loss of team members to insurgent attacks.

We would lose ourselves in a mission that consumed our lives, living and working together for years as we learned, through hard-earned experience, how to restore normal life to war-ravaged communities, how to build links to the outside world for local businessmen, and how to begin to provide the one thing frustrated citizens we engaged wanted most: access to prosperity.

We would create hundreds of new enterprises, restore employment to hundreds of thousands, and facilitate foreign investment of billions of dollars, in places written off as impossible to engage by the civilian bureaucracy.

We developed a doctrine and a methodology for how to revolutionize our foreign assistance to provide this access to the troubled countries of the world, at a fraction of the cost of traditional foreign aid programs, leveraging America's strength—its private sector.

This is our story.

WAR FRONT TO STORE FRONT

1.

NEW RECRUIT

I was leaving California.

    For the last several years, I had enjoyed, then endured, a front-row seat in one of the most remarkable business stories of the twentieth century: the rise and collapse of the communications networking industry.

    JDS Uniphase was a remarkable conglomeration of the elements of the communications network we take for granted every day. Whenever we surf the Internet, place a phone call, download a song or movie, pay a bill, or send an e-mail, we pass information that relies on the products of JDS Uniphase. Specifically, JDS Uniphase manufactures the lasers and components that enable light to be carved into its elemental colors (or channels), to transmit digital signals across those channels at speeds enabling billions of bits per second of data to flow through fiber-optic cable.

    I joined JDS Uniphase when its revenue had only recently crested $1 billion a year. By the time the Internet bubble burst in 2001 we were running at almost $4 billion a year.[1] As the company's stock grew, its acquisitions became more and more grand, culminating in the largest corporate acquisition in history (at the time) of SDL Incorporated, a complementary optical technology company. Using our stock as an incentive, we had been able to hire anyone we wanted, poaching top talent from world-class companies across industries.

We put in place standard accounting, human-resource management, engineering, and production systems that were deployed in all of our factories, enabling an order to be booked in our Ottawa, Canada, customer service center for a custom-designed technical device, and to ship that device a day later from a factory in China. It was a remarkably tuned supply chain with real-time access to information on all aspects of company operations at the fingertips of management. I had spent my career working in laboratories and factory operations throughout the world, operations that manufactured some of the world's most complex technology. JDS Uniphase was the ultimate realization of a modern optimized supply chain, linking manufacturing to demand with a minimum of wasted time and money.

At the peak of the Internet boom, the sky truly seemed to be the limit for us. Silicon Valley was experiencing an economic boom unlike anything anyone had ever seen: the network technology boom was accompanied by the dot-com boom and bubble. Almost as quickly as the networking sector rose, it collapsed.

By early 2001, I was running all of the customer-facing operations of JDS Uniphase, including customer service and inside sales (call center sales force) functions. The company was building factories dedicated to specific customers who continued to forecast near-limitless demand for highly complex components. Almost in unison, major customers began canceling orders en masse. Our backlog evaporated overnight. I recall sitting with supply managers from major companies who were canceling tens or hundreds of millions of dollars in orders, requesting compensation for our losses, only to be told we were out of luck.

In less than 90 days, revenue for optical components and subsystems used in optical fiber networks around the world dropped by more than 80 percent. The stock price collapsed. Stock options that had made many of us multimillionaires on paper were now worthless. Unlike many of the "darlings" of the dot-com world, however, JDS Uniphase was a company built on the physics and engineering of exotic high-tech materials, with far-flung research and development labs of scientists with co-located factories. For a high-tech hardware business to experience such a complete reversal of product demand was unprecedented.

The company immediately shifted from rampant growth into desperate survival mode. Over the next two years, as demand continued to fall, JDS Uniphase consolidated and collapsed its operations and research and development staff at an unprecedented pace. By 2003, the company had reduced its factory base from more than 40 operations to just 13 factories, and had consolidated most of its low-end manufacturing to newly established operations in Shenzhen and Fuzhou, China.

As part of my role, along with the rest of the executive leadership team, I had spent a lot of time shutting down operations and laying off workers. People who had been exuberantly engaged in growing a great enterprise one day were told weeks later they were out of a job. I laid off many people who would break down, beg for an explanation, literally plead with me to reconsider, as if I had made these decisions personally. I would try to explain that it was not personal. Too often, the person was one of the best people I had worked with in my career, but the financials simply wouldn't allow the company to keep its workforce intact.

I personally laid off more than 100 executives, senior managers, and professionals in a two-year period. Those 100-plus people will never forgive me. There is no sugarcoating it—we had moved American jobs to China in order to enable the company to compete in an industry where manufacturing costs were collapsing.

JDS Uniphase survived, a miracle of management leadership by the different executives I worked with and learned from, who had led the company through a period of rampant growth and then a terrible downturn, and had built a company capable of surviving anything. By late 2003, it was clear that now the company faced a long period of slow growth as the network communications industry began its gradual return to health. Several colleagues and I had a compelling idea for a technology start-up, and after a series of meetings on nights and weekends, we had a business plan and initial funding committed to get a new venture off the ground. For the first time in almost three years, I was getting positively energized about something again.

I then received a phone call that would change everything.

Scott Uhrig, an executive recruiter from Austin, Texas, reached out on behalf of a colleague at the Pentagon. Brad Berkson, responsible for overseeing logistics and material management for the Department of Defense, wanted to talk to me about our supply chain work at JDS Uniphase and similar challenges at the Department. I was intrigued. Our work at JDSU had been world-class, but because of the collapse in business had never received much attention. The opportunity to talk to someone in government, especially the military, sounded interesting. Maybe our work at JDSU could provide some lessons that would benefit the Defense Department.

After a lengthy first phone conversation, Berkson indicated that he wanted me to consider working for the Defense Department. I wasn't particularly interested, but decided to visit Washington. At the very least I wanted to see the Pentagon, so I took a few days of vacation and went to meet Berkson.

When it comes to "home-field advantage" for recruiting a new hire, the Pentagon is hard to beat. To walk halls walked by Marshall, Eisenhower, and Bradley, was awe-inspiring. The Pentagon made the work I had done in my past, work that I had been so proud of, seem small in comparison. Berkson had a compelling vision for improving defense logistics. He introduced me to many of his colleagues, most of whom had left industry to serve the country. They were an impressive group.

The job being offered was remarkable as well. I was asked to oversee the modernization of logistics and supply chain management for the Defense Department, the largest enterprise on earth, a good four times larger than the largest corporation at the time, IBM. Berkson explained the scale of the opportunity was unlike anything I would ever encounter, and how the work would have meaning I could never find in the private sector. How I could make a difference at a critical time in our nation's history.

I was sold.

I returned to California on a mission. I would move my family to Washington and serve my country. After guilt-ridden years of laying off Americans and moving jobs overseas, I realized that the opportunity for atonement was no small part of my motivation.

＊　＊

I assembled the team of colleagues I was planning to launch a start-up with, and told them the news. They were shocked; what made so much sense to me made no sense to them. How could I possibly walk away from starting my own firm? We were convinced we had a sure thing, but I was unflappable in my commitment to join the Department of Defense.

What ensued was a harbinger of things to come. From the time I told Berkson I would make the leap to join the Department of Defense, six months would pass before I received a firm offer of employment. I was being hired under a new authority granted by Congress to the Defense Department enabling the hiring of senior executives and "highly qualified experts" from the private sector at the highest grades of federal pay scales. In spite of this authority, compensation was shockingly low. The highest executive pay the Pentagon could offer was almost 70 percent less than I earned in my last year at JDSU. But for me, this was not about money, it was an opportunity to serve. While I waited for a formal offer, I continually engaged with Brad indicating my interest. I accepted the offer when it finally arrived.

I arrived at the Pentagon on the morning of August 2, my first day, to bad news. The Undersecretary of Defense for Personnel, Dr. David Chu, had issued binding policy about the hiring of highly qualified expert appointees within the Department of Defense. In this policy, Chu stripped the appointments of all executive authority, basically making the positions into essentially highly paid advisors.[2] No management decision making, direct management of federal employees, or executive oversight of government programs was to be permitted.

Chu took this step under pressure from the federal government's Senior Executive Service (SES) Association, an organization that advocates for the highest-paid civilian employees in the federal government. The SES Association felt the new senior hiring provisions passed by Congress threatened the traditional senior executive hiring process of the federal bureaucracy, which limits executive positions to internal government candidates, and had lobbied for the restrictive policy with Chu's senior staff.

Berkson informed me that as a result of this decision, and since I could not be placed into direct management authority, I would be denied an office in the Pentagon.

I had uprooted my family, sold my home, and sent all of our personal belongings across the country under a relocation program designed for new recruits. I had derailed my career and taken a massive pay reduction, only to arrive in D.C. to find my position had been stripped of any meaningful authority.

Moving into a cubicle in an adjacent complex of office towers near the Pentagon, fury collapsed into despondence. I talked to my wife, Cindy, at length. Together we decided to reconsider the whole decision, reverse course, and go back home to California. We would need a few weeks for our belongings to arrive, and then to arrange to move everything back home.

I explained my frustrations to Berkson, who asked me to do one thing before I threw in the towel: accompany him to Afghanistan. He was overdue to visit Afghanistan and review logistics operations there. I decided to go with him. At least I would see something during my short tenure in the Department.

✳   ✳

The Hindu Kush mountains surrounding the valley where Bagram Air Base is located are majestic, snowcapped peaks, and the elevation of 6,000 feet made the air thin and crisp. A former Soviet air base, the compound was completely surrounded by fenced areas indicating the presence of land mines left over from the 1980s, when Afghan Mujahadeen had fought to overthrow the Red Army occupation.

The base was next to a small village, and the local Afghans worked on the base. There was no tension present among them; all were friendly to a fault. Interestingly, there was no common "look" to the Afghans; their features ranged from faces I had seen in the subcontinent to east Asia to Europe.

Berkson was in his element walking among supply depots and storage yards, surveying operations. He knew the language of military logistics, knew what to ask. A former consultant with McKinsey & Co., Berkson had great instincts for quickly assessing a distribution or logistics operation and providing quick feedback on how to improve performance. After dinner with the base commander at the dining facility, we retired for the evening. We were given bunks in plywood structures that served as housing for visitors. Everything went well. But lying there that night, listening to the constant roar of F-15 jet fighters departing on missions, my resolve to go home to California returned. I had made a huge mistake; I didn't belong here. I like to build operations or organizations, not offer advice. If I couldn't be given authority, I had to go.

The trip to Afghanistan had only increased my resolve to move on.

At two A.M., I was awakened by a colleague shaking my arm. "Our flight has been moved up due to an emergency. We are wheels-up at 0300. Pack out, we have to go." I scrambled to get dressed and haul my gear outside. Our C-17 flight back to Ramstein Air Force Base in Germany had been pulled in: a soldier in a Ranger unit had been critically wounded and had to be evacuated to surgical facilities in Landstuhl, Germany. Our flight would serve as his medevac transport.

We boarded the aircraft first, and I took a canvas jump seat near the front of the plane. As I sat and arranged my bags for the long flight, hoping for some rest, a crew entered the aircraft carrying a variety of medical devices and equipment. They began plugging devices into the side of the fuselage of the C-17, a gurney rack, IV bottle holders, all sorts of monitoring devices. This took place directly in front of me, perhaps 10 feet away from my position facing the fuselage of the plane.

Once the gear was in place, two medical corpsmen carried the wounded soldier to the front of the plane, and connected his gurney to the rack that would hold him in place for the flight to Germany. Severely wounded, with blood soaked gauze bandages on his head and body, his condition was grave.

Suddenly a new figure entered the scene. A lean army doctor with a shock of grey hair approached, dressed in a jumpsuit—like the flight suits I saw the pilots wearing. The crew helped him get into a harness—a four-point restraint system with straps that connected to the roof and floor of the aircraft. This would hold him in place in the event of turbulence while he was caring for the soldier.

Shortly after the doctor was in place, we departed for Germany.

For eight hours I watched transfixed as this young soldier fought for his life. The doctor and nurses never left his side. The doctor was not a young man. He had to be at least fifty, and while he was lean and fit, by the time we landed, he must have been exhausted.

This doctor, I realized, could have been anywhere. He could have been living the comfortable life of a family practitioner. He could have been giving Botox injections and performing plastic surgery and making millions.

But he wasn't any of those things.

He had chosen to serve.

I was shaken to the core of my being.

For all my petty outrages, what in my life did I truly have to complain about?

I would not be returning to California.

✻   ✻

The Department of Defense is by far the world's largest industrial enterprise. Within its budget are the equivalent of multiple airlines, shipping companies, Walmart-scale distribution operations, technology centers, research and development laboratories, and factory depots capable of vertically integrated manufacturing and repair of any equipment used by our uniformed military.[3]

It is an awesome organization, capable of projecting force, and the material to support the projection of force, anywhere in the world. Unlike private-sector industry, however, the Department does not exist to generate financial profit from its business operations. Its business operations exist to support soldiers, sailors, airmen, and marines in their critical national security missions.

This difference in mission renders the standard management models used in the private sector limited in their application in the Department. While there are many things the private sector does that can be applied in defense industry, at the core of the business model is a fundamental conflict. Private business is about balancing risk against profitability. Miss that balancing act in the business world, and you may miss your profit target. Miss that balancing act enough in the private sector and your stock price falls, and you are out of a job.

In the DOD, business operations must balance risk against loss of life. Fail to have the necessary material or capacity when or where it is needed, given the budget provided by the Congress, and the lives of uniformed personnel, and possibly, national security, are at stake.

This extreme imbalance between risk and negative reward in the Defense Department makes change very, very difficult. The business operations of the Defense Department, for all of their perceived inefficiencies, have enabled our military to successfully execute missions of great difficulty in the past several decades. Resistance to change is supported by the perception that the current way works—and by another risk equation—"do you want to be the guy that breaks it?"

The Department's overall industrial enterprise is a loose and inefficient confederation of independent sub-enterprises—the military Departments of the Army, Navy (which includes the Navy and Marine Corps), and Air Force. Financially, each military department has an annual budget ranging from $150 billion to almost $250 billion per year, making each military department as large as the largest multinational corporations.

Over the years the Department has centralized some key functions. The Defense Logistics Agency was established in 1961 to consolidate the management of common supplies across all military services. Fuel, food, basic parts and supplies, housing material, and other commodities are centrally managed by the DLA. It has an annual budget of approximately $50 billion, making it one of the largest supply-chain management organizations in the world on its own merits.

The Defense Finance and Accounting Service, established in 1991, provides central financial transaction management for all of the Department of Defense. Supplier payments, payroll, and other common financial transactions are centrally managed by this organization.

Generally, the centralization of any activity is resisted by Military Departments—it is not uncommon for functions that are officially centralized by the creation of an agency or office to live on within a Military Department, sometimes for years, sometimes forever.

In this respect, the Department of Defense is a lot like a huge multinational holding company comprised of autonomous divisions. Think General Motors in its heyday, or General Electric today. A large conglomerate of businesses that have some things in common, but many things that are unique, and where each division is given great leeway to runs its affairs as long as it is profitable. A great division of a conglomerate company wants to be left alone—it generally doesn't want help from the corporate headquarters. So it is with the Military Departments and their relationship with the Office of the Secretary of Defense.

Unlike a big multinational corporation, the Department has no strong central leadership, both by design and in practical reality.

Although it reports to the president, the Department primarily answers to Congress, which sets its budget, oversees its major expenditures (and increasingly its minor expenditures) on weapon systems (and the jobs these programs create back home in congressional districts), and approves via Senate confirmation the appointment of its most senior political leaders who are selected by the president.

So at its top level, management of the Defense Department is vastly different from a corporation. Its chief executive (the Secretary of Defense) and his leadership team often don't know each other well, and sometimes act more accountable to the president—even if organizationally they report to the Secretary. They may, or may not, be qualified for their respective roles. Their tenure is short relative to the scale of their responsibilities.

In addition, management in any organization depends on the ability to offer incentives to the workforce, to reward outstanding performance, and to motivate nonperformers, either through positive incentives or if necessary by replacing them. The federal personnel management process essentially offers no such incentives. I had directly experienced the archaic hiring process, which made hiring external talent into government almost impossible.

But once within the government, I found that the ability to reward outstanding performance through basic management tools such as incentive compensation, annual salary increases, or performance bonuses, was also essentially impossible. The government bureaucracy was awarded a blanket salary increase annually, usually anywhere from 1 to 3 percent. The "General Schedule" performance management system allowed a performance rating and salary flexibility within 1 or 2 percentage points of this overall annual increase. And that was it. There were few financial or other tangible incentives offered to encourage outstanding performance.

Terminating poor-performing employees was more difficult still. It was easier just to "park" underperforming staff in "dead-end" jobs and work around them rather than terminate their employment.

The ability to drive rapid change, or "transformation," in such an environment is nearly impossible.

But people still try.

On September 10, 2001, Secretary of Defense Donald Rumsfeld

gave an address to the Department, in which he issued a call for the Department to modernize its business operations and eliminate waste.[4] The speech was compelling, delivering concrete data on the inefficiencies of DOD operations and the amount of time it took to design and deploy new weapon systems—which in some cases were at risk of technical obsolescence by the time they reached the field. He launched a major initiative to modernize defense business operations, from weapon system acquisition to financial management to streamlining installations and military logistics.

The very next day, on September 11, everything changed. The focus of the Secretary and his senior leadership was redirected to the response to the attacks in New York and on the Pentagon.

As the Pentagon geared up for war in Afghanistan, the management of defense business modernization was delegated to the head of Defense finance—the Undersecretary of Defense–Comptroller Dov Zakheim. Under his oversight, the Business Management Modernization Program (BMMP) was launched.

In launching the BMMP as an element of Rumsfeld's vision for improving efficiencies, Zakheim declared a target date for a remarkable achievement—the ability to audit cleanly the financial statements of the Department of Defense—by the year 2007.[5]

Auditing financial statements should be a basic part of managing any enterprise to ensure accountability. The Department of Defense, like most other federal agencies, cannot audit its financial statements—it cannot track its rolled-up financial reporting to the Congress seamlessly back to the transactions that trigger financial payments or obligations of taxpayer money. It is a remarkable state of affairs. It is also fairly easy to explain why this is so difficult.

The Department of Defense has always been an early adopter of technology. Mainframe computing systems were widely deployed by the Pentagon back in the 1950s and 1960s, and some remain in use to this day. Over the years and decades that followed, layer upon layer of additional systems were acquired, until the department became a spaghetti ball of systems and software dating from the dawn of automation to the present day of Internet-based computing. Over the years, as financial reporting was automated first at the local level, financials were rolled up to higher and higher levels of organization, but no department-wide standards for accounting classifications were established. As a result, human intervention and translation using everything from adding machines to calculators to spreadsheets were employed to translate layers of financial information.

In 2004, there were more than 2,000 individual business systems used to generate financial information critical to auditability across the Department of Defense. No standard financial coding structures existed, no common accounting codes or "charts of accounts" were in place. Just manual intervention via spreadsheets as information was rolled up and finally submitted to the top of the Department for consolidation and budget management.

At each layer of the Department overall, there was no motivation to standardize this flow of information to enable financial management to be automated or auditable. Easy access to financial information at higher levels of an enterprise makes it easy to move money from organization to organization, or from program to program. Better to stand pat with the old way of doing things, and protect your budget, than to make it easier for higher-ups to reallocate your funds.

The notion of auditing Defense financials was also questionable given the scale of the department. In terms of size, the budget of the Defense Department would rank as the 17th-largest nation on earth in terms of gross domestic product. The notion of financially auditing an organization with the scale of a large nation-state was hard to fathom.

The scale of the BMMP program was therefore remarkable. It sought to map every process used for any transaction that could trigger a financial outcome, across all of the military services and defense agencies. It would then redesign every process into a set of standards, forklift out the "legacy systems" that supported the old processes, and implement new standard systems and processes for the entire Department.

What seemed bold and visionary on paper was in fact far beyond the management capacity of the DOD, with its weak, decentralized management structure, to undertake. The absence of any authority to drive change into the autonomous military departments and their respective business operations made the likelihood of failure high from the beginning of the BMMP program.

Three years later, by late 2004, the BMMP program had followed an all-too-common path in government—it was floundering, failing to achieve any deliverables of consequence, and spending massive sums of taxpayer money. With a total budget in excess of $120 million a year, the program was completely adrift.

As President Bush won reelection, I prepared a set of aggressive recommendations for my new boss—Undersecretary of Defense for Acquisition, Technology, and Logistics Michael Wynne. A former General Dynamics executive with a broad business background as well as deep military ties, Wynne was a wise leader who understood well how the Department really worked and why any top-down approach would fail. Incorporating his advice, I recommended a sweeping redesign and down-scoping of the BMMP program, to align its efforts with the legally established management authorities within the Department.[6]

Defining a few critical information standards, getting them implemented, and then putting a process in place to increase steadily, over time, the number of these standards, would put the Department on a path to continuous steady improvement and increasingly transparent financial management. Such a process could become imbedded in the culture of the career bureaucracy, and could outlast political appointees who came and went. Had such an incremental, continuous improvement approach been taken at the launch of the effort in 2001, and had it been sustained for the duration of the Bush Administration, Zakheim's goal of auditability by 2007 might have been achievable.

By early 2005, I accepted a political appointment of my own, as the Deputy Undersecretary of Defense for Business Transformation, a role created specifically to lead business modernization and a restructured BMMP program across the Department of Defense. This was a significant increase in the scope of responsibility from the original position I had been offered by Brad Berkson, and that I had been so upset about being derailed just four months earlier.

✳   ✳

Thomas Modly was the Deputy Undersecretary of Defense for Financial Management. Recently appointed and responsible for improving the financial accountability of the Department, he had an extensive background in private-sector business, including a stint leading mergers and acquisitions for a technology company. Tom was a former naval aviator and had served as the Executive Director of the Defense Business Board. We met in December 2004, and instantly connected. Patient and thoughtful, but also passionate about the need for improvement in Defense business operations, he was an ideal complement to my sometimes over-aggressive personality. Modly and I were asked to jointly brief Deputy Secretary of Defense Paul Wolfowitz about our recommendations.

Consumed in the midst of an ever-worsening situation in Iraq and the aftermath of the U.S. presidential election, Wolfowitz demonstrated limited interest in our arcane discussion of management structures and process improvements within the Pentagon. But the meeting ended well for us. Tom and I were jointly named co-directors of the business modernization effort, and set about to consolidate all of the fragmented "improvement" programs within OSD offices, and to catalog all of the various improvement initiatives throughout the military services and defense agencies.

What we found was shocking. From the Office of the Secretary down through all of the Military Departments and subordinate offices and agencies, the DOD was spending more than $4 billion a year on improving its business practices. Much of this was in large-scale process-reengineering and systems-modernization projects, many of which had gone on for years. Backed by legislation, we moved to create tiered structures to oversee these initiatives, to establish concrete milestones and transition plans for old processes and systems onto new processes and systems, and to define a small standard set of critical information that would improve the overall management of the department while acknowledging the autonomy of the Military Departments.

Freed from "top-down" demands by the top-level Pentagon bureaucracy that sought to micromanage all aspects of their responsibilities, there was a huge release of momentum and support for our work within the Military Departments. By the fall of 2005, we had established management structures, standard meetings where progress was reviewed, and published to Congress a comprehensive but easy-to-read transition plan outlining where every defense improvement dollar was being spent, and what its deliverables and milestones were. This enabled us to measure our success against a baseline of commitment, to kill programs where necessary, and to hold contractors accountable to their commitments to the taxpayer.

At our request, newly appointed Deputy Secretary of Defense Gordon England approved our efforts to consolidate the disparate process, systems, and data standardization teams present within various independent offices in the Office of the Secretary of Defense into a new unified organization. That organization, called the Business Transformation Agency, was an aggregation of existing budget and personnel resources within the Department. It was established in 2005, with Tom and me named as co-directors. The goal of the BTA was to create visibility to all of the top-down Defense business process and systems-improvement efforts, drive them to succeed, or shut them down to save taxpayer money.

We set out to increase a sense of urgency within the business operations of the Defense Department. At the top of the massive bureaucratic pyramid of the Pentagon, it is almost impossible to link the mundane daily work to the soldier. But making that connection matters. In prior work environments I had actually held workshops where all employees had to walk through their daily work and map how doing it well mattered to a customer, and therefore to the bottom line of the company.

To create this link to the soldier in the field, using a model I had deployed at JDS Uniphase at the behest of then-CEO Kevin Kennedy, we created a warfighter support office within BTA. Composed of a team of former military personnel with business and/or systems experience, this team would have a role unprecedented for an organization at the top of the Pentagon. It was given the task to go forward to the troops in the field, as far forward as commanders would allow, to identify how the logistics, personnel management, or financial management policies, processes, or systems that were driven from the top of the Department were affecting them.

To lead this team we appointed a recently retired marine colonel named Bob Love. Bob was a smart, stubbornly passionate advocate for making things work better. He instantly grasped the concept of the Warfighter Support Office, and got it off the ground. Within a few weeks his team was engaging with deployed army units, naval forces, and marine units in forward locations.

Soon, the Government Accountability Office began to comment positively on the changes in Defense business management.[7] Trade press took notice, with beltway journals I had never heard of writing about our work.[8] We began to be called to testify before congressional oversight committees, which were uniformly complimentary of the changes that we had made and the alignment of the Department that had taken place so quickly.[9,10] After a year and a half of effort, Tom and I had established real momentum for sustained improvement in the business operations of the Department. The Congress, pleased with the progress of our joint leadership, codified the unorthodox comanagement structure into law in the National Defense Authorization Act of 2005.[11]

*   *

In January 2006, we were walking up a dry canyon, following a company of marines conducting live-fire training. As we moved, surrounded by trainers and coaches barking directions to individual marines, it was hard not to be impressed by the efficiency and professionalism on display.

We were visiting Camp Pendleton, home of the First Marine Expeditionary Force, soon to deploy to Al Anbar Province in Iraq, the most dangerous region in the increasingly troubled Iraq conflict. Marine units, mixing Iraq war veterans as well as new recruits, were going through intensive training, preparing for everything from combat operations to local community engagement. A model Iraqi village had been established at Pendleton, staffed with Arab American volunteers dressed as Iraqis, behaving as villagers would behave when engaging with young marines.

I marveled at the complexity of the job we were asking these young men to undertake—essentially to play the combined role of a lethally trained warfighter, a local police officer, and a community development expert, in a place where the language and culture was completely unfamiliar. I wondered how well a seasoned veteran police officer could do this job we were assigning to twenty-something-year-old marines. I was also deeply impressed with the level of effort the Marine Corps was undertaking to prepare these young men for their assignment. Most Americans had no idea what we were asking these marines to do in an effort to reverse the decline in security in Iraq.

I was here at the behest of Bob Love, who was establishing a practice of having his Warfighter Support Office engage with army and marine divisions prior to their deployment, to assess what if any gaps they saw in their material or business processes they would use to support their operations. Our tour of the combat training was a standard offering to visiting Washington dignitaries, one I was glad to accept. I was very happy with Bob's efforts—bringing the Pentagon bureaucracy close to the deployed forces was proving to be a larger success than I had hoped.

We were hosted by Major General Richard Zilmer and the commander in charge of logistics, civil affairs, and support operations, Brigadier General David Reist. Reist was being assigned an additional responsibility as part of his deployment. He would be in charge of something he described as an "economic line of operations," essentially looking at what could be done to help improve the local economy. As he explained this to me, I was only marginally interested. Mostly, I had come to see business and material management processes; economic development in a war zone was way outside my area of responsibility, but Reist persisted. He had the natural leadership persona of a high school quarterback. Outgoing and gregarious, he was easy to talk to and very willing to work with us.

We left Camp Pendleton with a to-do list of actions involving policies and practices that were hindering the efficiency of the marines from a business perspective. After returning to the Pentagon, I reimmersed myself in the daily activity of managing the business modernization program, which continued to build momentum.

That spring, Bob appealed to me to visit again I-MEF, this time in the deployed location in western Iraq. I told him I was interested, but I had no real intention of going to Iraq. My calendar was always full, but Bob began traveling to Baghdad late in 2005 with members of BTA focused on improving the processes and systems used to purchase goods and services within the war zone, referred to in the Department as "contingency contracting." The business systems used for buying things within the Department were designed for peacetime operations at home or on secure bases overseas. None of these systems was designed for use in combat environments where network access and basic automation was unavailable. As a result, soldiers and marines deployed in the field used paper-based systems to acquire the things needed for their mission, and paid the bills for those things in cash, creating huge opportunities for fraud and abuse.

Air Force Major General Darryl Scott took responsibility for all contracting in Iraq early in 2006. The finest business mind I have ever encountered among the uniformed military, Darryl set about to revolutionize contingency contracting in Iraq. He began tasking Bob and the BTA team to develop automated solutions for contracting in combat zones. In support of the Commander of Multi-National Force–Iraq, General George Casey, Darryl developed a policy that would become known as "Iraqi First"—the military was importing hundreds of millions of dollars of goods and services that could be provided by Iraqi businessmen at lower cost, and that could stimulate economic activity and help support community stabilization at the same time. BTA aligned its systems efforts for contingency contracting to support General Scott's vision.

After returning from one of his follow-up trips to meet with the marines, Bob made another appeal. General Reist had asked him for assistance with something unusual. Reist was seeking to assemble a group of tribal leaders from Al Anbar Province to meet with him in the neutral location of Amman, Jordan. Since the fall of the Saddam Hussein regime, most of the Sunni tribes of Anbar had resisted the American presence in Iraq, and were harboring or actively supporting Al Qaeda in its efforts to attack American forces. After three years of resistance, Reist, in his role as leader of civil affairs efforts in Anbar, had been directed by General Zilmer to open up a dialogue with the tribes.

Remarkably, he was held back by a bizarre constraint. In spite of the billions of dollars spent every month on the Iraq conflict writ large, I-MEF had no budget that could be used for a meeting with tribal leaders in Amman. Reist asked Bob if my office could provide the necessary funding for this effort. I asked Bob how much Reist needed. Fifty thousand dollars: a pittance within the Department of Defense. But it may as well have been a billion dollars. Money is appropriated by Congress to the Department of Defense for specific uses. You cannot take congressionally appropriated funds designated for one purpose and spend them on another, regardless of how small the amount. The marines had no budget appropriated for tribal engagement outside of Iraq, and neither did I.

I told Bob there was no way we could help Reist with his request. A few weeks later, the request came again, this time with greater urgency. Operations several months earlier to reoccupy the city of Fallujah, Anbar's largest city, and drive out Al Qaeda had created an opportunity for the marines to engage local leaders and solicit their support to keep Al Qaeda operatives on the run. The time for accelerating outreach efforts was now.

I spoke to colleagues in the Finance office in the Pentagon. They suggested a creative potential solution. If, as a normal part of our mission, we happened to hold one of our business modernization follow-up meetings with the MEF in Amman, Jordan, that would be permissible. If the MEF happened to hold coincident meetings in Amman with tribal leaders, using a conference room we had rented for our meetings after we had adjourned, that would be acceptable, as long as the purpose and heavy preponderance of activity in Amman was focused on business transformation activity.

Bob had in fact been holding a series of follow-up engagements with the marines. Holding them in Amman made sense from a number of perspectives: it allowed longer sessions in a more secure environment than Anbar, and allowed us to assess other Department supply chain and logistics operations from the port of Aqaba to the Jordanian border with Iraq.

And so it came to pass that the first Business Transformation Agency conference in the Middle East provided a venue for the first formal tribal engagement between the U.S. Marine Corps and the historical family leaders of the tribes of Al Anbar. I agreed, in addition to providing the funding and organizational support for this event, to attend and also to visit Al Anbar while I was in the region.

I arrived in Amman, and participated in a series of lengthy meetings on marine logistics, payroll, procurement, and other processes. The next day, as process meetings continued, I was invited to sit and observe as Reist met with the tribal leaders. A group of twenty aged Iraqis, most wearing traditional dishdasha robes and headgear, were present in a conference room. Reist opened with an appeal—to stop fighting America, and to work with the marines to evict the foreign radicals who had moved into Anbar to establish Al Qaeda's vision of an Islamic Caliphate in Iraq.

The participants reacted passionately, making angry statements in Arabic about all of the mistakes the United States had made, about the humiliation of Abu Ghraib and the loss of honor for the Iraqi people, and about how Iran was taking over the country, a sentiment that would be expressed repeatedly in coming years, and that I would learn was often code for Sunni anger at the rise of Shia leaders in Iraq.

But they also expressed weariness at the conflict and disgust with the behavior of Al Qaeda operatives, who were imposing rigid interpretations of Sharia law, marrying young Iraqi girls, and cutting off fingers and limbs for minor offenses such as smoking cigarettes.

The tribes of western Iraq were direct descendants of Bedouin culture, and were deeply proud, independent people. Saddam had largely left them alone, buying their support or complacency as required, in return for peace. Now their world had been turned upside down, and American mismanagement of the post-Saddam administration of Iraq had left them convinced we were either incompetent or that we had a master plan to subjugate them.

The engagement of tribal leaders in Anbar eventually evolved into a successful initiative called the Sunni Awakening, which created armed but friendly local forces comprised of young men from the tribes to actively root out Al Qaeda operatives. Like any success, many fathers of the Sunni Awakening have emerged in ensuing years. In fact from the very beginning of the Iraq conflict early in 2003, there were efforts made by diplomats, generals, and senior officials to reach out to Sunni tribal leaders. Reist's 2006 outreach efforts were carried on by his successor, Brigadier General John Allen, who eventually concluded that many tribal leaders who were meeting in Amman had effectively disengaged from Iraq and been away from daily life in Anbar for too long to exert much leadership. A new generation of Anbar leaders had emerged in their absence, and, in 2007, General Allen and a remarkable army colonel named Sean McFarland would forge trusted relationships with this new generation, from which would spring the Sunni Awakening.

Following the meetings, several members of my team, including Bob Love, and I departed Amman for Camp Taqqadim, Iraq, on a Marine C-130 transport plane. A steep, spiral landing at "Camp TQ" was followed by lunch and a meeting with the local logistics and material management commanders, the same crew we had met at

Camp Pendleton prior to its deployment. We were then transported via CH-47 helicopter to Camp Fallujah, where we were greeted by Major General Zilmer, his combat commander Brigadier General Robert Neller, and Brigadier General Reist.

Camp TQ was located on the banks of a large lake formed by damming up canals from the nearby Euphrates River. The water was crystal clear, and as we flew over the area the lake formed a striking and beautiful vista against the endless desert, reminiscent of a scene in Arizona, but against an almost white desert sand as opposed to the red hues of the American West. It was hot; the temperature was above 100 degrees Fahrenheit that day, even though it was only May.

Two senior leaders from my Pentagon office were with me on that trip: David Scantling, a former Hewlett-Packard executive and tech entrepreneur; and Kristopher Haag, a brilliant young systems engineering and supply chain management executive with an extensive background in operations management. That night, we found an empty patch of sand not far from our quarters, and Scantling fired up a satellite base station with Wi-Fi access for our laptops. The Milky Way was more vivid than I had ever seen it. It was a surreal setting. We were online in the midst of the western desert of Iraq, a mix of middle-aged businessmen, military officers, and a couple of support staff with a retired marine colonel, in the middle of the hottest area of a hot war zone. We talked for hours. The desert night grew cool by the time we finally went to bed.

＊　＊

The next morning, I was shocked awake before daylight by thundering explosions. Panicked, I leapt out of bed searching for a light—then rushed outside to take cover, as we were clearly under attack. To the politely subdued laughter of the marines, I was told it was only a volley fired from a nearby Marine M777 howitzer cannon.

Gathering my wits, I got dressed and went to a series of briefings from civil affairs units on the state of local economic development. The marines knew we were businesspeople, and their entire focus was on how we could help them get the local economies in the cities and towns of Anbar back on their feet. Absent a return of normal life, including jobs, schools, and other facets of normality, these communities would again become hotbeds of unrest, ripe for a return to insurgent activity.

It was also clear that the marines had no civilian support at all. In spite of public claims at home to the contrary, it seemed that other than a few diplomatic representatives of the State Department and governance experts from the United States Agency for International Development (USAID) based in the Anbar provincial capital of Ramadi, there was no expertise available to the marines to support basic local development activity.

The marines made it clear: they needed our help. Questions about how to assess businesses to determine if they could provide adequate goods or services, questions about pricing, payment, all of the complexities of managing supply relationships came to the fore.

In the spring of 2006, the United States economy was booming, with unemployment less than 5 percent. The irony that America, the pillar of global capitalism and the driver of globalization of economies around the world, had young marines struggling in the deserts of Al Anbar to get small businesses and large industries back online was an eye-opener.

What was more disturbing to me was the complete lack of awareness of this problem at home. The news media had actively reported the steady decline in security in Iraq for the last two years, yet the role of economic distress as a motivator of violence was never discussed. Long-suppressed Sunni-on-Shia violent sectarianism, Iraqi sympathies with radical Islamists unleashed by the removal of Saddam Hussein, and resurgent nationalism were all factors frequently discussed as motivation for increasing violence in the news media. But no mention of economic frustration was ever discussed.

I couldn't understand why this was the case, but the consequence of this lack of understanding was clear. If there was one thing America should be able to provide, it was ready access to business expertise for its men and women in harm's way.

2.
A GENERAL'S CALL

After two days in Fallujah, we departed for Baghdad—specifically for Camp Victory, a sprawling U.S. military complex housing more than 50,000 U.S. personnel located near Baghdad Airport, and about ten miles from downtown Baghdad. Spread among a palace complex surrounding small lakes that had been built as a resort by Saddam Hussein for use by his malevolent sons and inner circle of henchmen, Camp Victory was now a "little America" within Iraq. American fast food, coffee shops, massive health-club–style gyms, and a large department store PX provided soldiers and contractors with a few of the creature comforts of home.

We were housed at the Joint Visitors Bureau Hotel, a small "palace" on one of the larger lakes, across the water from the massive Al Faw Palace, home to the command.

The decor was a bizarre kitsch: gilded furniture and crystal fixtures looked opulent, but on inspection proved to be plastic or painted wood. We unpacked our gear, grabbed lunch at the massive dining facility, and began planning our next few days, focused mainly on meeting with C4 (logistics), C6 (information technology), C8 (financial management), and Joint Contracting Command under Major General Darryl Scott.

Almost immediately, our plans were changed. MNFI C9 (civil affairs) took over our agenda.

The Joint Visitors Bureau informed me that, as a high-ranking U.S. official, I was being requested to participate in a ribbon-cutting for a municipal facility built by the U.S. Army Corps of Engineers the next morning in a town called Tarmiyah. I pushed back, but they were insistent, stating this was important to Civil Affairs command and that my presence would be greatly appreciated. I relented. I had no idea what I was supposed to do, but I would go and try to put on a good face.

The next morning we departed via Blackhawk helicopter for Tarmiyah. Located in Salah ad-Din Province, Tarmiyah is a small farming community north of Baghdad near Tikrit, the hometown of Saddam Hussein. Salah ad-Din Province (named for the famous Islamic military leader known in the West as Saladin) was a hotbed of insurgent activity, and Tarmiyah had been the location of the former regime's nuclear enrichment laboratories shut down during the period of IAEA inspections after Gulf War I.

During the flight, I got my first look at Baghdad. A large sprawling city, it had no distinct architecture: instead appearing to be a hodgepodge of old neighborhoods, large subdivisions of larger homes (villas), and a variety of large buildings that appeared to date from the 1950s to early in the 1980s in style. The streets of Baghdad weren't empty, but there wasn't much traffic—either autos or people—for a city so large. The Tigris River bisected the city, its banks lined with tall reeds creating bands of green along each side of the waterway.

We landed in Tarmiyah and were greeted by a company commander within the 1st Brigade, 4th Infantry Division, which had secured the town earlier that spring, driving insurgents from Tarmiyah and shifting the town from a high-risk location for U.S. operations into a focal point for rebuilding the local municipal infrastructure. The overall stabilization effort, which included the rebuilding of schools and markets, was designed to demonstrate progress to the leadership within the Sunni-majority town and to gain their commitment to work with Shia majority leadership within the local district government.[1]

After landing I was immediately taken to meet with the mayor of the village. Grasping my hand, he gave the customary "three-kiss" Iraqi greeting that I would soon master—right cheek, left cheek, right cheek—then took my hand and led me on a short tour of his town.

Children flocked to us as we walked around his village hand in hand.

I could not understand a word he was saying, but in his eagerness to take me around his town, to have his photograph taken with me everywhere we went, he was genuine in his excitement. Children were surrounding us. Yet I was in a helmet and full body armor—the absurdity of the scene greatly bothered me. The morning sun was rising, driving up the temperature, causing me to sweat profusely under the layers of protection. It seemed to me that there was something completely incongruous about wearing body armor to meet with local citizens I was supposed to be engaging with on a personal level.

But that's how it was. The U.S. civilian entourage surrounding me, the Western media, all were wearing armor as well. So I played along.

I was discreetly given candy to hand to the flocks of children around us, as we went to the mayor's office, where we had hot tea and where platters of food and fresh melon were arrayed for us. We abruptly left his office, as the commanders informed us that the ceremony was to begin. Walking outside, we found a lectern had been set up in front of the new building, where a crowd had gathered along with a phalanx of video cameras and local media microphones. The mayor gave a speech, talking for about five minutes, thanking the U.S. for its support in securing the village and rebuilding its shattered infrastructure. He then looked to me and motioned for me to speak. I stepped to the lectern and did my best, making bold but general statements about the new facilities being a gift from the people of the United States, and how they represented a small portion of the commitment we were making to the future of Iraq. I kept my comments brief. We then stepped to the ribbon, each grabbing a pair of scissors, and completed the ceremony.

✳   ✳

Our last meeting on the schedule was an obligatory visit with senior command. Normally that would have been General George Casey, Commander of Multi-National Forces–Iraq, but he was unavailable so I instead was slated to have a short meet-and-greet with Lieutenant General Peter Chiarelli, Commander of Multi-National Corps–Iraq (MNCI). As MNCI commander, General Chiarelli was in charge of actual combat operations: the day-to-day management of the war on the ground. Most of the deployed military forces and associated air and ground assets reported directly to Chiarelli, who in turn reported to Casey.

This made Chiarelli a busy man. I expected a polite meeting, some small talk about what I had seen, a handshake, and a quick exit.

I was a bit nervous.

We arrived at Al Faw Palace, where I was met by General Chiarelli's staff, who escorted me into the massive edifice. Al Faw was the most grandiose of Saddam's palaces at Camp Victory, with an enormous domed atrium adorned with a massive fake crystal chandelier. I entered Chiarelli's office to find him giving instructions to a member of his staff. His office was filled with accoutrements of the conflict, acknowledgments from various Iraqi leaders, books, memorabilia, maps everywhere. It was a busy place, organized but not neat.

He rose and shook my hand in greeting. For the first time, I felt something I would later understand to be "true command presence," a sense of being in a place where truly serious decisions were made and where there was no time wasted on trivialities. The sort of place that is generally unfamiliar to Americans of this generation, no matter their role in life.

Chiarelli had a calm, steady demeanor but a high energy level as he motioned for me to take a seat on a small leather sofa next to a chair, which he took for himself. A few members of my team were seated several feet away, along with some of Chiarelli's military staff. After a little background discussion, I told him what we were doing, what we had found, and how I felt we could make improvements to several operational processes that would make support functions more effective for his command.

He then paused, and began asking me detailed questions about my background. He had clearly been told who I was and where I came from. He grew more animated as he began describing a particular problem he was having.

He believed that a major driver for the growing violence that was being visited on his forces was the complete collapse of the economy across the country. His troops were having to fight not just hard-core radical Islamists and terrorists, but increasingly were capturing people setting off explosives who had no motive other than money. Many were engineers or professionals who had been out of work, and would plead for mercy when captured, claiming they were feeding their families and required money. Too many young men were idle, he stated, and needed something productive to do. When questioned, they were clearly not hard-core insurgents, but with no jobs and no prospects after three years of American occupation, they had joined the insurgency.

He then grabbed a map. Pointing south of Baghdad, he described a place he had visited only a few weeks earlier. A bus factory, he said, that the State Department economic experts said was old and would never be able to build anything, but that didn't look that bad to him. Apparently it used to employ thousands of Iraqis, and now it was completely idle. Security in the area surrounding it was collapsing, and his troops were hearing the same story: there was no hope for a better future among the local leaders, so increasingly they were sympathizing with Al Qaeda or Shia terrorists who were attacking our forces.

I didn't like where this conversation was heading.

"I need you to go visit this factory."

"General, I appreciate the offer, but I'm a political appointee assigned to work on defense business operations. I'm not here to look at idle factories."

"You used to run factories didn't you?"

"Yes, but . . ."

"You know what a factory is supposed to look like, don't you?"

"Yes, but . . ."

"Well, nobody else around here does. We need somebody who knows what the hell they are talking about to go look at this bus factory and come tell me if there's any hope we can get people there back to work."

My mind raced. This was not part of the plan. But I wanted to impress this man. Something in me *needed* to impress this man. This wasn't corporate bullshit. This wasn't a corporate executive trying to wring a few more cents of profit out of every dollar by moving a factory to China.

"I've got boys dying down there, if you tell me there's no way to get something positive going at that industrial compound, then I've got to come up with something else. I need you to do this. Your country needs you to do this."

"How would I get down there?"

"I'll make a call and have my birds fly you down right away."

"What is the security situation?"

"It's bad, getting worse, and will continue to get worse unless we get something positive going. Are you going?"

I must be out of my mind to do this. "Yes. I'll go."

"Great. I want to see you as soon as you get back. Be careful." His staff entered the room and escorted me out.

✳   ✳

The temperature gauge on the shaded side of a nearby fabricated building read 135 degrees. The oppressive heat—furnace-like—resisted every effort to reduce its effect. Sweat soaked my clothing, a mismatched collection of a white dress shirt, tan cargo pants, and a pair of hiking boots sinking into the ankle deep dust pervasive everywhere in Iraq.

It was increasingly clear that this was not to be a well-choreographed visit to a ribbon cutting. I now wished I had refused Chiarelli. I knew I had no business doing this.

Five colleagues and I finished a premission briefing by the unit commander, whose team would be our protectors for the next several hours. All in their early twenties, hardened young men dressed in full, heavy, long-sleeved, digitally camouflaged army uniforms, and fully armored. They laughed at our jokes, the off-color banter increased, but you could sense the laughter was at least partly obligatory—the uncomfortable intrusion of civilians from Washington into their presence was clear in their faces when their guard was down.

We were at Forward Operating Base Kalsu, preparing for a convoy departure to Iskandiriyah, the City of Alexander. Located in northern Babil Province, its mix of Sunni and Shia Islamic faiths made it a major fault line of conflict in the collapsing security of 2006 Iraq. Combined with far eastern Anbar Province and the southernmost portion of Baghdad Province, Iskandiriyah formed a vertex of what had become known as the Triangle of Death, with an appalling rate of deadly insurgent attacks on our soldiers and marines.

In spite of the danger, none among those in uniform questioned our mission or indicated any lack of energy for the effort.

The "diplomatic" or protocol rank of my appointed position in the Defense Department made me the equivalent of a three-star general in terms of military hierarchy. At my age of 38, had I chosen a military career, and with unblemished outstanding performance, I might have held a rank of lieutenant colonel, *maybe* in the event of some stellar act of highly unusual performance and impeccable political connections, a colonel. Never that of a general, much less a three-star lieutenant general.

In Santa Clara two years before, I had felt my age becoming an increasing liability—something to be explained to the twenty-something wunderkinds who dominated the technical arena. But here, the opposite was apparent. Faces caught off guard betrayed something unsettling—surprise and disappointment. How could this guy be so important? He doesn't look important.

Softened by two years of working late hours in the Pentagon, my physical fitness had been completely lost. At 270 pounds, balding, out of shape, and pouring sweat, I did not cut an impressive figure.

The commander in charge of our mission, a lieutenant within the Fourth Infantry Division, Second Brigade Combat Team, and his team of seasoned noncommissioned officers (NCOs) and enlisted men, had all served at Kalsu for more than nine months. They put us through an unvarnished review of how our mission would play out.

"In the event of attack by small arms fire, stay in the vehicle at all times." "In the event of an improvised explosive device pay attention to your assigned leader, sergeant such-and-such." "In the event that the gunner is hit, you will need to assist in getting him out of the turret harness and into the vehicle, and in rendering necessary aid until medical care can be provided."

On it went. Most alarmingly—"Two of every three patrols and convoys on today's route have been hit by IEDs over the past several months."

Doors creaked under the weight of aftermarket thick armor plating. Designed for lightweight high-speed combat applications, the HMMWV (*Humvee*—or High Mobility Multipurpose Wheeled Vehicle) had been retrofitted into an armor-plated rolling brick in a losing effort to combat the enemy's primary weapon: the IED. The suspension groaned under the weight of the heavy plates and the turret added to the top of the vehicle. The gunner in my assigned vehicle manned a fifty-caliber machine gun, as he rotated the turret sitting in his harness his legs brushed against my own, seated in the cramped back right seat. We set off, the stifling Humvees wallowing through thick moondust roads as we departed the base. Weapons locked and ready, all humor vanished.

We entered a highway, and as the miles passed, the tension eased. Mud-brick houses, goats, and sheep, refuse littering any populated area. Satellite dishes everywhere. Ragged date palms near any source of water. Reed-clogged canals parting the dusty desert landscape and irrigating fields green with vegetables, melons, potatoes, and wheat, somehow growing in spite of the blistering heat. Farm plots were square green oases in an otherwise Star Wars landscape of endless baking desert dust.

We rolled through a small town. The streets were lined with people. No one smiled, only benign stares, or worse yet, cold glares. A child waved, his elders surrounding him pushed him away from street-side. My naive images of flags waving and liberation, and the staged reception I had experienced in Tarmiyah two days before, now confronted hard reality. We were clearly not welcome.

Every mile or so, a crater in the road marked the deadly application of insurgent force against our soldiers. Some of these blast craters had destroyed the road entirely, the sand-fill diameter an indicator of size and impact as we passed from pavement to fill to pavement, again and again.

The soldiers talked of their experiences, their suspicion of the local population clear in their dialogue. With no enemy to engage, with minimal understanding of the language and culture, they were the equivalent of police patrolling an alien beat, a beat where they didn't understand the language, the culture, or the faith. And all too frequently, their buddies were dying.

After passage through farmland and villages interrupting the endless flatland desert landscape, we pass through Iskandiriyah. The main street through town is filled with shops: bakers, butchers, dry goods, appliance dealers. The third-world village bazaar. Electrical wiring randomly strewn at every level above seven feet in the air. A nest of power cables entered every building. But where one would expect teeming activity on a weekday afternoon, the streets were sparse, and the men we saw wore ever more angry looks when they met our gaze. Our nine-vehicle convoy moving through town caused all activity to cease. The tension in the vehicle reached a peak.

A few miles from the center of Iskandiriyah, we pulled up to a giant building with a large entryway, the sort of facade one might find on an industrial headquarters building anywhere in the world. A single Iraqi man stepped down to greet us. As I walked to him, my ill-fitting helmet and body armor hiding my soaked head and clothes, Sabah Al Khafaji took my hand and greeted me. *Peace be upon you.* Holding my hand, he walked me into his building.

Dust covered everything. The fine desert dust of Iraq. Not the grainy sand one thinks of when one thinks of desert, but rather a true dusty sand, whose grit is only revealed when inhaled. The un-air-conditioned building baked in the heat. As we passed through the empty reception area we climbed a grand staircase, and were led through a door into his office. A single employee brought cold water bottles to each of us, and we were seated, a wall unit blowing cool air provided blessed relief from the heat.

I introduced myself and explained my visit. We were private businessmen from the United States, now working with the U.S. government, and visiting Iraq to see how well our troops were being supported. "General Chiarelli has asked us to visit your factory and report back to him about the operation and if it could be reopened. Maybe you can start by explaining why it has been closed. "

At this, Sheikh Sabah's eyes grew narrow, and he began to speak. His words were a constant flow, with no break for interpretation. As I looked to the interpreter for his translation, he tried to interrupt, but the Sheikh continued unhindered. Finally he paused. The interpreter looked mildly alarmed, as he tried to recount all of Sheikh Sabah's points before he began to speak.

"Our factory was built in the 1980s. It built tractors, trucks, municipal buses, irrigation equipment, and large iron and steel equipment as customers needed. We were partnered with Scania of Sweden, with Czechoslovakian companies, with Asian companies. More than 5,000 people worked here. This factory center was the industrial heart of Iraq. Nearby the Hateen munitions factory manu-factured artillery and weapons for our military. Your military bombed the munitions factory, and I understand this. We are all glad for the Americans when you came and removed Saddam. I am glad for this. You say you are American businessmen—I say 'Where have you been?' You are the first and only businessmen I have met since 2003."

At a pause in translation, I asked "Why is the factory closed?"

Sheikh Sabah fixed me with his gaze; his tone became another step more intense, as he said in English. "The Americans closed this factory. You closed this factory. My people have no work. Now they make violence on you. This is my home. These are my people. I had so much hope for this place, but that hope is almost gone."

He reached to his bookshelf and picked up a copy of the recently published Thomas J. Friedman book about business and globalization *The World Is Flat*, and, returning to Arabic, continued. "I've read this book. Everyone in business in Iraq was ready to do business when you Americans came. We did not think things could be worse than they were in the time of sanctions. But instead things are much worse.[2]

"What am I to tell my people when there is no work? What am I to tell them when there is no food? What am I to tell them when the mullah preaches that the Americans are here to enslave Iraq, and after three years our factories remain closed and our jobs are gone. Tell me, American businessman, what am I to say?"

This made no sense to me. Why would he blame us, blame America, for his factory being closed? Surely he was victim of some propaganda—some misrepresentation. New to the role of representing my government in a foreign country, I fell into a scripted response, explaining how the United States only wanted the best for the Iraqi people, and how with time they would see that their liberation would lead to prosperity. I then asked again why his factory was closed.

Sheikh Sabah's demeanor changed again. His weary expression returned, and he looked at me as one would look at any person expressing their confident opinion in spite of their ignorance. My pride felt the sting of the look. The unit commander leaned over and spoke in my ear. "We should try to keep this meeting positive, he is frustrated, don't take this personally." I looked the lieutenant in the face, surprised he would think I would react negatively, but remained quiet. He spoke to Sheikh Sabah, asking if he would give us a tour of the facility so I could see firsthand the capabilities of the factory. Sabah stood, calmed a bit, and again took my hand and led me on a two-hour tour of his facilities.

What I saw, minus the layers of dust, could have been in the American Midwest, or industrial zones of any major American city. Large lift cranes, a huge machine shop, a foundry for steel production, welding operations, assembly lines, an engineering department with a sea of drafting tables and design tools, and an automated line for vehicle painting. None of the equipment was less than 20 years old, some was older. But in business, 30 years is the normal capital life for heavy industrial equipment, and there are plenty of active manufacturing plants all over the world with equipment of that age. It was no Toyota or Honda factory in Kentucky or Ohio, but it was no lost cause by any means. In China I had seen far worse, with employees busily working away making goods to be exported abroad. Clearly thousands of people had worked here, from production workers to skilled machinists to engineers to managers and accountants.

But there were no workers anywhere, and it was obvious that there had not been work performed for a long time. I was confused. What had happened here? Semifinished production was everywhere. Vehicles were in various states of completion along the assembly lines. Valuable welding and assembly tooling was sitting as if abandoned while in use, but not looted. It was as if the workers had simply vanished while working, and three years of falling dust had been the only change since they disappeared.

As Sheikh Sabah ended the tour of his operations, he took my hand and we walked back to his office. His mood, which had grown animated as we toured the facility and he spoke of his operations during their heyday, had become somber. As we sat back in his office, he looked at me and spoke.

"I have had so many Americans from Baghdad come see this factory, but never any businessmen. Do you think my operations are hopeless?"

I told him my honest opinion: while the place wasn't new, and while it needed a good cleaning, and while I had no idea how skilled his workforce was, I saw no reason for the factory to be idled. I told him I had seen many factories in worse condition in Rust-Belt industrial zones in the United States that were still making products and making money. I told him that I had seen far worse conditions in Asia in factories filled with workers making products for their local markets. I saw no reason why something could not be done here, assuming there were skilled workers available to run the plant.

"You are the first American to say this to me," he replied.

I asked him why he wasn't running the operation. He explained that, because of policies implemented after the fall of Saddam, factories owned by the Government of Iraq were stripped of their money, and their worker salaries had been reduced. He did not understand why, but had been told that the factory workers needed to move out of state-owned industries and on to private-sector enterprises, but that there were no private businesses to hire the workers.

Gradually, his operation had come to a halt. As security began to collapse, he told his workers to stay home. The government was still paying them a monthly wage of less than half of what they had made prior to 2003, but they did not come to the factory. All of his lines were now shut down. Yet the Iraqi government was spending money on things his factory used to build. And coalition forces were spending money as well, importing equipment that he used to manufacture from regional countries. As an example, he noted that the City of Baghdad had recently purchased fifty municipal buses from a factory in Amman, Jordan. Sheikh Sabah could not make sense of this.

This had to be a mistake, I thought. I had personally worked to privatize and integrate a large, initially inefficient Chinese state-owned operation into JDSU. While that led to workforce reductions over time, it was a gradual process designed to soften the impact to the local community. The idea that the government would cut everyone's pay and send all of the workers at this factory home, essentially turning productive employees into welfare recipients, was crazy. Why would the government of Iraq do this?

Sheikh Sabah didn't directly answer that question. Glancing at the lieutenant he clearly did not feel comfortable giving a direct answer. He simply said I would have to ask Baghdad.

Looking me again directly in the eye, he asked me if I would help him get his factory running.

Once again I was asked a question I didn't want to answer. To say no would clearly leave him despondent. Chiarelli had asked me to see the factory, because getting it running again was important to his security strategy for the area. To tell Sheikh Sabah we would not help would clearly not advance Chiarelli's mission, and I could see no reason why the factory wasn't running already.

I returned his gaze, and said I would do everything I could to help.

As I departed Sheikh Sabah's company, I shook his hand. He held my hand for a long time, and looked me directly in the eye, again asking a question I would hear often in coming weeks.

"Will you help me?"

I replied that I would be back in a month, and would have ideas when I returned about what could be done. He looked at me dubiously, but thanked me for coming. As we lifted off in Chiarelli's Blackhawk helicopters, I saw Sheikh Sabah a final time. He did not look optimistic.

Our flight took us back to Camp Victory, where we went directly back to Chiarelli's office. I gave him my feedback, and asked him why the factory was shut down. He told me that because it was state-owned, the U.S. had a policy not to buy anything from it, and had discouraged the Iraqis from reopening it as well. As the State Department had the leadership role on all aspects of Iraqi reconstruction, MNFI could not change the policy. He had argued against it, to no avail. The policy had been implemented by the Coalition Provisional Authority immediately after the fall of Saddam. When he had managed to get State Department representatives to visit the site in Iskandiriyah, they had told him the plant was hopelessly out of date and could never compete with global manufacturers of industrial equipment or vehicles.

I told him my opinion, that not every factory that made goods in the world was a pristine showcase operation, and that there were many parts of the U.S. where older factory operations operated profitably and employed workers.

I wanted to meet the people who were advocating this policy. Surely something could be worked out. Chiarelli seemed pleased. I committed to go to Baghdad and see what I could do, and I also told him I would meet with Darryl Scott and work to determine what the Department of Defense was buying and importing that could be manufactured at the site.

We had one more day before departing Iraq to return via Jordan to Washington. I arranged to go to the Green Zone to meet the State Department reconstruction teams within an organization called the

Iraq Reconstruction Management Office (IRMO). Managed by a career Foreign Service officer, Joseph Saloom, IRMO consisted primarily of contractors and consultants hired under a special authority established for civilians who were deployed to Iraq as part of the Coalition Provisional Authority under L. Paul Bremer in 2003. This authority provided higher-than-standard base salaries for deployed civilians, as well as a 35 percent add-on to base salary for time in Iraq, and another 35 percent again if the continuous deployment to Iraq exceeded 42 days.[3]

Like most members of the Foreign Service I would get to know, Saloom was a friendly guy, very gracious, but he was instantly skeptical when he understood the topic I wanted to discuss. As I explained what I saw and began asking about the policy regarding industrial operations, particularly Iskandiriyah, he was quick to opine that the factories in Iraq were all old and antiquated and could never compete in global markets.

I thought the response was odd. It seemed rote. But he was helpful, and offered to get his economic team together to discuss the topic.

That afternoon, Bob Love, Kris Haag, David Scantling, and I sat down with the economic-development advisory team within IRMO. As we made introductions a few things became clear. There weren't very many people on the IRMO economic team, perhaps a dozen total. All were veterans of the Coalition Provisional Authority, and had been in Iraq since shortly after the fall of Saddam. Their backgrounds were either from academia or think-tanks; apparently only one had ever worked in business before. Most had never worked in government prior to CPA.

Their mood was gloomy. There was no life to their discussion. They seemed to be going through the motions. While they were cordial, they clearly weren't eager to discuss economic development with a bunch of guys from the Defense Department. One, in his opening statement, expressed confusion about why the Defense Department was asking about the subject at all—"Aren't you the guys who blow things up so others have to fix them?"

It was going to be an interesting meeting.

I talked about our backgrounds, and why we were there. I explained Chiarelli's request to us, which elicited scowls from several IRMO participants. I explained the viewpoint that much of the increasing violence appeared to be motivated by economic factors, and we wanted to understand what was being done to address this.

That statement sparked a flurry of visceral reactions, some rational, others not so much.

"The reason the economy is falling apart is because there is no security. You can't have economics without security; once there's security the economy will take care of itself. You DOD people need to get the security situation fixed and let us worry about the economy."

"You start opening up industrial operations for these people, and before you know it they will just manufacture weapons to kill our soldiers."

"These people don't have enough electricity as it is. You start opening factories and businesses, and there won't be enough electricity to light homes."

And, "Chiarelli must be a three-star idiot to think these people are killing our troops because they don't have work."

I was taken aback by the nature of the reactions. I asked about their travels around the country, and how often they got to go see towns and businesses, to see firsthand where there might be opportunities for positive effort to take place. This brought a litany of complaints about security, and how the security situation was so bad they weren't able to travel in the country. Most had not left the Green Zone in months; a few had never been "outside the wire." One had seen a factory in Baghdad, a large dairy processing plant that he described as the worst facility he had ever seen. Other than that, they had no direct experience with Iraq outside of Baghdad, or with businesses in Iraq.

Yet their opinions were firm and fixed. There was no room for debate or discussion. As far as they were concerned Chiarelli was simply wrong. They had the responsibility for economic development within IRMO, and they had no accountability to Chiarelli, Casey, or any other member of the military mission in Iraq.

I then raised the question of state-owned enterprises. I explained a little about my background working on economic development in China and on privatization of Chinese businesses, and asked why the Iraqi factories were shut down.

Again the response was visceral, and this time, ideological.

"This was a Baathist, socialist state. We learned in eastern Europe how to handle postsocialist economies. You shut them down, and get the old inefficient companies out of the way so the free market can emerge without having to compete with subsidized industry. CPA issued the orders to decommission the state-owned factories. They are all so old there is no way they can compete in today's world. They are shut down, and they will stay shut down."

There was no budging on this. I offered a viewpoint that comparing a shattered war-torn society like Iraq to eastern Europe might not be the best comparison. After all, there was no European Union sitting next door to Iraq ready to move in, invest, and hire Iraqi workers, as there had been after the Cold War in Europe.

"Iraqis don't have the skills necessary to compete in today's world. It will take years before they are ready. And they have no work ethic. You are wasting your time trying to get productive work out of Iraqi factories."

The former CPA advisors were advocating an economic model known as shock therapy. Shut down the remnants of state control and state subsidization, and let private enterprise emerge. Doing so enables industries that take advantage of a nation's inherent competitive advantages to emerge efficiently and create wealth. It was an ideological point of view, most frequently attributed to Milton Friedman and the University of Chicago School of economic thought, and effectively demonstrated in Chile following the rise of the military dictator Augusto Pinochet in the 1970s.[4,5]

Regardless of what they thought, Iraq wasn't some laboratory for a social science experiment. Iraqis were real people with real lives who had been full of hope in 2003, and now had been out of work for three years because of an economic theory advanced by a group of State Department consultants in Baghdad.

We were appalled, and increasingly angered, about what we were finding.

We kept our frustration largely to ourselves, kept the meeting cordial, thanked the group for taking time to meet, and left to go see General Darryl Scott one last time before departing for Washington.

I told Darryl what we had found in Iskandiriyah, and asked what he knew about the economic policies of IRMO. Darryl basically affirmed what I had learned from IRMO, that there was a binding

CPA policy still in effect forbidding U.S. government entities from doing any business with state-owned enterprises in Iraq. I asked him how many factories there might be in the country. He said he had heard there were hundreds, that they made just about everything, but he had no concrete data on any of them.

I thanked Darryl for his time, committed to get BTA working to deliver his automation requirements for his Iraqi First vision, and told him I was going to get the policy on state-owned enterprises reversed. The goal would be to get U.S. orders placed on factories that could build goods we were currently importing, start getting Iraq back to work, and getting the country back on a road to normal life—we hoped to reduce sympathies with insurgents and assist in the stabilization of the country.

He asked that I help get a policy issued by the Secretary unifying his authority over all contracting in Iraq. It seemed that although he was nominally the head of Iraq contracting, in reality, any organization within DOD with a budget could execute a contract for goods and services in Iraq, so dozens of different DOD organizations did just that. The fact that much of the Iraq contracting going on did not report to him rendered his role essentially powerless to drive a strategic impact. I committed to get a policy through the Pentagon if he would draft what he needed it to say. We would enforce the policy through the automated systems we would deploy. We set a goal of getting all of that done within six months, a warp-speed commitment in a government organization.[6]

With that last meeting completed, we departed for Washington.

* *

On the trip home, I finally had time to think. It had been a whirlwind experience, from the meetings with Reist and the tribal leaders in Amman, to the unexpected ribbon cutting in Tarmiyah, to the request from Chiarelli to visit Iskandiriyah, culminating with the remarkably disturbing meeting with the CPA staff in Baghdad.

I could not get the appeals from the young I-MEF marines in Anbar to help them with the local economy out of my head. I could not stop thinking about the Army 4th ID soldiers in the convoy from

FOB Kalsu who drove us through the countryside around Iskandiriyah, and told us about losing their buddies to roadside bombs. What could be more important than helping these soldiers and marines in a time of war?

If we could automate Joint Contracting Command under General Scott, creating online visibility of what the military was purchasing, and then redirect that demand to viable Iraqi factories, we could potentially make a major positive impact on General Chiarelli's operations.

To do that would require a lot of work. The system automation would be the first critical step—Kris Haag would tackle that. While that was underway, we had to see all of the factories—we would need to physically tour as many of the industrial sites as possible, determine which were capable of providing a good or service that the military was consuming, and then work with the plant managers to get the operation up and running again so it could execute orders. I would need people who knew how to assess factory operations—people who could stand up to what would be a lot of push-back from IRMO.

We would need to figure out how to plug these people into the command structure of the military mission. I had no idea how to do that—civilians typically did not embed with the military in a war zone.

Back in Washington, I asked for a meeting with Deputy Secretary of Defense Gordon England, to outbrief him on my trip to Iraq. England's extensive background in business, which included roles running massive manufacturing operations, made him easy for me to talk to. Savvy and wise from many decades of hands-on experience leading large organizations, he always had constructive feedback when Tom Modly and I would seek his engagement or support on business modernization.

This topic would be different. I was asking him to do something completely out of the ordinary—to endorse a plan that would send civilians from a politically appointed office under the Secretary of Defense into a war zone in an effort to kick-start economic activity. I proposed to use the massive pool of Department spending, which was more than $9B a month in 2006, as a stimulus, applying contracts for food, equipment, construction material, to anything that we could buy from an Iraqi business as opposed to importing it from other countries in the Middle East.

Secretary England instantly understood the problem and endorsed the proposed solution. He had been briefed repeatedly about the economic element of the stability problems in Iraq by commanders, but until now had no proposed solutions. To him, what we were suggesting just made good sense.

I explained the issues with CPA policies regarding state-owned enterprises, and he had an interesting response. He explained that it was a little-known fact that almost every factory currently used by Boeing, Lockheed Martin, Northrup Grumman, or most of the other large weapon-system manufacturers were at some point owned by the United States government.[7] In that regard, he had worked during his career for partially "state-owned" enterprises, even though the companies were "private"—so called "government-owned-contractor-operated" or "GOCO" facilities. He recalled how, over the years, many of our bellwether industries in the United States had been at one time or another launched by the government, or enabled by government contracts. Regardless, he had no interest in a theoretical debate when soldiers and marines were dying—if the CPA policy became an issue, he would deal with it directly himself in Washington.

A discussion ensued with his Chief of Staff Robert Earl about the best way forward. We would need a formal directive issued empowering our work. If we wanted to put a team to work in an active combat zone and use military assets, we needed orders issued that defined our role and responsibilities within MNFI, and ensured our support requirements were appropriately taken care of. Earl took the action to draft the directive for England to sign, getting input from MNFI as well as the necessary Pentagon offices. That directive would create a temporary Task Force to focus on economic-development support to MNFI.

Finally, England asked me how I would lead this Task Force and continue to manage my current duties overseeing Defense business transformation. I proposed that Tom Modly and I continue to formally "co-direct" the modernization effort, but that I focus primarily on the Iraq work, which I expected to take only a few months, and Tom would focus on the business modernization effort back in the States. He agreed with this proposal.

As I had feared, Tom Modly was not enthusiastic about these new developments. For almost two years, we had been inseparable partners, sort of a "Butch and Sundance" act. There had been serious bureaucratic and political resistance to our work across the Department, but the bureaucracy did not know how to handle two senior people at such a high level working so completely in concert with one another. We were back-to-back, swinging away at the system, forcing change at a pace that was unprecedented. The system did not like this one bit. Our ability to represent and marshal the resources of the two most powerful civilian organizations in OSD—Finance and AT&L—made resistance to change futile.

✳   ✴

Tom was torn between supporting the Iraq mission and our commitment to the transformation work within the Department. He had recently turned down a compelling offer to serve as the Chief Financial Officer of the Millennium Challenge Corporation, a new government sponsored company focused on third world development.[8] He had stayed in the Department out of loyalty to the transformation effort. He was justifiably concerned that if I was now focusing on Iraq, he would bear the brunt of the bureaucratic resistance on his own. I also knew that he was under increasing pressure from his boss, Defense Comptroller Tina Jonas, who had never supported his access to Deputy Secretary Gordon England—which violated her sense of hierarchy—nor the establishment of the BTA in the first place. We joked about this, and Tom tried to laugh it off, but it was no laughing matter. It was clearly wearing him down.

Although Tom and I shared access to England when we needed it, I also had the benefit of working for two great bosses that each served in the role of Undersecretary for AT&L, Mike Wynne and later Ken Krieg. They each gave me positive counsel, and helped me refine strategies and plans to better fit the unique challenges of the Department of Defense. Neither had any issue with my dealing directly with England.

As Robert Earl began circulating his memo announcing the establishment of the new Iraq Task Force, it became clear that I also was on the receiving end of a lot of political ill will. There were open questions within the office of the Undersecretary for Policy, Eric Edelman, about who I was and what business I had working in Iraq. The Defense Policy shop was traditionally the civilian organization that interacted with warfighting commands. People from AT&L and Finance managed the back-office business affairs of the Department—they had no business engaging commanders. It was all bureaucratic nonsense to me, and I said as much in meetings with representatives from Policy. In dismissing it I was playing a dangerous game of Pentagon politics—a game I did not understand at all.

I met with as many Pentagon organizations involved with Iraq policy as I could, in an effort to explain our work, including the Director of the Iraq/Afghanistan Transition Office led by retired Army Lieutenant General Claude "Mick" Kicklighter, which was responsible for working transition issues between State and Defense. Kicklighter had earlier led the Defense Department transition effort when the CPA was shut down and moved to the State Department.

The rising political and bureaucratic resistance manifested itself as the directive memo was reviewed across the senior leadership of the Pentagon. The name of the organization, which began as a simple "Task Force for Economic Stability in Iraq," began to morph as different offices started chopping away at the definition of our role. When the memo finally was issued, I was to direct the "Task Force to Support Improved Contracting and Stability Operations in Iraq." I was highly annoyed by the absurdity of most of the arguments over the name of the team, but did not want to make a major issue of it—a decision I would later regret.

Undersecretary of Defense for Acquisition, Technology, and Logistics Ken Krieg, who had replaced Mike Wynne a few months earlier, was direct in his advice to think hard before taking this on. Krieg was a prototypical CEO—easy to talk to, analytically smart, well spoken, and actively engaged and supportive of our business modernization work. He exuded integrity in every aspect of his management style. I loved working for him.

This time was no exception—he was clear in his feedback. I made a bulleted list of his points of advice.

- Be careful—you have a young family, and this will take you in directions you may not have thought about enough.

- You are already making a real difference here, something few people have the opportunity to do. Don't throw that away getting bogged down in Iraq.
- You cannot fix Iraq on your own, and it is not clear that the nation has the ability to fix Iraq at all.
- Don't let the thrill of getting asked to help by commanders in a war zone overwhelm your ability to think this through.
- If you do this, you are going to piss a lot of people in the Pentagon off, so think it over.

For the only time in my tenure working for or with Ken, I ignored his advice. I told myself that I would have our solution in place in a few months, and then I would be back in business in my regular job. Tom could hold down the fort for a few months.

On June 28, less than a month after I had returned from our first visit to Iraq, Deputy Secretary of Defense Gordon England issued the memo that established the Task Force.[9]

✳   ✳

It took a few weeks longer than I expected before we were ready to return to Iraq. Much of that time was spent working my network of contacts from the business world in an attempt to find people interested in our new mission. It was not an easy sell. Not because of fears of security, although those were part of every discussion, but rather because the idea just seemed to conflict with American notions of the Middle East. "They have factories in Iraq? I thought all they had was oil and camels." Variants on this theme were common responses to my appeals for help. I had held the same perception prior to visiting the place. Building a team would not be easy.

One thing that was critical, though, before departing was to assemble the initial group that had visited Iraq in June, and assign roles and responsibilities. Bob Love, Dave Scantling, Kris Haag, and my military assistant Lieutenant Colonel Tom Snyder were the initial four leaders who would manage operations, business development, contracting systems, and our military relationships, respectively.

While it would take several more weeks to get some business talent with manufacturing experience into the new team, I was convinced that I needed someone to join us right away to validate my own assessments. The factory I had seen in Iskandiriyah looked viable to me, but I wanted another set of eyes on that site, as well as any other operations I was to look at.

A couple of years earlier, I had met John Dowdy, an American senior partner with McKinsey & Co., now with global responsibility for McKinsey's economic-development practice, based in London. He had extensive private-sector experience, was easy to work with, and agreed to go with me on our next trip. I would later learn that he took vacation time to go along, as McKinsey would not sanction the visit because of security concerns—not the last time he would do this to support our mission. Having a senior McKinsey partner of his high status with me would provide an excellent "second opinion" of factory capabilities.

Through research, the team acquired information about all of Iraq's industrial capacity prior to 2003. Darryl Scott had been correct. There were literally hundreds of industrial operations, factories, and distribution centers, an economy's worth of capacity that had been owned by the government of Iraq, with only a few operations in private hands. The list was overwhelming. We decided to focus our attention on manufacturing operations, with a prioritization of factories that manufactured goods we thought could be ordered and consumed by our military operations.

We then began to research what had happened to the Iraqi economy before and after the fall of Saddam in 2003. What we learned, at the time, was an untold but significant contributor to the unrest and public dissatisfaction among Iraqis that emerged during the CPA occupation. Most Americans, by this time, knew that a key misstep by the CPA was the sudden decision to stand down the Iraqi Army and send all of the troops and their commanders home, essentially putting more than a million trained soldiers and their command infrastructure out of work. This decision had proven disastrous, as many of these angry former soldiers would join the insurgency in later years.

Most Americans also knew that the CPA policy of wholesale de-Baathification of the Iraqi government had been a mistake. This policy, which declared any member of the Baath party ineligible to serve in a government position, resulted in the elimination of the functioning Iraqi bureaucracy. The policy initially ignored the fact that many Iraqis joined the Baath party out of fear: you could not serve in government in Saddam Hussein's Iraq without pledging loyalty to the Baath party. De-Baathification below the senior level of the Iraqi government removed much of the professional capability of the Iraqi government to do anything, such as manage its budgets, transportation, police, and hospitals, to contract for services like new electrical power plants, basically to function as a government at all.[10]

Less well known here at home was the decision to apply economic shock therapy to the Iraqi economy, eliminating support to all state-owned industries. As essentially all industries in Saddam Hussein's Iraq were state owned, this was equivalent to suddenly shutting the economic engine of Iraqi society. More than 500,000 people worked in state-owned enterprises in Iraq. Within a few short months of the triumphant removal of Saddam Hussein, those workers were watching their places of employment shuttered.

The factories were often managed by senior Baathist officials, who used them to hire family members in the local communities. As UN sanctions took hold during the period immediately prior to Gulf War I, the industrial operations became increasingly critical to Iraq's internal needs; most goods other than food and medical supplies could not be legally imported. Iraq's factories combined with smuggling of imported goods to fill the gap created by the sanctions regime.

Like any industrial operation, the factories were the economic backbone of their communities, creating secondary and tertiary economic activity. Small local machine shops, suppliers, all sorts of private businesses depended on the large industrial operations for their own income. As in any country (including the United States), shutting down a major factory can devastate the economy of a local community—having far broader impact than just the direct employment of the factory itself.

So was the case in Iraq. After the fall of Saddam, in an effort to prevent Baathists from seizing funds from the government and fleeing the country, many government-controlled accounts in the large state-sponsored banks were seized by the CPA. The funds from these accounts were moved into a large pool of money called the "Development Fund for Iraq," or DFI, where they would be applied to the costs of the new Iraqi government yet to be established.[11] Many account balances for state-owned enterprises were swept up in this account seizure. All accounts receivable and accounts payable balances to and from state-owned enterprises were voided at the direction of CPA.

Policies were then issued, via CPA directives and subsequent State Department guidelines, that prevented coalition funds from being used to acquire goods or services from state-owned enterprises. Salaries of employees of state-owned enterprises declined by an average of 60 percent. Given the massive oil wealth of Iraq, the celebratory welcome that greeted the arrival of American forces in Iraq, and the commitment of international funds to rebuild the country's infrastructure, the outlook for the Iraqi economy was bullish in the early days of the CPA.[12]

A less-covered but equally unfortunate CPA order (CPA Order 12) unilaterally removed all tariffs for imported goods in an effort to further accelerate free market economic development. The effects were, once again, unfortunate. Prices for goods collapsed throughout Iraq, as cheap imports poured in from surrounding countries. Iraqi agriculture was especially hard-hit, as Iran and Turkey began mass imports of produce, rice, meat, and poultry. Iraqis who had lived for more than a decade under UN sanctions bought new appliances, electronics, and automobiles, all of the things they had been denied for so long. This drove demand for electrical power up exponentially, at a time when the power grid was already straining to provide only hours of power a day in most parts of the country. For Iraqi industries, the effect of Order 12 was devastating. Instead of a careful transition to a free market, consistent with other postsocialist states, Iraqi businessmen suddenly confronted wholesale collapses in the value of the goods they manufactured.[13]

With bank accounts and payables/receivables seized or frozen, Iraqi state-owned businesses had little-to-no working capital to buy raw material and pay outstanding bills to suppliers, and no revenue as their markets disappeared overnight. The majority of the professional class of engineers, accountants, managers, and other middle-class educated Iraqis soon found themselves unemployed and on the equivalent of welfare.

The unfortunate history of American engagement in the economic development of Iraq in the immediate aftermath of occupation in 2003–04 was described in brutal clarity in *Imperial Life in the Emerald City*, Rajiv Chandrasekaran's scathing review of the entire first year of the American experience in Iraq.

The reconstruction of Iraq's shattered infrastructure had an equally troubling history.

A frequent metaphor that was used by the United States in 2003 was the Marshall Plan, the massive redevelopment aid that was offered to postwar Europe after World War II and was credited with enabling Europe to emerge quickly from devastation and establish economic prosperity.

In reality, the approach to the post-Saddam reconstruction of Iraq was radically different than the Marshall Plan. The Marshall Plan was a commitment of financial aid from the United States, to be applied by the governments of Europe to their own reconstruction, with incentives and milestones that had to be met for additional funds to be released. This approach enabled postwar European governments to rebuild their own capacity, applying U.S. financial support to reconstruction using European expertise.[14]

Post-Saddam reconstruction funding was managed far differently. In the absence of a functioning Iraqi government following de-Baathification, the United States attempted to rebuild Iraq alone. The Iraq Relief and Reconstruction Fund (IRRF) was established by Congress following the fall of the Saddam Hussein regime. A generous commitment of aid from the American people, this fund would eventually reach $22 billion in size.[15] Rather than set these funds aside for the Iraqis to execute under American oversight, enabling the Iraqi government to build capacity and credibility, the United States contracted directly with large American construction companies to enter Iraq and execute major infrastructure projects.[16]

The World Bank estimated that the total cost to rebuild Iraq's shattered infrastructure, including electrical power, water, sewer, and transportation systems, in the first three years of occupation would exceed $50 billion.[17] To plan for the execution of these funds, the CPA, in collaboration with the U.S. Army Corps of Engineers and the U.S. Agency for International Development, assessed all of the needs of the country. While more than $20 billion was a generous commitment from the people of the United States, it would not be nearly adequate to rebuild Iraq.

As the various American organizations planned to allocate the IRRF funds, a typical bureaucratic approach was applied. Every organization involved in reconstruction activity received an allocation of the funds. This enabled projects to be launched to rebuild portions of every element of Iraq's infrastructure—e.g., some funding for electrical power, some for oil infrastructure, some for sewer, some for water, etc. Transportation and communications infrastructure received the smallest allocation of IRRF funding, with only 3 percent dedicated to these two areas so critical to private business development.

The objective, reasonable at the time, was to get work underway that demonstrated broad-based American goodwill to the Iraqi people. As Iraqi oil exports were expected to increase, generating massive wealth for a new Iraqi government, the Iraqis could take over and complete the reconstruction of their infrastructure. It was a rational approach to the problem.

History played out much differently than the CPA expected it to in 2003. Initial looting was followed by a collapse in governance across the country, exacerbated by the dismissal of the Iraqi military and the functioning Iraqi bureaucracy through de-Baathification. Widespread outbreaks of violence began soon thereafter. The American military presence, designed not for a long-term policing exercise, but rather for a quick regime-change followed by a departure, was nowhere near large enough to secure a nation of almost thirty million people, especially with the absence of Iraqi security forces—which had to be rebuilt. Violence begat violence, with tribal vendetta and sectarian vengeance taking hold as the numbers of Iraqis killed increased.

American firms that entered Iraq after being awarded CPA contracts funded by IRRF now came under attack. Major world-class companies, including Bechtel and General Electric, had projects attacked and employees killed as violence increased.[18] The leaders of these companies were appalled to learn that, upon calling for security assistance from Coalition Forces, they were told they were on their own; the Coalition simply did not have enough troops on the ground to secure all of the reconstruction projects underway. The companies began to depart Iraq abruptly. Those that stayed to complete their projects began hiring their own private security firms to protect their staff and project sites, blowing up their budgets for the projects, and significantly expanding a new industry of private armed security forces that exists in Iraq to this day.[19]

Eventually, the majority of the IRRF funding was expended. The problem was that the eruption of violence and the near gridlock of the de-Baathified-but-dysfunctional Iraqi government meant that there was no follow-on project work undertaken. Progress began to grind to a halt on rebuilding infrastructure.

Because of the approach taken in allocating the IRRF funds, no major element of infrastructure was actually fixed. It's no good, for example, if you are an Iraqi and you have no clean water, for a U.S. official to hold a ribbon cutting on a single water treatment plant that only services 20 percent of the need for clean water. You still don't have clean water. It's no good for the sewer system to be 20 percent more efficient because a few treatment plants are opened if you still cannot flush the toilet. It is especially no good for you to have one extra hour of power a day because power generation has increased by a few percentage points, when you only had three to four hours of power a day to start with.

The sums of IRRF spent seemed astronomical to everyday Iraqis— yet they could see no fundamental improvement in their circumstances. The most common refrain I heard in 2006: "The United States is the most powerful country on earth, and put a man on the moon. If you wanted to have the lights back on in Iraq after three years, they would be on."

Privately, Iraqis complained bitterly that the money must have been stolen by their officials, a belief that undermined their confidence in an already-shaky emerging democratic system.

It was a fiasco. A well-intentioned and expensive gesture of the American people, IRRF generated little resultant goodwill. Most IRRF-funded projects were eventually successfully completed and turned over to the Iraqi people. All over Iraq, there are successful IRRF-funded projects and many things to be proud of on a project-by-project basis, but the net contribution of IRRF to Iraqi well-being was regrettably hard to find.

As the CPA struggled to establish governance in 2004, election politics in the United States heated up, and the desire of the Bush Administration to declare sovereignty and turn Iraq over to the Iraqis early in 2004 grew dramatically. The prisoner-abuse scandal at Abu Ghraib pushed the decision ahead even faster. In an executive order, or National Security Presidential Directive (NSPD) dated May 11, 2004, President Bush directed the near-immediate dissolution of the Coalition Provisional Authority.[20] Responsibility for all nonsecurity or military operations within Iraq was transferred to the Department of State, specifically the Chief of Mission for the newly established American embassy in Baghdad. The former CPA organizations whose work was to continue would be moved into the Iraq Reconstruction Management Office (IRMO), reporting to the State Department.

By the winter of 2005, the executive order was further strengthened by NSPD 44, a broader directive that established long-term responsibility for reconstruction activity in all "post-conflict" countries transitioning to peaceful circumstances to the State Department.[21]

On its face, this order seems logical. The State Department is the cabinet agency responsible for advancement of foreign policy. The State Department had long advocated for increased responsibilities and associated budgets to enable it to operate in conflict zones, and to be on a more-level footing with the military as an alternative option for postconflict stability operations.

Yet as the State Department sought increased responsibilities in high-risk environments, policies were established within the State Department that made effective postconflict engagement impossible.

In August 1998, the United States embassies in Kenya and Tanzania were bombed by Al Qaeda operatives. More than 200 people were killed, including 12 Americans, and thousands more were injured. These events triggered a wholesale review of the physical posture of State Department personnel in high-risk environments. The review was conducted by retired Navy Admiral William Crowe, who determined that the physical posture of embassy structures and the security posture of embassy personnel was entirely too permissive to ensure their safety.

The report recommendations led to military-like security postures for all State Department installations to avoid future casualties, as well as highly restrictive movement policies for American personnel under Chief of Mission authority in high-risk countries.[22]

The effect of the Crowe recommendations has been dramatic. To visit an American embassy in the Middle East is to see a forbidding, highly restrictive, fortress-like structure. In postconflict environments such as Iraq or Afghanistan, embassies have prison-like architecture, with razor wire, multiple sequences of gates with heavily reinforced vehicle barriers, and guard towers monitoring the broad perimeter of the installations.

Embassy personnel largely stay within their compounds, venturing out only when necessary, to avoid any risk to their safety.

Given that the highest priority is to secure our diplomatic personnel, these security postures are aligned with that objective.

But to place an organization operating with this security posture in charge of the reconstruction of postconflict zones undermines the stated U.S. policy. You cannot build goodwill among a war-torn population if you do not engage with them on a human level. Occasionally touring areas in heavily armored vehicles accompanied by gun-wielding private security contractors, while wearing body armor and Kevlar helmets, does not build trust and goodwill. In places like the Middle East, where anti-American rhetoric from Islamist clerics is part of daily life, a restricted security posture creates even greater suspicion and resentment among the general public.

In Iraq, the Green Zone was an ever-more-dramatic manifestation of this policy conflict. An entire section of Baghdad occupying beautiful and valuable real estate along the Tigris River, had been walled away from the Iraqi people years before by Saddam, and was now sustained as a "forbidden city" by the American occupation. Thousands of American and Western diplomats, contractors, and thousands more military personnel occupied the Green Zone. It was not uncommon for an American to serve an entire yearlong tour of duty, yet never eat Iraqi food, meet an everyday Iraqi citizen, or see any part of Iraq outside of the Green Zone.[23]

Thousands of good-hearted, bright, and optimistic American civilians volunteered to serve in Iraq, filled with the expectation that they would work to rebuild a shattered society, only to leave a year later embittered and frustrated with the complete inability to achieve anything of substance, having been locked behind fortress walls for twelve months.

The environment we would be entering as we returned in July 2006 would prove even more challenging than the grim findings of our research had led us to expect.

3.

STATE OF CONFUSION

The founding members of the Task Force returned to Iraq to engage with the marines in Anbar Province, reviewing our new directive from Secretary England with General Reist and his commanders, and began discussing how we could more directly assist their economic-development efforts.

From Anbar, we returned to Camp Victory, where Bob Love worked to establish our operations. We were assigned office space at Al Faw palace. Bob had planned our travel to a number of industrial sites, including a return trip to Iskandiriyah. We also had our first meeting with MNFI Commanding General George Casey.

I had again been expecting a lukewarm reception, and a brief engagement, with Casey. Security was continuing to decline, especially in Baghdad, and the last thing a commander needed was another visitor from Washington. Casey exuded a reserved demeanor but beneath that had a high energy level, and a quick engagement style. Clearly already well-informed about our new effort, he was highly interested and wanted details on how quickly I felt we could field civilians with necessary experience to get progress going. He was very focused on Baghdad and how quickly we could engage there in support of the new counterinsurgency effort of a brigade he had deployed to augment Iraqi security forces in the city. He emphasized his full support to our efforts and encouraged me to contact him directly if I ran into any roadblocks as we launched our work.

I briefed General Chiarelli on our new mission, and on our plans. There was an intensity to the discussion. We were now beyond introductions; he viewed us as an operational capability that he needed right away. He asked us to move fast; progress was needed immediately.

I told Chiarelli that I believed there was an untapped reservoir of goodwill present in the American business community, which, if asked, would step up to support his soldiers and marines in the field. We pledged to build such a team to provide that support, and told him that we would go anywhere the troops would go, if they were willing to take us.

In that regard we were different than other civilian missions in Iraq. It was unreasonable to expect the State Department or U.S. Agency for International Development to provide expertise in an active war zone. Talented American diplomats or development experts who select a career in the foreign service or at USAID do so out of a desire to help people or serve their nation, to feed children, build schools, roads, or other infrastructure, in the poorest areas of the world. To overthrow a regime, establish partial security and governance, and then suddenly ask those organizations to take over was completely unreasonable. Employees at USAID and the State Department did not, generally, sign up to work in combat zones. Military personnel enlist with the knowledge they may be called on to work in harm's way. The State Department and USAID leaders in Washington who had lobbied to have control of Iraq reconstruction should have known better.

Our goal was to build a team of business experts who would join the mission knowing that they would work in harm's way, a team of volunteers willing to rebuild businesses in support of the troops, regardless of the risk.

I also asked that we not be treated as visiting Washington D.C. dignitaries. We would be establishing operations in Iraq, and needed to operate as a command resource, as part of MNCI/MNFI under direction from Iraq, not D.C. Deputy Secretary England would ensure we had necessary resources and support from the Pentagon, but within Iraq we would operate as an element of the command.

Chiarelli fully supported this, and told me he wanted continual updates on our progress and any barriers we encountered.[1]

As I left his office, my military advisor Lt. Col. Thomas Snyder was growing concerned. The command was in need of help, and we were the only civilians stepping up to offer anything. The expectations that would be placed on us were going to be heavy. I shared his concern, but saw no alternative to what we were doing. We had to try.

The following day we returned to Iskandiriyah. Sheikh Sabah Al Khafaji had been shocked when told we were returning so quickly by the local army units; he had expected nothing to result from our original visit the month before. I brought him a signed copy of the book he had shown me, *The World Is Flat*, along with some ideas about what we could do to get some production going on his shop floor. Sheikh Sabah again toured the entire compound with us.

John Dowdy and I photographed everything, especially the equipment, capturing information about its origin, serial numbers, manufacturers—everything we could. We looked at his inventory, to determine its condition and what could be used. At the end of a long day, Dowdy agreed with my initial assessment. While no Toyota plant, it was a viable industrial operation that could certainly be reopened given the chance.

Over the following two weeks, we visited several other major industrial operations. First was a clothing company in Najaf, The State Company for Ready-Made Clothing. Najaf is the holiest city in Shia Islam, and for centuries was the principal center of religious learning for Shia clerics. Following the fall of the Ottoman Empire, and British-led efforts to expel Shia insurgents fighting British rule, most of the religious leaders of Najaf were deported to Iran, contributing to a contemporaneous process of rapid expansion of a competing "school" of Shia theology in Qom, Iran. Now, eighty years later with the downfall of the Hussein regime, Najaf was reemerging as the major center of Shia learning. Najaf was the home of Ayatollah Ali Sistani, among the most revered clerics in all of Shia Islam, and a key source of influence in every aspect of Shia society in Iraq.[2]

This emergence of Najaf as a Shia center of learning had broad strategic implications for American foreign policy. The theology of Najaf viewed the role of faith as being above politics—to form the social bedrock on which political behavior should rest, but generally discouraging the role of clerics in direct political activity. This contrasts greatly with the politically oriented theology of Qom, which advocates direct clerical involvement in political life, as represented by the oppressive theocratic regime of Ayatollah Khomeini in Iran. Ayatollah Sistani had been a vocal advocate for democratic political institutions in Iraq—a powerful counternarrative to the approach of Iran.[3] From the perspective of advancing American interest in democratic institutions, anything that built up the economic (and therefore political) strength of Najaf was good policy.

Unfortunately, precious little had been done in Najaf since 2003 to advance the economic well-being of its citizens. Based on the perceived hostility of Shia politicians to the American occupation, we expected to receive a cold reception in Najaf, and to find a sweatshop for a clothing factory.

We were wrong.

Greeted by the governor of Najaf Province as well as the mayor of the city, we were treated like highly honored guests. Expecting to find a sweatshop, the clothing factory was literally state-of-the-art. The large facility was fully air-conditioned, with several hundred sewing stations, all sitting idle. The impeccably groomed general manager was stylishly dressed in an Italian suit, and eagerly showed us the entire facility, including his design studio. Fully computerized, the lab had a large laser-cutting machine to automatically convert his design team's clothing designs into fabric patterns. Dowdy recognized the high-tech Gerber laser-cutting equipment. The factory was pristine, and completely idled. I couldn't believe it.

The general manager showed us men's woolen dress suits that a small number of his workers had been manufacturing for sale in local shops. They could have been on the racks of any European clothing store. I asked about his workforce. He introduced us to his department heads. His head of engineering and his production manager were women, as were most of the factory workers, in defiance of all of our stereotypes about women in the Arab workforce. His managers all participated actively in the tour. The operation was spotlessly clean, with excellent material management processes. His only constraints were demand, and enough working capital to buy fabric. His usual sources of fabric were other Iraqi factories now also shut down.

Getting demand for goods from a brand new clothing factory capable of making high-end men's wear wasn't initially part of our thinking when we were brainstorming about how to restart industrial operations in Iraq.

Over a two-week period we visited several other major manufacturing operations. Several were decrepit, and in need of major capital investment, making it impossible for us to do anything to help. Some were like the clothing factory, and were pristine, and others still were more like Iskandiriyah: aging but not obsolete, at most in need of maintenance and cleanup.

Sometimes on these visits we would stay with forward deployed units, or at command headquarters sites in Mosul, Tikrit, Baqubah, Fallujah, Hillah, or Basra, depending on the proximity to the factory being visited. We would stay in tents or trailers, whatever was available. If there was a dining facility we ate with the troops. If not, we ate Meals-Ready-to-Eat (MREs). Our jet lag was extreme for the first week in country, so we would sit outside with our satellite dish and work online with Washington during East Coast business hours. Our travel was usually via Blackhawk helicopter or military convoys in up-armored Humvees. Convoys were especially nerve wracking. Often small arms fire could be heard as we would pass through villages, and the recent damage from IEDs including wrecked vehicles or damaged buildings were common sites as we rolled through cities and towns.

In every case we were impressed at the planning and execution demonstrated by our armed forces. Young men and women in their late teens or early twenties, they were completely professional, in spite of long hours, seven days a week in the most difficult of circumstances. They were genuinely appreciative of the opportunity to do something other than "kinetic operations," active military combat operations or patrols in hot areas. The chance to assist activities that would directly benefit the communities they were working to secure was a welcome break for them. It was a relief to see such an important part of our government where true accountability and performance management were still integral to the culture.

✳   ✳

The most troubling site we visited on our return trip was a large fertilizer operation in Baiji, in the northern region of Iraq not far south from Mosul. The Northern Fertilizer Company was a large urea plant that converted natural gas into granular urea for use as fertilizer. Built by M. W. Kellogg & Co. in the 1980s, the plant was still operational. The problem with the factory was that the gas supply had been cut off, leaving it without a source of raw material. The gas had been rerouted to a nearby large new electrical power plant at the direction of CPA back in 2004, in an effort to expand production of electricity. Without gas to maintain operations, the plant was falling into disrepair.

The power plant used large gas-powered thermal turbines to generate electricity. The gas that was redirected from the fertilizer plant, however, was filled with sulfur and other corrosive contaminants. It corroded the turbines, causing extensive continual maintenance and making sustained operation difficult. To be used for power generation, so-called sour gas has to be filtered of its liquids and contaminants to prevent corrosion. The damage to the equipment at the power plant cost significant amounts of money, money that was no longer available[4] as large-scale reconstruction budgets were largely expended by 2006.

So not only was the urea fertilizer plant shut down because of the gas supply being shut off, but there was little power being generated from redirected gas.

The story grew more depressing still.

The Northern Fertilizer Company factory in Baiji provided all of the fertilizer used for agricultural cultivation for all areas of Iraq north of Baghdad, approximately half of the country, including some of its richest farmland for grain and cotton farming. A sister factory in Basra, the Southern Fertilizer Company, provided the fertilizer for the rest of the country. Since Baiji fertilizer had shut down, crop yields in northern Iraq had fallen dramatically, as there was no fertilizer to distribute, and farmers, given the collapse in agricultural commodity prices, had little money to buy imported fertilizer. The growth in use of ammonium nitrate fertilizer for homemade explosives by terror networks made importation of fertilizer by farm co-ops and private importers to fill the gap in supply increasingly difficult.[5]

This was one of many examples where shutting down a factory

with a goal of creating a free market environment had a devastating downstream impact on the well-being of the Iraqi people.

Getting Baiji Fertilizer back up and running was another imperative, and solving that would not be easy. The military didn't buy a lot of agricultural fertilizer.

As we toured more and more facilities, another fact became clear. Iraq was not an eastern European–style socialist state as the CPA and now IRMO assumed. As we met with factory managers and learned about their operations, we found that virtually every site had a different relationship with the Baghdad government. Some were completely autonomous and could show us robust profit-and-loss data going back for many years. Some had sophisticated marketing capability and an aggressive approach to increasing their revenue. Still others were almost devoid of management skills and simply were told how many products to make and where to ship them, and how much raw material to buy and where to buy it from, the classic Soviet central-planning approach. The variance in these sites seemed to depend on the relationship the local population had with the Saddam government. Some areas were allowed to live in relative autonomy. Others lived under an iron fist. The factories seemed to reflect the political realities faced by the local communities.

It became apparent how useless it would be to try to modernize the Iraqi economy by CPA or State Department fiat issued by a few people sitting in Baghdad. Since there was no single operating model for Iraqi industry, trying to change the Iraqi economy via orders from an occupying authority in Baghdad was destined to fail from inception. Since the civilian advisors in Baghdad never visited operations because of their restrictive security posture, there was no way for them to know this. In addition, it seemed that every factory we visited had a variation that would complicate our simple strategy of using military demand to restart operations. This was not going to be easy. We were compiling a long list of challenges.

When we returned to the Green Zone, we reengaged with Darryl Scott, and synchronized on progress with systems for his Iraqi First program. Told about the clothing factory, he proposed they should begin making uniforms for the new Iraqi Army and Iraqi police. Hundreds of thousands of uniforms were needed, and were now being imported from the U.S. I was bewildered by that, but Darryl explained that under the Berry Amendment—legislation that protects American textile manufacturers and clothing companies—the U.S. military must acquire all clothing and apparel from American companies.[6] As the U.S. had been purchasing the uniforms for the new Iraqi armed forces and police, they were subject to the Berry Amendment. He was confident a waiver could be obtained if we pursued it in D.C. We would work in Washington with the policy offices to make that happen, and collaborate with the factory management team to get them ready to take on the orders, and Darryl would work the contracting. The Director of Defense Procurement and Acquisition Policy, Shay Assad, would prove instrumental to getting this waived and in future efforts to strengthen the economic impact of contracting in Iraq and Afghanistan.[7]

We reviewed the other operations we had seen and assigned the team to begin looking at what could be acquired that would meet military requirements for quality while creating Iraqi employment. We avoided redirecting any demand for goods manufactured in the U.S., instead looking at anything that was being acquired in the region (Kuwait, Jordan, or the United Arab Emirates, primarily) that could instead be purchased from an Iraqi business.

Our next meetings were to reengage with the U.S. Embassy. I met with the ambassador, Zalmay Khalilzad. A charming personality, Khalilzad extended a warm welcome. We talked at length in our first meeting, and he pledged his full support to our efforts, and assured me that the embassy would put up no barriers, regardless of what CPA policies had been. I was relieved. He also asked me if I would be working in Afghanistan as well. An Afghan American, Khalilzad had been the first U.S. Ambassador to that troubled country following the fall of the Taliban in 2002. I told him that we were business people, and I did not believe there was enough business in Afghanistan for us to be of much help. He disagreed with me and encouraged me to explore that country as well.

At that point I was still questioning my own sanity for stepping into Iraq. The notion of going to Afghanistan was out of the question.

For the duration of his tenure in Baghdad, Zal would be a good friend and supporter of our efforts. Unfortunately, his support did not translate into much action or support within IRMO, an organization that operated much as CPA apparently had, as an autonomous fiefdom accountable to no one.

Our meeting with the IRMO staff was far colder than the difficult first introductory meeting of a month earlier. It seemed that our new mission and our vocal opinions about the viability of Iraqi industry had triggered a lot of traffic from the State Department in Washington asking questions about the state of factories and the continued adherence to CPA policies. The economic team was openly hostile, asking us why we wanted to restore socialism in Iraq. They insisted we were wasting our time on Iraqi industry, that we had no idea what we were talking about, and that the Department of Defense needed to "stay in its lane" and out of economic development.

Dowdy then engaged, expressing the same point of view I had shared before. We showed them pictures of operations we had just seen, and we explained what we were learning about the differences in operating management from site to site. It made no difference.

I was growing concerned. My strategy was to put a team together, demonstrate how we could get some of the factories up and running, hire some expertise, get IRMO on board as a partner, with Darryl Scott driving the contracting side of the effort, and then transition the whole program to IRMO and stand down our new Task Force as soon as possible. That would enable me to go back to focusing on Pentagon business transformation, having made a contribution to the war effort.

It seemed like a perfect solution.

But IRMO would not play along. I made my pitch. The State Department was always complaining because Defense had all the money and resources. I would go and hire business volunteers, willing to work within the Defense Department for security posture, and able to travel with the troops, but assign them to report to the IRMO economic reconstruction team for strategic direction. That way, any success would accrue to IRMO, the IRMO principals could stay inside the wire in the Green Zone, but we could drastically increase their staffing and enable real improvements in the Iraqi economy. No one would declare anything CPA had done a failure; this would just be an adaptation of strategy, a shift in approach resulting from a deeper understanding of certain operational realities for Iraqi industries.

I may as well have made my offer to a brick wall. To a person, the

IRMO staff declined. No reason was offered, just a simple rejection of the proposal. Over the next few days, as individuals, we tried to carve off individual IRMO staff and leaders and convince them in one-on-one meetings, but they never changed their stance. IRMO was absolute in its belief that we were wrong and had no desire or intent to change direction.

Our last meeting in the Green Zone was with the Iraqi Deputy Minister of Industry and Minerals, Dr. Sami al Araji. With a PhD from Michigan State University, Dr. Sami was a rare example of an Iraqi leader who had managed to navigate through the pre-Saddam and post-Saddam era and maintain his influence. Part of this was due to his competence, and part of it was because of the influence of his family. The al Araji family is one of the most influential in all of Iraq; its members occupy leading parliamentary, military, and ministerial positions throughout the Iraqi government. The IRMO office had arranged for me to see Dr. Sami. I was eager to have this meeting. The Ministry of Industry was responsible for almost all of the state-owned enterprises we were interested in reopening. Getting this relationship off to a good start was absolutely critical. I had hoped to meet with Dr. Sami's boss, the Minister of Industry himself, Fawzi Hariri, but he was unavailable.

*   *

I entered a conference room and waited for him to arrive. Almost half an hour after our appointed meeting time, he finally appeared, looking disheveled and annoyed. He complained about the treatment he had received getting into the embassy. Apparently he had been subjected to a full search, and an extensive verification of his identity before being allowed to enter, even though escorted by a diplomat.

We made introductions, and I explained my purpose for the meeting. I told him I believed many of the industrial operations could be reopened in support of his ministry, and that I was establishing a team for just that purpose. I talked of the sites we had visited, and then asked him for his thoughts and advice, and how we should proceed.

He looked at me for a long time, and began to speak, giving me generic platitudes thanking me for visiting his country and showing interest. As he continued, however, his voice began to rise, his anger rising with the volume. "Do you know how many damned Americans I have been called in to here to meet in the past three years? At least a hundred. All of them just like you—you come here, you drag me into a palace that belongs to my country but that now you guard with dogs, you frisk me like a criminal and humiliate me, then you tell me you want to help? And then you know what happens next? NOTHING! Not one thing! I have no use for your words! I know that when I leave, I will never see you again. You will go back to wherever you came from, show everyone your pictures of your adventure, and forget you ever came here. I wish you would all go home and stop wasting my time!"

"Dr. Sami, I'm sorry but that is not what will happen this time," I replied.

"I guarantee that you will never come back. If I thought that I could collect the debt, I would bet any amount of money that you will never come back here again."

"I guarantee you I will be back here in two weeks."

"I do not believe a word you say. There have been one hundred like you. You are number one hundred and one."

At that, I had nothing left to say. I would have to prove him wrong. Had I been in his shoes, I would have said far worse.

✳   ✳

Sold on the merits of our program, and the potential impact it could have on a matter of international importance, Dowdy convinced McKinsey & Co.'s senior leadership to allow him to put together a team to work in Iraq. Within a few weeks, he had assembled a strong group of consultants from the McKinsey global manufacturing practice, ready to deploy into country for extended six-week assignments, rotating out with replacements ready to pivot in to maintain momentum.

It is hard to overstate the courage of McKinsey & Co. in stepping up to support our mission. This was not "green-zone" work. It was as high risk as any other noncombat activity that was taking place in Iraq. The headlines in 2006 were a drumbeat of negativity, making engagement in Iraq all but impossible for corporations to consider. It would have been perfectly rational for an august, starched firm like

McKinsey to say no to our request for help. Yet it did not—and in stepping up it played an instrumental role in changing the course of the nonmilitary mission in Iraq.

In another demonstration of courage and commitment, Bob Love decided that, rather than do rotations in and out of Iraq, he would take on the role of operational leader on the ground. His military background would be critical to building successful engagement as a resource to MNFI/MNCI, and ensuring responsiveness to their requests for support. This represented a real sacrifice for Bob. He had recently retired after a twenty-year career in the marines, a career that included a combat deployment to Iraq in 2003. Now he would be returning as a civilian. He would complete the establishment of our operations, provide oversight to the McKinsey team that would be performing factory assessments, and liaise on a daily basis with General Scott's contracting command to begin to identify demand sources for Iraqi factories.

I would shuttle between Washington and Iraq, meeting with the business community when at home, as well as the Pentagon bureaucracy, while also providing overall direction to the work in Iraq, engaging with senior command as well as Iraqi business leaders and senior officials, to restore normal demand to Iraqi industrial operations and eventually reduce any dependence on U.S. military contracts for production demand.

I discussed our phased strategic approach with Gordon England, who reached out to Thomas Donohue, the Chairman of the United States Chamber of Commerce. Donohue hosted a reception inviting a number of senior U.S. business executives to a dinner with England and me, where we described the challenge and solicited advice. The attendees were, as expected, surprised to learn of the economic element of the problems in Iraq. Their advice was to identify products that American industry could buy, that would meet American standards, and that could tap into American industrial demand. As companies began acquiring goods from Iraq, relationships would be established that would lead to additional future business opportunities.

This would begin one of the most important elements of our work over the coming years. Most business leaders were not unlike me: willing to respond to requests for help, especially if those requests could be fulfilled with normal business activity, such as supply relationships. For years to come, the U.S. Chamber would be an active advocate for U.S. business engagement in Iraq, in partnership with the Task Force.

I also reached out to Stuart Bowen for advice and support. Appointed by the White House as the Special Inspector General for Iraq Reconstruction, Bowen had crusaded against many failed projects and initiatives in Iraq. Rather than repeat mistakes already made by others who had tried to assist the Iraq mission, I spent several sessions with Bowen seeking his advice on how to ensure we avoided problems. He attended several of our early meetings with business groups, lending credibility to our program, and providing assurance to companies that we would work to ensure their protection from any of the project-execution problems so many other companies working in Iraq had encountered.

At this point, the Bush Administration made clear that we were permitted to focus on every industry in Iraq, excluding the oil and gas sector. The reasoning behind this was clear. The Department of Defense could not work directly to engage the oil sector given the widely perceived motives for the removal of the Saddam Hussein regime: that America had fought the war to seize Iraq's oil reserves. I had no argument with this at the time. Our work would be complicated enough and there was plenty to focus on without getting in the midst of the oil industry and the endless State Department–led efforts to resolve the legal framework in Iraq that would enable rapid oil industry development.[8]

After further discussions with Deputy Secretary Gordon England, I decided that our initial focus would be on industrial operations: machine shops, metal works, and heavy equipment manufacturers. These were industries that would have the best chance of thriving in the future Iraqi economy. The huge petrochemical industry development that would inevitably emerge in coming years would consume any productive capacity in heavy industries. If we could get some heavy industries running, and then establish supply partnerships with Western firms, we would demonstrate the viability of Iraqi industries and restore employment to thousands of Iraqi professionals.

In September, the first Task Force factory teams reached Iraq, and began industrial assessments. From September to December, the Task Force completed basic assessments of more than sixty factory operations, across every sector of industry excluding high-tech. I personally participated in thirty-two of these factory assessments. The sites were prioritized based on information from the Iraqi Ministry of Industry indicating they were most viable and able to restart production quickly. The factories were distributed throughout Iraq. In visiting the sites, we grew to know the country in a way few Western civilians ever had. There was almost a routine to the process: hours of frustration and anger expressed by a plant manager, followed by a tour of the operation, and then dinner with the senior management team. By the end of a day at a site, rapport would be established and relationships built that would endure for far longer than we expected at the time. Even in areas that were undergoing extreme violence, we would find industrial operations sitting undamaged. In October, Tom Modly joined me on a visit to Iraq. He wanted to see firsthand what had diverted my attention from our work reforming the Pentagon bureaucracy. He also recognized the risk that he would come away from the trip as driven to support the Iraq mission as I had become.

The marines took Tom and me to a factory in Ramadi, the provincial capital of Anbar Province. Ramadi was experiencing extreme amounts of violence, as many of the remaining Al Qaeda operatives that were pushed from Fallujah, and many new Al Qaeda recruits entering Iraq from Syria, were converging on Ramadi. The marines were looking for anything positive that could augment active military operations to turn the tide in Ramadi.

The convoy to Ramadi was highly tense, as it involved a slow two-hour drive from Camp Fallujah along the main Anbar highway following the Euphrates River valley. We were to visit a glass-and-ceramics factory that had been the primary employer in the city prior to 2003. The highway was a frequent target for IEDs. As we entered the city, the streets were almost empty, except for small roadside stands where gasoline was being sold in soft drink bottles along with bottled water and cheap groceries. The few people we saw were darting between buildings—there was no sustained street presence. The tension in the Humvee was thick as we rolled into the city, as the marines were expecting violence to erupt at any moment. One of the marines, when asked if he had visited the city before, ominously replied that his convoy had been hit every time he had been on that road.

Fear hung in the air. There was an oppressive feeling to the place.

In coming years, after literally hundreds of visits to places throughout Iraq, we would develop a "sixth sense," an ability to read the "vibe" of a place and to know when danger was imminent. At this early point in our work, we had no such intuition, but in Ramadi intuition wasn't necessary. We were clearly in danger.

Putting on a "game face," inside I grew increasingly uneasy. I could not understand why we were in Ramadi. Clearly the entire town was in a state of siege. There was no sense in seeing anything; any factory would surely be looted of anything of value. The marines had related stories to us of homes and vacant buildings being stripped of anything of value, including even copper wire, which was sold for scrap by desperate families looking for any source of income.

We arrived at a Gothic-looking facility on the outskirts of town, across the Euphrates River from the city center. Entering, we were discouraged. The building housed a massive sheet-glass manufacturing plant; its equipment was full of frozen glass. The marine commander from the local unit explained that the factory had been suddenly shut down when power was cut off during the 2003 invasion, causing molten glass to freeze up in the equipment. The building appeared to have been shelled or rocketed, as evidenced by large holes in the roof. Birds were roosting throughout the facility, their droppings and feathers covered everything.

Ramadi had been a center for glass manufacturing, as the local sand had a high quality silica content especially desirable for glass production. But this factory was a complete write-off. The sheet-glass equipment was decades old, and obsolete technically. Any effort to restore Ramadi's glass industry would have to start from scratch and would require at least $50 million in new investment. We had been wasting our time, at high risk to ourselves and the marines. We told the marines as much, and indicated that we needed to go.

The marines insisted on taking us to an adjacent site. A large rectangular building, about the size of a football field, was padlocked shut. As we approached the facility, small arms fire erupted around us, causing us to rush to a wall near the building entrance to take cover. The marines maintaining a secure perimeter around the building were growing agitated as we waited for what seemed like an eternity for someone to cut the lock on the facility.

When the door was finally opened, Tom and I looked in shock. The factory was literally pristine. Brand-new ceramic manufacturing lines, with new computer-controlled equipment, were sitting as though the workforce had just walked off the floor. Only the settled dust indicated that the site had been vacant for any time at all. New modern sinks and other bathroom fixtures were stacked neatly. As we walked throughout the plant, I could not understand how this site had been untouched.

The plant had been established in 2000, as an expansion of the glass industry into ceramics production. New high-grade Italian equipment had been acquired, the workforce had been trained, but the factory had been abandoned in 2003. This site could be started back up immediately. All that was needed was electrical power and a source of demand.

We found similar examples of this throughout Iraq. Regardless of how nihilistic a particular group may appear, there was still a desire to maintain the potential for future economic well-being. People in leadership still felt they had something to lose, in spite of the chaos and violence. For me, this was a cause of real optimism.

If we could identify and tap into this "hidden" leadership structure present in Iraq's communities, and demonstrate we were working for the long-term economic benefit of the people in the area, we could become a potent tool for reducing support to violent actors.

✳   ✳

As we continued to assess factories, seeing operations firsthand revealed the flaws in our overly simplistic strategy, and resulted in changes to our plans. In many cases, getting demand restored to a factory was not going to be sufficient to restore production operations. After two to three years of idleness, factory equipment had to be cleaned. Spare parts were needed. Many sites had no raw materials or existing inventory of supplies necessary to begin operations. While these issues were significant, they could be resolved for very small amounts of funding. In most cases less than a few hundred thousand dollars was needed to restore employment for hundreds or thousands of workers at a single site.

Unfortunately, the Government of Iraq had no budget for the Ministry of Industry except for the reduced salary payments for the employees. CPA orders from 2003 had eliminated the Ministry of Industry budget. For simple logical reasons, I was not worried about this. Given the staggering amount of money that was being spent on the war effort within DOD alone, which was at a monthly run rate exceeding $9 billion, I was confident we would be able to scrape small amounts for spare parts and supplies to get a few factories up and running as part of initiating our work.

We began to understand aspects of the Iraqi economy and Iraqi politics through our work with the factories. In the past, under UN sanctions, Iraqi factories could not export goods, nor import supplies. Their only trade relationships were with other Iraqi factories. Cotton gins would supply fabric mills that would supply clothing factories, which in turn would supply Iraqi retail outlets. Metal works would supply industrial supply companies that would supply equipment manufacturers. Petrochemical plants would supply raw material to a variety of other industries. Distributed across the country, these trade relationships among Iraqi factories were part of the commercial fabric that created mutually beneficial relationships among Iraq cities, provinces, tribes, and sects.

When the factories were shut down, not only were local communities devastated by unemployment, but also much of the trade among the various communities of Iraq gradually ceased.

Regardless of the society, trade is a critical element that binds a people together. If states in the U.S. were no longer trading with one another, how long would the Union stay together? How soon would the differences among the various cultures within the relatively homogenous United States start to overwhelm public debate? Getting Iraq's factories up and running would not only restore local employment, it would also enable the gradual restoration of trade within the country—and help to reduce the boiling sectarian frustration that was feeding terror networks and fostering anger at our troops.

We began to map the intracountry trade relationships based on our engagement with Iraqi factories, with a new goal of working to restore such operations that had been negatively affected by the cessation of production. We found many operations in which trade across Sunni and Shia regions of the country had been eliminated.

In October, the Task Force contracting systems team led by Kris

Haag delivered an automated solution for central coordination and execution of military contracts. This system was delivered three months ahead of schedule and formed a backbone of information that enabled General Scott to understand, for the first time, how to strategically apply military spending as a tool of economic stabilization. Kris's team, in particular a brilliant young technical manager from Canada, Darren Farber, began upgrading the new system at General Scott's request.

With this system in place, the Task Force could begin identifying demand opportunities for Iraqi factories. Working with Sheikh Sabah in Iskandiriyah, Bob Love enabled the welding and metal works production lines to be restarted to build containerized housing units, or CHUs—military jargon for mobile homes or house trailers. One thing the United States had demonstrated in Iraq was the ability to establish huge military and civilian compounds comprised of CHUs, with hundreds of units in the Green Zone as well as Camp Victory. Until 2006, all of the thousands of CHUs in use throughout Iraq were acquired from factories in Kuwait or Jordan and imported to Iraq. Now they would begin to be manufactured in-country. Within six months, 400 workers were back on the job in Iskandiriyah building CHUs. Although much work remained to get Iskandiriyah restored as a major industrial operation, 400 new jobs was a good start.[9]

There was another pattern among Iraqi factories that was becoming clear. Factories in the south of Iraq, in predominantly Shia areas, tended to involve higher levels of employment. Manual assembly operations, labor-intensive factories, machine shops, sewing centers, all tended to be in Shia areas. In the Sunni north and west, factories tended to be large mineral- or chemical-processing plants and cement factories, with fewer but higher-skilled professional employees. These operations were less labor intensive, and required massive amounts of electrical power for sustained operation.

In 2003, after removing Saddam, the coalition found a large imbalance in the allocation of available electrical power across the national grid, with a disproportionate amount flowing to Sunni areas of the country as compared to southern Iraq. The CPA redirected electrical power, attempting to evenly distribute available electricity among all Iraqis, regardless of geography. This redistribution made restarting much of the industrial base of northern and western Iraq impossible.

There was simply not enough electricity to fire up the idled industrial plants in the west and north.[10]

It was critical that our work not be perceived as benefiting only Shia areas of Iraq. But many factories in the south were labor-intensive, and used relatively little electrical power. If the Task Force could only restore operations in southern Iraq, we would foster resentment among Sunni Iraqis. The only way forward we could see was to work to foster private investment in cement plants and chemical operations. An investor would have to co-locate a power generation facility with an industrial plant, which would require the Ministry of Industry to have to offer highly favorable terms for investors accustomed to having grid-based power. We assigned a team to begin working on a strategy for this approach right away.

I began to meet directly with Iraqi ministers and senior officials, and was frequently invited to their homes for dinners, which would often last late into the night or early morning, with broad discussions among attendees. I encouraged them to converse freely even when I could not understand; I gradually began to follow conversations after months of such engagements. They would shift to English then back to Arabic, depending on the subject. I was getting an invaluable education in the "after-hours" decision-making process so critical to working effectively in Iraq.

Through these engagements, I met dozens of Iraqi parliamentarians, ministers, and deputy ministers, as well as leading clerics and businessmen from throughout the country. I began to comprehend Iraqi politics better, and the worldview of Iraqi politicians, which had been so heavily influenced by their difficult lives working in resistance to Saddam for so many years.

Many of the new generation of Iraqi leaders had spent their lives residing in Damascus or Tehran, and had only infrequently visited modern commercial centers in the region like Kuwait, Dubai, or Abu Dhabi before returning to Iraq in 2003. As a result, their worldview of how Iraq could fit into the global economy was often far too restrained. We spent many hours discussing Iraq's potential economically beyond a role as an oil producer, something the Iraqi leaders believed in, but had no concrete ideas how to make into a reality.

4.

PRESSURIZATION

I raq is, like most of the world, fanatical about football—or soccer as Americans call the sport.

No matter where we traveled throughout the country, Iraqi children could always be seen kicking soccer balls wherever there was a bare spot of sand, from gritty urban areas to remote farm communities.

One of the most popular gifts our troops would give to Iraqi children were soccer balls—a gift to build trust and confidence in America's presence throughout the country, a trust that was rapidly fading with increasing violence and unrest.

The soccer balls being handed out by coalition forces to Iraqis were made in China.

In the past few months, we had discovered factories throughout the country capable of making just about anything. Surely we could find a factory in Iraq that could make soccer balls, and put some people back to work.

We located an idled factory in Baghdad with the necessary production line and, working with the military, placed an order for several thousand Iraqi-made soccer balls. The plant manager was thrilled to have his line running again, and committed to a delivery date several weeks after the order was placed.

When the day arrived, Bob Love and one of his brightest team leaders, Shawn Winn, traveled to the factory to pick up the order. The soccer balls were neatly boxed and stacked, waiting for our arrival.

The plant manager proudly handed one to Love. He looked it over, his face growing ashen, then angry.

Stamped on the side of the soccer ball were the words "Made in China." Clearly the manager had taken the money from us, bought cheap Chinese soccer balls, and pocketed the difference.

Instead of a quick success, we would have to explain an act of corruption at a factory we were trying to reopen.

Panicking at Love's distraught reaction, the plant manager grabbed him by the arm and walked him out to the factory floor. He showed the line, which had clearly been recently used, walking him to the end, where a machine stamped each ball with the "Made in China" label.

Love and his team were bewildered. Why, they demanded to know, would the factory stamp "Made in China" on a soccer ball made in their own factory. His head bowed, the plant manager replied, "Mr. Bob, please understand. No Iraqi child would want an Iraqi-made soccer ball."

Iraq was a shattered society. Year after year of sanctions dating back to 1991 had left Iraqis with no goods to buy other than goods made in Iraq, goods often of inferior quality. Like consumers anywhere else, Iraqis wanted something new. Their self-confidence and sense of their own ability to make something worth buying had been stripped away.

"No Iraqi child would want an Iraqi-made soccer ball."

You could have removed the world "child" and the words "soccer ball," replacing them with any product, and hear the same sentence from anyone in Iraq.

The same American policy that had scuttled operations at almost all Iraqi factories in 2003 had also opened the borders of Iraq to complete free trade—with no tariffs or trade restrictions for imported goods. These open borders that allowed goods to pour in at below-market cost only exacerbated the problems faced by Iraqi factories—factories that had directly or indirectly employed the majority of Iraq's professional workforce outside of the oil industry.

In our short time working it was now becoming clear that there were no simple solutions to the problems facing the Iraqi economy—no quick fixes to be had. Three years of bureaucratic missteps were not going to be reversed easily.

Rebuilding the Iraqi economy was going to take a lot more than restarting factories that should never have been closed. It would take electricity. It would take private investment.

Most important, it would take a restoration of confidence in a people shattered by hardship and deprivation.

✳ ✳

As our initial efforts built momentum, our meetings with Iraqis became more and more energized with a flood of ideas and appeals for help. Word of our mission spread among Iraqis and among the military commands. Army divisions were agitating for us to accelerate our engagement in their particular areas of responsibility. We could not keep up with the demand.

At the same time, Baghdad was growing increasingly dangerous. When traveling to other military bases in the country via Blackhawk helicopter, or to industrial sites in Baghdad, we would fly over the city, often multiple times a month. The rapid decline in street life revealed how much security was declining. Most of the city appeared barren. No one was walking the streets, and the few cars were driving at very high speed. Ad hoc roadblocks were everywhere, some manned by police, some by civilians, some to protect neighborhoods, some to shake down travelers for cash before allowing passage through a particular area of the city. A palpable sense of fear had settled over the city.

When we would stay in the Green Zone, we would be assigned a room at night in a trailer. When the sun set, alarms would sound a warning of incoming rockets, usually launched from Sadr City by Shia Mahdi army militias, but sometimes from Sunni neighborhoods. When alarms sounded during daylight hours, procedures called for a quick dash into a concrete "duck and cover" bunker. But at night, you were to stay put in your quarters. Too often, the following morning, one or more trailers had been blown up, with crime-scene tape preventing onlookers from gaining access to the grisly scene. Usually within forty-eight hours, KBR cranes would efficiently arrive to lift out the wreckage of the destroyed trailer, and drop in a new one.

It was nerve-wracking. We would usually work late into the night inside the palace itself, retiring to bed at two or three A.M. The 107-mm rockets commonly used by insurgents could not penetrate the palace, and our jet lag made sleep impossible anyway. As the attacks became more and more frequent, tension among embassy personnel grew, and tempers flared.

The more we worked in the Green Zone, the more we began to understand the embassy and its daily activity. As the hundreds of American civilians rarely met with Iraqis, they had little direct access to information about what was going on in the country. But a key element of the roles of IRMO and embassy staff was to provide updates on progress in their respective areas of responsibility, sending reports up the chain of command that could be incorporated into online reports (cables) back to Washington. As the Task Force grew more and more active in its engagements around the country, the IRMO, embassy, and MNFI civil affairs staffs began to demand reports and attendance at meetings by Task Force personnel.

This seemed, on its face, like a reasonable expectation. But soon we were overwhelmed. In 2006, there were twenty-seven meetings every week on economic development within the embassy compound. We were expected to attend all of them. Not a single Iraqi participated. The meetings consisted of civilians and MNFI civil affairs military officers, who rarely went outside of the embassy compound, briefing each other, usually compiling information from the Internet or media publications that were translated and reviewed. Hundreds of different people participated in these meetings. As a small team, with a core leadership of six overseeing a total team of about sixty industry, factory, and military contracting experts in the fall of 2006, the Task Force had no ability to staff the meetings in the embassy.[1] After a few weeks of trying, we gave up.

This generated even greater resentment of our work. We were operating completely outside of the restrictive security policies of the embassy, freely meeting all over the country embedded with military units in the field, collaborating directly with senior Iraqi officials, provincial leaders, businessmen, and tribal sheikhs, and the lower-level embassy staffers felt they were intentionally being kept in the dark. I was meeting directly with Ambassador Khalilzad and several of his deputies, keeping them briefed on our activities. Bob Love was meeting with senior leaders as well. But there was no way to "feed the beast"—

the huge civilian bureaucracy trapped in the Green Zone, starving for information. And the beast was getting increasingly upset at not being fed.

*   *

We identified, out of the dozens of factories we assessed, ten that had high potential and required minimal effort to get running, that would put more than ten thousand Iraqis back to work. Once this "top ten" list was complete, we would move on to additional operations throughout the country. The factories in the top ten list included Iskandiriyah, Najaf clothing, Ramadi ceramics, and Baiji fertilizer, among others. Each required a small amount of funding to get raw material or some spare parts to get running. Tracking the status of these top ten factories became part of our regular updates to MNFI and MNCI commanders.[2]

In Washington, the bureaucracy was moving at its usual glacial pace in getting the Task Force the resources needed to make a difference. Just as when I was hired, the personnel management process was painfully slow. We were using McKinsey & Co. consultants to do initial factory assessments, but to restart operations we needed to hire seasoned factory managers from a variety of industries. We were having no problem recruiting volunteers to join our team, but it was almost impossible to hire them quickly. It was a similar problem with support staff, personnel to "feed the beast" in the Green Zone, with its endless demands for updates and briefings.

To speed up the process, we ended up hiring factory experts as contractors. We assembled an impressive team of highly experienced factory executives and shop floor engineers, all ready and willing to deploy with the troops in areas of violence. It was inspiring to see this group answer the call to serve. To lead them, I reached into my own Rolodex and recruited William Duncan, an executive I had met at JDS Uniphase who ran a $1 billion operation in Ottawa, Canada, and whose experience included stints in factory and supply chain management at McDonnell Douglas and other industrial companies.

For support staff the situation was more complex. The federal hiring process simply would not respond to our need to move quickly, and the staff at the embassy refused to work with nongovernment staff members. I could not substitute contractors for leadership personnel to work in direct collaboration with the embassy. The military command was more flexible about this. They did not care about the personnel status of our team; they just needed talented people deployed as soon as possible.

In less than six months our mission had experienced significant expansion of scope. From a beginning focused on automating military contracting and creating central visibility for contracts for General Scott, we had expanded to encompass the reversal of misguided CPA policy for Iraqi industrial operations. Now we were working not only to restart Iraqi factories, but also to create supply partnerships with American firms. Yet our human and financial resources were lagging our workload by about six months. All the while, the military command, embassy staff, and Iraqi leadership were asking for more and more assistance.

※ ※

As I tried to secure small amounts of funding to get factories restarted, I hit a legal roadblock. No matter how hard we tried, there was no funding that the lawyers in the Pentagon would allow us to apply to buy raw material, or parts, or to pay for servicing equipment in Iraqi factories. This was absurd to me. The Department was spending a staggering amount of money, not only on "kinetic" military operations, but also on construction projects, road building, schools, hospitals, and any number of humanitarian relief projects. But the Defense Department fiscal lawyers would not budge. Their interpretation of congressional intent for funds appropriated to the Department, even for local projects, did not include restarting factories.

For the lack of a few hundred thousand dollars per site, our top ten list of "quick-hit" factories that would get momentum going for our work was now at risk. In spite of the ongoing sponsorship and support of Deputy Secretary England, and the commander of all coalition forces in Iraq, General Casey, we were stalled over an amount of money that would not represent ten minutes of Defense Department spending in Iraq.

The bureaucracy was crippling our mission.

My anger at the Pentagon bureaucracy manifested itself in my front office. Half of my team was focused on Iraq, and half was still focused on my original mission, defense business modernization. Recruited to join my business transformation office in 2005, many had left behind desirable jobs in other parts of the government or the private sector and bought into our vision of reforming the Pentagon. Now my primary focus was elsewhere. When people returned from extended stints in Iraq, I would give the Iraq-focused staff ample time off. In Iraq, the team worked 24/7, with little sleep, at nearly constant risk of violence. So when they arrived back in Washington, they were allowed extra days off and permitted to sleep in until their hours adjusted. This caused real resentment among the staff members who were not focused on Iraq, but I had no patience for it. A rift emerged within my own front office support staff that would grow deeper in the months ahead.

Before his retirement that December, Donald Rumsfeld visited Iraq for a last time to say farewell to the troops and the senior commanders. While I had worked in his Defense Department since August 2004, and had, in partnership with Tom Modly, revitalized the failing business modernization initiative launched at his direction on September 10, 2001, I had never met Donald Rumsfeld. This was no small irony. Much of the enmity I was getting from the State Department was attributed to their perception that I, as a senior political appointee in the Defense Department, was a "Rumsfeld guy."

Rumsfeld arrived in Baghdad late in December for his farewell visit, staying at the Joint Visitors Bureau Hotel at Camp Victory. I received word through my staff that he had requested a meeting with me. After two years, I would finally meet Secretary Rumsfeld. I arranged for the entire team, including our industry group, to convene in a dining room at the palace, so they could all get a chance to meet the Secretary.

I had been staying at the JVB Hotel while in country, leaving my belongings in my quarters for days at a time while we traveled throughout Iraq. I arrived late on the evening of December 17, checking in at the "front desk" with the Kansas National Guard unit that had been our hosts every month since the start of our mission. The young enlisted soldier who had handed me my key in every prior visit looked pale, informing me, "I'm sorry, sir, but I don't have a key for you." I asked what the problem was, and he told me I needed to speak to his commander.

This was odd.

I went to the commander, who took me aside, and told me that he was afraid I must have been fired. I assured him this couldn't be the case, but he was certain he was right.

Tired and covered in dust from a long day in the field, and now annoyed, I strode down the hallway toward the rooms usually reserved for high-level visitors. I had every intention of confronting somebody for an explanation. As I walked, a member of my staff grabbed my arm, and explained what happened. "Secretary Rumsfeld's advance staff arrived earlier today, and they took over all the rooms. They walked in to your room, grabbed your bags and belongings, and threw them into the hallway. They told the Kansas National Guard staff, 'These belong to some guy named Brinkley, get them out of here!' The hotel staff thinks you must be getting fired."

Rumsfeld's staff was notorious in the Pentagon for "wearing Rumsfeld's rank," and running roughshod over anyone they felt they could. Clearly that had happened here.

Grabbing all my bags and gear, I walked up front and asked the National Guard units for a tent or a trailer—whatever was vacant, away from the palace. Relieved, the soldier handed me a key, and gave me directions.

While I was trekking to my new quarters in a distant trailer unit, Rumsfeld swept into the palace dining room, greeting my team warmly and shaking every hand. I remained in my quarters for a few minutes to clean up and to calm down from my offense at having been slighted by Rumsfeld's staff. Before I joined the team back in the palace, Rumsfeld had left for a farewell dinner with General Casey.

I still had never met Don Rumsfeld.

✳   ✳

In March 2006, Congress had established a commission to review the state of the Iraq conflict and make recommendations on the way forward. Known as the Iraq Study Group, this commission was due to release its report before the end of the year.[3] I was concerned that the state of the Iraqi economy was not being represented in the discussions. I met with several of the support staff members for the commission at the United States Institute for Peace to discuss our findings and our work to restore economic activity, and set about attempting to meet with the members of the commission.

One of the members of the commission was Robert Gates. A former CIA Director in the administration of George H. W. Bush, Gates was serving as the president of Texas A&M University. I arranged to visit College Station, Texas, to meet with Gates, to provide input about our work in Iraq.

When I arrived at his office that October, Gates welcomed me, and then we walked to a nearby food court in the student center. Surrounded by students coming and going, we sat at a table, ate fast food, and talked about Iraq for more than two hours. I was brutally honest in my assessment of the situation in Iraq with regard to the nonmilitary effort. At the end of the conversation, I felt drained of information—and realized I had learned little to nothing about what the commission was thinking or might conclude in its report. In true "Agency" style, Gates had kept me talking and gathered all the information I had to offer. But I could tell that my insights about the economic aspects of the problems in Iraq were news to him. I left feeling I had not wasted my time.

Two weeks after my trip to College Station, the Bush Administration announced the resignation of Donald Rumsfeld as Secretary of Defense, and the nomination of Robert Gates as his successor.[4] My meeting with Gates and its timing were a complete coincidence. But the bureaucratic perception in the Pentagon that I was somehow connected to him did not hurt as I tried to push faster action on our hiring and funding issues.

With Rumsfeld's departure, Tom Modly's role in business transformation efforts soon changed. He led the Transition Support Team for Secretary Gates for several weeks before departing to return to the private sector. He had faced heavy bureaucratic resistance to our efforts on his own for most of 2006, with little to no support from his leadership, and after five years in the Pentagon was ready to move on. A new director of the BTA, David Fisher, was hired, reporting to me. Elizabeth McGrath, a senior career civil servant with deep knowledge of Pentagon budget and accounting processes, moved into a leadership role as my deputy, focused on overseeing business transformation programs during my absences in Iraq. For the remainder of the Bush Administration, the BTA delivered significant accomplishments across a range of business operations throughout the department. But with Tom's departure and my immersion in the Iraq mission, the accelerating momentum Tom and I had established for reforming the Pentagon bureaucracy was lost.

※   ※

General Chiarelli remained firm in his support of our work, making the case for our efforts in the media with far greater credibility than we could have mustered on our own. He continued to ensure our work had the full support of his civil affairs officers and units, and that our logistical support was given the same priority as other noncombat military missions. Both Generals Casey and Chiarelli hosted frequent sessions with our team, and would specifically invite our industry experts and advisors to discussions about the state of the economy and the opportunities present in Iraqi industry. They also communicated to the Pentagon civilian leadership the critical nature of our work, ensuring that the bureaucracy could not shut us down.

Chiarelli was the first combat general I would get to know. He was burdened with an incomprehensible responsibility, making decisions every day that affected the lives of soldiers and marines under his command, in the midst of a rising death toll caused by a now-blazing insurgency. Some days, before a periodic review of our progress with him, would be filled with particularly grim news of U.S. casualties. On such days, Chiarelli would be especially reserved, his eyes heavy with the burden of command.

He would still meet, giving us direction and time for strategic input. In spite of the lack of adequate forces to secure the country, he never showed any lack of confidence to his subordinates, especially my team of civilians. Working so closely with a combat command, I felt as though we were being drawn into a circle few civilians, certainly few outsiders like ourselves, ever got to see.

I remembered how upset I used to get about things in my old days at JDS Uniphase, how important the decisions seemed at the time, and how mundane that life seemed now.

The more I worked with the commands, and with our troops in the field, the more I grew to love the military. The young soldiers and marines we met in the field never failed to demonstrate professionalism, even when their faces betrayed fatigue and weariness, and sometimes sorrow, over their increasingly frustrating mission. In an age of an all-volunteer force, most Americans are far removed from the life of our military servicemen and -women. We were being drawn into a world most civilians today never experience.

As in Washington, where I had forced myself to learn the language of the Defense Department and the U.S.-based military support organizations in logistics, finance, and acquisition commands, I now worked to learn the language and structures of the combat military. Roles and responsibilities of commissioned and noncommissioned officers, and their own vernacular, became second nature to me. The colorful language and humor of combat-deployed forces also became second nature.

As a team, we grew extremely tight-knit. Working within this environment, placing ourselves in harm's way with the troops, a tight familial bond formed among us. We worked constantly. Jet lag reduced our sleep to a few short hours a night, with the day starting early on military time at 0700 regardless of when we would finally fall asleep. The exposure to constant violence eventually became routine, and we stopped thinking about the risks of our work. We simply began doing our jobs, along with the troops who did their jobs.

To help manage the stress of our work and to combat jet lag, I would go to the gym on whatever base we were staying at, where I would work out for hours with the troops. By January 1, 2007, I was down to 220 pounds, having lost 50 pounds in six months.

I immersed myself in the study of the region, devouring every book I could find on the Arab world—historical and political—and the Islamic faith and all of its sects. I also made every effort to learn Arabic, an extremely difficult language to pick up. Even when frequently immersed among Iraqis speaking no English it took months before I could follow the train of conversations.

Chiarelli's tenure as corps commander was slated to end in December. Much was being made about the change of command back in the States. The transition from Casey and Chiarelli to new commanders was being heralded as a new start in Iraq, but being there the situation was far more complicated. For months, MNFI and MNCI had been pulling forces into Baghdad—there simply were not enough troops available on the ground to enable Baghdad to be secured and a counterinsurgency strategy to be applied. Chiarelli had championed counterinsurgency concepts for some time, and as an element of this had championed our entire effort. I was concerned we would lose support as the command turned over.[5] As our initial sponsor, he had developed a seamless relationship between us and his command, and we needed this relationship to continue with his replacement, Lieutenant General Raymond Odierno. As a two-star general in 2003 and 2004, Odierno had led the 4th Infantry Division into Salah ad Din Province north of Baghdad, the ancestral homeland of Saddam Hussein, who was captured under Odierno's command. The intensity of combat operations during the early campaign under Odierno earned him a reputation as a ferocious battle commander, not necessarily a counterinsurgency expert.

My initial meeting was formal but productive. At six-five, fully built with a shaved head, and a quiet and intense personal style, Odierno had an intimidating presence. He indicated full awareness of our work, and gave us the task of aligning our efforts with his new divisional commanders' efforts to restore normality as his troops worked to reestablish security.

Odierno's chief of staff, Marine Major General Thomas "Tango" Moore, was less sanguine about our mission. While he indicated we would continue to receive support, he made clear that the focus of MNCI would now be on kinetic operations, not on perceived soft-power efforts. It was clear that we were identified within the new MNCI command staff as a remnant of the last command. This is something we would experience multiple times in coming years. In this respect, military commands are no different from any other organization. When a new leader takes charge, the current "carry-over" staff has to prove itself all over again, and initiatives that were overtly tied to the "old guard" have a hard time keeping their place in the hierarchy of priority and support.

As Chiarelli left Iraq, it soon became clear that the intellectual drive for economic stabilization within the overall campaign effort would go to General Casey's newly announced successor, General David Petraeus. In his first stint as a commander in northern Iraq in 2003, Petraeus had seen the need for rapid economic development to follow the downfall of the Saddam Hussein regime. He had launched innovative efforts to drive funding and resources into areas near Mosul as diverse as agriculture and tourism. In this regard, Petraeus was an early proponent of economic development as a critical factor in stabilizing Iraq. A Princeton PhD, Petraeus had subject-matter expertise on economic development.

I first met Petraeus in a private dinner in Washington, prior to his deployment to relieve General Casey. Petraeus questioned many of my baseline assumptions, not in a manner that indicated a lack of support, but to verify I knew what I was talking about. He had an unusual command of detailed information for a four-star general, reciting statistics and cases from his prior engagements in Iraq, and from his recent assessments of the current economic situation. Petraeus was clearly accustomed to dealing with Washington political appointees who lacked ground-level understanding. It was clear I would have to earn Petraeus's support for my involvement in his area of responsibility.

As the evening ended, he ended the discussion positively, and I felt that the Task Force would fit well into his strategic vision.

✳   ✳

In the fall of 2006, I had received a briefing from one of the leading agricultural-development institutions in the world, the Borlaug Institute for International Agriculture, based at Texas A&M University. Named for Norman Borlaug, a Nobel Laureate who led the technical effort that caused the "green revolution" and eliminated famine in the Asian subcontinent, the Borlaug Institute is a remarkable institution.[6] Staffed by American agronomists recruited from land-grant universities throughout the United States, Borlaug researchers are a combination of "Indiana Jones" expeditionary personalities with doctoral-level expertise in soil and crop science. They work throughout poverty-stricken areas of the world, often in harm's way, to modernize farming practices and improve food production, alleviating hunger and disease. The land-grant agricultural institutions of the United States are a tremendous but little-known national foreign policy asset, one that had not yet been deployed to Iraq.

Jerry Jones, a senior advisor to the Secretary of Defense, introduced me to Ed Price, the Director of the Borlaug Institute. Price met with me to explain how Iraq's agricultural sector had collapsed, and how critical it was to restore farming as a major element of economic opportunity. I had been particularly interested in understanding how to prioritize our factory work to benefit to the agricultural sector—i.e., focusing on textile mills, food processors, fertilizer plants, etc. After our initial meeting, Ed had stayed in continual contact with me, sharing ideas and advice on our work.

Early in February 2007, Price contacted me to describe an opportunity. It seemed that there had been an international blight affecting seed potatoes commonly planted in Iraq, causing a major shortage for the upcoming planting season. If we wanted to do something meaningful for Iraqi farmers, finding an alternative source of seed potatoes was a good start. As Baghdad, Anbar, and Babil Provinces were areas of heavy potato cultivation, and as these provinces were some of the most violent areas of the country, doing something for their farmers would fit well into the counterinsurgency efforts General Petraeus would be pursuing. Price had identified one alternative source of seed potatoes from a strain proved to grow in Iraqi conditions, but the only supply available was in Newfoundland.

Since the launch of the Task Force, I had sent monthly status review memos to General Casey and General Chiarelli, and continued to do so with the new commanders. I included a line about the seed potato issue and opportunity in my first monthly update to General Petraeus. Petraeus noticed this, and forwarded it to his subcommands for review and action.

What happened next was unexpected. Eager to impress the incoming MNFI commander, the command staffs in Baghdad shotgunned the note about seed potatoes all over the entire command and embassy community. Before I could react, the entire MNFI organization was scurrying to understand the problem, and directly contacting Ed Price for additional information. Price provided details on the source of alternative seed in Nova Scotia, and logisticians began working out the details of transporting seed potatoes to Iraq.

It was like watching a train wreck via e-mail that I couldn't stop.

The numbers were ready twenty-four hours later. Logisticians estimated that sixty-three dedicated sorties of C-17 transport aircraft would be required to fly to Nova Scotia to get the potatoes to Iraq in time for spring planting season, which would end by April. The cost of this would run into millions of dollars. U.S. Transportation Command, and its subordinate Air Mobility Command, had already replied with incredulity about the whole idea.

The IRMO agricultural advisor, an individual with a background in dairy science who rarely if ever left the Green Zone, issued a blanket pronouncement that the whole issue was fiction, as everyone knew that Iraqis ate rice and not potatoes. His viewpoint was widely circulated, to nods of agreement among other denizens of the Green Zone and Camp Victory. He was also unaware that the U.S. Agency for International Development had supported field tests of alternative varieties of potatoes for Iraq.

Iraqis are, in fact, very active cultivators and consumers of potatoes. Price, feeling terrible about the whole fiasco, forwarded a formal letter from the Iraqi Minister of Agriculture asking him to help find an alternative source of seed potatoes that year.[7] But the IRMO agricultural advisor had never met the Minister of Agriculture, explaining that since he was a member of the radical Shiite Sadrist political party, he could not meet with him.

Had the advisor been engaged with the Ministry of Agriculture, as his job required him to, he would have known about the seed potato shortage months earlier, in time to enable the replacement seed to be sent at low cost via ship instead of airlifted—a perfectly rational solution to a simple problem. Instead, the potato harvest in the summer of 2007 collapsed, leaving farmers in rural areas of Baghdad, Anbar, and Babil Provinces, the heart of the Sunni "Triangle of Death," in even greater economic distress. As potato harvests are labor intensive, and as potato processing is labor intensive, it is hard to estimate how many workers were actually affected by the crop failure, but it would number in the thousands.

Thankfully for American morale, there was no shortage of potatoes in the Green Zone that year. Frozen Idaho potatoes continued to arrive daily, shipped from cold storage in Kuwait, for the french fries in the embassy dining facility.

✳   ✳

As our work gained attention at home, the appeals from the U.S. Chamber of Commerce began to attract support from American industries. Major firms including Caterpillar, Cummins Diesel, and a variety of midsized American manufacturers showed an interest in engaging in Iraq.

I made an appeal that would be repeated often in coming months. I offered to take executives to Iraq, to see firsthand the operations we believed could supply goods to the U.S., or serve as partners to open markets for American goods in Iraq. The American companies could then decide if it made sense based on firsthand knowledge.

Our first delegation of American businessmen was held in January 2007. Six executives from American companies joined the delegation, along with representatives from the U.S. Chamber of Commerce. We stayed at Camp Victory, hosted by the JVB Hotel staff. Lieutenant General Odierno and his divisional commanders were fully engaged, with additional command meetings on economic strategy by General Casey, Major General Joseph Fil, commander of Multi-National Division—Baghdad, and Major General Zilmer, Commander of IMEF Multi-National Forces–West in Anbar Province.

Together, this delegation would tour the restarted industrial operations in Iskandiriyah, as well as Baiji Fertilizer, a large industrial work in Taji called Nassr Automotive Industries, and a food-processing facility in Irbil, Kurdistan. The Kurdistan Regional Government set up a large evening reception, inviting Kurdish businessmen from all over the surrounding area to meet this first American business delegation to the KRG since 2003.

This first delegation was designed to "shake out" our thinking, and to get some additional advice on what to do. Thomas Donohue Jr., the son of Chamber of Commerce President Thomas Donohue, and CEO of Adelphi Capital, provided a lot of advice—a role he would play for years to come. But the participants also would serve as "credible" voices, not from the government, to communicate what they saw back at home, to their peers and colleagues in various industry groups and forums.

The scale of our effort was overwhelming to them. We had more than fifty industry experts working to get operations restored with no dedicated funds to buy spare parts or raw materials, working on industries as varied as chemical processing, carpet weaving, textile manufacturing, heavy industry, and food processing. I could honestly have used five hundred industry experts. The visiting executives could see the impact on the local community our mere engagement was having. The delegation was warmly welcomed by Iraqis everywhere they went. This flew in the face of their expectations of hostility based on the news coverage at home. More important, the visitors could see the positive impact of our efforts on the morale of the troops, at the command level and in the field, who communicated their support for what we were doing and asked for more engagement by American business.

Having run sales operations in the past, I was thinking like a sales manager. Sales is a game of percentages. If you want to land a customer quickly and don't have time for lengthy relationship building, you have to engage a lot of potential customers with your sales pitch. To me, if we wanted to establish business relationships between American companies and Iraqi businesses, we would need to get a lot of American companies over to Iraq and hope that a few of them would follow up and do business. This traditional sales-oriented thinking would create yet another mistake in leading the effort, which would irreparably damage my working relationship with many of Odierno's staff.

I began planning for a large delegation to visit Iraq—something far larger than had ever been attempted. We issued a blanket invitation via the United States Chamber of Commerce to American businessmen to engage in support of the troops. The appeal went out to other business groups as well, including Business Executives for National Security, and the Business Roundtable. When the invitation rolled in, we had a delegation of more than fifty business leaders from across American industry, including a number of agricultural-sector companies. We augmented this large delegation with an additional team of agricultural faculty from American land-grant universities as well as the Borlaug Institute. The total size of the delegation would exceed sixty high-profile visitors to Iraq.

Bob Love worked around the clock to create a multifaceted engagement program, with groups of executives sent to different areas of the country, with Task Force leaders, to see manufacturing operations, agribusinesses, farms, and other businesses. It was a massive operational undertaking, requiring complex logistical coordination with multiple commands for housing, food, security, and movement.

For a week, we consumed a number of the helicopter assets normally reserved for civilian movement of State Department personnel, creating no small amount of annoyance at the embassy. The State Department, surprised at the level of engagement the Task Force had generated, sent a senior Foreign Service officer with us, something I welcomed with open arms. Todd Schwartz, a seasoned expert on the region, became a long-term ally for our work after engaging with the delegation.

The visit went beyond our wildest hopes in terms of impact. This was not a low-level set of company representatives. Through the efforts of the Chamber and other organizations, we had senior executives from major American multinationals, seeing the real Iraq for the first time. Exposed to the good and bad, but from a hands-on view, the delegation was worth the effort if only to communicate the reality of the Iraqi situation at home, where the heated debate over the surge continued. Our work was no longer Pentagon spin; I could now refer skeptics to representatives of highly regarded American enterprises to validate what we were reporting.

But the consumption of the command staff at MNCI and MNFI was extreme. Not only had they redirected helicopter assets, at the expense of State Department use, they had also worked long hard hours to support a highly complex nationwide mission. General Tango Moore expressed his concern to Bob Love, who relayed Moore's frustration to me. I told Bob to inform General Moore that he should want 5,000 businessmen in Iraq, not just 50, and we would not reduce the size of the delegation. This foolish aggressive behavior on my part burned up a lot of the goodwill of the new staff working under MNCI.

The delegation was in Iraq when General Petraeus arrived to assume command from General Casey on February 10. The potato episode had just occurred and now there was a huge business delegation in Petraeus's Area of Responsibility. This was not the best timing on my part.

Petraeus arrived to a reception we were holding, and greeted all of the attendees warmly but hastily. Colonel Michael Meese, a strategic advisor to the new command, was a member of Petraeus's highly regarded "council of colonels," a group of thought leaders with doctoral level education in fields relevant to counterinsurgency and stabilization. I met him that evening, establishing a relationship that would prove invaluable many times over the years to come.

✳   ✳

The delegation visited many sites during its week in country. One particularly harrowing engagement took place in Baqubah, the capital city of Diyala Province. As operations were heating up in Baghdad in a broad effort to clear the city of Al Qaeda, many were fleeing northeast into Diyala, specifically gathering in Baqubah.

Our experience rolling into a large electrical transformer factory was every bit as unsettling as our first visits to Ramadi and Iskandiriyah. Ambient fear filled the city, and the troops that were managing our visit were highly tense. As we arrived at the compound, the front gate was blocked by a large concrete "jersey" barrier, similar to those used to block construction activity on American highways. After a long pause, the military unit commander made the decision to leave our vehicles and walk up the half-mile-long drive into the compound.

As we walked, I could see we were at great risk. There was not a sound, no birds were chirping, no stray dogs, no sounds at all. The fields to the sides of the driveway were littered with trash and burnt out vehicles, each a perfect hiding place for a sniper or to place an IED.

Mark Treanor, a senior vice president with Wachovia Corporation, the East Coast banking giant, and several other executives walked with me as we finally reached the large buildings of the compound. Entering the headquarters facility, we were led by the unit soldiers up to the office of the general manager. He was literally in a state of shocked panic to see us there.

Pointing to bullet holes in the window of his office, he told us that only the day before he had taken sniper fire while in his office. His workforce had been on site a week before, but now were all at home, having received threats that if they boarded a bus to go to the factory they would all be killed. His phone line had been cut off the day before, and he was convinced that he would be killed if he left the factory. After long discussion, he agreed to walk us through his facilities.

This was yet another surprising tour of a viable Iraqi factory shut down because of failed economic policies. The production lines made transformers used for electrical grids. In the 1980s, the factory had a joint-venture partnership with Mitsubishi of Japan, and was building Mitsubishi designed transformers and other electrical equipment. The gear they were producing was high quality. In a country with no electricity, now importing electrical equipment to maintain its failing grid, having this factory shut down made absolutely no sense. The site, at its peak, employed more than 2,000 skilled professionals, engineers, and production workers. It was part of the industrial backbone of the community. Now dusty and in need of some cleanup and repair, it was clearly not obsolete.

The manager completed his tour quickly, and bade us farewell. I told him we would be back soon, and that we would make his factory a priority for restoration of production. He openly stated that he could not believe my words, but hoped they were true. My heart was pained leaving him. I honestly did not know if we would ever see him again given the way Diyala was falling into violence.

Less than two weeks later, Task Force team leader Dave Scantling had a satellite dish and Internet phone service installed at the factory— enabling the manager to call for help from the nearby military base when under attack. Years later, after the Task Force had completed a number of projects at his site, and after his factory had received private investment proposals from multinational companies, he told me that our simple act of getting a phone installed had been the first sign of hope he had seen in months, and had enabled him to start the long restoration of his factory to full production.

The delegation ended with a large press conference for international and Iraqi media held outside near a large lake on Camp Victory. Several members of the delegation spoke of their observations, and their confidence that economic development would help restore normal life and improve security in the country. More than half of the companies represented in the delegation initiated business engagement in Iraq following their trip. In spite of this success rate, I never again attempted such a large delegation—

from then on we would bring smaller targeted groups to Iraq focused on specific industries, a strategy that had a high success rate and created far less of a burden on command resources.

*   *

By March 2007 we were now eight months into our work, in a perpetual fog from jet lag because of rotations back and forth to D.C., and physically breaking down from constant sickness and the weariness of hauling duffle bags with two weeks of clothes and communications equipment everywhere we went. Understaffed, underfunded, and under-resourced, we were cracking under the strain of endless demands for more help in the field, and lack of effective bureaucratic support at home, in spite of Deputy Secretary England's direction to the bureaucracy.

Our work continued to progress, and we began to see the improvements in spite of the lack of funding. We also finally began to get a sense of the total true unemployment picture in Iraq.

The World Bank was reporting total unemployment in Iraq at 18 percent, but there was no place we could find in Iraq where anywhere near 82 percent of the working-age population was employed. Even Kurdistan, which was booming compared to the rest of Iraq, had a higher unemployment problem than 18 percent.

We then received a briefing on statistical unemployment from COSIT, the national statistical agency of Iraq. Working under a grant from the United Nations, they confirmed the estimate of unemployment at 18 percent. But they also reported a statistic called "underemployment," defined at the time for Iraq as greater than fifteen hours of work a week. This statistic was used to identify a break-over point of income, below which a risk of hunger might take hold. The underemployed represented an additional 30 percent of Iraqi workers. Added to the base unemployment statistic of 18 percent, and we had 50 percent of the population effectively out of meaningful work.[8]

We then learned that the COSIT statistics did not include workers in state-owned enterprises. Asked why, we were told again the purpose of the measurements was to determine risk of hunger or deprivation. Employees of state-owned enterprises were receiving approximately 40 percent of their original income, even though almost all state-owned factories and businesses were closed. In any other society, these workers would be classified as unemployed and receiving welfare payments. In Iraq, they were counted as employed workers. More than 500,000 workers fell into this category, out of a total Iraqi workforce of 6 million. Adding this category of workers raised real unemployment in Iraq to almost 60 percent.

Understanding these statistics added a level of clarity to the challenge of stabilizing Iraq. Imagine the impact of 60 percent unemployment to any society. Imagine how many police would be needed to secure any American city with 60 percent unemployment. This was the challenge our young soldiers and marines were facing, with the added complexity of a culture and language they did not understand.

*   *

In spite of a lack of funding, we were able to place orders on a number of sites. Containerized Housing Units (CHUs) were requested from Iskandiriyah and from the Nassr industrial operations in Taji. Clothing orders were placed for Iraqi uniforms in Najaf. Fabric to supply the uniforms was ordered from a large textile mill in Hillah, a town in southern Babil Province that was the site of the ruins of Babylon. Leather boots for the Iraqi military were ordered from the leatherworks in Baghdad that had provided mislabeled the soccer balls. And in the west, we were working actively with the marines to restore power in the far western town of Al Qaim, which had access to power from the Syrian grid, and had a large cement factory and a phosphate plant, each of which were in good condition but had been idled.

In my biweekly updates with General Petraeus, he continued to probe for details and to exhibit subtle skepticism about our work. I was unable to "connect" personally with him the way I had with Chiarelli, to establish an intuitive sense of alignment to his command intent. Finally, we were able to arrange a site visit for him to go with me to Najaf to tour the clothing factory and see firsthand the impact of our efforts. His public affairs staff arranged for NBC News to send a camera crew and correspondent on the trip. Petraeus's cultural advisor Sadi Othman traveled to Najaf as well. Othman had served every military leader and ambassador as the principal interpreter and advisor, liaising with Iraqi officials of every level and political faction since 2003. This visit to Najaf would begin a long-term collaboration with Othman for the Task Force that would last for years to come.

By this time, Najaf was running two full shifts, with more than 1,800 workers back on the job. We toured the facility together, reviewing its state-of-the-art design capability and production operations. The vast majority of the workforce were women, including almost all of the engineers and management staff other than the general manager.

Petraeus was clearly and visibly impacted by the operation. Finally, I felt he understood the value of our mission in a far deeper way than my update reports could have provided. On the flight back, I reiterated my commitment to ensure we restored normal life throughout Iraq, as had been done in Najaf. From that day forward, we became an integral part of his mission. NBC reported from the Najaf clothing factory that evening on the NBC Nightly News, but the majority of the story was not about the factory, but instead about violence of the day back in Baghdad. No matter. Our goal of demonstrating the value of our work to Petraeus had been achieved.

If only we could be as convincing in Washington, we could get somewhere.

✳   ✳

Our initial prioritized "top ten" list of factories needed just under $6 million in funding to get them fully operational. Now, in alignment with the new campaign plan, we had developed a priority list of factories for each divisional command. We estimated that within a year, applying $100 million in funding would enable almost all major industrial operations in Iraq to be reopened to a degree that would restore significant employment in areas of unrest. Although this amount seemed large, it was a tiny amount relative to the $12 billion being spent every month in 2007 on military operations in Iraq.

Journalist Fareed Zakaria ran an op-ed in *Newsweek* in which he highlighted our efforts as a surge element that might work.[9] Rudolph Giuliani and Newt Gingrich also weighed in, jointly publishing an op-ed in the *Wall Street Journal* making a case for jobs as a key to stability in Iraq, and highlighting the Task Force effort as worthy of support.[10] There were a number of other individuals, Democrats and Republicans, who directly spoke on our behalf with representatives and senators. It made a big difference.

Working with the Legislative Affairs Office in the Pentagon, draft language requesting an appropriation of $100 million in the supplemental war budget set to pass in May was submitted, late in the cycle for submissions. The Senate Armed Services Committee fully supported the appropriation, and inserted language into the supplemental budget law. The House committees and subcommittees, including Armed Services, Foreign Operations, and Appropriations, all were against giving the Defense Department economic-development funding. Legislative Affairs advisor Esther Swartz, who had worked with me for more than two years on business transformation legislative support, was confident that the two sides would appropriate at least $50 million once they met in conference to pass final legislation.

Further complicating our request for funding was a late request from the State Department asking for $250 million for a private investment fund for Iraq. Modeled after successful efforts applied in eastern Europe after the fall of the iron curtain, the request sought to create a source of venture funding for Iraqi entrepreneurs.[11] USAID would administer these funds.

This proposal was an initiative driven by a newly appointed American ambassador to Iraq, Ryan Crocker, and had the active support of our new colleague in Baghdad, Todd Schwartz. Crocker was a quiet, reflective personality with a deep history in and knowledge of Iraq and the broader region. Completely fluent in Arabic, Crocker would receive all of our delegations to Iraq, and was an ardent supporter of our work, in spite of the active resistance of subordinate organizations within the embassy.

Both Crocker and Schwartz asked me to support their effort to get approval for the investment fund. I thought this was a great idea, and hoped again it could serve to provide a platform for collaboration with the embassy, and a potential path for me to hand off the work of the Task Force. I lobbied actively for their funding, to no avail.

A series of scathing reports on the failure of reconstruction efforts by the Special Inspector General for Iraq Reconstruction, Stuart Bowen, was filling the pages of newspapers at home. Project after project was called into question, with clear violations of safety, health, and basic construction standards cited. Bowen was unflappable in his determination to root out waste, fraud, and abuse among the contractor community in Iraq.[12] But these high-profile cases did no favors to efforts to maintain or gain additional funding. As the explanation given by organizations like the Army Corps of Engineers and USAID in their own defense was a lack of adequate management resources to oversee projects, Congress was not inclined to add additional responsibility to USAID, especially in an area such as private investment.

The debate over the surge, followed by the emerging campaign rhetoric caused by candidates beginning to jockey for the 2008 presidential election, kept the 2007 Defense Supplemental budget on hold until late in the spring. When it finally passed, on May 27, 2007, the Task Force received $50 million in a one-year appropriation to facilitate the revitalization and reopening of Iraqi industries[13].

The money requested by the State Department for a private investment fund was not approved. This was not well received within the embassy in Baghdad.

From the time the law was enacted to provide the $50 million appropriation, two months would pass before we would have the actual funding transferred into accounts where it could be applied to purchase items for reopening factories. General Petraeus was slated to testify to Congress on the progress of the surge in October. That gave us only a few short months to try to deliver as much progress as possible, in contribution to the economic elements of the counterinsurgency strategy. I called our team together at our industry team headquarters at Camp Victory, and described the challenge to them.

By now, the industry team of manufacturing experts had been working for almost a year, deployed full-time in Iraq. They had surveyed more than seventy factories, and identified exactly what was needed to reopen each of them, including vendors and suppliers of parts and raw materials. I challenged them to make one hard push to get as much done as possible by the end of September.

Bob Love was exhausted. I was exhausted. The entire team was exhausted.

In spite of their exhaustion, they stepped up to the challenge.

5.

BUILDING MOMENTUM

Sometimes it is logical to step above a foreign policy and look at it all through a purely economic lens, through the eyes of an investor seeking a return on his investment.

Twelve billion dollars a month on military operations—*$144 billion a year*—to secure a $40 billion economy. If this were a private enterprise, with that poor a return on invested capital, you would short the stock. Of course the mission in Iraq was not about making an investment for financial return. There were security and humanitarian aspects of the mission that cannot be measured financially. But looking at it financially was a useful exercise in one respect. How much less would we have needed to spend on military operations had we approached the mission differently from the beginning—had we focused on economic well-being leveraging our own economic strength instead of placing the entire burden on the military.

America's economy was booming in 2006–07. A tiny percentage of the hundreds of billions of dollars in agricultural products, parts, clothing, or other raw materials that American companies purchased abroad from countries all over Asia, if redirected to Iraq, would put all of Iraq back to work, at a fraction of the cost of our military operations. A step like that would send a powerful positive message to Iraqis— fulfilling their expectation of 2003 that they would be plugged into the global economy, and undermine the radicalization efforts of Al Qaeda and Shia militias.

Most important, it would save the lives of our armed forces by removing economically motivated violent actors from the battlefield, enabling the military to focus on the far smaller number of radical Islamists bent on nihilism.

It sounded simple. It wasn't. Not by any measure.

As our first efforts to reopen Iraqi industries gained momentum, and as capacity to build products was restored, we increased our effort to establish supply relationships or joint ventures with Iraqi companies. The offer to American business leaders was simple: I would personally host their visit to Iraq, traveling with them into the country and taking them throughout Iraq to see firsthand the opportunities we believed were compelling. They would meet with senior U.S. commanders, with the prime minister and other key ministers, and with Ambassador Crocker. We wanted their advice, and we wanted them to consider doing business in Iraq if they were convinced, as we were, that there was money to be made.

This offer to *visit* Iraq was surprisingly well-received. From January through August 2007, we hosted more than one hundred senior company representatives—at a time when the headlines at home about Iraq couldn't have been much worse. As more and more business leaders visited, some patterns became clear.

As most had no exposure to or experience with the military, and as our society has become increasingly disconnected from the military in the post-Vietnam era of the all-volunteer force, getting to see and understand how our military worked in action was inspiring. That alone was often worth their visit—it provided a low-cost means for elite American leaders to see the conflict in Iraq firsthand, and to appreciate what our military was undertaking every day in extremely difficult circumstances.

I would always receive advice on my mission from executives. We would take executives to business enterprises, either recently reopened factories or private businesses all over the country. I cannot recall a single delegation that didn't leave behind many suggestions or ideas for how to accelerate our work. We incorporated all of this input into our efforts with Iraqi business leaders.

Finally, every delegation reinforced what we believed: while there were areas in Iraq that were too dangerous for business investment, there were other areas that were sufficiently stable, where profitable operations could be established, and that it was a mistake to ignore the stable areas out of fear driven by headlines highlighting violence in other parts of the country.

Even when American executives saw opportunity, and understood the tremendous long-term upsides in a country with the world's largest undeveloped oil reserves, they were plagued with the same problem our military and diplomatic organizations faced: American and international public opinion.

On returning home, an American executive proposing to engage in business in Iraq would invariably encounter two foes—a board of directors that was at best evenly split along the lines of American public opinion about the entire Iraq mission, and a general counsel terrified of the risks and liabilities the company could incur if the worst happened and someone were injured or killed. The polarization of American public opinion didn't stop at home. Employees, board members of companies, all were equally opinionated about the perceived debacle in Iraq, and they took these opinions to the workplace. It was impossible to harness the goodwill present to support the troops in the face of such negative public opinion. And every night public opinion declined more—as the worsening security situation dominated the headlines.

In this environment, the key was to get enough initial "first-movers" into Iraq to take away the sense of bewilderment companies faced when they wanted to engage.

*   *

When driving through Iraq, it was common to see early Soviet-era Czechoslovakian tractors rusting in fields. Most plowing was done with draft animals—horses or oxen—much as it had been for thousands of years. The first thing any Iraqi farmer asked about when meeting with us was how they could get mechanized farm equipment. From irrigation to plowing to harvesting, the potential for a large market for agricultural equipment was clear. Under UN sanctions it had been impossible to import any equipment for mechanization of agriculture.

Case New Holland is a storied American company, the merger of two great tractor and heavy equipment producers—Case Tractor, of Racine, Wisconsin, and New Holland Tractors, of New Holland, Pennsylvania—each with more than a century of history supplying agricultural and construction equipment.

Case New Holland saw Iraq's potential from the inception of our mission. Senior executive Joseph Samora and technical teams from CNH, as well as from its new Italian parent holding company Fiat, visited Iraq on multiple occasions in 2006 and 2007. Their intent was to establish assembly operations in Iraq as quickly as possible, understanding that if they created jobs, the goodwill they would accrue to their brand image would be immeasurable as Iraq emerged from violence in coming years.

Early in summer of 2007, the Task Force partnered with CNH to introduce assembly of New Holland farm tractors in the idled tractor assembly lines in Iskandiriyah. By this time, using our own spending and redirecting orders from imports to Iraqi suppliers, the Task Force had successfully put more than 1,000 workers back on the job in Iskandiriyah, building containerized housing units (CHUs) for military bases, large storage tanks and pressure vessels for the Ministry of Oil, assembling trucks for use by military logistics contractors, and other one-off orders. But to have the old Soviet-era tractor assembly line back up and running was a major objective. Interest was solicited from all of the American tractor manufacturers, but only CNH answered the call to engage in Iraq.

By the fall of 2007, State Company for Mechanical Industries in Iskandiriyah was assembling New Holland tractors, using imported partially assembled tractor kits initially, and then increasing the complexity of assembly as workers became familiar with the modern designs. Within two years, thousands of New Holland tractors were in use across Iraq; it became common when traveling through the countryside to spot blue New Holland tractors. Knowing where and how these tractors were assembled, and the workers whose livelihoods were restored, was very rewarding.

But more important, the restoration of agricultural production, and the improvements in farm yields, resulting from the opening of this market for Western goods, would dwarf the impact of the factory workers being reemployed. As we began to understand this nonlinear impact ourselves, we began to explore how to directly support agribusinesses at the source of agricultural production, not just via mechanization, but through direct improvements of technology at each stage of agricultural production.

Another major benefit of the CNH tractor assembly program in Iraq was the establishment of an indigenous demand-driven business. Earlier Task Force guests, Caterpillar and Cummins Diesel, had set up operations in Iraq almost immediately after visiting the country. But where Caterpillar and Cummins had entered Iraq to service and support power generation equipment originally imported as part of the U.S. mission, and expanded their business from this base of U.S.-purchased equipment, CNH established its presence based on the merits of the Iraqi market itself and its potential for significant growth. The fact that this growth was not driven directly by the hydrocarbon economy was equally valuable to our overall program, as it helped counter the perception at home that Iraq was destined, at best, to eventually become an oil-based command society—subject to the well-known detrimental effects such societies often display throughout the world, such as concentration of power, corruption, lack of regard for human rights, and lack of opportunity for the bulk of the population.

In each of these cases—CNH, Caterpillar, and Cummins, the Task Force had facilitated the establishment of business relationships in Iraq for well-known American companies. These "ice-breaking" relationships helped to accelerate our efforts at drawing additional businesses to Iraq. With existing American companies setting up operations, taking a leap into business in Iraq no longer seemed so outlandish.

✳   ✳

A major challenge to building momentum with the business community involved fears of widespread corruption. As Iraq's economic fortunes worsened following Gulf War I, smuggling and black market importation of sanctioned goods stimulated a culture of corrupt behavior among Iraq's ruling Baathist officials. Ten years of this activity had a tremendously corrosive effect on public behavior, creating a culture in which the general expectation of payoffs was part of any government transaction.

Following the fall of the regime in 2003, the CPA and subsequent State Department anticorruption efforts established institutional structures to root out corrupt behavior. These structures were predominantly punitive in their approach—Iraqi inspection and audit organizations with sweeping powers to jail offenders were established. In the initial euphoria following 2003, it appeared that significant change was possible and that systemic corruption was losing its place in the culture of public life. As the United States began moving literally billions of dollars of cash into the country to pay for governmental and military salaries, for contractor invoices, and for goods and services to support the U.S. mission, reports of corruption grew rapidly.[1]

The destabilization of the country and loss of faith in the central government that was accelerating as security began to collapse in 2005–06 resulted in a major increase in institutional corruption throughout the national and provincial governments.

As we studied this problem, social scientists advised us that in situations where faith in the future has been lost, corruption increases. Only through restoring confidence in the future of the state can the motivation of officials to "take what I can get today, because there may be no tomorrow" begin to be removed from political life.[2]

For American and international companies from Europe and nations such as Japan and Korea, systemic corruption posed a major barrier to willingness to enter the Iraqi market. Within the U.S., the Foreign Corrupt Practices Act, passed in the late 1970s in response to widespread reports of U.S. corporate payoffs to foreign officials, severely penalizes companies for any corrupt behavior with foreign officials.

As news reports focused on widespread corruption among Iraqi officials, companies had another reason to be reticent about engaging in Iraq. This was a problem that had to be solved. At minimum, we needed to provide assurances that any transactions companies entered into that were facilitated by the Task Force would be "safe" from corrupt activity.

At a review of our programs and progress with Deputy Prime Minister Dr. Barham Salih early in summer of 2007, he asked what we could do to help the Iraqi government execute its budget. Oil prices were rapidly increasing, and the Iraqi government was taking in increasing amounts of revenue, but very little of the budgets passed by Parliament were actually being executed.

To put it simply, the Iraqis lacked the ability to spend their own money.

As an American, this was a novel problem to consider. If there is one thing the American government has no problem doing, it is spending taxpayer money once Congress appropriates funds. But in Iraq, de-Baathification of the government had removed most of the experienced leaders who made decisions on large-scale procurements. Essentially, the Iraqi government had been stripped of its most-experienced bureaucrats. In their absence, lower-level functionaries lacked the necessary skills and confidence to pull the trigger on major acquisitions of goods and services.

This was increasingly a crisis for the Iraqi government. The Parliament was passing budgets with fanfare, announcing plans to build power plants, schools, hospitals, roads, and infrastructure of every sort. But the population was seeing nothing result from this. Rather than assume the government lacked competence, the average Iraqi assumed the worst. In Sunni western Iraq, the man on the street concluded the Shia-led government had sent all the money for projects to the Shiite south of the country. In the Shia areas of the south and the Kurdish north, the man on the street assumed that the Maliki government had stolen the money. In every case, confidence in the government was collapsing.

In response to the appeal from Deputy Prime Minister Salih, we began assessing the U.S. effort to train the Iraqi bureaucracy. It was underwhelming. USAID had a $300 million contract with a major Western firm to provide training and education on procurement and budget execution. This training activity was classroom based. Iraqi government personnel would enter the Green Zone, go through checkpoints and physical searches to get to the training center, sit in class all day, and then go home. After a few weeks, they would receive a certificate and return to their jobs.[3]

This program had been in place for three years, and had trained tens of thousands of Iraqi government staff members. Yet budget execution as a percentage of total appropriated funds remained flat at about 30 percent, with no improvement. Clearly, classroom training was not having the desired effect.

We then began meeting with the ministerial personnel, and learned something profound. Most of the newly trained staff knew how to execute their particular jobs, but were afraid to do so. An unintended consequence of anticorruption efforts was suddenly revealed. In an environment where the only incentives for behavior are punitive, and there are no rewards for positive activity, the wisest thing for a bureaucrat to do is nothing.

So that is what most Iraqi bureaucrats did. Nothing.

We acquired the services of a major Western accounting firm, Grant Thornton LLP, to engage in direct ministerial budget execution support. Our approach was unique. We gave the Grant Thornton staff members broad guidance, but told them that their daily chain of command would be with selected ministers overseeing ministries with large procurement budgets. Their specific direction from the Task Force was to sit in the ministries, outside the Green Zone, working side by side with the workforce. They were to provide "on the job" counsel, rather than classroom training. And they were to provide, using the credibility of their role as certified public accountants, certification of transactions executed by honest bureaucrats, protecting them from false accusation of corruption for work done well.

Within three months, Grant Thornton, under the leadership of Scott King, had fielded more than 150 accountants and consultants across the ministries of Planning, Industry, Electricity, and Trade. Passionate, driven, and charismatic, Scott King was a former Air Force officer who had become highly successful in private-sector life. He embraced the mission of the Task Force, and the Procurement Assistance effort, and established trusted partnerships with key Iraqi ministers, especially the Minister of Planning. Almost immediately, budget execution began to improve. The honest bureaucrat was now confident in his role, had ready access to technical support from an authoritative advisor when it was needed, and was assured of protection from any false accusation. The dishonest bureaucrat now had accounting firm consultants looking over his shoulder, monitoring transaction execution, and directly reporting to the minister on status at the close of each day.

Critical to this process was the "shielding" of Task Force or any

U.S. government staff from any transactional details. We had to avoid any hint that we were influencing, or attempting to influence, daily work within ministries. The ministers had to trust that the accountants and advisors worked for them. All that I received from Scott King were monthly summary reports of activity and metrics indicating the status of overall execution within each ministry—enough to effectively monitor Grant Thornton's performance, but not to be aware of any transactions.

With this new approach in place, the Iraqis began buying things. And as their budgets increased, the size of their orders began to grow. We learned something else at that point: Iraqis loved American products. Unlike just about any other country in the world, Iraq still uniformly believed the best goods in the world were American. Walled off from information about the rise of Japan as an economic power, and the increase in quality of European, Japanese, and Korean goods, Iraqis wanted to buy American. This tendency would create a huge competitive advantage for American companies willing to take a risk. All we needed now was for companies to take that risk.

Grant Thornton, in working with TFBSO to establish the Procurement Assistance Center, was another example of an American firm that stepped up in the face of great risk and hardship to support our mission. It joined TFBSO in the worst of the conflict in Iraq, and made an immeasurable contribution to the U.S. mission.

✳   ✳

By May 2007, the Task Force had used every bit of creativity it could muster to get production going in Iskandiriyah. Orders for everything from house trailers to sheep-dip tanks for pest and disease control to oil field equipment were being manufactured at the site. But Iskandiriyah, like every other site we would work on, could not survive if it did not develop its own markets. Our goal was to get production running again in Iraqi factories, and then to get outsiders interested in using the production capacity to build products for sale in Iraq or internationally.

The team of industrial experts and consultants, led by stellar private-sector executives who had joined the government for reduced pay, including Gerry Brown, David Kudla, Steve Geary, and Bill Duncan, worked at great personal risk almost around the clock to find creative ways to generate demand for factories throughout Iraq. Gerry Brown, in particular, was remarkably effective at getting international companies to engage. His most important success was the reengagement of Daimler Benz. Back in the early 1980s, Daimler Benz had developed a plan for manufacturing trucks in Iskandiriyah, in a joint-venture arrangement. That plan fell through because of the Iran-Iraq War. Gerry had reopened the discussion with Daimler, which visited Iskandiriyah in July 2007 to see the facility and determine if the old plans could be reinitiated.

Through its efforts, and in spite of a lack of dedicated funds to help its factory restart work, the Task Force managed to restore production at more than a dozen industrial operations by the summer of 2007.

Our program to restore industry and rebuild the Iraqi economy also had specific focus areas for the government of Iraq. The restoration of the financial account balances each factory had held that were seized by CPA in 2003, giving factories the working capital needed to restore their operations, was critical. We also publicly advocated the implementation of normal trade policies within Iraq: eliminating the "zero tariff" regime that the CPA had implemented that had devastated the industrial and agricultural sectors and replacing it with a normal tariff regimen, using mirror-image tariff schedules with its neighboring countries.

Iraqi Finance Minister Bayan Jabr was willing to help with restoring the financial accounts for the factories. I assigned some accountants to dig for information on the amounts that were seized in 2003. Information was hard to obtain, but we eventually identified $71 million in funds that had been swept from the accounts of Iraqi factories and placed in the Development Fund for Iraq by the CPA. The Finance Minister agreed to work to have this money restored to the Iraqi factory bank accounts.

I was thrilled with this news. While $71 million was not a lot of money when spread across more than 200 factory operations, and while it would only begin to assist in restoring Iraqi industry to modest levels of production, it would send a resounding positive signal and give plant managers some control over their own operational destiny again.

Within a few weeks, my excitement faded. Transferring money back into the factory accounts at the Iraqi state-owned banks would take a great deal of time. Each bank was independently managed, highly inefficient, and slow moving. Accounts within the Development Fund for Iraq were overseen by a multinational bureaucratic structure that did not make decisions quickly.

Over dinner that June, Finance Minister Jabr informed me that he was going to restore a full operating and capital budget for the Ministry of Industry of $300 million for operations, and $150 million for capital expenditures, in support of our program. He then told me that, pending the approval of the budget, he had approved a short-term loan program allowing state-owned factories to acquire near-zero-interest loans to restore production, from funds he had identified and distributed to Rafidain Bank.[4]

Minister of Industry Fawzi Hariri and I were ecstatic at this news. Jabr was doing more than just replacing the seizure of funds, he was funding and empowering the Ministry of Industry to get his factories running again, get Iraqi professionals back to work, and start the privatization of Iraqi industry. Jabr, Hariri, and I agreed that we would collaborate to begin establishing private-sector joint-venture investments in restarted factories, beginning with cement operations, to get the factories on a path to private ownership over time.

By midsummer, more than 2,000 Iraqi companies had registered to do business with the United States via Task Force systems. Darryl Scott was driving $100 million a month in contracts into these companies, a direct economic stimulus that leveraged a small portion of the monthly cost of military operations to help create employment. By bidding on these contracts, Iraqi companies had to adopt standard U.S. terminology and business practices in order to achieve high ratings, and access to additional future contracts. Month after month, hundreds of additional Iraqi firms registered to do business with the United States.

The benefit of this "Iraqi First" approach was significant. Iraqi companies now were getting an "on-the-job" lesson in how to do business using highly rigid standards, even more rigid than what they would need to compete in the international market for private-sector business. Furthermore, the eagerness with which Iraqi businesses were bidding on American contracts seemed to defy conventional wisdom at home that Iraqis were universally hostile to Americans.

This base of Iraqi businesses provided another opportunity to shape the Iraqi economy in a positive direction. For decades, Iraq had been a cash-based society. The only banks in Iraq were large, highly inefficient, state-owned banks such as Rashid Bank, Rafidain Bank, and the Agricultural Bank. Tied to ministries, these banks served to manage the finances of state-owned enterprises, and as payroll operations for Iraqi industry. Since 2003, these banks had been essentially running as dedicated operations for internal Iraqi government transactions. Under international debt-protection regulations established by the United Nations, Iraq could only transact commerce with the outside world via a single correspondent banking relationship between the Trade Bank of Iraq, and JP Morgan of New York. All letters of credit and loans in dollars were executed via the Trade Bank of Iraq.

For contracts with the U.S. government, payment was made to Iraqi businesses in cash. Many scandalous accounts of missing "bricks" of U.S. dollars had been uncovered since 2003, and the U.S. still flew in pallets of dollars to pay for goods and services.

For Iraq to take its place in the global economy, the Iraqi economy would have to move away from a cash-based transaction environment to an automated modern banking infrastructure.

Working with the Treasury Department liaison at the embassy, William Baldridge, we saw an opportunity to link the Iraqi First program to the banking issues in the country. Baldridge had an extensive background in assisting developing countries build financial infrastructure. The idea was to require Iraqi companies, once they were awarded a contract from the United States via the Iraqi First program, to open an account with one of the new private banks that were emerging around Iraq, where they would be paid electronically instead of with cash. Through this approach, Iraqi private businesses would stimulate the growth and capitalization of the private banking sector, and the U.S. would eliminate the distribution of cash for payments around the country. Baldridge reviewed the possible private banks, identifying approved partners for this new program.

Kris Haag, who had led the effort to automate the contracting process with General Darryl Scott, now was assigned full-time to focus on modernizing the Iraqi banking sector, with Darren Farber bumped up to take over contracting systems and automation. Haag and Baldridge established a consortium of selected private Iraqi banks and installed a basic electronic funds transfer infrastructure enabling them to receive electronic payments using international standard Society for World Interbank Financial Telecommunication, or SWIFT, transactions.

With this new structure in place, within twelve months, more than 95 percent of payments to Iraqi businesses, totaling more than $1 billion annual run rate, were flowing through private Iraqi banks. With this new liquidity, Iraqi banks could begin to act like normal financial institutions anywhere in the world, offering loans and entering into correspondent bank relationships with international banks. More important, this effort removed hundreds of millions of dollars of cash from the battlefield, cash that freely flowed to support insurgent activity and purchases of equipment needed to manufacture improvised explosives.

Haag's effort helped demonstrate an effective interagency partnership with the Department of the Treasury, an important accomplishment given the difficulties we were having at a working level with the State Department. Now, threat-finance teams from Treasury and other U.S. agencies had the ability to monitor electronic financial transactions, gaining insight into how money flowed within Iraq among terror networks and insurgent groups. Deputy Treasury Secretary Robert Kimmitt was a major supporter of our work, even attending a kickoff meeting we held in Amman, Jordan, with private banks from throughout Iraq, to invigorate this work and demonstrate its strategic importance to the entire U.S. mission in Iraq.

We were starting to understand how the military "economy within an economy" could be used to take on problems creatively and provide financial incentives to shape economic activity. For three years, hundreds of millions of dollars had been spent on educational programs, seminars, and advisory services browbeating Iraqis about the need to adopt new legal structures, new banking practices, new business processes. Now, we were merely using the activity of transacting business, with simple conditions for winning future business, to shape behavior in a positive way. It cost a fraction of the money and effort, and was proving to have a far greater positive effect.

For two years I had been working around the Pentagon bureaucracy, largely avoiding roadblocks, gamesmanship, politicking, goldbricking, and red tape nonsense. As our Iraq mission began to succeed, I had a growing sense of confidence that I had mastered how to operate without triggering problems. But I soon waded into the kind of morass that discourages everyday Americans from risking a stint in public service.

✳   ✳

Arriving in Baghdad at our new facility one night in the summer of 2007, I could see something was amiss. Members of my military staff filled me in on the problems. My military assistant, among other military Code of Conduct violations, had been actively cohabitating in my absence with a junior female member of my team, a young married political appointee assigned to my office who had worked on the Iraq team since the start of the Task Force a year earlier. An elite young American, with education from the University of Florida and Yale, a private pilot, and a member of the United States Winter Olympic Skeleton Team, she had traveled throughout Iraq in support of the Task Force.

Under general orders within the Iraq area of operations, cohabitation was forbidden among Defense Department personnel. Under U.S. military law, adultery is a criminal offense, subject to prosecution under the Uniform Code of Military Justice. Many military careers have been derailed over adultery charges.

Now that other military staff had brought the issue to my attention, I had no choice but to act. As a senior official, when acts in violation of standing military orders or military law were reported, by law I was required to take appropriate measures. I sat down with them both and asked them for an explanation. I had not accused them of anything. I simply asked if they were involved, and told them that if that were the case, I understood but that we would need to make organizational alignment changes to deal with it.

My military assistant launched into a tirade, declaring our mission a failure, the Iraqis to be corrupt and incapable of civilized behavior, and accusing me of lying to the American people and prolonging the war with my hopeless mission. The political appointee followed with a tirade of her own. I replied angrily in response to them, which escalated the confrontation.

When working in a combat environment, you literally put your life in the hands of your support staff. Rapport and trust builds, and even though there had been indications that the military officer, an Iraq combat veteran, did not appreciate the intent of our mission, I looked at both of them as trusted confidential staff.

I met with them again a few hours later, this time at the embassy compound coffee shop. I informed them that I was sending them home, and that I wanted them to get some rest before taking any next steps. I told the military officer that regardless of what happened next, that there was no way he could continue to work with us given how he felt about the mission, and that I would arrange to return him to the army for reassignment elsewhere. He nodded in agreement and stated that was fine with him. The political appointee stated that she was exhausted and ready to do something else anyway.

I let the rest of the Task Force leaders in Iraq know what had happened. I then phoned Washington, letting my team in D.C. know that the two would be coming back to D.C., and would be on leave for two weeks until I got back. I explained the situation, but declined to formally document what had happened for the time being.

I felt that their behavior was at least partially a consequence of the bizarre circumstance of our mission, having civilians and military personnel thrust into a high-pressure setting twenty-four hours a day, constantly exposed to violence. Both had made contributions to our mission. I did not want that to end badly for them. I was hopeful that, with a couple of weeks to sleep and recover, they would calm down and a rational way forward that dealt with the problem could be found.

While I remained in Iraq, the two individuals came into my office at the Pentagon, instead of taking time off as instructed. Gaining access to my calendar and e-mail, they built a chronologically aligned set of accusations, dating back over six months, accusing me of all manner of wrongdoing, and claiming that our mission was a failure. Each personal accusation was fictitiously tied to an actual event that took place, a meeting or gathering, in Iraq, Jordan, Dubai, or Washington, lending it a sense of credibility to an uninformed reader. They distributed it within the Pentagon. They turned it in to the office of Deputy Secretary England. England's chief of staff, Bob Earl, handed it over to the office of the General Counsel, and called me to ask what the hell was going on.

The document was unsigned and lacked structure other than its chronology. It was page after page of unformatted rambling text. As the political appointee had handled my media schedule, she had all of the contact information for the press corps covering the Iraq conflict. Virtually every press outlet of significance received a copy.

They distributed the document to every business executive who had visited Iraq over the past year. Defense Business Board members, the United States Chamber of Commerce, all received their wild accusations, accusing me of all manner of wrongdoing.

When I returned to Washington, I arrived at the Pentagon to find lawyers from the Office of the General Counsel waiting to see me. They entered my office, took a seat, and proceeded to somberly inform me that I was under investigation for a variety of alleged acts. I was told that the individuals who had filed the allegations were under whistleblower protection, and that any effort on my part to attempt to discredit them or engage with them in any manner could be construed as a criminal act, subject to referral to federal authorities for prosecution.

I was astounded. I had taken clear, if moderate, disciplinary action based on allegations of wrongdoing in a combat zone. Several people had been informed of this. How on earth was a management structure supposed to work if employees, when disciplined, could simply respond by fabricating allegations about their supervisor?

I was given no access to the accusations, and had no idea what I was even being accused of. At that point, I still had been given no information informing me that the unsigned accusations even existed.

I was subjected to a four-hour interrogation by investigators from the office of the DOD Inspector General. I was placed under oath, and endured a bizarre set of questions. I had no attorney present, and no idea how serious my situation was. I answered every question truthfully and honestly, denying all of the absurd accusations, confident that the process would clear up the situation if given a chance to work.

My senior leaders were called home from Iraq, and for the next two weeks, my leadership team was subjected to a similar interrogation. Everyone was rattled. The timing could not have been worse for our mission. We were in the midst of trying to execute the funding we had worked so hard to get from the Congress, only now to be consumed with an investigation.

I spoke to Deputy Secretary England, who was disturbed by the allegations, and the distraction they were causing. An emerging success that he had sponsored was now at risk. Lieutenant General Chiarelli, now serving as the senior military advisor to Secretary Gates, looked me in the eye and asked, "Is any of it true?" I supposed he had to ask, but the words cut me to the core. I shuddered to think of what Gates must be thinking.

I retained the services of a legal team, providing them my copy of the accusations, along with other documents and information about the situation. Given there was no evidence to support their false allegations, the legal team was not worried about the outcome. They would look into the matter and get back to me. A few days later, they had troubling news. The political appointee was not any of the things she had claimed on her résumé. She was not an Olympic team member, had never attended Yale, the University of Florida, or any American college or university according to reference clearinghouses. She had no private pilot's license.

Her entire résumé was fiction. Somehow she had received a White House appointment and a security clearance with a falsified résumé.

In spite of this new information, I was told I could do nothing. The General Counsel's office had made clear that anything I did to impugn the credibility of my accusers could result in criminal prosecution.

6.
DARK DAYS

Random false accusations are increasingly a part of life in any management role, in the private or public sector. I later learned that there are classes for senior career civil servants where they are taught how to handle inevitable false accusations and the investigations that result from them. There are processes in place to handle such things, and if wrongdoing has occurred, to deal with them appropriately. As a result of the news media acquiring the accusations, the investigation became public—another violation of Pentagon policy as internal investigations are supposed to be kept confidential pending an outcome. Arriving at the Pentagon on Monday morning after the story broke, I confronted my new reality. All of my perceived "top cover," political support, suspected ties to Secretary Gates and the administration, were now gone. I was, but for the continued support of Deputy Secretary England, completely alone.

My Iraq mission had always been inexplicable to the Pentagon bureaucracy and many administration political appointees. Senior political appointees simply did not do operational things anywhere. They especially do not engage in combat zones, involving themselves in tactical activities at risk of violence, or worse yet for a politician, failure. I had annoyed almost all of them at one time or another, with my aggressive, overbearing style and endless challenges to the structures and processes of the Pentagon bureaucracy. Many had always suspected I would come to a bad end, and now their suspicions were proving true.

I had grown too confident, after three years of working in the Defense Department, that I was good at "gaming out" scenarios, and being prepared for possible bad outcomes. The outcome I was now experiencing had never occurred to me as being even a remote possibility.

Had I followed the book and written them up formally for reprimand and sent them home by officially relieving them of duty in writing, instead of verbally communicating it to senior staff, I would have been protected. Instead, because of my ill-considered effort to avoid damaging their careers—my reaction to the situation as a business executive rather than a high-ranking Defense Department official—I had taken less-formal action.

I sent a note to several members of the command in Iraq, explaining what had happened, in case they were hearing about it. General Petraeus sent a note of encouragement in response and told me to keep focused. Several others did the same.

My wife, Cindy, was my strength throughout the ordeal. Nothing about the entire experience of moving from California had gone as we had planned. For two years I had worked late hours at the Pentagon with Tom Modly on business reform. Now for a year I had been in a war zone, gone half the time from home, roaming around with troops at risk of injury or death. When home, I had been in a jet lag–induced fog of inattention, constantly worrying about the news of the day from Iraq, fighting battles within the Pentagon, and worrying if my people were safe. She had taken on all of the responsibilities of home and family, and put her own successful career on hold indefinitely. She had not signed on to be a military wife. This was supposed to be a two-year stint of service inside the Pentagon, followed by a return home to California.

She never questioned the mission. She never asked me to resign. She told me again and again that none of the media noise mattered. She was, as always, strong through all of it. But I knew how much this situation, and the possible impact it could have on our children, worried her.

✳   ✳

Although my circumstances had changed drastically in Washington, in Iraq things were fairly normal. Our industry team was working literally around the clock to get the funding we had recently received turned into small orders for material, equipment, or maintenance to help restart factories throughout the country.

At the request of local units, we began holding ceremonies at factories, where we would present large signed "checks," ceremonial representations of the allocation of funds to help get production going again. I was surprised by how much excitement these ceremonies generated. Where there had been work around the country to build infrastructure, often this work was not presented publicly as security declined, out of fear that the project would be targeted for destruction or violence if it was clearly associated with the American mission.

Our donations were mostly small, a few hundred thousand dollars in most cases, up to the largest project we launched—$6 million for restoring production at Baiji Fertilizer. I attended almost every ceremonial presentation. In every case, the local community would show up, along with local media, and the entire work force of the factory would be present. Throngs would shake our hands, thanking us again and again for helping them. Such a small gesture generated so much goodwill.

Of course, the gesture received a lot of criticism at the embassy. Our "big checks" were widely ridiculed within State as cheap publicity stunts. In March 2007, a new ambassador, Ryan Crocker, had been appointed to take over for Zalmay Khalilzad. Zalmay had never wavered in his support, but his support had made little difference within the embassy groups that opposed our work. Crocker became a great supporter and advisor to me throughout the duration of his tenure. Crocker and his staff even presented one of our "big checks" to the manager of the Diyala Electric factory, the same manager who had been terrified to receive us only six months earlier.[1] Under Crocker's leadership, the open hostility directed to our work gradually subsided.

I now had no support staff, and needed someone to help me liaise with the command staffs in MNFI and MNCI. Bob Love offered up a recent addition to his team at Camp Victory: Beth Law, an Army Reserve lieutenant colonel on a six-month assignment from the Alaska Army National Guard.

A tall woman, with big, bright red hair, an outgoing personality, and very direct command style, Beth had an interesting story. A high-school dropout from Arizona, Beth had struggled early in life to find her way. She enlisted in the army, during the last days of the Women's Army Corps in 1977, after getting her high school GED. Through her continued service in the army, she accomplished amazing things. She acquired a college degree, completed a graduate degree, and became one of the first female helicopter pilots in the army, flying UH-1 "Huey" helicopters on drug interdiction and other missions all over the United States. She went from an enlisted soldier to Officer Candidate School, became an officer, and had worked her way up to the rank of lieutenant colonel. When her husband Steve Law, an army aviator, was assigned to Iraq, she arranged to be assigned to Iraq as well. The Task Force had selected her from a list of available officers provided by the army personnel office.

In my first meeting with her that August, I was in a bleak mood and had no desire to work with anyone in a close support role again. Looking intensely at me, she said, "Everybody knew those two were trouble, but no one thought they would do that to you. You have no idea what this mission means to the troops. Don't let two liars destroy you and what you are accomplishing here."

Getting to know Beth, and seeing the reaction from the Iraqis to our efforts to restore their livelihoods, helped me get through that time. They provided needed reminders at a difficult time that our mission was about service, and that with service comes challenges. While I was distraught at my circumstances in Washington, my problems paled in comparison to what our soldiers in combat faced every day, not to mention the struggles of daily life for Iraqis.

Beth quickly reestablished good order within our operations, and worked with our newly assigned contracting officer, Air Force Lieutenant Colonel Mark Baird, to get recently acquired facilities for TFBSO—an abandoned set of villas once occupied by members of the Hussein regime near the southern edge of the Green Zone that we had essentially seized—up to a livable standard with plumbing and electricity. Baird, who had taken over for Lieutenant Colonel Tom Snyder, was working around the clock to get our industry projects funded in support of our manufacturing team.

I then received some good news. Matthew Schoeffling was a young leader working in Defense Policy. A gifted linguistic prodigy, Schoeffling was fluent in four dialects of Arabic, as well as Farsi, Mandarin Chinese, Japanese, Spanish, and Portuguese. A Georgetown PhD, he had lived in Saudi Arabia, Syria, and Egypt, and had worked extensively in Iraq. Weary of Pentagon advisory work, Matt introduced himself, and after his first visit to Iraq with us in July, had convinced his management to let him transfer to the Task Force. The impact of this decision was huge for me. Schoeffling was an elite talent. For him to be willing to place his career on the line by joining my team was a desperately needed vote of confidence.

Minister of Industry Fawzi Hariri, Minister of Finance Bayan Jabr, and I had held a few joint press conferences in prior months, describing our work and our collaboration. These were unusual events. Outside of General Petraeus and Ambassador Crocker working with Prime Minister Maliki, Foreign Minister Hoshyar Zubai, or the Defense Minister Abdul Qadir, it was very uncommon for U.S. officials to appear jointly to describe programs with senior Iraqi officials. I tried to always hold these events at an Iraqi government location, like Adnan Palace or the Parliament Building, both in Baghdad. Hariri now offered to come to the United States, and to hold a similar press engagement at my side in Washington.

On September 4, Hariri and I held a joint press briefing in the Pentagon briefing room. Televised by C-SPAN, and widely covered online, Hariri and I made our case for our efforts and their emerging success. Most important, in an act that I would never forget, Deputy Secretary of Defense Gordon England launched the briefing with an introduction of our work, and a strong endorsement of my efforts.[2]

Fawzi Hariri took a great risk by visiting Washington and standing in the Pentagon, for all to see, beside me. He was living in a Baghdad still racked by violence, in which government officials were targeted for attacks almost constantly. He was risking his safety to stand up for me, in his role as a minister, to ensure that our work to restore Iraq's industries was completed. But he also stood up for me as a friend.

By the end of September, we had successfully restored production at sixteen industrial operations throughout Iraq. More than 5,000 employees were back on the job in those operations. But because of unfortunate media leaks about our "top ten" list and its projected restoration of 10,000 jobs, our work was publicly perceived as falling short. Our projection had been made when we thought we had access to funds to start operations quickly in January, before lawyers told us we could not use available funds for our work. But such explanations don't matter in times of controversy. Any nugget that could be used to discredit our program was quickly seized.[3]

✳   ✳

Those 5,000 employees were in sustained jobs in factories that made goods of value. They were not temporary construction jobs. They were not temporary security contracts to put young men carrying guns for militias to work carrying guns for someone else. They were real jobs in a real economy. It was a beginning.

Still, my industry team, led by Bill Duncan, had literally worked around the clock during August and September to get as many results as it could, and team members were getting tired. Steve Geary, a seasoned supply chain management pro from Boston, had also pushed himself to the very limit of endurance, focusing on ramping up production in Iskandiriyah. The whole group was completely drained. By November, twenty of the thirty industry team members had gone home, most not to return.

My own future was now unclear. I had never intended to work in Iraq for a full year. I had confidently told Undersecretary Ken Krieg one year earlier that I would be back in the Pentagon focused on business modernization within a few short months. Fourteen months had passed since that conversation, and I had hoped to hand the mission off to someone else before Christmas.

That plan was now complicated. I was under the cloud of an ongoing investigation. To depart the mission before I was officially cleared of wrongdoing would invite speculation that I had been forced out because I was guilty of something. I needed to stay on until the Inspector General issued his report clearing me of wrongdoing. I was informed that Inspector General Mick Kicklighter had told Secretary England that there was apparently no merit to any of the allegations, but that his organization was talking to everyone mentioned in the twelve-page document to ensure no one could say the case was "swept under the rug." He could not project how long that process would take. I grew increasingly gloomy as I realized it would not be resolved quickly.

✳   ✳

For most of 2007, night after night, sirens would wail over the Green Zone in Baghdad as rockets rained down, targeting the embassy compound, but striking randomly throughout the entire area. Our new headquarters facilities were on the far southern end of the Green Zone, about two miles from the embassy, still housed in the Republican Palace. Starting in September, however, the number of attacks began to decline. They continued to drop until, by October, the nights were blessedly quiet.

The surge had begun to work. General Petraeus and Lieutenant General Odierno had executed a strategy of placing troops on almost every city block of Baghdad, co-locating our forces with Iraqi Army units and Iraqi Police stations. With this backup, the Iraqis began to restore security, and neighborhoods began to return to normal. Overhead surveillance systems monitored any rocket launches, enabling quick deployment of combat forces to roll up insurgent cells.

Gradually, peace was being restored in Baghdad.

Fardh al Qanoon, it was called. Arabic for "Restoring Law," it was the name applied to the Baghdad Security Plan.

You could see the difference when flying over the city. Where only months before the streets had been deserted and a sense of fear hung in the air when driving through Baghdad, now many major portions of the city were beginning to fill with pedestrians and cars again.

The commands that led the military effort of 2007 to turn the tide of violence in Iraq were a remarkable collection of leaders. I had the good fortune to get to know many of them. Division commanders developed comprehensive counterinsurgency strategies for each region of Iraq, and as security was restored we were called on to engage in support of their efforts.

I began to rebuild a manufacturing team, as Multi-National Division–Baghdad Deputy Commander Brigadier General Vince

Brooks, a stellar intellect and leader responsible for securing Baghdad, linked TFBSO to his stabilization strategies.

Some of these efforts were focused on factories that simply should never have been closed, that had operations that were perfectly capable of thriving in the new Iraq. An example of this was the Heavy Engineering and Equipment Supply Company in Baghdad's Doura neighborhood. Largely idled since 2003, HEESCO is a huge industrial facility, capable of building major steel infrastructure for the construction and oil and gas industries. In April 2007, after terrorists destroyed the Sarrafiya Bridge over the Tigris River in northern Baghdad, HEESCO engineers and production workers began replacing the metal work. In less than a year, the bridge reopened early in 2008.

Restoring full production to HEESCO was critical to revitalizing the Sunni-dominated neighborhood of Doura, which was being cleared of Al Qaeda operatives. Formerly a mixed community of Assyrian Christians, it was now entirely Sunni. The hope was that by restoring operations and employment, normality could be restored as well, and neighborhoods could be repopulated.

The first time I walked around HEESCO I was impressed. The workforce had been assembled for our visit. The engineering and professional staff was young and cosmopolitan, and gave excellent reviews of its capability. When staff members showed me around the facility, they took me to the engineering department, which was a sea of old-fashioned drafting tables. The engineering team was still using ink-on-paper for its design work, something that had not been done internationally in more than twenty years. The core engineering skill of the staff was excellent, but the technology was completely out of date. TFBSO acquired computer equipment and computer-aided design software along with training for the workforce at HEESCO. We also acquired new oxygen tanks and retrofitted the oxygen-welding systems for the factory, enabling the restoration of full production operations. Several months after our work began at HEESCO, I visited the site with Multi-National Division–Baghdad Commander Major General Joseph Fil. The team was welcomed with open arms, and the relationship with the military command was clearly very positive.

We undertook a number of projects in Baghdad that we knew, in years to come, would probably not thrive economically. In

Khadimiyah, an important historic site of the shrine of the seventh and ninth Shia Imams, a large cotton factory and a companion wool factory employed thousands of production workers. There was little hope for the long-term competitive position of either the cotton or the wool factory; its looms were forty to fifty years old and in need of complete replacement.

TFBSO was asked, as an element of restoring local economic activity, to work on the factory. The Task Force acquired a large boiler to clean cotton, replacing a damaged boiler, and enabling weaving operations to begin again. The impact on the community of our positive gesture was an element of local stabilization. The economic impact may have been temporary, but it was important nonetheless, as it improved community well-being and helped establish security and stability in the area. In support of Fardh al Qanoon, TFBSO undertook a number of such projects: doing things that may not have made sense in the long term economically, but made a great deal of sense in the context of a counterinsurgency strategy to restore normal life.

Another example of this approach was in the infamous town of Abu Ghraib, where a dairy operation had been destroyed during military operations. In 2004, the United Nations had acquired state of the art dairy pasteurization and packaging equipment, which was in storage, pending the construction of a facility suitable for dairy production. The Task Force was asked to see what could be done to rebuild the dairy. This became one of only two construction projects that the Task Force funded in Iraq. TFBSO built a large structure to house the dairy, in partnership with the U.S. Army Corps of Engineers. This was another example of a project that would not have been launched for purely economic reasons, but that was seen as showing the local community that positive steps were underway to restore normal life.

With the industrial revitalization effort now delivering results throughout the city, procurement assistance efforts starting to improve budget execution within the ministries, our corporate engagement effort ramping up, the private banking initiative pulling U.S. cash off the street and automating the banking system, and the Iraqi First program driving millions of dollars in U.S. contracts to hundreds of Baghdad-based companies, TFBSO was delivering broad support to the Fardh al Qanoon campaign. But much work remained. Everywhere we turned, it was clear that the basic infrastructure to support sustained economic development was lacking.

Baghdad had experienced no new commercial construction on any scale for three decades. For companies seeking to do business, there was no office space, no industrial parks, and no ready-to-occupy rental property enabling even a representative office for a corporation to get business underway. While security had improved dramatically, the public perception would lag reality for a long time to come, making it difficult to convince companies to establish sustained operations. Our villa compound turned into temporary operating quarters for companies, who would send representatives into Iraq on a rotation, staying with TFBSO as needed. It was a crowded, busy scene, requiring us to expand into an adjacent building, which was quickly upgraded to our "2-star" motel standard with electricity, functioning plumbing, Internet access, a decent kitchen serving local cuisine, and not much else. But it was enough to sustain our progress.

✻   ✻

One of the companies that visited Iraq was ABC Carpet and Home of New York. An elite retailer of home fashions and hand-woven carpets, ABC Carpet and Home's store on Broadway is a remarkable establishment, with several stories of high-quality home furnishings and decorations. The CEO of ABC, Graham Head, had a passion for economic revitalization in impoverished areas of the world, where native crafts could be sold in Western retail establishments, generating needed income. He immediately offered advice and assistance to our efforts, a role he continued in years to come.

Iraq, like most other countries in the Middle East and south Asia, had a centuries-old tradition of weaving carpets. Under the Hussein regime, home weaving was industrialized, with large factories built that possessed dozens of weaving looms, large and small. Saddam ordered that all production of carpets be dedicated strictly to decorating his palaces and government facilities. Over time, the artistry of Iraq's carpet industry gradually faded, as most of the rugs produced in the industrial operations were an odd Iraqi kitsch: woven portraits of Saddam, of grandiose battle scenes from the Iran-Iraq War, of the "mother of all battles—Gulf War I," or from tourist sites such as the Ishtar Gate at Babylon or the ancient ruins of Ur. Occasionally, though, a beautiful silk or woolen rug would be produced on special order from a Baathist official for his home, or for a government building.

When TFBSO visited the first carpet-weaving operations in 2007, we could see that the entire industry would have to be rebuilt. It was not an early priority as the effort would be intense, and the product clearly would not sell in international markets. What was unfortunate was that most of the workers were war widows, many with children, now out of work. The largest of the operations, and the headquarters for the State Company for Hand Woven Carpet, was in Khadimiyah, but there were factories scattered around the country.

Graham Head introduced us to the lead carpet buyer for ABC Carpet and Home, Richard Ringrose, who began working with Gerry Brown. An Englishman, Ringrose is truly a world authority on handwoven carpets, able simply to look at a rug and tell you everything about it: the source of its wool or silk, its dye composition, and most impressive, exactly where it was woven, down to the town or village of origin. For decades he has roamed the world, acquiring carpets and working with local communities to create artistic rugs for sale at Harrods of London and ABC Carpet and Home in New York.

Ringrose, after hearing my pitch, surveyed the eclectic decor in my Pentagon office. Looking disapprovingly at a rug on my floor, he asked where it came from. When I first visited Kurdistan in 2007 and held an all-day meeting with the Kurdish government ministers at the request of Ambassador Khalilzad, I had been given a small rug as I boarded the plane to depart—a common gesture in the region. I took it back to Washington, where it covered a portion of the office floor. It was a good conversation starter when people would ask about it. I used it to pitch Kurdistan as an entry point into investing in Iraq.

When I explained all of this to Ringrose, he laughed out loud. I asked him what was so funny, and he said, "Well, besides being a bloody ugly rug, that carpet is from Iran. It's from a small village in a region of Iran called Kermanshah. It's about forty years old, and not worth a dime."

Ringrose agreed to have a look at the carpet-weaving operations in Iraq. After a visit, during which he saw the operation and the weavers at work, he brought in weaving experts from Turkey to look at the operation. They decided to take on the task of trying to restore the carpet industry, but not to weave cheap kitschy rugs. Their vision was to work with Iraqi industry leaders and weavers to rebuild the lost art of Iraqi carpet weaving.

The oldest-known handwoven carpet in the world is in the Hermitage Museum in St. Petersburg, Russia. Found in an archeological site in the Pazyryk Valley of the Atlai Mountains of Siberia, the carpet dates to 500 B.C., and was located in the tomb of a Scythian prince. The carpet, which is artistically beautiful with red, green, blue, and golden colors, is believed to have originated in the area surrounding ancient Babylon at the time of the reign of Cyrus of Persia, who is believed to have introduced carpet weaving to the Persian Empire from Babylon.[4]

Ringrose acquired detailed photographs of the Pazyryk carpet, and had "knot" diagrams created that would re-create the weaving of a replica of the carpet. He then accompanied the Task Force on a trip to Kurdistan, where we sought out local shepherds to acquire wool from the variety of sheep present in Iraq since antiquity. Natural dyes from regional vegetable matter were acquired, chosen to match the exact colors of the Pazyryk rug design. I visited the carpet factory in Khadimiyah about every three months. As the project came together, and I saw two Pazyryk rugs on the looms for the first time, it was hard not to be overcome with emotion at what the work represented culturally, artistically, and from a humanitarian perspective. An art that had been stripped away by violence and war and depravity was coming to life again.

As the factory began producing replicas of ancient rugs, Ringrose visited the British Museum and the Louvre to capture images of other ancient Mesopotamian art, which were then converted into carpet patterns for new carpet designs, based on images from Iraq's ancient past.

Every rug delivered has sold within days of hitting the shelves in New York.

✱   ✱

In January 2008, Major General Darryl Scott ended his two-year tour of duty as the commander of Joint Contracting Command–

Iraq. Darryl and I had discussed at length the possibility of his next assignment being with TFBSO. My original sponsor, Mike Wynne, was now serving as the Secretary of the Air Force. With the support of Wynne, I was able to get the Air Force system to assign Scott to my office as Deputy Director of the Business Transformation Agency. This freed up another two-star general, Army Major General Carlos "Butch" Pair, to shift to a six-month tour of duty in Iraq, allowing Bob Love to pivot home for a well-earned break.

A year earlier, we had made requests across all of the military departments for personnel support. Now, at the beginning of 2008, a full contingent of officers arrived. Finally we would have what we had always lacked: a fully staffed organizational structure that could effectively "liaise" with the multiple tiers of commands, and better "feed the beast" in the Green Zone that constantly demanded information.

With General Pair on the ground running day-to-day operations in my absence, and plenty of senior leadership to manage our projects, I was able to focus on strategic initiatives, and on engagement with Iraqi leaders at the national, provincial, and local levels. Beth Law had brought order back to my front office and to the overall operational mission support in Washington. Matt Schoeffling was providing invaluable strategic vision and counsel to the overall mission, enabling us to target our efforts in a manner with greatest overall impact on political stability.

Through the first several months of 2008, security in Baghdad steadily improved. The atmosphere in Baghdad had changed dramatically. On a trip into the "red zone" to tour one of the commercial districts, I was getting out of my armored SUV, when I looked around and saw children flocking to the car. Kids always came up to us when we would walk the streets, sometimes seeking candy or money, but often just to walk along with us as we toured an area visiting local businesses. On that trip, the local Provincial Reconstruction Team (PRT) members arrived, along with soldiers from the neighborhood outpost. The PRT members were in full armor and helmets.

My security detail handed me my helmet and body armor. I put it back in the car. At that moment, I saw for the first time the absurdity of it all. We were there to help the citizens of Baghdad. Our soldiers were combatants; they had every reason to wear armor. But as civilians, we were there to build trust, to engage. Instead, we looked like astronauts exiting our spacecraft, wrapped in layers of protective gear to walk among the aliens.

I imagined the horror I would feel if something happened, if a sniper opened fire, or a bomb went off, and I awoke surrounded by dead children who had flocked to my side, while I survived wrapped in my cocoon of body armor. I would rather die than experience such a moment.

The security detail protested, but they worked for me, so there was nothing they could do when I told them to get back to work. The soldiers shrugged their shoulders and began walking ahead. The PRT members looked at me as if I was insane. As I walked the street that day, and entered shops and talked to locals and drank tea and engaged as a human being, for the first time I felt completely at ease.

I would never wear armor in Iraq again.

✳   ✳

Now that security had improved, we could work more openly in Baghdad. We began thinking of the necessary business infrastructure required to successfully enable companies to operate independently in Iraq. With the recent launch of commercial air service to Baghdad by a TFBSO investor, Gryphon Air, and the rapid negotiation of international routes to Iraq by Etihad Airways, Austrian Airways, and Gulf Air, it appeared air travel was coming together. What was completely lacking was decent, safe hotel space.

TFBSO worked with the Iraqi government to identify a tract of land suitable for a large hotel complex in the Green Zone. We then actively solicited international investment to build a hotel, using private funding. After significant effort, an American consortium that included capital from U.S., Jordanian, and Lebanese investors stepped forward. Initially the consortium attempted to negotiate a hotel-operating agreement with Marriott Corporation. General Petraeus and I met with William Marriott in Washington, D.C. to encourage Marriott to consider the project, and for several weeks it appeared that the first new major construction project in Baghdad in three decades would be a Marriott. The bombing of the Marriott in Islamabad late in 2008 caused the participation to fall apart, subsequently to be replaced by Rotana, a luxury hotel chain based on Abu Dhabi. The project, however, was approved, with ground broken late in 2008 for construction, and scheduled to be completed in 2015.

The project was important for other reasons that had to do with more than just building a suitable hotel for business travelers. Early in 2007, Iraq established a National Investment Commission, and appointed Ahmed Ridha as its first commissioner. Given the task of facilitating foreign direct investment in Iraq, Ridha had worked for years in Abu Dhabi on the Chamber of Commerce, making him unique among Iraqi leaders in his knowledge of modern investment practices in the region. He was also close to Nouri al-Maliki, making him unique among Iraqi leaders.

Maliki, the Iraqi Prime Minister, led a relatively small Shia faction within the Iraqi government known as the Islamic Dawa Party. A compromise candidate for the position of Prime Minister, he was selected after months of impasse over forming a new government after the national elections of 2005. As part of this compromise, competing Shia political factions settled on Maliki, who had been a Dawa Party opposition figure prior to 2003, living in Damascus and Tehran at different times.

Dawa, a Shia Islamist faction that was heavily funded by Iran, had won only a minimal number of seats in Parliament in the national elections. Most of the powerful positions within the Iraqi government had gone to larger parties, including the Shia Islamic Supreme Counsel of Iraq, the Sadrist Party led by the Shia firebrand Moqtada al Sadr and backed by the Jaish al Mahdi militia, and several Sunni parties.

As outsiders, and especially as Americans, it is common to think of Iraq in terms of its primary religious sects—Sunni and Shia. But within the majority Shia population there are layers of ethnic and sub-sectarian complexity that is too often ignored. Generally speaking, the Islamic Supreme Council of Iraq (ISCI) represents the upper and middle class of Shia, merchants, traders, religious leaders, and government bureaucrats. The Sadrists generally represent the poor and downtrodden, the underclass of Iraqi Shia society. With their base largely in impoverished areas such as the Sadr City neighborhood of Baghdad, Hayyiniyah neighborhood in Basra, and the marsh regions of southern Iraq, the Sadrists are deeply conservative and hostile to Western cultural and political influence. Dawa is the "middle-actor," the smaller party heavily backed by Iran that serves as a compromise between the larger ISCI and Sadrist factions when compromise on political matters is needed.[5]

Ridha was the first Iraqi official we worked with who was closely aligned to the prime minister's Dawa party. He was eager to demonstrate progress, and proved to be a reliable partner in the early days of the National Investment Commission.

Deciding how to lease nationally owned land had to be figured out. The Iraqis were wary of being taken advantage of, and there was no way to assess the value of large tracts of real estate in Baghdad for commercial development.

We assigned a team, led by Scott King, to survey practices and real estate leasing rates for the surrounding countries, based on the proximity of land to valuable assets such as government facilities, riverfront property or river views, and highway or air transport infrastructure. This information was used to provide the Iraqi government with a baseline of knowledge on how to value land for real estate development negotiations.[6]

Sometimes these efforts were not well received by potential investors. The Iraqis required a lease payment on state-owned land, for up to a fifty-year lease, renewable for an additional fifty years at the discretion of the investor. Those payments were set at reasonable levels based on the analysis framework the Task Force provided. Many investors who had shown interest in building on state-owned land in Baghdad were angered by this; they were expecting the Iraqis essentially to give away land in return for investment, not to charge a lease payment.

For the Iraqi government, giving away free land was not possible. Land prices were skyrocketing as security improved throughout the city, a sign we viewed as a positive market indicator of confidence in the long-term economic prospects of the city. Giving away land for investment was not good policy, nor politically tenable, for the Iraqi government.

Negotiations between the American investment company and the Iraqi government were painfully slow. The Iraqis loved to argue the same terms, again and again, as if empowered to finally make decisions that had long been only permitted at the very top of the Saddam Hussein regime. But the process provided a concrete mechanism for the Iraqis to haggle out and develop their own opinions about what they wanted in commercial transactions. It was the beginning of the long process of establishing Iraq's own "boilerplate" set of legal terms and conditions that could be repeatedly applied in future negotiations. But the negotiations were excruciatingly painful for the investors, and not a lot of fun to watch for TFBSO. Finally, at the point at which everyone was ready to walk away, the Iraqis signed the deal.

The hotel investment project initiated our collaboration with the Overseas Private Investment Corporation, a United States government agency offering low-interest financing for private-sector development in high-risk areas of the world. OPIC stepped up to finance 50 percent of the Rotana Hotel project. Establishing relationships between OPIC and the Government of Iraq was critical to Iraq's economic development, as OPIC represented a credible financial institution whose presence in Iraq would build confidence among private financial institutions about the feasibility of investing in Iraqi projects.

✳   ✳

By the end of 2007, the Task Force had grown to more than 250 professionals; an industrial revitalization team led by Bob Love and Lieutenant Colonel Mark Baird, budget and procurement assistance led by Scott King, Iraqi First contracting support led by Darren Farber, private banking and financial infrastructure development led by Kris Haag, investor support led by David Scantling, and a dedicated team of investment advisors based in the capital city of the Kurdistan region, Irbil. John Dowdy, and two new McKinsey partners, John Stoner and Jerry Lundquist, continued to provide strategic advice, especially to the Ministry of Industry on privatization of industry.

TFBSO also launched a business-training effort for factory-management teams, teaching basic principles of marketing, sales, distribution, and how to manage a profit/loss operation. John Stoner led this effort, along with other advisory efforts within the Ministry of Industry. The goal was to prepare management teams to adapt to a new free market competitive environment as operations were privatized over time.

The breadth of effort had risen based on requests for support, from the command, from the State Department, or from the Treasury Department, all of which we were now actively collaborating with. IRMO remained a critic, but had largely grown quiet as our breadth of effort increased and results rolled in.

From those separate efforts, a structure began to emerge that provided an initial "doctrine" or methodology for how to approach postconflict stabilization. It was clear to me that, given my unfortunate circumstances in Washington, I was not going to be able to hand over the mission to a replacement anytime soon. It was also clear that no other U.S. government organization would ever step up to assume responsibility for our work. The only thing to do was to establish, within the Iraqi government, the capability to do our work without outside assistance. That was a sounder strategy anyway, but now I was thinking of our mission as a model for effective "nation building"—with the end result being a functioning, sovereign economy capable of thriving within the global economic community.

At the request of the Ministry of Planning, TFBSO's Scott King worked to establish "Provincial Procurement Assistance Teams," two-to-three person cells, located in each provincial capital, to assist provincial governors with executing the provincial level budget.

To prevent conflict, I had established the Procurement Assistance Center (PAC) as a collaborative effort with the State Department. TFBSO provided all but 5 percent of the budget for the PAC, as well as the life support and permissive security policy enabling the effort to work successfully while embedded in Iraqi ministries. By putting up 5 percent of the budget, we enabled State to claim the effort as part of its overall "capacity development" strategy for the Government of Iraq. We kept its "TFBSO" ownership generally quiet at the working level within the embassy. As new embassy staff members and military leaders would rotate in, they often would not know that the PAC was even a TFBSO initiative. Ambassador Crocker frequently incorporated PAC statistics and successes into his updates back to Washington, as State Department successes. This demonstrated the spirit of cooperation I had hoped to achieve with IRMO back in early 2007; a quiet Defense

Department effort working under State Department sponsorship, with State getting "credit" for its successes.

The seeds of new interagency conflicts, however, were sown as the PAC began to deliver concrete results.

The United States Agency for International Development had been generally friendly to our efforts in Iraq since their inception. The USAID Iraq country director in 2006, Bambi Arellano, was a wise, experienced development expert with broad experience in the region. She and I had met frequently, and shared many of the same frustrations with the remnants of the CPA, particularly IRMO. Unlike CPA, with its gigantic contractor-managed trailer park surrounding the Republican Palace, and its closed-door security policy that prevented easy engagement with Iraqi leaders, USAID had hired Iraqi labor to build small houses in a miniature neighborhood in the Green Zone at a fraction of the cost of the CPA trailer park, a good distance from the embassy. It was a far healthier work environment, and USAID was much more positively oriented about working in Iraq than the grim mood that had pervaded the embassy staff when we arrived in 2006.

Now, however, our good relations with USAID were fading fast. USAID had fallen increasingly under the control of restrictive State Department security policies in the wake of kidnappings of USAID financial advisors working at the Finance Ministry in 2007. It now had largely been locked down and prevented from engaging outside of the Green Zone and the nearby walled USAID compound in the Mansour neighborhood of Baghdad. Arellano had gone on to a new assignment and been replaced by a country director who, given the restrictions now in place on outside engagement, seemed primarily interested in surviving his one-year assignment in Iraq.

USAID had renewed a massive contract to provide classroom-style capacity development training for the Iraqi government in financial management and budget execution, a contract valued at more than $200 million. Now, at less than 10 percent of the expense, and at far greater effectiveness operating under a permissive security policy, the TFBSO PAC was making the USAID-sponsored effort look ineffective and expensive by comparison. USAID began actively opposing PAC efforts, a hostility that soon spread to other TFBSO initiatives.

The new Provincial Procurement Assistance Teams drew the ire of yet another failed experimental organization in Iraq, the Provincial Reconstruction Teams, or PRTs. PRTs were a brainchild of Zalmay Khalilzad that had been first applied in Afghanistan under his leadership, and transferred to Iraq when he became the ambassador in Baghdad. A great idea in principle, the notion was to place teams of civilian experts in governance, reconstruction, and development into every provincial capital of Iraq, to assist the establishment of competent provincial governments.[7]

The problem with PRTs was that the same restrictive security posture that had made the Green Zone a walled fortress was now duplicated in provincial capitals all over Iraq. Mini-embassy compounds were established, sometimes on military installations, always under highly restrictive security procedures, with little daily engagement with local populations. When the small civilian teams were allowed to venture out, it was only in heavy armor with either full U.S. military or private-security contractors providing movement support. The image for the local populations could not have been worse.

In 2007, coinciding with the much-debated approval of the "surge" in military forces, Congress approved an increase in funds for the PRTs. Rather than staff the PRTs through a recruiting process, the State Department issued memorandums to the other agencies in the federal government requiring each to provide staff for the PRTs on a nonreimbursable basis (each federal agency had to pay for the personnel sent to work on PRTs). The bulk of this requirement fell on the Defense Department.[8] I was asked to participate in the Pentagon effort to review this request from the State Department. Defense personnel was treating the requirement like a staffing exercise, searching through the rolls of reservists and civilian volunteers looking for two hundred people willing to work for six to twelve months on a PRT. By this point in the war, after so many rotations of skilled reservists, the quality of the available personnel was not especially high.

I attempted to argue for a different approach. Congress had appropriated more than $300 million for the PRTs. That seemed like a lot of funding, but spread over 18 provinces, it amounted to less than $20 million per province. The bulk of that funding would be consumed by the security, food, and living expenses necessary to maintain fortified compounds, leaving a small amount to actually deliver any value to the local province.

I argued that the whole effort should be rethought. If we had eliminated the word "team," and simply stated that each province would be provided $20M in support for reconstruction and governance development, we would build goodwill with provincial leaders and avoid creating mini–Green Zones all over Iraq. Benchmarks could be defined for provinces to meet before receiving allocations of the promised funds.

I also argued that the entire effort should be renamed. The United States had no intention of "reconstructing" any province of Iraq. To name a small team of civilians a "provincial reconstruction team" simply created an impossible expectation among the local populations in the provinces, ensuring a perceived failure no matter how effective the team was. Better to call them what they were: provincial advisors, if you had to have teams at all.

My arguments fell on deaf ears. Staff members were assigned and the expanded PRTs were created. Provincial governors generally disliked the new PRTs and said as much in meetings throughout the country. They were viewed as an alternative power structure in competition with newly formed provincial governments, rather than as partners. There was, generally, little collaboration with provincial leaders on the projects that were undertaken, which tended to be classroom training exercises, strategy development projects, or small experimental pilot economic projects. While there were cases where talented individuals were able to overcome structural restrictions and have positive local impacts, these were the exception and not the rule.

The establishment of TFBSO Provincial Procurement Assistant Teams was done outside of the PRT structure, at the request of the provincial governors. The elected provincial councils were allowed to interview and participate in the selection of the PPAT staff, which was formally placed under the direction of the provincial government. Performance management would be provided by TFBSO, and rolled up to me for review, but only at a summary level—neither I, nor any TFBSO leaders, would have visibility to individual transactions, to avoid any hint of influence over provincial decision making. PPAT staff members were assigned to provide support and transparency assurance to provincial budget execution, just as PAC staff provided for ministries in Baghdad. Within months of their establishment, provincial budget execution performance began to improve.

The embassy Director of Provincial Reconstruction, who oversaw all PRTs, was livid over our approach, and felt her "ownership" of all provincial reconstruction activity had been undermined. She demanded that we have the PPAT staff members report to the local PRT managers, and provide the local PRT with access to all of their detailed information about provincial budget allocation and associated projects, a request that I ignored as it would have destroyed the entire initiative.

And so it went. We realized that our mission would go on indefinitely until we had an organization we could transition our work to. And it was clear that no U.S. civilian agency was going to step up to take on our work—and that even when we could achieve breakthroughs in our relationships with elements of the U.S. government, other relationships would break down as new staff members continually rotated into and out of Iraq. Our only choice was to enable the Iraqis to take on our work. Across ministries and provinces, we were now putting the resources in place to do just that.

7.

THE BUSINESS OF DIPLOMACY

In 2008, as momentum continued to build and the positive results of our work become increasingly clear, Deputy Secretary of Defense Gordon England gave TFBSO the task to begin working with the Japanese government to assist them in executing a committed $5 billion in soft loans for Iraqi reconstruction initiatives, initially promised in 2003. After more than two years of deployment of forces, Japan had withdrawn its contribution of 600 troops working in the southern city of Samawah in July 2006. So far, none of the soft loan funding had been applied in Iraq because of delays in resolving outstanding debt obligations as well as security concerns within the Japanese government. In conjunction with Deputy Secretary of State John Negroponte, Secretary England had been encouraging the Japanese to begin launching projects to apply the soft loan funds, especially in southern Iraq.

England offered the Task Force as a vehicle for the Japanese to reengage in Iraq with minimal risk. This would be a new and unique role for TFBSO, and given our limited involvement in strategically important southern Iraq so far, could open up that area for broader TFBSO efforts. I recruited a political appointee serving as the Deputy Assistant Secretary of the Navy for Logistics, Nicholas Kunesh, to lead the effort. Nick had an extensive background in maritime logistics, was a veteran navy aviator, and had worked in Japan for several years for large industrial companies. Conversationally fluent in Japanese, Nick was willing to take on the opportunity to work with the Japanese government.

Within a few months, the Japanese government had come to agreement with the Government of Iraq on how to apply the first set of loans, totaling $1.2 billion. The majority of the projects were to be executed in the south of Iraq, in and around Basra, initially focusing on restoring full capacity to the industrial port of Umm Qasr.[1]

Until that time, TFBSO had minimal engagement in Basra. Assigned to the British military forces for security operations after the invasion in 2003, the city of Basra was now almost completely under the control of Shia militias, which had imposed harsh religious restrictions on the local population. No reconstruction activity of any consequence had taken place in Basra since 2003.[2]

This was strategically unfortunate. As the commercial lynchpin to Iraqi's economic future, Basra was far too important to ignore. Iranian media and trade have heavily influenced Basra, so allowing it to be ignored and to fall into the hands of militias only reinforced suspicions among the long-oppressed Shia of southern Iraq that the coalition could not be trusted to keep them safe.

Matt Schoeffling, in his first assignment within TFBSO, led the establishment of Task Force operations in southern Iraq with Nick Kunesh. Based at the port of Umm Qasr and Basra International Airport, TFBSO established a compound that served as a springboard to engage in the city of Basra and surrounding communities. Kunesh, working with Matt, began liaising with key Japanese contractors, selected to execute the projects funded by the soft loans, providing space and support to get them up and running in southern Iraq. The Japanese International Cooperative Agency, as well as major firms including Nippon Koei, JGC, and Mitsubishi Heavy Industries, all established operations in southern Iraq through the support of TFBSO.

This engagement was a reminder of something I knew from my private-sector life, but had forgotten given the perceived strict separation of private-sector industry and government within the United States. In most countries, the economic interests of industry serve indirectly to drive the interests of government. To rebuild Iraq's relationships with the global economy, it was critical to get international industry—not just American industry—engaged. In this respect, the support given to the Japanese soft loan program by TFBSO helped establish economic ties between Japan and Iraq that were far broader than just the foreign aid provided by soft loans.

Matt, Nick, and I visited Japan in 2008, holding meetings with Japanese companies and government leaders to encourage their reengagement in Iraq. This served several strategic purposes for the mission in Iraq. The United States, faced with growing budget pressure, needed to get other international parties involved in Iraq to share some of the burden of stabilizing the country. The presence of a broad range of international companies engaging Iraq further strengthened the message to Iraqis that, once violence subsided, they had the opportunity for a bright prosperous future within the global economy. Finally, as Japan was a coalition partner of the United States, our support was good American-Japanese diplomacy.

Within a year, TFBSO had hosted several Japanese business delegations and assisted in the launch of soft loan–funded projects exceeding $2 billion in southern Iraq. Our effort culminated in sponsoring a delegation of Japanese officials in Baghdad early in 2009. To make them welcome, we hosted a formal Japanese reception for Iraqi officials, provided fresh sushi flown in from Kuwait at our personal expense for the Japanese visitors, and essentially faded into the background during the event, to ensure that the ceremony was clearly Japanese and not overtly American.[3] Nick Kunesh was the only non-Japanese invited to address three separate Japan-Iraq business forums in Amman, Tokyo, and Basra, to promote Japanese commercial development in Iraq.

In 2008, a similar diplomatic benefit emerged for the United States and Iraq as a direct result of TFBSO engagement. Daimler Benz, after long discussion and multiple visits by technical staff and managers to Iskandiriyah, was now making a decision on its Iraq strategy. In the summer of 2008, Joachim Schmidt, a senior Daimler executive and the head of international operations for the company in the region, visited Baghdad as a guest of TFBSO and signed a memorandum of understanding to establish truck-assembly operations there.[4] This engagement had unforeseen additional benefits.

As a result of the reengagement of Daimler, several Iraqi officials were invited to visit Stuttgart to tour Daimler facilities and further discuss a broad relationship—especially for industrial-vehicle operations. This invitation was soon broadened by the German ambassador to incorporate government-to-government economic relationship discussions. TFBSO worked directly to support the visit to Stuttgart, and to support the ambassador's efforts to broaden the mission. In the fall of 2008, the Government of Iraq and the Government of Germany signed an economic-development agreement, pledging to work to restore industrial capacity to Iraq.[5] That agreement has led to more than $1 billion in foreign direct investment by German interests since 2008.

The Japanese and German examples demonstrated the formative and unique roles TFBSO played in the stabilization of Iraq's economy. In these cases, there would have been no way for other U.S. government agencies to directly support other nations' business interests. The U.S. Commerce Department could never have hosted Japanese or German businesses in Iraq, for example, as it would have directly conflicted with its core mission of broadening American industrial engagement abroad. Because the mission of TFBSO was to quickly restore economic stability and create conditions for growth in the economy following the establishment of security as an element of counterinsurgency, using any means to get private investment—American or international—was not only completely reasonable, but also the best way to support U.S. interest with the least expenditure of taxpayer dollars.

＊　　＊

A principal benefit to the Task Force of the work in support of the Japanese soft loan initiative was the establishment of TFBSO operations in Basra Province. Operating out of the port of Umm Qasr, TFBSO launched industrial revitalization initiatives at nine factories that had been idled or operated at near-zero capacity since 2003. As much as idled heavy industrial operations made little sense in other parts of Iraq, they were especially hard to understand in Basra. Basra Province, a land area about twice the size of the state of Delaware, contains as many as 100 billion barrels of oil under its sands. The historic port city of Basra, located on the Shatt al Arab waterway near the Persian Gulf, had once been home to a rich cosmopolitan culture and had centuries of trading history with surrounding countries. It is inevitable, given global demands for energy resources, that Basra will eventually be a major city in the region and a center of industrial activity. To leave its industries idled for the better part of a decade following the overthrow of Saddam created a huge missed opportunity.

TFBSO set about restoring production at operations ranging from a large industrial equipment manufacturer to the nation's only petro-chemical plant that made high-density polymers (plastics) used in a variety of applications, to the large idled Basra Iron & Steel State Company, a huge Soviet-style steel mill that had been offline for more than a decade. As in other operations in Iraq, the goal of our work was to acquire the minimal equipment, raw material, or maintenance service needed to get production operations up and running, and then to work to reconnect suppliers and customers to maintain production. Once operating, we correctly believed that the factories would be easy candidates for foreign investment. As the oil industry would be centered in Basra, there would be near-unlimited demand for any industrial production in the province in the future.

Most of these projects were on the outskirts of the city or between the city center and the port of Umm Qasr. The complete lack of security in the city made it impossible even to assess opportunities there in 2007 and early in 2008.

The reasons for the collapse in security were complicated. Basra Province was allocated to the British for ongoing reconstruction and security following the downfall of the Hussein regime. From an initial presence of more than 40,000 troops, the UK had reduced its presence to less than 4,000 by late 2007, with all of its forces confined to bases in the city and at Basra International Airport.[6]

Early in 2004, British commanders were confident that they could apply the lessons learned in northern Ireland to draw in community leaders, create effective engagement, and establish stability. But in 2006, the British military made a strategic decision to permit the presence of armed militias in the city, which shortly carved out entire neighborhoods as territories. Corruption grew rampant, with random checkpoints throughout the city and countryside established to shake down citizens for money or to identify members of families or sects for abuse or worse. The British bases were shelled nightly by rockets and mortars, with no return fire to discourage the attacks permitted by British politicians, who were under increasing pressure at home to withdraw all UK forces. In the summer of 2007, all UK forces withdrew from the city to a single base at the airport, leaving Basra to the complete control of militias.[7]

Security and stability collapsed, and radical Shia militias quickly imposed rigid interpretations of Islamic law on the local population, killing more than forty women in a matter of weeks for violations of dress codes. For this historically important port city, it was a shameful failure on the part of the coalition.

For TFBSO, this collapse in security made our work in Basra difficult at best. Driving through the city, it was hard to believe any Western engagement had happened at all. The entire city was piled high with garbage; its historic canals were open, stinking sewers. Children and adults scurried from building to building; street life was minimal. Buildings still bore the scars from shelling during the Iran-Iraq War two decades before, and rubble was visible in every neighborhood. There was no evidence of any reconstruction.

Driving through the city, I thought about the population, and what they must be thinking of the United States. After the First Gulf War, the United States had encouraged an uprising in southern Iraq in an effort to overthrow Saddam. When he retaliated with helicopter attacks and tanks rolled into Basra, the U.S. stood by while Shia were slaughtered. Now, a full five years after Saddam had been overthrown, Basra was still living in complete squalor and chaos. Iranian propaganda continually repeated the line that the U.S. was in Iraq to subjugate the Iraqi people. I could not help thinking that if I were a Basrawi, I wouldn't have trouble believing this, given what had taken place so far.

As we drove through the city, the eyes of young men on street corners and at "checkpoints" made clear we were unwelcome.

It was also difficult to meet with the British commanders, who were clearly driven to complete frustration by their inability to engage in securing the province. I would meet with them frequently when in Basra, and each time I would notice further declines in morale. I saw firsthand that there is nothing worse for an army than to be held idle while security collapses around it. Accustomed to the remarkable infrastructure, from dining facilities to weight rooms to recreational facilities on large American installations in Iraq, it was a different experience to visit the British base in Basra. Morale was low, in spite of the best efforts of commanders to keep their troops motivated, and the level of infrastructure and support was clearly far less than Americans were afforded.

But on the occasions we were able to collaborate with the British, we were always tremendously impressed with their ability to get more done with less. I felt genuine empathy for the British soldiers and commanders in Basra. It was clear that, properly resourced with enough troops, they would never have let the situation in Basra degrade as it had.

✳   ✳

In March 2008, everything in Basra changed. The Iraqi Army entered Basra in a surprise military operation later referred to as Saulat al Fursan—the Charge of the Knights. Two brigades from Anbar Province were first to enter Basra, with a clear objective to restore order and clear Shia militias—particularly Sadrist Jaish al Mahdi militia—from the city.[8] This operation, the first significant military campaign led by Iraqi forces, was supported by coalition air assets and, later, by special operations forces. Within a week of the launch of this campaign, a cease-fire was negotiated by the Sadrist leadership. Iranian weapons as well as evidence of operational support to militias were found throughout the city in the following weeks, as weapons caches were seized and order was restored.

It had been more than six months since any sustained fire had taken place in Baghdad, but with the launch of operations in Basra, sirens were going off continually, with rockets launched from the Sadr City neighborhood of eastern Baghdad in retaliation against the Iraqi government for its operations against the Sadrist militias in the south. Overhead surveillance systems usually provided quick information on the location of origin for rocket launches, but the country was experiencing drought, and as winter turned to spring and winds kicked in from the west, huge dust storms settled on the city, rendering the surveillance systems ineffective. As the sun would grow dim from the dust, a feeling of dread would pervade Baghdad, and soon the sirens would sound and the telltale impacts would follow.[9]

As this cycle of attacks began, we returned to the mindset we had held during 2006 and 2007, when rocket attacks were part of daily life when visiting Baghdad. Entering the U.S. Embassy Compound at the Republican Palace during the period of the renewed attacks for a meeting with Ambassador Crocker, we found a disturbing scene. Since the rocket attacks had largely ended over six months earlier, many embassy staffers had returned home and been replaced by new personnel, most of whom had never experienced the nightly terror of waiting for the rocket impacts to sound after the sirens would start wailing. When they fled their unarmored trailer houses, cots were set up for them throughout the palace building, and the halls were lined with people sitting against the walls, visibly emotional and distraught.

Less than a year earlier, the daily rocket fire had been so constant that there was a fatalistic mood among the embassy staff members as well as military personnel. You learned just to ignore it and go on with your work. Now, a sense of fear pervaded the place.

During this period, a key TFBSO leader, Air Force Lieutenant Colonel Mark Baird, who had taken over our finances and our contract management when Lieutenant Colonel Tom Snyder moved on, was standing outside a home in the Green Zone meeting with the CEO of one of our most reliable contractors, Groundworks International, Greg Holmes and his wife Zoraida. He had stepped outside for a phone call on his Blackberry, only to have the call get disconnected—a common occurrence on Iraq's overloaded mobile phone network. Perhaps ten seconds after his call was disconnected and he had returned into the house, a 107-mm rocket landed one foot from where he had been standing talking on the phone, blasting out the windows of the home and covering everyone in glass. Had he stayed on the phone, he would have been lost. It was the nearest of many near misses for TFBSO personnel at that time.

Lieutenant General Lloyd Austin had assumed command of MNCI from Lieutenant General Raymond Odierno in February 2008. Austin was another example of a warfighting commander with a remarkable breadth of knowledge and understanding of economics and governance. I met with him monthly on our progress, as I had with other MNCI commanders dating back to 2006 with Lieutenant General Chiarelli. As Basra calmed down following the conclusion of the Charge of the Knights campaign, TFBSO was confronted with an opportunity. Austin asked what TFBSO could do to help in Basra. As the U.S. military was only present in a limited supporting role to the Iraqi military, and as there was no U.S. civilian presence there, he needed us to step up and assist wherever possible. We immediately expanded our existing operations in Basra to including banking automation and investor support—building on the foundation Matt Schoeffling had established more than a year earlier.

* *

In the spring of 2008, I hosted a visit by Tom Pritzker. Pritzker is best known for his role as chairman of Hyatt Hotels but also serves as chairman of the industrial conglomerate Marmon Group. In addition to overseeing these multinational companies, Tom had built Triton Containers, the world's largest container-leasing company, as well as the first national health care PPO, and a number of other thriving businesses. Bill Strong, the vice chairman of Morgan Stanley, joined Pritzker at the Pentagon, where I made a pitch for them to visit Iraq and assess business opportunities—an offer they eventually accepted.

Touring Baghdad and Basra, Pritzker was particularly intrigued by our challenge and quick to offer advice and help. Hyatt eventually submitted a proposal to take on renovation and operation of the historic Al Rashid Hotel in Baghdad. We also looked at the former Sheraton Hotel on the waterfront of the Shatt al Arab in Basra, a huge structure in an ideal location that had been stripped down to bare concrete by looters during the chaos of Basra in 2005–08.

The Pritzkers would host the Iraqi minister of tourism in Chicago in 2009, and they continually offered to engage in supporting the restoration of antiquities and archeological sites as contributions from their foundations. Active across a variety of foreign policy boards and organizations such as the Center for Strategic and International Studies as well as the Council on Foreign Relations, Pritzker was intrigued by our mission and our approach to development—involving the private sector and working to create a sustainable economic base in war-torn countries instead of simply providing charitable aid.

Pritzker would again visit Iraq, and later Afghanistan, traveling in areas of violence at great personal risk to better assess business and economic opportunities. His support in Washington helped build our credibility among both elite business leaders as well as the foreign policy "establishment" in New York and Washington. His first delegation to Iraq, which included Strong as well as the CEO of the fertilizer giant CFS Industries, Steve Wilson, wrote an op-ed in the *Chicago Tribune* on their return sharing their generally favorable observations of Iraq compared to their expectations and encouraging investors to engage.[10]

Our most-focused and significant effort in Basra involved a massive idled steel mill. I took this on as a personal challenge. In 2008, Iraq was importing steel at the rate of six million tons per year. The global steel market was booming as Chinese consumption increased exponentially, and prices were near all-time highs. A steel mill in Basra would run at full capacity as the country rebuilt its oil and gas sectors as well as its infrastructure. It was a can't-miss proposition for foreign investment.

I reached out to the world's largest steel company, ArcelorMittal, which had recently acquired International Steel Group of the United States, giving it major status as a domestic steel producer. ArcelorMittal Chief Financial Officer Aditya Mittal visited Iraq in 2008 at the invitation of the Task Force with a team of his engineers and managers, who then submitted a visionary proposal to Fawzi Hariri to rebuild the steel industry in southern Iraq. The proposal, which generated a publicly announced memorandum of understanding, called for more than $3 billion in investment to create a steel facility capable of producing more than 1.5 million tons per year of industrial-grade steel suitable for oil-sector and industrial applications.

Within weeks of submitting this proposal, the New York investment bank Lehman Brothers failed and the global financial crisis of 2008 began. The global economy entered a steep recession and credit crisis. Steel prices fell by almost 80 percent from their peak levels by the fall of 2008. Instead of expansion, like its rivals in the industry, ArcelorMittal regrouped and pulled its proposal from consideration. Excitement in Basra at the steelworks was replaced by disappointment.

The spring of 2008, however, brought one other breakthrough for

TFBSO. For months, since hosting the investment conference with the Ministry of Industry in Dubai, TFBSO had a team of advisors and accountants working with Fawzi Hariri to review proposals. In March 2008, the first private joint-venture investments in Iraqi state-owned factories were finally signed after a marathon negotiation in Amman, Jordan, supported by accountants from Grant Thornton led by Scott King. Cement plants in Karbala, Qubaysah, and Al Qaim were to be revitalized by major international companies from Europe in partnership with Iraqi investors, for amounts each in excess of $100 million. It was a ringing vindication for our program, and proof that the transitional approach of privatizing state-owned enterprises was sound. The Ministry of Industry would receive annual income from the operators of the facilities, which could be used to initiate operations in other idled factories belonging to the ministry, which could then also be privatized.

We were thrilled with this news. Qubaysah and Al Qaim were in Anbar Province, the center of the worst violence of 2006 and 2007, and where, because of electricity shortages, TFBSO had been able to do far less than we had hoped to restore production to idled large factories. These cement plants would have dedicated power plants built as part of the negotiated agreements with international operators. We felt we had finally contributed something significant in Anbar. It was the first of many things to come.

As the broad-ranging impacts of our work became increasingly apparent in command briefings back to Washington, I was busier and busier giving updates to the National Security Council leaders responsible for the Iraqi mission at the White House. Meghan O'Sullivan had been an early member of Bremer's team in Baghdad during the CPA days, but unlike many former CPA members, she had been a strong supporter of our work from its inception. An Oxford PhD, O'Sullivan had a reputation for fearless engagement with so-called radical factions, especially perceived radical Shia elements of the Iran-backed Badr organization, and continued to visit Iraq frequently. In May 2008, Meghan departed the NSC, where she was the presidential advisor on Iraq and Afghanistan, to assume a faculty role at the Kennedy School of Government at Harvard University. Her replacement, Army Lieutenant General Douglas Lute, was also an active and vocal supporter of our work during the last year of the Bush Administration.

When I would update them on our progress, both O'Sullivan and later Lute would provide a lot of positive feedback, and occasionally mention a desire to have me brief President Bush directly. I viewed these suggestions as polite throwaway comments. It is common for senior political appointees to hold out an engagement with a senior official as a reward, but nothing usually comes of it. I had learned over the years that this was a standard Washington routine: well-intentioned and harmless, but also not to be taken seriously. I rarely saw Defense Secretary Robert Gates. I certainly would not be seeing the president. And I was quite happy about that. I was perfectly content to report to Deputy Secretary England and to have the opportunity to interact frequently with leaders such as Joint Chiefs Chairman Admiral Michael Mullen, and General David Petraeus and their respective organizational leaders. By this point, I had far exceeded any expectations for senior-leader engagement based on my initial job at the Pentagon in 2004. I always thanked O'Sullivan and Lute for any positive feedback and suggestions and went on about my business.

✳   ✳

In Baghdad, intermittent rocket and mortar attacks continued for weeks, gradually tapering off, but not stopping altogether. In late May, Baird, Bob Love, Beth Law, Sonja Stephens—my long-time executive assistant now working in Iraq—and I were outside at our compound two miles from the embassy on the edge of the Green Zone. Suddenly the too-recognizable *whish* of rockets passed near overhead, with an impact very close to our headquarters. Standing and moving quickly inside, another impact followed seconds later.

Within minutes, we were informed that the rockets had landed near our dining area a few hundred yards down the road from our headquarters building. Several of our support staff members had been injured by shrapnel, one severely, who was being rushed to the U.S. Combat Support Hospital. Minutes later we were informed that he had been killed.

Dionasis "JoJo" Saguid absorbed a lethal impact of shrapnel from the blast as he bravely leapt to cover his female coworkers. The workers were part of our extended team, in near-constant interaction with us on a daily basis. The father of two children, JoJo had defied a ban on Filipinos working in Iraq imposed by the government of the Philippines in 2004, in an effort to provide for his family by working for a U.S. government contractor.

By the summer of 2008, the Task Force was more than 400 people strong, with a presence in every province of the country, working across every sector of the Iraqi economy except for oil and gas. Those 400 people were operating extensively outside of walled compounds, interacting freely with everyday Iraqi business leaders, farmers, merchants, and government personnel. Yet after two years of operations, our first casualty of violence in Iraq had been in the supposedly safe Green Zone, where he was the random victim of a rocket probably launched at the Republican Palace that missed its mark by more than two miles.

＊　　＊

The Task Force members had grown increasingly interested in agriculture as they began working in factories around the country. Sites like fertilizer plants, textile mills, and food-processing operations all were either suppliers or consumers of Iraqi agriculture. As these operations were shut down, the impact on Iraqi farms had been severe. MNFI commanders had asked me if TFBSO could engage in an agricultural assistance effort (for more than a year), but we were so busy with our other programs we simply could not take on yet more work. I was also unconvinced that we were the right people to do this.

A call with a J.C. Penney executive almost changed my thinking about this in 2007. West Point graduate and senior executive James Kenney had indicated a desire to help the mission in a discussion with General Petraeus early in 2007, who in turn asked me to reach out to Kenney. He and I had a long phone conversation, in which he affirmed our analysis that Iraqi clothing companies would not be able to thrive in the long term given the flood of cheap clothing and the near-infinite manufacturing capacity in east Asia.

He did, however, tell me that organic cotton was in extremely high demand for use by high-end environmentally friendly garment manufacturers, and commanded prices per ton as much as six times greater than regular cotton. If we could provide organic raw cotton, or better still, woven fabric or clothing of an acceptable standard made from organic cotton, demand would essentially be unlimited. He told us we would need to find some niche that Iraq could satisfy if we wanted to get the textile sector back on its feet. Organic cotton could be just such a niche.

To be certified as organic, a field that has been treated with chemical pesticides or fertilizers must lie fallow for three years. Only natural products, well defined by international standards, can be used to fertilize or control pests once a field is planted at the end of the fallow period.[12]

This sounded perfect to me. Because of the collapse in farm production across Iraq, and the closure of almost all cotton gins and textile mills throughout the country, a large portion of Iraq's cotton farms had been fallow since 2003. If we could get idled cotton farmers trained in organic cultivation and get the farms certified, we could rebuild the cotton sector and put thousands of farmers and farm employees back to work.

When I returned to Washington, I visited with several experts in organic farming and cotton cultivation. I then received a call from a friend on the Senate Armed Services Committee staff, stating that unless we wanted to have our mission funding pulled we had better back off of our efforts at cotton farming in Iraq. We had apparently attracted the attention of the cotton lobby, with my wide-ranging inquiries in town about cotton cultivation with various agricultural bodies and the USDA triggering a response.

We were running afoul of the Bumpers Amendment, a law passed in the 1980s, in an effort to prevent American foreign aid from being used to assist in the development of any agricultural production that could potentially compete with American farm products in international markets.[13]

For commodities that are essentially sold in global markets or exchanges, including all grains, corn, and oilseeds, as well as farm products such as flax or cotton, this prohibition prevents the application of U.S. funds appropriated to USAID or the State Department for agricultural development.

The logic of this law is clear. It makes sense that American farmers, faced with increasing global competition, do not want their tax dollars expended on creating yet more competition. But in a war zone, with a burning insurgency killing our troops and costing hundreds of billions of dollars, preventing the restoration of normal life to farm communities is exceedingly shortsighted.

It is evident that in every society in times of war, most of its soldiers come from rural communities. This is true of the American military, and equally true for every society. If you want to deny radical leaders access to a ready pool of willing recruits, one way to help do so is to make the farm communities prosper.

USAID and USDA could not, by law, help any effort to create a viable prosperous cotton industry in Iraq, even if it was organic cotton in short supply around the world. The Defense budget had no funds available for direct support to cotton farmers. My industrial revitalization funding was all now being applied to reopen factories, and regardless, I would never get approval from Pentagon fiscal lawyers to use those funds for direct farm support.

It was a shame. Cotton cultivation in Iraq remains depressed, with production levels in recent years at less than a third of historic peak production. The regions of Iraq that historically grew significant amounts of cotton remain some of the most troubled parts of the country, areas such as Kirkuk and Diyala Provinces.

We did, however, aggressively work to provide agricultural support to commanders. I had received a green light to hire experts to work in areas clearly tied to the military mission, as such areas were permitted to use Defense Department general funds for the Iraq conflict. To ensure that any agricultural experts we hired could not be construed as undertaking "foreign aid" activity, we used a different management model than for our other lines of operation. I committed to hiring agricultural experts, drawing on American land-grant universities as a source of expertise, and directly embedded these staffers within units of the military.

To make this work, I entered a partnership with the U.S. Department of Agriculture to hire agricultural experts. USDA had been under a lot of pressure to provide additional agricultural support for Iraq and Afghanistan through its Foreign Agricultural Service.

But the Foreign Ag Service was founded to create new markets for American agricultural products, and was a small, elite organization of specialists in agricultural economics, with a miniscule budget. There was no ready "bench" of foreign agriculture development experts at FAS ready to parachute into war zones to assist farmers. At best, the FAS was able to place a few experts on one-year assignments in the embassy or on Provincial Reconstruction Teams, where the security restrictions made their ability to engage very limited at best. USDA was willing to partner with TFBSO to find a solution to this problem.

By the summer of 2008, world-class international agriculture experts from universities including Virginia Tech, Penn State, Mississippi State, Oklahoma State, University of Maryland, and Texas A&M were working throughout Iraq. More than 40 different faculty members worked as part of the TFBSO/USDA agriculture team. Rod McSherry, the USDA attaché assigned to the embassy in Baghdad, was an instrumental partner in this rare model for intergovernmental cooperation.

The agriculture team, in partnership with and in support of our troops, worked in the most dangerous areas of Iraq in 2008–09. In partnership with provincial officials and farmers, they wrote comprehensive agricultural development plans for governorates of Anbar, Babil, Basra, Najaf, Mosul, Salah ad Din, Diyala, Baghdad, Dhi Qar, and Wasit. Working with agriculture colleges in cities of Ramadi, Najaf, Basra, and Baghdad, the team provided textbooks, and modernized curricula, and taught seminars on topics ranging from water resource management to soil science to yield improvement across a variety of commodities.[14]

Most inspiring were the tactical projects the team completed throughout the country. Fish farms, farmers markets, produce-processing operations, and farm improvement projects by the dozens were completed across the country. Unit commanders were able to quickly apply funds used for local projects to opportunities identified by the TFBSO ag team. The total cost of this initiative was less than $8M over two years, but the return on that investment was immeasurable.

In the summer of 2008, Congress appropriated another $50M in funding for capital expenditures by TFBSO[15]. This time, the funds were far less restrictive—with a broad mandate to restore Iraqi industries including factories, farms, and other economic sectors. With this funding, we launched one of our most significant programs in the agriculture sector, a program that would eventually affect trade policies for the entire country of Iraq.

By the middle of 2008, the industrial operations in Iskandiriyah had more than 3,000 employees assembling and/or manufacturing a variety of industrial goods, vehicles, house trailers, Case New Holland tractors, steel assemblies, and oil field equipment. We learned of efforts by Iraqi farmers to acquire greenhouses to create winter growing seasons for fruits and vegetables, and to extend the spring growing season into the early summer by shielding crops from the blazing sun.

With a small investment in metal-bending equipment and raw materials, TFBSO established an industrial-sized greenhouse manufacturing operation in Iskandiriyah. Dr. Ahmed Araji, an Iraqi American University of Idaho professor of agriculture working for TFBSO, engaged with the governors of every province to establish a business development program for vegetable cultivation. The Task Force donated hundreds of industrial-sized greenhouses to each province. The governorate sold the greenhouses to farmers at half cost on a three-year payment plan. This payment-plan approach ensured that the farmers were motivated to establish produce-cultivation businesses. The future income from the repayment of the three-year financing would be used to acquire additional greenhouses.

A remarkable example of the impact of this program can be seen in Karbala. The holiest city in Shia Islam, Karbala is the site of the shrine of the first Shia Imam and grandson of the Prophet Muhammad, Hussein ibn Ali, killed in a one-sided battle resisting the establishment of dynastic rule of Islam in the year A.D. 610.[16] Every year, millions of Shia Muslims make a pilgrimage to Karbala, often walking hundreds of miles to visit the shrine of Hussein. Given the importance of this city, and the ongoing hostile relationships with Iran and its position as the defender of the Shia, the United States would have done well to shower Karbala with support and development—doing so would have resonated throughout the Islamic world and sent a clear countermessage to the claims of Iranian leaders that the United States, the so-called "Great Satan," is at war with Islam.

The city of Karbala sits between the Euphrates River and the vast deserts of northern Saudi Arabia. To provide a barrier to the encroachment of the desert sand, the provincial leadership of Karbala planted a fifteen-kilometer belt of date palms and olive trees encircling the southwestern quarter of the city. With the TFBSO donation of greenhouses, a vegetable-cultivation center was created adjacent to the greenbelt of trees. Today, hundreds of industrial greenhouses fill the desert, and an entire vegetable cultivation industry has emerged in Karbala, creating economic opportunity for thousands of farmers, handlers, and distributors providing a source of income selling fresh produce to feed the millions of pilgrims that visit the city.

Two years after this program was launched, I visited Karbala and saw the results. Greenhouses stretched across the desert landscape southwest of the city. The gratitude of the community to this American donation of an economic livelihood to some of the poorest inhabitants of the city was heartfelt. And, most important, as production of vegetables and fruits grew in Karbala and in similar settings across Iraq, farmers' demand grew for fair prices compared to cheap imports from Iran.[17]

In 2010, the government of Iraq finally established mirror-image tariff regimes with Iran—putting the Iraqi farmer back on an even playing field with his competitors to the north and east, after seven years of unfair trade. The emergence of vegetable cultivation in some of Iraq's most important and politically influential regions, enabled in no small part by the greenhouse-distribution program, provided the political pressure needed to resolve that longstanding mistake of the early years of the American occupation.

❋   ❋

It was springtime in Washington, the 2008 campaign season was in full swing, and conversations within TFBSO were shifting to a new subject: how to manage a transition of our work to the Iraqis, or if necessary, to MNFI, USAID, or the embassy. Our assumption was that, as a political appointee, my tenure would clearly end on January 21, along with that of all of the other senior leaders in the Office of the Secretary of Defense. The mission was unprecedented: politically appointed officials simply did not do tactical work in the Department of Defense, much less in an active combat zone. Absent a proactive transition plan led by ourselves, the mission would be at risk of ending abruptly, leaving too much work unfinished and too many commitments in Iraq unfulfilled.

This was an unavoidable distraction, and it had operational impacts. Security in Iraq was continually improving as the benefits of the surge took hold, yet we were reluctant—outside of our new work in Basra—to further expand our efforts in spite of continuous appeals from divisional commanders to do more and more work. With more than 400 team members already in the country, keeping momentum on the programs already underway was difficult enough. By this point, I had spent an average of eleven days a month working throughout Iraq, for twenty-three consecutive months dating to my first engagement in May 2006. As Iraq was eight hours ahead of Eastern Standard Time, I had lost all sense of a Circadian rhythm, and basically slept whenever I was able to lie down or find a quiet place. At 188 pounds, I was in my best physical shape since high school, but was physically and mentally exhausted. There was no sense in expanding our mission even more given the inevitable end of our team with the upcoming change of administration.

The organization had changed fundamentally since its inception. With Major General Butch Pair running operations in Baghdad, and with a full contingent of military officers to staff TFBSO operationally and liaise with commands, we now had much better lateral communication with each tier of MNCI and MNFI commands, as well as with the embassy, which remained largely sequestered in spite of security improvements. I was relieved not to have to spend so much time in the operational details of daily activity. It freed me up for far more engagement with businesses, Iraqi ministers, provincial governors, and local leaders, when in country. When at home, I could devote significant time meeting with company leaders and recruiting potential investors to engage in Iraq. But we were slowing down. The pyramid organizational structure so comfortable within the military command and control doctrine resulted in far less efficient flow of direction across the extended organization. We had lost our start-up feel and we were becoming bureaucratic. My role became more strategic, and our management shifted to monitoring metrics and progress to our internal and external plans, we were naturally losing the entrepreneurial vibrancy that had made the effort unique in 2006 and 2007.

The benefits of TFBSO efforts to date were now rolling in, however, across every sector of the Iraqi economy. The Iraqi ministries were shifting from an existential mindset, under constant threat of lethal violence, to getting on with the work of rebuilding their country. There was an excitement in the air in our meetings with ministerial officials, as if they realized that finally they could get to work. Efforts now accelerated within ministries for the privatization of industry, budget execution, training in market-based economics, and establishment of the national investment commission and its subordinate provincial investment commissions.

Our credibility was increasing in Washington. Even the constant naysayers were silent, as the improvements of the surge were becoming apparent at home, and as General Petraeus increasingly and openly identified TFBSO as one of many successful elements of the overall strategy for counterinsurgency.

In one of my near-daily meetings with Deputy Secretary England's Chief of Staff Robert Earl that April, he looked surprised as he informed me that the White House had requested a briefing from me.

The meeting was set for March 12. Always supportive, Deputy Secretary England gave me his advice on what to say and do, and what to present. Twenty minutes had been scheduled—apparently an unusually long meeting with a lower-level official. Presidential meetings involving non-cabinet appointees are typically formal affairs set up as brief "atta-boy" discussions, in which a short discussion takes place followed by a photo and then the meeting adjourns. The entire proceeding would typically take only a few minutes. To dedicate a full twenty minutes for a full-on briefing was apparently atypical.

I was beyond grateful for England's support. Cabinet secretaries and deputy cabinet secretaries generally do not like surprise requests for briefings from the White House involving their subordinate staffs. If a White House briefing takes place, a cabinet secretary arranges it.

As usual, I spent the better part of early March in Iraq, returning to D.C. on a Friday so I could spend the weekend with my family. As Wednesday, March 12 approached, I became anxious. Since joining the department in 2004, I had grown accustomed to meeting with all manner of senior officials, both at home, and abroad. I had testified before congressional committees before cameras. I had given lengthy press conferences in Washington and in Baghdad. I thought I had grown beyond the "butterfly" stage of nervousness. But this time was different. I felt the pressure of going into the most powerful office in the world.

I almost never prepared for a briefing, beyond a basic organization of topics to cover, priding myself on my ability to simply discuss any topic I was involved in off-the-cuff. But this time, I prepared, and prepared, and prepared again.

I had visited the West Wing many times for meetings with the NSC leadership over the past two years, and had arranged a tour for my family shortly after arriving in Washington that included a peek into the Oval Office. Seeing the Oval Office on a tour is a far cry from entering the Oval Office for a meeting with the President of the United States.

The president and I shook hands, and he quickly motioned for everyone to be seated in a manner that indicated we were on a schedule that was intended to be kept.

I took the single seat next to the president, to the left of the fireplace above which hangs a famous portrait of George Washington. Deputy Secretary of Defense Gordon England and Secretary of Defense Robert Gates took seats on the couches to my right and left, with National Security Advisor Stephen Hadley and his staff seated next to them. Deputy Secretary England made some introductory remarks regarding my work, and I began my briefing.

The environment was difficult. My seat was just far enough from the president that it was hard to show the few slides and photographs I had brought. My structured approach I had practiced over and over was hindering my conversation. As I attempted to cover each sector we worked on, the discussion stopped when I recited statistics from our work on state-owned enterprises. Clearly the president had been prepared to question me about that.

He sharply questioned why we would want to get state-owned factories up and running again. I explained our approach and how it differed from earlier efforts, how a transition from socialism over time would reduce violence and lower unemployment, buying time for stability to take hold. I recited our statistics on private investment and the initial deals for joint ventures in state-owned factories, and our expectation for more. On it went. I had been expecting, based on popular media images, to find a kindly individual with little curiosity about details in President Bush. What I was experiencing was instead reminiscent of a grilling I would have gotten in a private-sector setting from a skeptical CEO. Armed with charts, and graphs, and prepared for any question on points of fact with my carefully prepared scripted remarks, I was able to answer his questions with facts, but I was not connecting with him at all.

Less than ten minutes into a twenty-minute briefing, the conversation was not going well. He had clearly seen my charts before, in a read-ahead book prior to the meeting. I looked at the president, and his eyes seemed to betray impatience with the discussion. I took a long pause, and looked to my right and left, where the Pentagon senior leadership sat. Gates was looking straight ahead and slightly down. England was looking at the president, but not at me.

I was going down.

I thought of what usually transpired in this room. How many recitations of statistics, of graphs, of charts showing great results and improvements, were paraded before this man every day? How sick and tired he must be of it all. How numbing it would get. It was the eighth year of his administration, and of all of his strategic decisions, the public opinion of the Iraq war was most damning. How weary he must be of briefings full of charts and statistics telling him how wonderful everything is going when the world clearly thought otherwise.

I also realized that from his perspective, my presence there could make no sense. What was a Pentagon political appointee doing talking about economics in the first place? Why was the Defense Department, with its endless pleas for more funding and supplemental budgets for military operations, spending time and money on economic development? Wasn't that the job of the State Department?

My pause extended to a point where the silence almost became uncomfortable for all in the room. I put down all my graphs, photos, and charts, and I told the president that I wanted to tell him a story. He looked surprised, and before he could reply I began telling the story of Iraqi soccer balls, our first effort to buy goods made in Iraq for our troops to hand out to children in the streets, which so perfectly illustrated the damage that war and endless sanctions had done to the commercial soul of Iraq and its people.

Building my narrative to the stamping of the soccer balls with a "Made in China" label, and the heartbreaking explanation of the factory manager that no Iraqi child would ever want something made in Iraq, I shifted my gaze to look President Bush in the eye and told him that all the Iraqi people need is time and space to rebuild their confidence and to take their place in the world economically, and that we are now providing that time and space. His eyes softened, and he sat back in his chair as I recounted our work in private banking, in agriculture, in foreign direct investment, and in budget execution assistance. I explained how we were a team of more than 400 professionals, largely from the American private sector, with international business experience who had volunteered to go into harm's way side-by-side with our troops during the worst of the violence. Businessmen and -women just like he had once been, we had stepped forward to fill a gap in our nation's foreign policy capability.

He leaned forward and grew ever more engaged as time went on. Secretary Gates began to comment on the importance of the work, and how it was a complement to the tremendous gains being made in security on the ground. The mood shifted to one of positive energy as the meeting rolled beyond twenty minutes. Forty-five minutes passed before our discussion concluded. His last question was whether I, were I still in private business, would invest in Iraq. Jumping up, the president went to his desk, and presented me with a few mementos from the oval office, shook my hand, and thanked me for all I was doing while we posed for a photo.

As we exited the Oval Office, Secretary Gates and Deputy Secretary England were clearly pleased.

As I returned to the Pentagon via the Metro, I reflected on how far my journey had taken me from the cubicle in Arlington's Crystal City, after I moved from California to find that my job had been stripped of authority back in 2004. It had been a wild ride and I was completely exhausted both physically and emotionally, but with 2008 being the last year of the president's term, I could see the end of the road ahead.

8.

OUR BEST YEAR YET

In August 2008, a year after I had dismissed two staff members, triggering a series of events culminating in an investigation by the Department of Defense Inspector General's office, I had at last received the final report on the outcome of the investigation. I had waited and waited for the report; finally I would have a document I could circulate, trumpeting to everyone what had happened and why. I had never really been the same since the whole situation had erupted. I had stopped "performance managing" employees entirely—preferring just to avoid any negative consequences of normal management actions by ignoring or working around team members whom I would normally have dismissed from the organization.

For a year, the endless process was constantly in the back of my mind, even though the outcome was never in doubt. It had created a financial burden as well. My legal bills had climbed into the tens of thousands of dollars, none of which could be reimbursed. It was hard to contain my frustration at the circumstances.

The report cleared me of the allegations. But it did so in a manner that was impossible to use easily for a public defense. Every allegation was listed, with a subsequent legalistic statement defining how the allegation had been investigated, and that the investigation had failed to substantiate the accusation. It was simply an investigation of the charges, not an investigation of how ridiculous the whole thing was. The IG had done its job, but I was left without the simple statement I wanted—a blanket declaration of innocence I could broadcast to anyone who had questioned my integrity.

On further reflection, it became clear to me that, just as Ken Krieg had warned back in the summer of 2006, I had pissed off a lot of people in the Pentagon with my work in Iraq and my vocal advocacy for changing course on Iraq policy. When the opportunity came, no one pulled me out from in front of the bus, instead watching as it ran over me. That was an important lesson. In a political system, there are a hundred ways you can get broadsided, and there is no way to predict which one will hit you if you lose too many supporters.

＊　　＊

When Washington was at its most frustrating, I would pivot back to Iraq where a different set of challenges was always waiting. One of the first factories we had reopened in 2006 was Ramadi Ceramics, the plant that we had visited with the marines in the capitol of Anbar in August 2006, the first time we had experienced small-arms fire on any of our missions. Located in a high-risk area, the plant was difficult to visit, but full of brand-new equipment. Plus, it had been a major employer in that strategic city. I had assigned engineers to work with the plant to get it running, we had arranged for the employees to travel to Italy for retraining on the Italian-made production equipment, bought minor spare parts and some raw material, and confirmed with the marines that the power supply to the plant was steady (as ceramics kilns required steady uninterrupted power).

The problem then became marketing. The factory management apparently had no experience in selling the finished goods—sinks, fixtures, and toilet bowls—to the newly emerging private construction sector. We provided coursework for them in how to identify markets and how to sell, but so far they were building products with no customers.

As Kurdistan had a major housing-construction boom underway, we had begun working with several of the construction investors there, and the Kurdish private construction firms committed to buy any fixtures made in Ramadi. I figured that if we could "prime the pump" for the factory with some high-volume orders and begin the process of having the factory interact with private-sector customers, it would enable them to develop, over time, needed skills in sales and customer service. Introductions were made, and my reports from staffers indicated that everything was progressing, which I incorporated into the other project updates I provided Petraeus in my monthly reviews.

Petraeus learned otherwise during a report on economic progress in Anbar from the marines in the summer of 2008. In his usual probing style, he inquired about the state of the ceramics plant, and was told they still had no markets for their products. Armed with this nugget of data, he dropped it in my lap during one of my routine updates on our progress. I hadn't asked my staff about Ramadi recently. My last visit there had been a couple of months earlier, so I promised to get to the bottom of it.

I left annoyed. If we were so synched with the marines, as my team insisted was the case, why would Petraeus be hearing about problems at a sink and toilet bowl factory before I would be? Among all the projects I had reviewed with him, page after page of important initiatives from real estate projects to steel mills to truck factories to major supply agreements with international firms, why was I getting asked about toilet bowls?

I indelicately delivered that question to Regina Dubey, a former Senate Armed Services Committee staffer who now oversaw all TFBSO operations in Anbar Province. She let me vent, and then quietly explained how the orders from Kurdistan had not emerged, because sample fixtures from Ramadi never seemed to get delivered to Erbil even though the factory insisted they had been shipped multiple times.

My annoyance increased. At that time we had more than 200 projects and programs underway across Iraq; surely with our logistical prowess we could figure out how to ship a toilet between two cities, even in Iraq.

Finally we arranged for a sample to be delivered directly to TFBSO headquarters in Baghdad, where we would arrange for it to be taken to Erbil ourselves. When I arrived in Baghdad that month, Regina met with me at our compound, and in updating me on her Anbar efforts, informed me that the long-awaited sample fixture had arrived, and would be sent directly to Erbil as soon as possible. Once construction companies approved the quality, we could expect large-volume orders to

Ramadi Ceramics to follow quickly that could be shipped in dedicated trucks, avoiding any more logistical difficulties.

The next day, Regina asked to see me. She looked distraught. "It seems that we have lost the sample from Ramadi—it arrived yesterday, I saw the crate, but now it's gone."

We walked outside, where piles of construction material and stacks of lumber covered the grounds. The building next door to our compound was being renovated for our expansion, and construction crews were working onsite to finish the renovation.

I had a bad feeling.

Going next door, we found a suspicious, opened crate in a pile with a lot of packaging for other plumbing equipment. When we rushed into the building to the bathroom upstairs, the mystery was solved. Lined up in the stalls were three standard Western commodes, and one very ornate Iraqi-style toilet, each newly bolted to the floor. The construction workers had found the crate, assumed it was for their construction project, and installed it. They had since made good use of it, even though the water was not yet turned on in the building.

There was a long pause as emotions cascaded through our minds, from shock to frustration to resignation. All we could do was laugh. After two years of problems getting this factory running, from nearly getting shot, to electricity that wouldn't stay connected, to getting visas and transit to Italy for the workers, to the endless effort getting a sample fixture shipped to Erbil, this project had set the record for the most absurd barriers to success.

That evening, I removed the line on Ramadi Ceramics from my update briefing to Petraeus. For the duration of the mission in Iraq, I never asked my staff about Ramadi Ceramics again. The factory was running, the Iraqis had the names and contacts for construction companies, and from now on, it was up to them to get their products sold.

✳   ✳

By this time, Petraeus's nomination to serve as the Commander of United States Central Command had been announced, and he was soon to depart his role as MNFI Commander in Iraq. Prior to his departure, in September 2008, I hosted Deputy Secretary England on a farewell visit to Iraq, and Petraeus held a formal dinner in his honor, co-hosted by Ambassador Ryan Crocker.

As the event got underway, Petraeus and Crocker began their remarks and the group converged near them. Their seamless interplay was always impressive to see, Petraeus primarily in the leading role, Crocker mainly providing support, but with the two of them occasionally reversing roles. Their ease with each other was well known to me, but watching them and reflecting on the last two years, I could not help but contrast their collaboration with the painful conflicts between the Pentagon and the State Department that had preceded them.

As topics of discussion came up, it was interesting to observe Petraeus engage the Iraqi dignitaries present. Subjects of the day ranging from the value of the Iraqi dinar, to infant mortality, to the number of soldiers injured and the circumstances of their injury were engaged by Petraeus, who had complete command of all facets of security, economy, and political life, at a level of detail that was uncanny.

His numerous tours of duty in Iraq, combined with his obsessive need for detailed information, gave him a near-encyclopedic knowledge of the country and its complex nested political structures. This detail orientation, his ambition and competitive drive to prove his naysayers wrong, and his insistence on personal accountability for mission success in every aspect of his operations combined to create a leadership personality uniquely suited to the challenges Iraq faced when he assumed command.

In the nineteen months I worked for General Petraeus in Iraq, and in every subsequent meeting I had with him in his role as Commander, CENTCOM or Commander, International Security Assistance Force Afghanistan, he always saw TFBSO as an asset, and continually supported our expanded efforts across various economic sectors. His leadership style with me personally created immense internal pressure not to fail the mission or him as its leader, to do whatever it took to ensure success.

✳   ✳

Election night, November 4, 2008, marked what I thought would be the certain end of my tenure within the Department of Defense.

Senator Barack Obama was elected by a sizeable margin over Senator John McCain, ensuring a rapid full departure of any political appointees from the Bush Administration. Though I was not appointed for political reasons, I was part of the Bush Administration and would certainly be required to depart the government.

I was very comfortable with this. I had come to Washington four years earlier to work on the business practices of the world's largest bureaucracy—the Pentagon—only to have also launched a wartime support mission that had required twenty-eight consecutive months of travel to Iraq for two-week stints. I was so far beyond exhausted that it was hard to remember what a normal sleep cycle felt like. The constant worry about the hundreds of TFBSO personnel working outside the wire in Iraq, and the constant fear that every phone call would be bad news, was a heavy continual burden. It would be a relief to be free of it, to find a normal life again.

Returning to Iraq that month, newly appointed MNFI Commanding General Odierno and MNCI Commander Lieutenant General Austin were less sanguine about the prospect of our mission ending abruptly. Earlier that year, as part of our transition planning effort, I had worked with MNFI Deputy Commander Major General David Perkins to attempt the transfer of the TFBSO agriculture program led by the Borlaug Institute to USAID. USAID leadership along with the USDA representative in Baghdad had pledged to maintain the same level of field support to the troops, embedding the agriculture experts within deployed units just as we had done. Within a month of the transfer of the program, it collapsed and all of the agricultural work we had initiated came to an end. While our Borlaug team had done amazing work and completed dozens of projects and initiatives, it was work that should have continued long into the future.

MNFI had real concern that the rest of our critical programs would see a similar fate. In my monthly review, General Odierno informed me that he would be requesting that I stay on for a lengthy transition period into the new administration. I pledged to do all I could not to let the mission fail.

Privately, I was worried. There was little prospect of a new political appointee in the Obama administration taking this job. Had I been presented this job, as it now existed, as an opportunity before I was in government, I would have laughed out loud. The "opportunity" to spend half one's time in a combat zone outside of protected compounds, and the other half fighting for resources in the immense Pentagon bureaucracy and trying to convince companies to invest in Iraq? On paper it looked insane, especially now when the Obama campaign had made clear that it was going to wrap up the war in Iraq and draw down troops while increasing the focus on the conflict in Afghanistan. Ending the Iraq conflict had been a pillar of Obama campaign foreign policy since the primaries.

On the other hand, if TFBSO were to be handed off within the Pentagon to a nonpolitically-appointed leader, it would end up in a lower-level organization, where the bureaucracy of the Defense Department would crush it. We had barely survived this long as it was, with a direct line of reporting to the Deputy Secretary of Defense providing top cover for our unorthodox operating model. Moving it down in the organization below the level of political appointees could effectively kill the mission.

The risk for me was that staying on in an effort to "hand off" the mission could be an open-ended commitment. I had no stomach for any more problems within the Pentagon bureaucracy, problems that could only get worse as a Bush Administration appointee in a new Democratic administration.

Soon, matters grew even less certain. Rumors began circulating after the election that Defense Secretary Robert Gates would be asked to stay on in the Obama Administration. At first I found this unbelievable; the political system simply does not work that way. Even in times of war, a new president replaces the cabinet of his predecessor with his own team. But as days passed, the rumors grew, culminating in a public announcement that Gates would be staying on. It was an impressive decision by the new president, demonstrating sound leadership over partisanship, something almost unheard of in Washington. But now, instead of a reliable departure on January 21, it was increasingly likely that Gates would expect me to stay on in transition.

Gates's Chief of Staff Robert Rangel confirmed this suspicion to me early in December, informing me that my name had been provided to the White House transition team as critical to stay on for several months to enable a seamless handoff between administrations. A few weeks later, members of Gates's staff informed me that both General Odierno and CENTCOM Commander General Petraeus had made an appeal to Gates to retain me as part of his new organization. According to Gates's staff, when asked why it was so important, Odierno indicated that our presence not only added tangible value to the mission, but also served to motivate the other civilian bureaucracies to step up and do their jobs. Petraeus further opined that our acceleration of economic progress served as a concrete indicator of hope to the leaders in Iraq that, if they did their jobs, Iraq could assume a solid position in the global economy, and that the morale impact of this hope alone was worth our minor expense compared to the overall cost of the war effort.

By Inauguration Day, it was clear that I was staying put for a while. It really wasn't presented as a choice to me; clearly, departing would be irresponsible. I bade farewell to the members of the Bush Administration whom I had worked with for the past four years, including Brad Berkson, who had taken on the role of director of program analysis for Secretary Gates a few years before, and Jay Gibson, who had taken on elements of the role formerly held by Tom Modly in the finance organization after Tom's departure. Jerry Jones had been a long-standing advisor and counselor since I first joined the department, with decades of experience in navigating the bureaucracy he shared freely with me. Most especially I hated to see Mark Kimmitt go, who was now working as Assistant Secretary of State for Political/Military Affairs but had become a staunch friend and ally during his tenure as a Deputy Assistant Secretary in the Defense Policy organization. Mark had experienced his own challenges attempting, as a recently retired army brigadier general, to get the Pentagon civilian bureaucracy moving in support of the war effort. I would miss him greatly.

But most of all I would miss Gordon England. He had remained in my corner through thick and thin, was always available to provide counsel, never ducked a hard decision, and had keen business leadership acumen. Strategically he had endorsed and championed our mission from the moment I had returned from my first trip to Iraq back in June of 2006. Had I not enjoyed so much command support, I would have been fearful of staying in the Pentagon without England there to provide cover for our effort.

❋ ❋

As the new Obama team members started arriving in the Pentagon, I found that, contrary to my expectations of a hostile reception, our work was highly regarded and my presence was welcomed. Michele Flournoy, whom I had met in her prior role as a founder and director of the Center for a New American Security (CNAS) on visits to Iraq, was taking over as the Undersecretary of Defense for Policy. CNAS had been a supporter of TFBSO efforts in the past, providing a venue for our engagement in their seminars as an alternative point of view on postconflict stability operations. John Nagl, a brilliant retired army lieutenant colonel and a senior leader at CNAS, had provided counsel to us on a number of occasions. It was good to know that Michele would be part of the Pentagon senior leadership.

After briefing Flournoy, she indicated we should carry on our work as if there had been no change, and that the nature of our efforts were completely consistent with new administration policy on Iraq, which would focus on drawing down the military engagement while ramping up economic ties and strategic partnerships. While it was not clear where our mission would eventually end up, she was unequivocal in her support and in making clear that we needed to carry on our work.

As the dust settled, it became clear that the new administration might in fact be an easier place for us to operate in than the last. For TFBSO, the end of the Bush Administration created a number of new challenges. The military, expecting our mission to end with the change of administrations, did not arrange to replace the officers who had fully staffed our mission in 2008 as their assignments to TFBSO ended. In the span of thirty days, I lost a two-star general, two colonels, four lieutenant colonels, and a corresponding number of lower-level military personnel. Of the eight senior civilians who ran TFBSO's programs, only two remained. The others accepted jobs elsewhere, in anticipation of the TFBSO mission's ending and its work being transitioned to other organizations.

Matt Schoeffling, Kris Haag, and I were the only remaining senior leaders to oversee the mission in Iraq. Beth Law remained the operational bedrock for daily activity. Esther Swartz continued to provide strategic advice on matters of the budget and our congressional engagement. Gerry Brown continued his remarkable work as our "sales force" lead, continuing to land engagements with major multinational companies. Mark Baird was promoted to full bird colonel—the second officer under my leadership to be promoted to that rank—and moved on to a new role leading space systems and space launch vehicle development programs.

Our organization essentially had a clean slate. The negative effects of this were instant. Suddenly, an organization of more than 400 staffers operating throughout Iraq was in need of new managers. I flattened the organization structure, and Matt, Kris, and I immersed ourselves in managing the details of our programs and the daily management of activity across all sectors of the Iraqi economy.

Unexpectedly, the Task Force's work began to accelerate. Once again we were operating like a start-up. Agility increased as pyramidal structures were broken down, and while our bureaucratic communications were negatively affected, our execution of projects and programs was vastly accelerated. It was the classic managerial tradeoff—structure versus lean operations—and in this case, I was pleased to see the agility restored that was characteristic of our early efforts.

The Iraqi government was making progress as well. Security had continued to improve throughout 2008, and ministries were operating at full efficiency for the first time. Decision making remained slow, and negotiations over transactions within ministries remained painful, but progress was obvious. Within the Ministry of Industry, twelve private-investment transactions were completed in large state-owned industries—including the Diyala electric plant that manufactured transformers, as well as the Baiji fertilizer, Al Qaim phosphates, and Fallujah cement companies in Anbar Province, among others. The total investment commitment resulting from these signed agreements exceeded $800 million. Our approach to transitional privatization was working.

Another major challenge confronted us when we returned to Baghdad in January 2009. The State Department, expecting TFBSO to be shut down, had offered our renovated facilities to several different countries as a potential location for their embassies. Getting the regional countries, especially the Persian Gulf neighbors such as Qatar and the United Arab Emirates to establish embassies and normalize relations with the government of Iraq was a major priority for the State Department. Expecting our mission to end, I had told Ambassador

Crocker that if we had to give up a facility to get the UAE to open their embassy, I would not complain.

Early in December of 2008, I was told that the UAE had sent a communication to the embassy accepting the offer of our facilities for their use as an embassy. We still had our small compound at Camp Victory near the airport, as well as a number of sites throughout the country, but now we were effectively shut down in the city of Baghdad. When asked to stay on, the first order of business was to find a new place to operate our headquarters. I returned to Baghdad in January, and while having dinner with an Iraqi official, the ambassador from the UAE arrived. Striking up conversation, I congratulated him on his new facilities. He looked confused, and then informed me that he had no intention of moving into the buildings I was describing and had no idea what I was talking about.

It seemed the UAE was not moving into our buildings after all. We were homeless, it appeared, for no reason.

Our contractor-for-life support services sprang into action. Leasing two villas adjacent to each other in the Green Zone, we had a small "motel-style" structure built in the backyard, with thirteen rooms of the quality of a three-star hotel, and fully renovated villas providing living quarters for TFBSO staffers as well as dining and meeting rooms. The new compound was a major improvement. We moved into our new accommodations late in February, back in business sixty days after being left homeless.

Six months later, I drove over to our old compound. Several hundred thousand dollars had been spent renovating the facilities, which were in excellent condition when we departed. After six months of vacancy, they were now completely falling apart. Fixtures and woodwork had been stolen, sewers were backed up again, and weeds had overtaken the open areas. It was as if we had never been there.

✳   ✳

As we dealt with the organizational challenges and started driving the Iraqi mission forward again, we ramped up our efforts at foreign direct investment and noticed something remarkable. The election of Obama had taken away much of the residual "venom" from the public perception of our mission in Iraq. Most of the time, when engaging companies about doing business in Iraq in the past, the reaction had been initially negative. Public opinion toward the Bush Administration had been highly polarized about Iraq, and that extended into corporate executive offices and boardrooms. But with the new administration, suddenly companies that would not answer our calls were engaging with us.

Within months, new major corporations were traveling to Iraq with TFBSO to assess opportunities to launch operations. Stan Lumish and Eric Clark managed engagement from Google, Microsoft, and IBM, with Google launching an Iraqi version of its search engine, and Microsoft opening a training center in Baghdad for young Iraqi technicians.[1] In 2008, the Task Force had facilitated successful commercial reengagement in Iraq with General Electric Corporation, with General Petraeus personally appealing to GE CEO Jeffrey Immeldt to return to the country and provide leadership to the efforts to rebuild the electrical system. TFBSO provided full support to GE through its engagement back in Iraq, culminating in a $4 billion transaction for large electricity-generating turbines manufactured in Greenville, South Carolina.[2] Through 2009, we supported G.E.'s ongoing relationship with the government of Iraq in terms of financial payment and continuous installation challenges. Honeywell, Boeing, and a number of midsize investment funds and private equity firms visited Iraq.[3,4] We were also increasingly hosting regional investors, including major sovereign-wealth funds from the UAE and investors from Turkey. These firms and investment companies would have a comprehensive engagement with Iraqi officials: tours of facilities reopened by TFBSO, meetings with local chambers of commerce and investment councils in particular cities, and a reception with Ambassador Crocker as well as General Odierno.

The Task Force successfully engaged with the Export-Import Bank of the United States, hosting Director Bijan Kian and facilitating the engagement of EXIM Bank to reopen Iraq for export-lending credits for American manufactured goods. It was another example of interagency partnership by TFBSO.[5]

Yet another example of this interagency collaboration was our work to reintroduce the United States Geological Survey to Iraq. Water resources and nonhydrocarbon minerals were critical to the future of the Iraqi economy, and the Iraqi Geological Survey was in need of a partnership to modernize its technology and practices. Major General Butch Pair had suggested we engage with USGS shortly after his arrival in Baghdad in 2008. He visited USGS and established a solid partnership that eventually led, in 2009, to a project to survey water resources and mineralogy of Anbar Province and the Kurdistan region of Iraq in partnership with the Minister of Industry and Minerals, funded by TFBSO, with the Task Force also providing security and living accommodations for the survey work.[6]

As our work ramped up, my personal status remained uncertain. Secretary Gates then provided clarity. In April, he issued a memorandum to the entire civilian and military leadership within the Department reinvigorating the mission, clarifying its importance, and announcing the realignment of TFBSO to report directly to him[7]. This memorandum electrified our efforts in theater: any residual uncertainty about my status or that of the organization was now removed. For me, the opportunity to serve directly under a historic figure like Robert Gates was a chance in a lifetime. I was one of the few senior Defense Department political appointees from the Bush Administration that remained with Secretary Gates.

As more and more companies engaged, our facilities were constantly full. Firms that had already initiated business in Iraq with the support of TFBSO now needed their own place to operate, yet the complete lack of availability of decent office space was a major impediment. Working with the National Investment Commission (NIC), TFBSO renovated an abandoned compound to serve as both a headquarters facility for the Investment Commission, with an adjacent building that provided office and living space for companies to open their offices in Baghdad. The goal was to offer "incubator" space for companies making the leap into Iraq, providing them network, living, and office space as well as food and access to transportation, until they were able to locate their own offices elsewhere in the city. Companies were required to pay a monthly fee for their use of the incubator offices. It was an innovative solution to the problem.

The TFBSO business incubator was soon fully occupied, with GE, Daimler-Benz, and Eaton Corporation among the occupants. Gerry

Brown led the effort to establish and operate the incubator facility.

As our investor engagements accelerated, we launched focused efforts on women's business development, in partnership and support of an effective nongovernmental organization, Women for Women. Sara Steele and Lee Sanderson, as an outgrowth of our work supporting investment, developed specific programs focused on women's economic development and access to opportunity. These programs would provide a foundation for future larger-scale work beyond Iraq.

The newly appointed National Investment Commissioner for Iraq was none other than Dr. Sami al Araji—the passionate former Deputy Minister of Industry whose frustration had boiled over in our first meeting two years before. In addition to building a new head-quarters for the NIC, the international accounting and consulting firm PricewaterhouseCoopers won a Task Force–tendered contract to work within the Commission in support of Dr. Sami, training his team in proposal solicitation, financial analysis, and marketing techniques. Tom Modly, now well over a year removed from his former role in government, led the PricewaterhouseCoopers team in Iraq—a welcome addition to the leadership of the Task Force effort. Our goal with the NIC was to make Task Force investment support obsolete—to create an Iraqi team capable of managing foreign investment without U.S. assistance.

Our industrial projects and banking efforts were now wrapping up, with the final industrial restart initiatives led by Regina Dubey. Building on the work done to automate banking and eliminate the use of cash for payment of Iraqi firms that were contracted under Iraqi First to deliver goods and services to MNFI, Kris Haag now expanded the use of electronic banking to encompass personal credit card transactions. Haag worked with private banks to establish a consortium for shared electronic banking infrastructure called AMWAL.[8]

AMWAL is similar to consortiums used around the world, including firms in the United States such as Cirrus or Plus, that provide transaction processing for banks, reducing the costs of running their own infrastructure. Haag then invited Visa, MasterCard, and American Express representatives to Iraq. By the fall of 2009, Visa and MasterCard were offering card services through private Iraqi banks. TFBSO then kick-started the deployment of card-scanning devices at retail establishments, hotels, and restaurants throughout the country. Each of these steps helped create a more normal business-operating environment in Iraq, enabling noncash transactions and helping to modernize Iraq's financial sector, which had operated on a cash-based system for decades.

✳   ✳

One project that nagged at me was the restoration of Basra Iron & Steel, the huge facility that ArcelorMittal had shown an interest in prior to the collapse of the global steel industry. I was hell-bent on getting that factory restored to production, and the only way to do it was through private investment. We looked at the global steel industry; it was experiencing a complete glut of capacity now, and all of its companies were suffering from depressed stock prices. We would need to get a company involved that could afford to see the strategic opportunity Basra afforded.

Late in 2008, I had received a visit from a Korean American businesswoman named Sunyoung Chang. The daughter of a Korean military founder of the modern Republic of Korea, General Kyung-Soon Chang, Sunyoung was interested in facilitating visits to Iraq by Korean industries. I believed that South Korea, given its history of occupation and economic hardship followed by rapid modernization, industrialization, and democratization, would be a great potential partner for Iraq from a business-development perspective. My earlier experience seeing firsthand the effectiveness of Korean forces at reconstruction efforts in Kurdistan were also encouraging. A coalition partner, South Korea had realized no tangible benefit at that point for its efforts in support of the Iraq mission. Sunyoung Chang traveled to Iraq as a guest of the Task Force in 2008 and then participated in a large Korean business delegation to Iraq in 2009 that included major Korean companies Pohong Iron & Steel (POSCO), LS Industries, LG, and Hyundai Heavy Industries. POSCO was particularly interesting to me given our interest in restarting the Basra steel mill. POSCO was a top-five international steel producer, with major investment interest held by the American conglomerate Berkshire Hathaway. Sunyoung then arranged a visit for Matt Schoeffling and me to Seoul to meet with leading Korean industrialists, as well as senior government officials. We pitched investments in Iraq as a strategic interest for Korea—as a country with no hydrocarbon resources and excess refining capacity, a strategic partnership with Iraq would be of great mutual benefit. While we had no involvement in the oil and gas sectors in Iraq, the goodwill that South Korean industry could generate by helping revitalize profitable manufacturing sectors in Iraq would be of great strategic value. General Chang, now in his eighties, served as our host and provided us with direct access to a number of senior business officials with major Korean companies.

A few weeks later, we hosted representatives of POSCO and later of Korean conglomerate STX for their first visits to Iraq. Traveling with POSCO executives to Basra Iron & Steel, we entered the plant where the management was assembled to greet the entourage. The Iraqis spoke English with, perhaps, 70 percent proficiency. The Koreans had an equal amount of proficiency. I had no staff members with me, so I did my best to bridge the communication gaps. After touring the massive compound, the group returned together, at which time the POSCO executive in charge of their international operations spoke. I watched as he began to define a vision for the Iraqi leadership—a vision based on Korea's own "Miracle on the Han River"—with the rapid establishment of world-class industries following the Korean War, culminating in Korea's assumption of a place among the world's most-economically advanced nations. He told the Iraqis that the vision would be to build a Miracle in Basra, to create a world-class steel industry, with a modern industrial center surrounding it, much as had happened in South Korea. As he spoke, in spite of the differences in the language and the brokenness of the communication, the Iraqis grew more and more excited.

It was a remarkable thing to watch. We were linking together, at the most tactical level of business, two societies that had had little historical engagement. The Iraqis at Basra Iron & Steel were local factory leaders, none had ever traveled to east Asia, none had ever met any Koreans. These Koreans were engaging with Iraq for the first time. Their cultural backgrounds were as different as they could possibly have been. But when they began talking about steel and about building an industry, their differences fell away. Conversation became animated, engineering diagrams were pulled out, and factory equipment was discussed in excited tones. I sat back and watched it continue for another two hours. It was a wonderful human moment, and a highlight of my entire tenure leading TFBSO.[9]

*   *

Lieutenant Colonel Beth Law would often join me, Matt Schoeffling, Eric Clark, and others in our late-night trips to work out at the palatial gyms on U.S. military installations in Iraq. As the spring of 2009 progressed, I noticed she grew more and more fatigued. She had worked for almost two years at my side, fourteen to sixteen hours a day, as energized by the mission as any of us. I relied on her completely; she was instrumental to the success of our mission, and to my ability to oversee our far-flung operations. She had become well known among the Iraqi leadership and within the command, having brought the right balance of structure and discipline to our senior leadership team while maintaining our entrepreneurial energy and spirit of individual initiative. After gym time, several of us would sit on the rooftop of our facility in Baghdad, recapping the day and unwinding until well after midnight, when our jet lag would finally fade and we could get some sleep.

One night when we were all at the gym, and she was jogging on a treadmill, I noticed her breathing was labored. Talking that night, she said she thought she might have an infection in her lungs. That would not be surprising—we were all constantly fighting off some sort of bug in Iraq—either from food or water, or from breathing allergens from dust storms. Seeing a doctor on her return to Washington, she was diagnosed with a probable fungal infection in her lungs. But over the following days and weeks, medication did not help. Her breathing became more and more labored, even when climbing a flight of stairs she would become short of breath. I was becoming worried. After traveling to Iraq in May, she went to another doctor, who performed a biopsy on her lung tissue.

The news was devastating.

In July, after tissue analysis by doctors at the Army Institute of Pathology, Beth finally had her diagnosis—a rare lung cancer called bronchoalveolar adenoma carcinoma (BAC), in her case characterized by the rapid emergence of small tumors throughout both of the lungs. She was at Stage 4—the most advanced stage of diagnosis. Her doctors at Walter Reed Medical Center gave her a year or two, at most, to live.

Beth Law is one of the most remarkable people I have ever known. A living example of can-do spirit, with a steadfast refusal to buckle in the face of impossible odds—her entire life has been a battle to overcome circumstances that would have overwhelmed anyone else. She and her husband Steve had both served their country with distinction. Now she faced her biggest challenge yet. And her army doctors provided her little hope of overcoming this challenge.

One of the investors we had met back in 2008, who became a major supporter of TFBSO and made initial investments in private telecommunications network infrastructure companies in Iraq, was a Californian named Llewelyn Werner. Lew Werner visited Iraq multiple times, looking at investments across a variety of sectors from food processing to entertainment to information technology. Werner had a larger-than-life personality, a long active history within Democratic Party politics, and a diverse investment background in technology and defense-related industries. At different times he had provided critical support for us with congressional leaders—especially from California—when we were fighting for funding or support. On hearing of Beth's diagnosis, Werner stepped in and contacted world-renowned oncologists at Cedars Sinai Medical Center in Los Angeles, including one of the authorities on BAC, Dr. Ronald Natale. Natale agreed to meet with Beth, and promptly redefined her treatment protocol, making clear that the disease could be, at least, managed, and that she could indeed fight it.

Beth went on medical leave to fight for her life, and I never attempted to replace her, as I simply could not see anyone else filling her shoes. Matt and I would, from now on, manage the overall operation of TFBSO on our own. She was the last military advisor for TFBSO.

✳   ✳

Under the Status of Forces Agreement signed in 2008, which defined the role of the United States military in Iraq for the next three years, U.S. forces were required to depart all Iraqi cities by July 1, 2009.[10] There was a significant amount of nervousness about this for TFBSO. As security had improved throughout Iraq, we had stopped using military assets to move around the country whenever possible. Our last missions that required direct military support took place early in 2009. But it was always good to know that we could call on the military for quick support in the event we encountered a problem.

Now, that would be more difficult. To enter an Iraqi city, the U.S. military had to get approval from Iraqi commanders—something that was generally never denied, but which took time. This was a good thing. The objective of the U.S. mission was to build up Iraqi forces to a point where it was not necessary for U.S. forces to operate in the country. Now TFBSO would operate as we did in Basra—absent the presence of any significant U.S. military presence. As in Basra, the transition was a nonissue for us.

As an element of the Obama Administration effort to demonstrate a strategic long-term commitment to Iraq, while maintaining its focus on drawing down military forces, plans were made for a major Iraq investment conference to be held in Washington, D.C. The State Department, with the Commerce Department in support, was given lead authority for the event, which was planned for September 2009.

TFBSO had worked closely with the Commerce Department since the inception of our mission, hosting their business delegations and collaborating on smaller events in D.C. The objective of the event was to invite hundreds of Iraqi government officials and business leaders to Washington for several days of engagement with interested American companies and investors.

I viewed this, as with many other matters in 2009, as a chance to demonstrate again our desire to collaborate quietly behind the scenes to support the State Department. I persuaded Secretary Gates's office to provide funding from his personal discretionary budget to cover the cost of the conference, as neither the Commerce nor State Departments had budgeted for the event.

For most of August and September, TFBSO dedicated a majority of our personnel in Baghdad and in Washington to the event. Scott King, Gerry Brown, Hope Jones, Sonja Stephens, and a number of others led the effort to make the event successful. My only condition for all of this support was that TFBSO work in the background. We wanted this to be a State Department event, sponsored by State, and managed by State. I hoped that all this effort, including the funding provided, would demonstrate once and for all our strong desire for interagency partnership.

Secretary of State Hillary Clinton, National Security Advisor James Jones, and Commerce Secretary Gary Locke all addressed the gathering. Companies that had worked in Iraq with the support of the Task Force were present, more than fifty in total, along with many firms invited or attending that had never engaged in the country. Several business leaders we had worked with for years in Iraq and who were like family to us were in attendance[11].

At last, as I had desired to do in our early meetings at the embassy in Baghdad with IRMO, we had successfully and quietly provided support to our government partners.

As the event drew to a close, it was clear that 2009 had gone far better than we had hoped given the change in administration. There had been no bureaucratic fights to fight, no interagency conflicts, no impediments to our work thrown into our path. The Iraqi government had been focused on the work of governing the country, and our partners in the ministries were getting better and better at their jobs. Business transactions were being executed throughout the country. So far, it had been a remarkable year.

But the event marked a high point for our work with the Iraqi government. As we returned to work in Baghdad, the political atmosphere declined dramatically with the approach of national elections scheduled for January 2010. The ministers who had frequently shared meals as a large, boisterous group with us together at our home in Baghdad would now only meet separately, as each represented a different political party vying for power. It reminded me of the fall campaign seasons I had experienced in Washington in 2004 and 2008, when government basically stalls in the latter half of the year while the bureaucracy waits to see who will prevail at the polls, and partisanship is at its most extreme.

With the cabinet ministers' attention now focused on campaigning, the pace of executing ministry business across the Iraqi government slowed to a crawl. I was looking forward to the election, as I hoped a new government would shake up some of the critical ministries that had seen little progress so far, such as transportation, electricity, agriculture, and trade. But mostly, I wanted the elections over with quickly and a new government seated so that we could all get back to work again.

New to Iraq, and new to diplomacy, my tour of the village of Tarmiyah, May 2006.

Promising Sheikh Sabah al Khafaji to return to the State Company for Automotive Industries, Iskandiriyah, June 2006. Idle operations in Iskandiriyah would eventually assemble Daimler and Scania trucks, as well as Case New Holland farm tractors and industrial greenhouses, through TFBSO efforts.

Bob Love and Tucker Bailey touring Basra Refinery during initial assessment. TFBSO engineers and analysts assessed more than 70 industrial operations throughout Iraq in the first six months of the mission.

Multi-National Corps–Iraq Commander Lieutenant General Raymond Odierno welcomes the first delegation of investors to Iraq, January 2007. Delegates included Institute for Defense and Business Chairman Bill Powell, fourth from left, and Thomas Donohue Jr., fourth from right.

TFBSO staff members negotiate with nomadic shepherds in the mountains of
Kurdistan to acquire native wool for use in restoring carpet production.

Task Force for Business and Stability Operations–Baghdad and Central Iraq team poses at the Republican Palace, 2008.

Children in close proximity to gas flares, a common sight in southern Iraq. The flares release volatile compounds into the air, a health and environmental catastrophe. Pediatric cancer incidence rates in southern Iraq are among the highest in the world.

From left, Regina Dubey, Scott King, and Sara Steele, touring development site in Baghdad, 2009.

Aerial view of large scale greenhouse vegetable cultivation near ancient ruins
of Babylon in central Iraq. TFBSO deployed thousands of industrial-sized
greenhouses across every province of Iraq as part of agricultural development
initiatives.

Deputy Secretary
of Defense Gordon
England visits TFBSO
headquarters, greeting
Minister of Planning
Ali Baban and Central
Bank Governor Sinan
Shabibi, September
2008.

With President Bush, Deputy Secretary of Defense Gordon England, and
Secretary of Defense Robert Gates in the Oval Office, May 2008.

Bob Love leads a business delegation of visiting an agricultural site in South Sudan, 2009.

Emily Scott leads sampling mission to Khan Neshin Mountain, Helmand Province, Afghanistan, July 2010.

Babylon Hotel bombing site, and remnants of the vehicle. The arrow indicates the office location of the TFBSO meeting with hotel management at the time of detonation.

Drilling for Lithium in a western Afghanistan salt lake with geologist Bob Miller. For months, all TFBSO staff participated in mineral-sampling missions after hiring was frozen by Pentagon lawyers in May 2010.

ISAF Commander General David H. Petraeus welcomes TFBSO-sponsored investors Howard G. Buffett and other business leaders to Kabul, August 2010. Jack Medlin of the U.S. Geological Survey is shown behind Petraeus and Buffett.

TFBSO Leaders say farewell to Iraq under the crossed swords memorial, Baghdad, January 2010. From left: Matthew Schoeffling, David Scantling, Robert Love, John Stoner, Gerry Brown (face obscured), Scott King, Ed Price, David Kudla, Jerry Jones, Regina Dubey, John Lyons, Tom Modly, and Paul Brinkley.

With Punjab Governor Salman Taseer announcing launch of TFBSO business development efforts in Lahore, Pakistan, May 2010. From left, Barney Gimbel, David Kudla, Matthew Schoeffling, Paul Brinkley, Governor Taseer, Chairman of the Pakistan Board of Investment Saleem Mandviwalla. John Dowdy is at far right. Taseer was assassinated by terrorists within months of this photo for his progressive stance regarding religious tolerance in Pakistan.

9.
OUT OF AFRICA

In October 2008, in an effort to establish a more-coordinated command structure for U.S. military operations in Africa, United States Africa Command—AFRICOM—was established, with its headquarters in Stuttgart, Germany.

With AFRICOM's creation, the residual goodwill among many army and marine commanders familiar with the Task Force generated interest in how TFBSO could assist that mission. We were swamped, and the election was approaching along with a transition to a new administration, but the appeals were continual. Bob Love was seeking approval to meet commanders in Stuttgart at least to hear them out. In the fall of 2008, I relented.

Unlike in Iraq, where the huge military presence and ongoing military operations made it possible for the Department of Defense to establish a semiautonomous organization like TFBSO, AFRICOM had no active combat operations underway in Africa. I made clear that any work by TFBSO outside of contracting and systems support to the command would have to be clearly sponsored with formal invitations from the State Department and from the U.S. ambassador to the nation where any such work would take place. TFBSO resources and efforts would be, in this model, adjuncts to the embassy and part of the overall diplomatic mission.

I felt confident that these guidelines would prevent any TFBSO engagement in the countries in Africa. The idea that we would be invited into African countries by American ambassadors, given the endless difficulties we had experienced with the embassy in Iraq, was impossible for me to entertain.

To my thinking, Africa was surely the effective domain of other existing aid agencies and nongovernmental organizations. TFBSO had been established to fill the gap in our foreign policy institutions for societies that were just emerging from widespread violence—places that were still too dangerous to expect development professionals to go, but where accelerating economic progress would directly accelerate stabilization. With a few exceptions, African countries—to my thinking— did not fit this model. Surely USAID, with its large budget, and with the Bush Administration's focus on African aid and development, was taking care of Africa from an economic-development perspective.

I was wrong.

Over the next year, increasing numbers of requests arrived from embassies in Africa and from State to provide support to economic-development activities. In partnership with AFRICOM and the State Department, the Task Force began sponsoring events in the U.S. for African leaders seeking increased commercial ties to American companies. The newly appointed U.S. Special Envoy to Sudan, Scott Gration, was particularly engaged with TFBSO. This relationship led to direct TFBSO support to Obama Administration engagement in Southern Sudan. TFBSO sponsored a business delegation to Southern Sudan early in 2009 that generated agricultural projects in excess of $100 million. Building on our established relationships with American university agricultural and engineering programs, the Task Force reinforced an academic partnership between Virginia Tech and the University of Juba in Southern Sudan that had been previously encouraged by congressional leaders.

A similar business delegation visited Khartoum, Sudan, in 2009, coordinated by TFBSO, with American multinational companies focused on irrigation equipment, fruit processing, harvesting equipment, and gum Arabic processing. Three major American firms were awarded licenses to operate in Sudan and began the work of establishing business operations as a result of this delegation.

The work was not limited to Sudan. TFBSO provided assistance in Rwanda, with the support and encouragement of the U.S. Ambassador to Rwanda, Stu Symington. The Task Force sponsored business engagement in Rwanda for Marriott Hotel Corporation and facilitated development of relationships with NGOs and commercial businesses. Working again beyond just American industry and academia, and leveraging our relationships with international companies developed during our work in Iraq, TFBSO linked Rwandan silk and textile factories to major Italian partners, enabling expansion of their business operations. A business delegation to Rwanda was sponsored as well. In one case a business executive was so impressed with the efforts of TFBSO that on a subsequent trip he brought his family to Rwanda and was hosted by President Kagame and Ambassador Symington.

One of the most interesting projects in Rwanda involved the potential for developing natural-gas clean-energy generation using methane present at the lower levels of Lake Kivu. Thousands of years of vegetative decay have resulted in the absorption of billions of cubic meters of methane into this lake, which is surrounded by high mountains and is adjacent to the largest mountain gorilla reserve in Africa. Occasionally, methane bubbles up from the lake and accumulates in low-lying areas, occasionally with deadly results to local populations. Clean extraction of this methane for energy generation would provide a cheap source of electrical power for Rwandans as well as surrounding countries, creating income for Rwanda as well as economic development.

This work was kept low profile, out of the media, in an effort to maintain the trust we were building with the State Department. But it was not unknown. Leaders within the Congressional Black Caucus were aware of this work, having received a briefing on our programs, especially in Rwanda's energy sector.

Operating in Africa exposed TFBSO to the reality of our development agencies' operating models when working outside of an active conflict zone like Iraq. While we expected to find a much different engagement by USAID, for example, in Africa, the situation was not what we expected. The experience of local communities with American development aid was, at best, one of charitable contributions of health-care support and food assistance. There was little to no engagement in activity to develop sustained enterprises that would enable a country to move beyond a need for foreign aid. One of President Kagame's favorite quotes was, "send trade—not aid." The popular use of "capacity development," hiring foreign contractors to teach government employees how to do their work, is widely used in African countries, with some examples of effectiveness, at great expense. Direct facilitation of business investment and development is a low priority for development agencies in African countries. In places of moderate risk compared to Iraq, such as Sudan, all U.S. civilian agencies including USAID were required to abide by a restrictive security posture, with little "normal" public engagement by government personnel.

The effort was expanding rapidly, in spite of minimal resources allocated for the work. Our total cost of work in support of AFRICOM was less than $1 million over a fifteen-month period, with the effort led by Bob Love supported by one dedicated staff member, Courtney Vicario, and selected members of TFBSO when they weren't in Iraq or Afghanistan, and the contracting support team led by Darren Farber. But the return on this cost and minimal dedication of resources was remarkable. I received heartfelt letters of thanks from U.S. Special Envoy to Sudan Scott Gration and from Commander of AFRICOM General William "Kip" Ward for our work in support of missions in Africa.[1,2]

✳   ✳

A humorous adage I often heard while in government, "the worst thing you can be in Washington is right," seemed to me to have an unfortunate variant: "the worst thing you can be in Washington is successful." Clearly we were on a path to delivering real value and successful programs in Africa, but to realize the potential we would have to get a budget and formal endorsement, triggering an inevitable government interagency conflict.

Tired after yet another year of continual travel, frustrated with our inability to scale up an effort in Africa in spite of obvious need, and ready for new challenges, Bob Love tendered his resignation from government service in December 2009. Under the terms of his senior executive appointment, he was forbidden to engage in any way in meetings or discussions with his former organization for one year after his last day, a policy designed to prevent "influence peddling" by former government executives. In this case, we were losing a pillar of TFBSO, with all of his experience and history with me forming and driving our mission in Iraq followed by his remarkable work in support of AFRICOM and multiple U.S. Embassies in Africa. It was a major loss for the organization.

With his departure, and the increasing scrutiny of our work in support of AFRICOM, our engagements in Africa abruptly ended. All of the potential benefit that was building was lost.

But beyond the direct impacts to the missions in Sudan and Rwanda, the Africa work was eye-opening to me. For the first time, I had seen that direct, collaborative partnership with the State Department was not only possible but also relatively easy in places where there was no history of cabinet-level interagency conflict, as we had inherited in Iraq given the early problems between State and Defense in 2003 and 2004.

It was also apparent that our approach to economic development, with highly tactical focus on business-to-business engagement and connecting international companies to struggling countries, was not needed just in postconflict environments, and that the gap we were filling in Iraq existed throughout the developing world. These realizations would fundamentally change the way we approached our work in the months and years ahead.

10.
INTO AFGHANISTAN

At the end of every presidential campaign, before the new administration takes office, *Newsweek* magazine publishes an issue filled with essays on topics ranging from domestic affairs to economics to foreign policy. Intended to be a sort of notional advisory issue to the new administration, it attracts thought leaders from across the political spectrum to contribute. After the election, I was asked by Fareed Zakaria, then the editor of *Newsweek International*, to contribute an op-ed piece about the situation in Iraq. Since my first meeting with Zakaria in 2006, he had served as a source of counsel and advice on many aspects of our work in Iraq and in Washington. The piece ran in January, prompting the following note from General Petraeus.[1]

From: Petraeus, David H. GEN USA
To: Brinkley, Paul, Mr.
Cc: McKiernan, David D. USA GEN COMISAF
Sent: Mon Jan 05 06:58:37 2009
Subject: Great Piece

Paul, great piece on investing in Iraq—which made this morning's Early Bird. Well done on that—and on all that you've done to help companies invest in Iraq and complement our effort there.

Now, while maintaining the momentum in Iraq, how about turning your sights to creating a similar endeavor in Afghanistan, which arguably needs the help even more and will be even more challenging?

Pls let me know. We're all pleased the SECDEF is keeping you on; now we need to get going on Afghanistan and to keep you on longer!

You may achieve great heights in the business world again; however, you'll never work on missions of such importance to our country and the world!

Best—Dave Petraeus

It was not the first time we had been approached about Afghanistan. Zalmay Khalilzad had requested that I look at supporting the Afghanistan mission as early as 2006, when we were just getting started in Iraq. After our mission had achieved recognized success in 2008, several members of the Defense Policy organization responsible for Afghanistan had approached, making appeals for us to assist.

I had dismissed all such requests. My knowledge of Afghanistan led me to believe there was no value TFBSO could add there. We were mostly business people, working to restart a preexisting industrial economy. Iraq had a large professional class, a depressed and aging but viable factory infrastructure, and a clear economic asset—oil and gas—that could drive a rapid turnaround once security was restored. To my knowledge, Afghanistan had none of these basic elements of a modern economy. From the outside looking in, what Afghanistan needed was remedial development from competent aid organizations.

I drew together my brain trust of Matt Schoeffling, Kris Haag, John Dowdy, Scott King, Tom Modly, and Darren Farber to discuss this in depth. Farber offered interesting perspectives. Unbeknownst to most, TFBSO actually had been quietly helping in Afghanistan for a long time, through its support of Darryl Scott and his successor commanders of Joint Contracting Command, which was responsible for military contracting not only in Iraq but also in Afghanistan. At great personal risk, Farber had traveled all over Afghanistan, visiting small remote U.S. combat outposts to deploy automated systems for remote contracting. He believed there was a lot more TFBSO could do in Afghanistan to support the mission. Unlike what we had found in Iraq in 2006, we already had a solid base of data regarding Afghan companies from the systems and databases Farber had already deployed.

In spite of Farber's head start on gaining knowledge of businesses there, I remained skeptical.

One thing we all agreed on was that there was no way we would walk into Afghanistan blind and start trying to launch programs based on input from outside sources. I had learned better from my own difficult experiences in Iraq. If we were going into Afghanistan, we would do it right. We would enter on one condition. We wanted three months to put a team of experts in agriculture, industry, and natural resources on the ground and to quietly develop an understanding of opportunities for economic development across the country. At the end of that three-month period, a comprehensive report would be provided on our findings, along with a plan to pursue any work we felt would add value to the mission.

I made clear in our proposal to CENTCOM Commander General Petraeus and to the American Ambassador to Afghanistan Karl Eikenberry that if we believed we could not contribute value, we would say so openly and that would end our engagement. The last thing they needed was false hope. If we couldn't assist, we wouldn't waste their time. I also requested, building on our experiences in Africa, that before we would visit Afghanistan we receive a formal invitation from Ambassador Eikenberry to prevent any negative reactions within the State Department.

While these proposals were submitted, we were rebuilding our Iraq team and focusing on the acceleration of our work in Iraq. I could not see how, given our loss of resources at the end of the Bush Administration, we could possibly take on another country. But I was confident we would find, after reviewing the situation on the ground in Afghanistan, that we were the wrong team and that this would simply be a short-term distraction while we worked to keep our Iraq effort on track.

By early spring, we were discussing our first engagement trip to Afghanistan. I planned to take Matt Schoeffling, Ed Price (Director of Borlaug Institute), John Dowdy (McKinsey & Co.), Scott King (Grant

Thornton), and two senior leaders from the U.S. Geological Survey I had met as we launched their engagement in Iraq, John Devine and Jack Medlin. Air Force Lieutenant Colonel Julie Lopez had recently replaced Mark Baird as our military contracting and financial management lead and would travel with us as well.

Jack Medlin is an interesting character. He had worked for decades all over central Asia, and had an encyclopedic knowledge of the geology of the Hindu Kush and Himalayan regions of Asia. A tough, fascinating person, he reminded me of Ed Price, whom I thought of as the Indiana Jones of developmental agriculture. Now I thought of Jack Medlin as the Indiana Jones of geology. Brilliant men with doctorates in their respective scientific fields, they were also fearless and full of stories of close calls they had experienced in their decades of fieldwork in dangerous places.

Medlin and Devine asked me to join them at USGS headquarters in Reston, Virginia, to discuss the geology of Afghanistan. After a few weeks of pushing out the date of the meeting, I agreed to go. I didn't have a lot of optimism about the meeting, I was mostly being polite. But what I would learn in that meeting would change everything.

✳   ✳

It turned out that in 2004, the U.S. Geological Survey was asked by USAID to perform an assessment of the mineralogy of Afghanistan. For thousands of years, mining of precious stones, gold, and rare metals had taken place throughout Afghanistan. The Soviets had done extensive drilling in certain locations there, revealing a world-class iron-ore deposit near the ancient Buddhist monuments of Bamiyan in the north of the country, and a world-class copper deposit about fifty miles south of the capital city of Kabul. The Afghan Finance Minister at the time, Ashraf Ghani, provided funding for the expanded USGS survey of the mineral deposits of the country, in hopes that it would lead to opportunities for the staggeringly poor nation to create economic growth and a source of revenue for the government.

The United States Navy provided P-3 Orion submarine hunter aircraft for the USGS survey, which was done using precision thermal and magnetic imaging equipment. Overflying the country in a grid pattern for many weeks, USGS gathered the most comprehensive remote data set on the mineral wealth of Afghanistan that had ever been accumulated on any country.

On analyzing the data, what USGS found was stunning. The overhead surveys indicated that the country was laden with high-value minerals: gold, copper, iron, rare-earth elements used in high-tech and defense applications, lithium, radioactive elements, gemstones, and oil and gas. There was not a single location in the country that was not in reasonably close vicinity to a deposit of significance. USGS analyzed the data thoroughly and provided a comprehensive set of reports to USAID as its deliverable for the project.[2]

And that was that. The reports were turned in late in 2006. For three years they sat on the shelf. No one in USAID had any idea what to do with them once they were delivered.

I listened to this presentation, fascinated by what I was hearing. Afghanistan was almost totally dependent on foreign aid for every aspect of its security and development, and had no source of wealth on which to build an economy. Yet I was now being told, almost eight years after the United States had deposed the Taliban and occupied the country, that there was a source of indigenous revenue available that could serve as a basis for a self-financing nation, but that it had not been developed.

Not so fast, Medlin and Devine said. What we had was overhead survey data gathered using the most advanced remote-sensing equipment. Although that provided powerful information about the potential for economically viable mineral wealth development, it was insufficient. Field surveys had to be undertaken. Sites that looked promising based on overhead survey data would have to be physically inspected and drilled if possible, with samples taken and assessed for their quality and compared to the expected quality based on the remote sensing results. Only then would we be able to project any value of mineral wealth or its potential economic viability.

Fair enough, I thought. We could even incorporate some initial fieldwork into our three-month study. Medlin and Devine agreed with this approach.

✳   ✳

It was July before we made our first trip, arriving in Kabul on July 7, 2009, for a whirlwind engagement throughout the country.

We had a full agenda: every day in a different city, hosted by a different NATO military organizations. We first met with International Security Assistance Force–Afghanistan Commander General Stanley McChrystal, who pledged to provide any resources necessary to enable us to do our work. McChrystal was well known to me, from both Iraq and from the Pentagon. He had led the most lethal efforts of Joint Special Operations Command in Iraq during the most difficult days of 2006–07, and was credited by many with breaking the back of Al Qaeda in Iraq. I had gotten to know him better in his subsequent assignment as the Director of the Joint Chiefs of Staff in Washington, where I would meet with him as part of my ongoing engagements to keep the Joint Staff informed of our work. Lean, intellectually focused, and with an earnest personal style, McChrystal was easy to like. We arranged an "outbriefing" at the end of our tour of the country with McChrystal and with Ambassador Eikenberry to review our initial thoughts and to lay out the ninety-day assessment plan.

From the very beginning, it was clear that this mission would be different from that in Iraq. Ambassador Eikenberry, a recently retired army lieutenant general who had previously served as the commander of ISAF, hosted a formal reception for us at his personal residence at the embassy in Kabul. His wife arranged a dinner, which included the senior leadership of the embassy as well as a large number of Afghanistan's ministers. I was moved by the level of support that Eikenberry was offering us as we launched. I was asked to give some remarks to the group, which numbered about fifty people, after a kind introduction from Eikenberry. I spoke briefly, pledging our commitment as an element of the nonmilitary effort to assist Afghanistan in building an independent economic future for its people.

That meeting was our first encounter with Afghanistan business and government leaders. It was not what my media-driven impressions had led me to anticipate. Almost all of the Afghan ministers were from the United States or the United Kingdom; all were Western-educated, many were successful businessmen who had returned home after 2001 to help rebuild their country. Minister of Mines Wahidullah Shahrani, Minister of Agriculture Asif Rahimi, and Noor Delawari, the president of the Afghanistan Investment Support Agency, were all present. Speaking with them at length, I was struck by the level of their strategic vision for the country. They were aware of our work in Iraq, and eager to talk about collaboration on private-sector development. To a person, they viewed this as having been neglected by the international community to date.

That night the weather was cool and the sky very clear. Kabul was also not what I had expected. The natural setting of the surrounding Hindu Kush mountain range was breathtaking in its beauty. The following morning, we had an early departure for Helmand Province via C-130 transport. The scenery of the mountainous country between Kabul and Helmand Province was spectacular: jagged snowcapped mountain peaks surrounding narrow river valleys green with vegetation and telltale green plots of land indicating the presence of small farms and rural villages.

I was energized by the reengagement with our military mission again. The troops were enthusiastic about our arrival. Our reputation from Iraq was well known, and it was clear the military, even at the working level, was pleased that we were engaged. We arrived at the British Air Base at Camp Bastion, and were transferred to the adjacent U.S. Marine base, Camp Leatherneck, where we were met with another friend from our days in Iraq, mission commander and Marine Brigadier General Lawrence Nicholson.

Camp Leatherneck, located about thirty kilometers south of Lashkar Gah, the capital city of Helmand Province, sits in utter desolation in a blistering flat desert landscape, not unlike the flat desert of Anbar Province where I first worked with the marines years earlier. I marveled at how the marines always seemed to end up with the most inhospitable terrain. The marines were deploying to push out resurgent Taliban elements that had reclaimed major areas of Helmand Province in the past two years. The epicenter of poppy cultivation and heroin production, Helmand was the drug capital of Afghanistan, and the narcotics trade provided a steady flow of income to the Taliban.

In the Pentagon I had often heard about the poppy trade in Helmand Province, and the long-standing efforts of U.S. and international agencies to try to eradicate poppy cultivation. That seemed like an exercise in futility to me. Absent another cash crop capable of generating needed revenue, what did we expect farmers to do? Starve? For years, the Drug Enforcement Agency had agents working in Helmand Province, at times trying various strategies including large scale spraying of poppy crops with herbicides, no doubt winning hearts and minds of impoverished Afghan farmers. I marveled at the notion of American law enforcement agencies attempting to stop the drug trade in Afghanistan, given the complete collapse of security in Mexican border towns in recent years. If we could not police our own border and assist a neighboring country in putting down a narco-economy, what hope did we have of doing so in a country like Afghanistan?

For the cost of the programs to eradicate poppy, it seemed to me that we could simply pay more than market prices to subsidize other crops—essentially to pay farmers the same prices for other crops that they were getting for poppy cultivation. American agriculture had often been subsidized for far less compelling strategic reasons. Given that we had troops in harm's way in Iraq, why would subsidizing alternative crops to poppy be problematic? While that sounded great on paper, I would soon see why that strategy was too simplistic.

Now, under marine engagement, a counterinsurgency approach was being defined. It was not clear to me how this would work yet, as other than poppy I did not see what economic alternatives would exist to cut off the funding of the Taliban. Establishing security made sense, but the follow-on elements of a counterinsurgency strategy of governance and economic development were not clear.

As we met with more civilians in Afghanistan, two things did become clear. The general caliber of American civilians in Afghanistan was far above the general caliber of those deployed to Iraq. I would learn that this was another result of the "good war" status that Afghanistan had enjoyed. The best and brightest in the development community had gravitated to Afghanistan, avoiding Iraq entirely. They were well-educated and motivated, with an understanding of local dynamics far beyond what we encountered in Iraq, and I began to warm up to the idea that civilian engagement in Afghanistan might just work.

The second observation involved the security posture. While still highly restricted, U.S. civilians were afforded some level of leniency to move about the countryside in Afghanistan. It was clear in meetings that would take place with Afghans that the U.S. civilians had forged solid relationships. I was relieved to see this, after more than three years of watching the futility of civilian engagement in Iraq. Furthermore, because Afghanistan had never devolved into the sort of open warfare that had erupted in Iraq in 2005–07, the posture of private security services was far less intimidating in Afghanistan. The ambient level of hostility one felt on the streets was an order of magnitude less than one felt in Iraq. It created a far healthier working climate than we were used to experiencing.

The following day, the local representative for USAID, Rory Donohue, took us on a tour of the city and to review several USAID-funded projects. Bright and energetic, he was eager to describe his projects and programs to us. Driving through town, it was clear why my simplistic ideas about paying farmers to grow crops other than poppy were not feasible. Several neighborhoods in the city had opulent large villas, each surrounded by high walls and security guards. Drug lords in the city were clearly thriving on the opium trade and had no intention of allowing poppy crops to be replaced. There could be no simple solutions.

But there was also plenty of evidence of obvious steps that had not been taken. A large cotton gin within the city was idled, with large bales of cotton rotting nearby. Asking why the gin was idled, I heard a refrain from my early days in Iraq: the gin was owned by the government of Afghanistan and therefore could not be given assistance by the U.S. government, given U.S. policy regarding state-owned enterprises. The local flour mill was also out of service. So even if a farmer wished to grow something other than poppy, the local processing plants that could turn his produce into a valuable commodity were shut down. I was distressed at the notion of the United States spending millions of dollars to eradicate poppy plants while leaving the processing centers for other crops shut down.

Donohue took us to several USAID pilot agricultural projects in the countryside surrounding Lashkar Gah. An experimental farm attracted particular attention from Ed Price, who described it as a show project for official delegations, rather than a farm that could assist Afghan farmers. Many of the experimental crops being grown were sub–Saharan African plants, ill-suited for large-scale cultivation in Afghanistan. A poultry farm for egg and meat production clearly was operational, but it was unclear how that large expensive model farm could serve as a guide to poor Afghan farmers seeking to earn a living growing something other than poppies. These projects looked impressive, but on asking about next steps, the nongovernmental organizations (NGOs) funded by USAID that ran the projects had no plans. Each was a stand-alone model project, not tied to an overarching agricultural development plan or to a local development strategy.

Our last engagement in Lashkar Gah was a large travertine processing plant. Travertine is a semiprecious mineral formed by the compression of sediments, in this case forming a beautiful green translucent stone similar to marble. Jack Medlin and John Devine were eager to see the processing plant. The plant manager greeted us and gave us a tour of his simple operations, which consisted of basic cutting and polishing equipment no fewer than twenty years old. Large blocks of uncut travertine were piled outside. The site of the mine for the travertine was in the Chaigai Hills of southern Helmand Province, straddling the Pakistani border.

Medlin and Devine emphasized how much this stone would be worth on international markets, properly mined using modern cutting equipment instead of explosives that fractured the stone. It would also employ hundreds, even thousands, in good-paying jobs. Now, the factory was good for small jobs carving vases and platters for domestic markets—nothing more. I asked about plans to expand or develop the market for this stone, but as with agriculture there was no plan for developing basic industries in Helmand.

✳　　✳

From Helmand our team traveled to Herat—a historic center of Persian culture in far western Afghanistan near the border with Iran. The highlight of our first visit to Herat was a tour of its well-developed industrial park near the Italian military base and the Herat Airport. Filled with small-to-midsized industrial factories, the park was a remarkable counter to our expectations of Afghanistan as a purely rural agricultural society. Several factories were filled with women working on assembly lines doing light assembly work or food preparation. All of the industrial operations had been established since 2001, the result of investment by Afghan businessmen who had returned home, many from the United States.

More than 200 small-to-medium-sized industrial businesses were operating in the industrial park, which looked as if it could be on the outskirts of any Midwestern U.S. city. Workers were intensely engaged in their jobs, production was in full operation, often with full automated assembly lines. I could not have been more surprised.

The welcome we received was equally surprising. Of the nine factories we visited, each plant manager greeted us with an excited welcome and tour. We were the first American business leaders to visit Herat, and every businessman we met wanted to discuss how he could expand his operations.

In our discussions it was clear that these factories were serving a strictly local market of two to three million residents of Herat and its neighboring provinces to the south and north. The only external trade taking place in Herat was with its neighboring country, Iran. This represented a pattern we would see repeatedly in Afghanistan.

In spite of the strategic placement of the city near the border with Iran, there was only a single U.S. diplomat assigned to the city and a single USAID advisor. Meeting with them, they were highly engaged and supportive of our work, and seemed relieved that U.S. resources would be dedicated to economic development in the west of the country. I was surprised by the U.S. posture. While it was true that most of the insurgency was in the south and east, it was equally important that cities that were stable such as Herat be engaged effectively and that they begin to prosper. This clean, beautiful, ancient city should have been a showcase for international economic engagement by now, but instead it had been neglected. It also reminded me of the stance of the coalition in Iraq with respect to Basra.

The cities that bordered Iran such as Basra in Iraq or Herat in Afghanistan would have been ideal places to demonstrate international goodwill, undermining the radical Iranian regime in its efforts to cast the U.S. missions in the region as being at war with Islam, or making efforts to encircle and subjugate the Iranian people. The cost, relative to the overall price of the failed reconstruction efforts in both countries, would have been minimal if it had involved the solicitation of private engagement. Instead, these cities had gone neglected and were still economically decrepit, reinforcing the narrative of the Iranian government.

NATO forces at the military base in Herat were highly restricted, with little engagement in any activity "outside the wire." Our visit had been the first extensive mission outside of the base for many of the Italian soldiers. The lack of civilian resources and reconstruction activity within the military mission were frustrating given how permissive the security situation was in the city.

The following day, we were received by the Herat Chamber of Commerce, a group of local business leaders who hosted our meeting in a decent business hotel in the city center. In a now-recurring theme, the hosts indicated they had waited for years for business engagement— something they had expected from the beginning of the post-Taliban period. They flooded us with ideas and requests for engagement in specific businesses and for access to capital to enable them to expand and reach new markets within Afghanistan. The capitalistic entrepreneurship we so often found lacking in postsocialist Iraq was abundant among the Afghan business community. After hours of discussion over lunch and then tea, we departed with a growing sense of opportunity. How could we ignore these requests for assistance we were encountering among Afghan business leaders?

We found similar engagements with business leaders in the northern Afghan city of Mazar e Sharif and in a tour of businesses in Parwan Province. Another highlight of our engagement was a drive into the Panjshir Valley—one of the northern strongholds that was able to repel Soviet invaders and never fell under Soviet occupation. An idyllic river canyon cascading down from the highest peaks in the Hindu Kush Mountains, Panjshir was incredibly pristine and beautiful.

The International Security Assistance Force mission in Afghanistan was truly international with almost 50 nations participating, along with U.S. troops. During our trip, every evening was spent with a different national element of NATO command—sort of an "Epcot" experience of different European food, culture, and engagement at every stop.

✳   ✳

We returned to Kabul for meetings with the business community and extended tours of the city. Surrounded by mountains, the city itself was still in pretty bad shape. It reminded me of Basra with its open sewers and lack of sanitation. New shopping centers had sprung up throughout the city, but the infrastructure was poor—roads were jammed with traffic and pedestrians. Carts pulled by donkeys and oxen intermingled with late-model vehicles on the city streets, all interrupted by the wail of sirens when official delegations would move through the traffic.

The Kabul River flowed through the city center, its banks lined by a boulevard of what looked like a once-charming riverfront commercial district that was now gray with accumulated soot from wood fires and pockmarked with evidence of shelling and gunfire, but teeming with street vendors and pedestrians moving among the merchants. Garbage filled the river.

I was annoyed. Afghanistan was supposed to be the "good war," the war that the entire international community had supported. International aid agencies and nongovernmental organizations had been spending billions of dollars in Afghanistan since 2002. Where were the results? The streets were barely paved and were riddled with potholes. There was no basic infrastructure. How was this possible? Kabul was the capital city, the epicenter of the entire international presence in Afghanistan. Where had the money gone?

If I were a citizen of Kabul, I would wonder why things were not in better shape by now after almost a decade of foreign occupation.

A striking mosque marked the end of the boulevard, which led to city streets that were equally jammed with traffic, and traffic circles that served as hubs for the confluence of movement of a mass of humanity. I was struck by the busyness of the streets. Men were carrying burdens of everything from construction materials to bundles of dry goods, fruits, and produce on their backs, hustling through the streets, or they were pulling large carts that were impossibly overloaded with goods, right through the automobile traffic.

The city was clearly overwhelmed with far more humanity than its streets and infrastructure could handle. The hillsides of the low-lying mountains that bisected the city were covered with mud-brick houses, clinging to the hillsides at impossible angles, with dirt paths winding among them. Children and burka-clad women could be seen climbing the paths, carrying five- or ten-gallon jugs of water as they navigated the steep walkways.

After nine days of intense engagement a consistent pattern had emerged. Contrary to our expectations, every Afghan city we visited had a solid base of business leadership and light industrial capacity that could serve as a foundation for sustained growth. Afghanistan's government leaders were generally more forward thinking and modern in their worldview regarding economic development than their counterparts in Iraq. The business infrastructure was above average, with multiple airlines offering intra-Afghan and international air services that were of an acceptable standard for a developing country. Cellular phone and data coverage service, which had only begun after 2001, was available nationwide, with a national fiber-optic ring in place for high-speed data services in the cities. Afghan business support institutions were well designed and organized; basic processes like permit issuance and licensing were streamlined.

Although there were far too few international civilians—we saw no evidence of the highly publicized civilian surge as yet—the quality of the civilian development talent present within the international community was higher than we were used to from our experience in Iraq. We hoped that the civilian surge would add the needed personnel to really make the development objectives successful.

Afghanistan, however, lacked any viable economic strategy or plan to build an economic base that would enable the government to finance its own security and development. It was disappointing to sit in review after review of comprehensive security plans and to sit through hours of reviews of pilot projects—all well intentioned—yet see no one discuss how to create a source of long-term wealth for the Afghan state.

✳   ✳

We ended our first engagement by having a lengthy review of our initial observations with General McChrystal and Ambassador Eikenberry. We were confident that we could deploy talented business, agriculture, and geology teams that could define detailed economic-development plans at the local and national level. We made a firm commitment to launch our ninety-day assessment. We also told them that they could expect a plan to establish an economically viable Afghan state as a product of our ninety-day effort.

The feedback from McChrystal and Eikenberry could not have been more supportive. I left energized, but mentally overwhelmed. I knew that achieving the goals I had laid out to Eikenberry and McChrystal was possible, and in many ways would be easier than our work in Iraq had been. But Matt, Kris Haag, Regina Dubey, and I were consumed managing the Iraq mission. Now we faced the work of creating an organization capable of overseeing two national economic-development efforts. Given all of the support we appeared to have from the State Department and the new administration, I was hopeful that we could pull it off.

Returning to Washington, we assembled our observations and plans into a comprehensive strategy and vision for the establishment of a sovereign Afghan economy capable of supporting its own security and development needs for the foreseeable future. Doing this would not be quick or easy, but it was imperative to the success of the U.S. mission. As we built the plan, we began briefing it within the Pentagon to various leaders, culminating in a briefing to Secretary Gates and Admiral Mullen that included much of the Pentagon senior leadership.

In 2009, Afghanistan's nominal Gross Domestic Product was approximately $10 billion. Our analysis showed that fully 60 percent of this GDP was the direct result of foreign aid. An additional 30 percent was the direct and indirect result of poppy cultivation and the production and export of illegal narcotics, specifically raw heroin. Only 10 percent was legitimate, self-sustaining economic activity. A nation of more than twenty million citizens had a legitimate annual economic output of only $1 billion.[3]

Let that number sink in. Fully seven years after the United States and a United Nations–supported coalition had deposed the Taliban and fostered the establishment of a democratic regime, Afghanistan's legitimate nominal Gross Domestic Product was approximately $1 billion per year.[4]

The percentage of Afghan GDP represented by foreign aid, at approximately 60 percent, was the worst in the world—placing Afghanistan at the bottom of a list of peer countries including Somalia, Rwanda, Sudan, and Mali.

The United States was spending, in 2009, almost *$4 billion per month* on military operations to secure a $1 billion economy.

Worse still, the annual budget of the Afghan government was almost entirely based on international donations. With a total annual budget of less than $1 billion, and less than 20 percent based on tax revenue, there was no hope that the Afghan government could pay for its own development and security within any reasonable time frame.

The nation was an economic charity case. A beggar nation. The Afghan government of President Hamid Karzai, which was attracting so much international attention for its failure to establish legitimacy, was lacking the most fundamental base of legitimacy for any state—an indigenous source of revenue for allocation by elected officials to the benefit and security of its citizenry.

Imagine living in a nation in which your national government was totally dependent on charitable donations from other countries for almost every dollar it spent. Would you respect that government? Would you believe that your officials were acting in the interest of the people, or in the interests of the donor nations? Would it matter to you who your leaders were? Would you not assume they were puppets of the international donors who were propping up the government? Imagine yet again that after seven years, this situation had worsened, and that your nation's dependence on foreign aid and foreign military assistance had only grown. Would you view your leaders as legitimate, much less effective? Would you believe that the international community had your best interests at heart?

The most fundamental responsibility of a government is to provide responsibly, through appropriate taxation and associated revenue generation, autonomous security and stability for its citizens. Afghanistan lacked any sense of economic sovereignty. From the perspective of our analysis, the failure to address the absence of a viable economic base on which to build legitimate government institutions was fundamental, and ensured the eventual failure of the Afghan government. As far as we were concerned, you could hold elections in Afghanistan forever, but you would not establish legitimacy for its elected officials. Until the Afghan people possessed a base of economic activity capable of funding an autonomous government, there can be no viable nation-state in Afghanistan. In 2009, there was no plan to achieve such economic autonomy.

Pomegranates shipped to fresh produce markets in India were not going to do the trick.

The goal of our strategy was therefore to provide a roadmap to economic sovereignty for the Afghan nation. To enable Afghanistan to stand on its own. To eliminate its dependence on foreign charity. This was the foundation of our entire strategic and tactical plan.

Our second observation focused on the nature of international foreign aid and its effectiveness to date. Since 2002, donor nations had spent billions of dollars on aid programs in Afghanistan, but little went directly to stimulate meaningful economic activity. Analysis of the United States Agency for International Development (USAID) budget was informative.[5] Through 2008, USAID had allocated approximately $6.5 billion in assistance to Afghanistan. Of this, only 5 percent was for agricultural development, and an additional 6 percent was for economic-development support through advisory services to the Afghan ministries.

With 85 percent of the people dependent on agriculture for their livelihoods, spending only 5 percent of the development budget on agricultural development was remarkable. What was spent on agriculture was focused on commodities such as fruit and nut cultivation, a segment that affected very few Afghans. Most Afghans cultivate grains, oilseeds, or livestock. Failing to invest in these areas meant that most Afghans experienced little to no daily impact of the international presence on their economic well-being. Of the remaining USAID budget, about 40 percent went to road building and electrical power generation projects. But as in Iraq, the need for basic sewer, water, transportation, and electrical infrastructure was so great in Afghanistan that these USAID programs were simply too small to create a visible impact on daily life.

The balance of the USAID budget went to fund advisory staff, primarily in Kabul, where thousands of contractors were employed by relief agencies and nongovernmental organizations. Kabul was a veritable alphabet soup of international relief organizations, spending hundreds of millions of dollars a year on human rights, education, ministerial support, and rule-of-law advisory services. While these programs were noble in their intent, and while each of these focus areas were important bedrock for a viable future Afghan economy, the results of the investment were hard to see.

As in Iraq, civilians generally had deployment terms of a year or less. Their security postures were too restrictive for genuine engagement, with most civilians locked behind walled compounds with heavily armed guards. One could almost predict the effectiveness of a program by the longevity of its civilian leaders; those whose leaders had remained in Afghanistan long enough to understand the culture tended to be effective, and the term of service needed to be effective was far longer than a year. Unfortunately, most programs failed this measure and simply served as job-rotation programs for Western consultants, and for the thousands of Afghans who migrated to Kabul for employment, either directly for relief organizations, or indirectly in the booming artificial Kabul foreign aid–based economy.

The presence of so much foreign aid flooding into such a small area was distorting Afghan society. Kabul was overwhelmed by people pouring in from throughout the country seeking work. But the work was not sustainable. At some point the system was destined to crash, and when it crashed, Kabul would crash with it. A city of fewer than 1 million residents prior to 2002, Kabul was by 2008 a teeming metropolis of more than 8 million, but its infrastructure was designed for 10 percent of that. Streets were constantly gridlocked on workdays, the canals and waterways were open sewers, the air was thick with smoke on winter nights from wood fires, and garbage was strewn throughout the city.

The Afghan foreign-aid economy was a house of cards. An international exit would cause an economic collapse, and the resultant misery would provide fertile ground for radical elements to reemerge. That exit was inevitable: at some point the international community would depart with its massive budgets for military and development operations. Absent a legitimate indigenous economy to replace this spending, there was little hope that the billions of dollars and thousands of lives invested in Afghanistan would not eventually have been in vain.

Our third principal observation was a by-product of massive military spending. Darren Farber had analyzed military spending since the inception of Afghan operations in 2002, and what he found was troubling. Most military spending, as well as international development funding, was spent on imported goods and business services. Very little was spent on Afghan businesses. International companies had entered Afghanistan and established operations, importing thousands of workers in pursuit of contracts with the United States and coalition governments, while Afghan businesses had too often been left on the outside looking in. Commodity after commodity demonstrated this pattern, regardless of how simple the item. Even basic construction materials were being trucked in from neighboring countries instead of procured from Afghan businessmen.

Cement was a good example. Imports of cement had increased 94 percent per year since 2002, to a level approaching a million tons a year in 2008. Afghan production of cement had remained flat at fewer than thirty tons a year since 2002, in spite of the presence of idle cement operations. Many simple commodities showed these results, from gravel to brick. Most of this construction material came from Pakistan, which was reaping hundreds of millions of dollars of direct economic stimulus resulting from the export of basic construction material to Afghanistan.[6]

More troubling still was the concentration of spending on a small number of Afghan firms. In areas where Afghan businesses had managed to establish sales relationships with the United States, they quickly became a single go-to source of supply, causing resentment from other local tribal leaders and businessmen. The constant rotation of contract management commanders and staff within the military and civilian missions made it impossible to sustain knowledge of local businesses. Often the easiest thing for a new contract staffer to do was award a contract to a bidding firm that had a prior record of successfully delivering a good or service. The unintended net effect was a heavy concentration of spending on an alarmingly small number of Afghan firms.[7]

Our final strategic observation involved the troubling lack of commercial activity between the ethnic and geographic regions of Afghanistan. In Iraq, as a result of the unfortunate shutdown of economic activity after 2003, commercial activity between and among religious sects and tribal groups had been stopped but was relatively easy to restore. In Afghanistan, it was not clear that such "intra-Afghan" trade relationships had ever really existed on any scale. From our analysis, it was very clear that meaningful levels of intra-Afghan trade had been almost absent since the Soviet invasion of 1979 until the present time.

From our perspective, this was a very troubling issue.

It is hard to think of a viable nation-state that lacks a vibrant level of intranational trade among its peoples. Yet Afghanistan had no real history of this sort of economic interaction. While there were some exceptions, generally all economic activity in a particular city or region was local. Where any trade existed, it was with the neighboring country, not with distant provinces.

The forbidding geography of Afghanistan had created this economic separation over the centuries. Separated by vast distances interspersed with rugged mountains, the subcultures of Afghanistan were largely autonomous and independent from one another. As a result, mutually beneficial trade relationships had never developed on any scale.

Often, people would contradict this observation by citing the "Silk Road" economy of the Middle Ages and earlier, a romantic notion that captures the fancy of Western development agencies, but this is a false comparison. The Silk Road was a transit route for the movement of goods from east Asia to markets in the Mediterranean and Europe. Caravans of silks and spices would be forced to pay tribute as they passed through each autonomous region along the Silk Road, generating local economic benefit but not in the sense of a trade partnership. The sort of trade necessary to knit together a society is a trade relationship—the transfer of an indigenous good for money or for another indigenous good from a neighboring society. The Silk Road is not a comparison for this sort of economic activity. In fact, the Silk Road economy model is exactly the wrong model if a goal is to create a viable Afghan state. The ancient "highwayman" economy that exacted a toll for passage cannot generate significant economic wealth for Afghanistan in a world with any number of alternative trade routes for goods.

Creating an economically sovereign Afghan state would require two difficult steps: identifying and developing a source of indigenous revenue for the Afghan people to eliminate their stifling dependence on foreign aid, and establishing a basis for intra-Afghan commercial activity that would create mutually beneficial economic activity among the troubled ethnic and tribal factions of Afghan society. Although these objectives seemed overwhelming in their scope and complexity, our studies defined a path that, with time, could achieve both of them.

The bedrock of our tactical plan was the development of the mining sector. Our initial field surveys, taken in partnership with the United States Geological Survey, were validating the overhead magnetic and thermal imaging data USGS had collected three years earlier. The country literally abounded with mineral wealth. Our team now included some of the most elite mining-industry leaders in the world, and what they had told us was remarkable. Copper alone provided an example. A single world-class copper deposit could be expected to generate more than $2 billion a year in contribution to GDP. Afghanistan had four such deposits, only one of which had even been known prior to the USGS data collection effort: the Mes Aynak deposit south of Kabul. Initially drilled by the Soviets, the mine had recently been awarded for development to the Chinese state mining company MCC. There were a number of secondary copper deposits of high grade. Most of the copper deposits were located with gold. Some of the samples we were gathering indicated high levels of ore purity. With gold trading at more than $1,000 an ounce, gold deposits could generate quick economic benefit to the Afghan state, as well as local employment.

World-class deposits of iron ore, cobalt, lithium, and a number of other commodities in high demand were identified. We were deploying field geologists to sample each of these sites, drilling where possible, in partnership with the Afghan Ministry of Mines and the Afghan Geological Survey. We were also hiring legal, financial, and marketing experts from leading mining-development firms to advise the Afghan government on how to develop these deposits in an economically and environmentally responsible way.

The USGS estimated the "in-ground" value of the total mineral wealth at just less than one trillion dollars. In addition to this staggering national asset, there were estimated reserves of one billion barrels of oil in northern Afghanistan, with wells that had been drilled by the Soviets still capped since their departure in 1989. While nothing on the scale of Arab countries, for a nation importing almost 100 percent of its fuel and energy, leaving capped oil wells undeveloped made no sense. With oil at about one hundred dollars a barrel and no exploratory drilling required for initial development, Afghan oil provided both a near- and long-term opportunity for economic benefit.[8]

Developing mineral deposits and oil and gas fields would not be achievable for several years. Infrastructure including rail networks and pipelines would be needed. While it was possible, with improved security, to facilitate eventual private investment in these sectors, we needed to demonstrate rapid benefits to Afghans in support of the counterinsurgency mission.

Our assessment of industrial operations provided a path forward. Food-processing operations would serve as sources of demand for Afghan produce and grain grown in other areas of the country. We would directly facilitate access to markets within Afghanistan for existing industrial and service businesses seeking to expand beyond local communities. We believed that if we could establish a few examples of intra-Afghan commercial activity between regions of the country, the natural entrepreneurial orientation of Afghan business leaders would follow these examples and scale up these relationships over time.

Wherever possible, we identified and defined opportunities for international market access for Afghan products, particularly carpets and fruits. In spite of the well-publicized focus on fruit and vegetable cultivation, no international export business relationships had been defined for Afghan produce farmers. While these would not generate major effects on GDP, they would demonstrate a change in the international approach to business in Afghanistan and buy time for longer term, larger initiatives to take hold.

Mining had both midrange and long-term economic potential. For commodities such as cobalt, gold, and possibly lithium mining, the amount of capital investment required was small. Ore could be removed using trucks, and "artisanal" techniques (picks, shovels, wheelbarrows) could be used initially to extract material. These would generate immediate cash flow to local communities, create positive momentum, and illustrate the feasibility of mining in Afghanistan for larger industrial-mining expansion and development over the long term.

Copper, iron, and other heavy metals, as well as potentially complex mining for rare-earth elements used in high-tech applications, would take longer. Railroad infrastructure would be most critical. If the international community had spent every penny of aid on building rail networks in Afghanistan since 2003, by 2009 Afghanistan would have had a legitimate GDP ten times larger than its actual size, as the ability to transport heavy mineral ore required rail networks. But there were plenty of cases in equally difficult security and geographical environments around the world in which private industry had developed infrastructure to enable mining of less-rich deposits of minerals. If security continued to improve, we were hopeful that this pattern would repeat in Afghanistan.

Finally, we emphasized the importance of establishing clear positive economic momentum throughout the country, not just in the areas of violence where U.S. troops were focused. To facilitate this national-level approach, TFBSO would set up operational centers in each major city in the country, beginning with Kabul, Jalalabad, Lashkar Gah, Herat, Mazar-e-Sharif, Kunduz, and Kandahar. Our goal was to fully staff these centers within three months, a warp-speed commitment from a governmental perspective, but one we were confident we could achieve. During the assessment period, the team in D.C. had worked to get a pipeline of professional talent ready to scale up and deploy in support of the mission. With the assistance of a newly hired team of advisors to work with the local communities, TFBSO would field a new, open approach for engagement in the localities of the country.

Shortly after we delivered our briefing, Secretary Gates issued a memorandum firmly reinforcing our work, its scope across all economic sectors, and its criticality to the missions in Iraq and Afghanistan. The memo authorized TFBSO to support command objectives for Operation Iraqi Freedom, as well as Operation Enduring Freedom (the Afghanistan campaign) and its "successor operations," and reinforced our reporting relationship directly to Secretary Gates.[9] I was no longer a "carryover" Bush Administration appointee wrapping up Iraq work with an obscure Task Force. We were now elemental to the broader Defense Department mission throughout the region.

I prepared to return to Iraq and Afghanistan on my normal monthly rotation, filled with renewed energy and with a growing feeling of invincibility. In Iraq, we had contributed to the military turnaround of a failing mission, something beyond anything I had expected to do when I had left Silicon Valley five years before. Now we were poised to make a contribution to the long-term stability of the broader region. I was growing confident again.

11.
LAND OF THE PURE

With respect to the security interests of the United States, there is no more dangerous country on earth today than Pakistan. With an enormous population of almost 180 million people, nuclear weapons, a major youth bulge, widespread poverty and unemployment, and ethnic and sectarian radicalization increasing every year since the end of the Cold War, Pakistan is fertile ground for terrorist organizations seeking recruits to wage violent jihad on neighboring India and on Western interests.

No greater example of this could exist than the events of November 2008 in Mumbai, India, in which Pakistan-based terrorists launched shootings and bombings in a coordinated attack that once again brought India and Pakistan to the brink of open war, with all of its unthinkable nuclear consequences.

The tribal areas on Pakistan's border with Afghanistan form a largely ungoverned region that serves as a home base for radical insurgent groups seeking to overthrow both the Afghan and Pakistani governments. Most of what passes for schools in these ungoverned regions are religious *madrassas*, often financed by Islamic fundamentalists in Saudi Arabia and the Gulf Region, in which jihad against the West is taught as the duty of every young Muslim.[1]

Bombarded with satellite television images of growing prosperity and perceived decadence throughout the world and with little prospect for a better life, there is widespread sympathy for the cause of insurgents in many regions of Pakistan. Pervasive official corruption in almost all Pakistani institutions further inflames the growing rage of the people there. Providing an alternative vision of a future in which young Pakistanis have a reason for hope is critical to undermining this public sympathy, essential to the long-term stability of the region, and necessary if we wish to prevent the emergence of a nuclear-armed failed state.

It is widely believed that increasing Pakistani radicalization partially has, at its roots, economic causes. The economy was simply not able to absorb a growing population of young Pakistanis who are increasingly frustrated at the economic prosperity taking hold in India—too much of which they erroneously attribute to increases in trade with the United States. Any effort to reduce the "pool" of recruits for terror cells would have to include an economic element.

I had succumbed to appeals from Richard Holbrooke, augmented by prodding from General Petraeus, to engage in Pakistan. The Obama Administration had made it clear that it was viewing Afghanistan and Pakistan as a unified mission, and if we were going to maintain our newly established momentum I needed to make sure that our team was aligned with that thinking.

There was also cause for hope for Pakistan. Progress was being made. The military dictator Pervez Musharraf had yielded power one year earlier to the elected government of the Pakistan People's Party.[2] Although this created some cause for optimism, we knew there could be no quick solutions there.

It would be hard to imagine a more complex, even absurd, relationship than the one that had emerged between the United States and Pakistan since the events of September 11, 2001. With its largely ungoverned Pashtun and Baloch tribal areas widely acknowledged as safe havens for Taliban, Islamist, and militant tribal groups that continued to destabilize Afghanistan, Pakistan also served as a principal logistical route for NATO forces to move matériel into the Afghan theater of combat. Under the new administration, with its emphasis on the Afghan conflict and with Holbrooke leading the charge, the United States had launched a multifaceted engagement strategy with Pakistan. This strategy, with its characteristic "carrot and stick" elements to encourage Pakistani alignment to American interests, combined vastly increased targeted killings of terrorist militants using drone aircraft over the northern tribal areas with a threefold increase in development aid.

The "carrot" portion of the foreign aid strategy had recently culminated in the passage of a massive American foreign assistance commitment, known as the Kerry-Lugar Act, which committed $1.5 billion per year in nonmilitary aid for a period of five years.[3] The bill was laden with conditions placed on the Pakistani government in return for the disbursement of funds, most involving the development of democratic institutions, rule of law, and reduced influence of military leadership on Pakistani politics. The bill had generated a great deal of public debate in Pakistan, where many felt that the conditions placed on the aid were onerous and impinged upon Pakistani sovereignty. The aid bill had also stirred resentment in neighboring India, where many wondered why the United States would offer so much assistance to a nation that was widely perceived to harbor terror networks hell-bent on attacking both America and India—as the recent attacks in the city of Mumbai had demonstrated.

After months of e-mail and dialogue with U.S. Coordinator for Nonmilitary Assistance Robin Raphel—a friend and colleague, and a supporter of our work dating from her time in Iraq in 2007—as well as the Commerce Department attaché in Islamabad, Will Center, we received the necessary formal invitations to engage in Pakistan. As the United States had no ground forces in Pakistan, we were essentially "seconded" to the embassy, completely under "Chief of Mission" authority while in the country. As we had learned in Africa and now in Afghanistan, this approach would help us avoid the interagency conflicts we continued to experience in Iraq.

A former Assistant Secretary of State for South Asian Affairs, and carrying the rank of ambassador, Raphel was best described as skeptically optimistic. She took a long view of everything and was highly suspicious of quick fixes. But she believed that an important cause of unrest and sympathy with radical actors in Pakistan stemmed from economic uncertainty and hardship, and that taking steps to address that hardship was critical to the future of the American relationship.

She was also frustrated with the inability of American aid institutions to deliver tangible, visible results within a credible time frame. Pakistan was overrun with advisors and consultants, but there was little being done that was tangible.

Our first meetings were in Islamabad with Pakistani officials, including Minister of Finance Shaukat Tareen, Minister of Agriculture Rafique Jamali, and the head of the Board of Investment for Pakistan, Saleem Mandviwalla. The timing of our engagement in Islamabad could not have been better from the perspective of the Pakistani government. Two weeks before, Secretary of State Hillary Clinton had barnstormed the country in a series of high-profile public engagements. Although this had attracted some attention in the U.S. media, I had no sense of the impact of Clinton's visit until I arrived in Islamabad. Even though two weeks had passed, there was palpable energy with respect to her meetings and dialogue. The direct nature of her feedback in public forums, her absorption of direct confrontation and criticism of U.S. policy, and the commitment of a new chapter in U.S. relationships had created a moment for concrete steps to be taken.

Our arrival so soon after she had departed was perceived as an example of rare quick American follow-up. Much of the feedback to Clinton had focused on economic ties with the United States. Pakistanis were well aware of the burgeoning American trade relationship with India, and the rapidly rising standard of living of their bitter rival to the east. They could not understand why America, the long-standing Cold War ally of Pakistan, was now building apparently seamless economic ties with India.

In my meetings with Pakistani officials, it quickly became clear that while Clinton had been well received, there was a lot of work to do to build any real trust. I heard a litany of complaints about the expenditures of USAID funding on consultants and advisors at the national and provincial level, and about USAID grants to nongovernmental organizations focused on rights, democracy development, and other "soft objectives." What was needed was direct assistance in infrastructure for power generation, and for enhanced trade status with the United States, allowing unfettered access to American markets for Pakistani textiles.

In addition to these two major areas of interest, there was great frustration at the push by the U.S. to establish "enterprise zones," or free trade zones with preferential U.S. tax status, in the tribal areas of the north. No matter the affiliation of the political or business leader I met with in Islamabad, there was clear antipathy to the northern areas, and passion for establishing such zones in the Punjab or Sindh Provinces, where there was also great poverty and growing sympathy with radical Islamist organizations.

As earlier in Iraq and Afghanistan, we were in listening mode in this initial engagement, capturing information and withholding opinions. It was clear that our work in Iraq was well known to the government and business leaders, who were quick to propose ideas about private engagement using examples from our work in Iraq.

The businessmen from Peshawar were equally encouraging, but vented their frustration at the preponderance of military action in the tribal areas, and the lack of any improvement in the lives of the citizenry. The resentment over drone attacks was vocal and direct.

✳   ✳

Flying via commercial carrier to Lahore, we encountered truly world-class transportation infrastructure. Lahore was a culturally rich city, a mix of colonial-era red sandstone palaces, incredibly ornate mosques, and boulevards separating a mix of traditional markets and modern shopping centers. Will Center and Saleem Mandviwalla accompanied us, introducing us first to the progressive governor of Punjab, Salman Taseer. Taseer, himself formerly a business leader, graciously received us at the historic governor's mansion in Lahore.

After dinner, we talked at length, where he focused much of the discussion on agricultural development and the concerns about loss of leadership in global textile markets. Imagine, he described, the climate for young Pakistanis, inundated with images of prosperity flowing from Indian television and Bollywood movies; the perceived heathen Hindu Indians growing rich while the Pakistani economy declined in relative per capita income. It was wise counsel and consistent with our observations in Iraq and Afghanistan. Our foreign policy apparatus was not equipped to support tactical economic engagement. As we drove around the city, the disadvantages of Iraq and Afghanistan were absent. The streets were clean, sidewalks were filled with a mix of people; I could see no reason why American businesses could not succeed here, as they were clearly succeeding in India, if the climate of hostility and public perception of risk could be reduced. Matt and I walked through markets and toured public parks and infrastructure, without any security or support, and were greeted warmly; there were no hostile eyes watching us.

The Lahore business community welcomed us graciously and crowded around us in meetings, eager to talk to Americans. Group gatherings with local business clubs were followed by private dinners or meetings with leading businessmen and investors. Most of the executives were involved, either directly or indirectly, in textiles or agriculture. The request for preferential trade status with America for Pakistani textiles became a familiar refrain. But another line of discussion also became uncomfortably familiar. I had noticed this first in Islamabad, and, by the time we had spent a few days in Lahore, it became disconcerting. Almost every business leader focused his energy on complaints about India. Many businessmen or -women we met would launch their discussion with a tirade about how America was in the clutches of nefarious Indian actors. They could recite the statistic that "27 American officials within the Obama Administration are Indian spies," naming them from memory. Once pleasantries were dispensed with, regardless of the audience, the conversation frequently shifted into denunciations of India and America's blindness to its efforts to hijack our foreign policy.

I found these lines of discussion curious at first and would redirect the discussion back to local businesses and where there were opportunities for tangible actions that would lead to significant improvements. After days of hearing it over and over again, in Lahore and later in Karachi, I grew weary of the constant haranguing about India.

I had done my homework before visiting Pakistan, and was not naive about the climate between India and Pakistan; I expected such sentiments from government or military officials. But recent outreach between Indian and Pakistani business leaders had left me optimistic that the business community would not be so focused on India.

These were not military leaders. They were not government officials. They were businessmen and businesswomen, gathered to discuss business-to-business engagement with American industry with a team that had a proven track record of such engagement in far less compelling environments. They were the economic elite of Pakistan's most powerful states, usually the most pragmatic representatives of a society given they have the most to lose. And yet they could not articulate a vision for their community that was not based on an Indian counternarrative. I wondered how on earth this beautiful nation, with all of its obvious advantages, was ever going to overcome this psychological barrier to its own success.

But through all of the dialogue, we did learn a lot. Cotton and textiles in particular were more complicated than described. Cotton cultivation was expanding, but at a reduced rate compared to other nations, partially because of the introduction of genetically modified cottonseed in developed countries including the United States and China. Genetically modified cotton seed, particularly the pest-resistant varieties of BT cotton, is resistant to boll weevils and other insect pests, as well as certain insect-borne fungal diseases that have reduced cotton yields throughout the world for all of history. Pakistan lacked access to these new varieties, for legal as well as contractual reasons. As the primary holder of the patents for BT cotton, American companies had been in long negotiations with Islamabad about licensing cotton seed.[4] Will Center had worked with U.S. corporations to try to arrive at mutually agreeable terms for the Pakistanis, but nothing had been concluded yet after many months of discussion.

Textile production was also a complex story. The introduction of Chinese textile mills along with other east Asian sources of production had created tremendous competition for Pakistani cloth as well as clothing. While some of the countries that had captured market share from Pakistan for American clothing were, in fact, benefiting from recently normalized trade (such as China and Vietnam), several others with long-standing normal trade relations with the U.S. (Bangladesh for example) were seizing market share in the absence of any favorable treatment from the United States. Irrigation and water utilization were also a major focus area of concern. I was eager to get our agriculture team as well as our U.S. Geological Survey partners into Lahore to visit farms and to get a deeper understanding of problems and determine what was possible.

The work in Pakistan, if undertaken at all, would clearly differ dramatically from Iraq and Afghanistan. We would never muster the resources to engage Pakistan at a level needed to make a difference beyond the local level. But we could potentially break the ice as we had done in Iraq. If we could demonstrate goodwill in a few key industry sectors and forge some new relationships with American businesses that proved profitable and beneficial, we could start the beneficial cycle of improved economic relationships. As our discussions in Lahore continued, I grew optimistic that this could be possible.

❋   ❋

In Karachi, we encountered an entirely different business climate. A sprawling metropolis of more than twenty million inhabitants, Karachi lacked anywhere near the infrastructure to support so many, but its position as the commercial capital of Pakistan had remained intact. The business community in Karachi was far more diverse and international than that in Lahore. And many executives representing the Pakistan divisions of American companies were present. Major American blue-chip companies including IBM, Proctor & Gamble, Cisco Systems, and many others were represented. The discussions with the executives were illuminating.

Most of them expressed frustration and resentment at their inability to get their American parent companies to invest in Pakistan. Although they had a sales office or a distribution operation, and perhaps nascent service businesses in place, it was far less than their available market demand would support. But a familiar refrain was heard: proposals to their corporate parent in the United States to increase market share or expand operations were invariably shot down over perceived security threats, risk-averse legal advisors convinced of heightened potential for corruption, and the general pall of a negative international perception that had settled over Pakistan in recent years.

Like the more extreme examples of conflict zones such as Iraq and Afghanistan, Pakistan was fighting its public image as a dangerous place, an image that had been etched into the American imagination by any number of events, from the horrific kidnapping and murder of journalist Daniel Pearl, to the Pakistan-borne attacks on Westerners in Mumbai, to the continued threats of Islamist extremists who found sanctuary in the country.

The Karachis were clearly grateful for our apparent concrete effort to start engagement with American businesses, stating repeatedly how much of the anti-American problem in Pakistan was because of the absence of American voices in the public debate. They repeatedly cited Hillary Clinton's recent visit as an example of the dialogue needed to counter the extreme voices that painted America as hostile to the Pakistani people.

But it was also clear that the desire of business leaders to have American attention was part of the broader crisis of Pakistani identity, the same crisis that manifested itself in the constant remarks about India. The business community seemed as focused on the "power" implications of American engagement and what it meant for their self-image vis-à-vis India as they were about a financial return on investments. They did not seem to see that the solution was to create financial incentives to entice investment. Investors do not, generally, care about a country's political aspirations. In Pakistan, this often seemed completely confused. I made these points in my discussion: American companies were not investing in India or outsourcing low-wage work to India because the United States sought political alliances with the Indian nation. If anything, the reverse was true. America's relationship with India had grown more strategic as the economic ties between the countries had increased. If Pakistan sought to be seen as a great nation, the first step was to begin the process of enticing international economic engagement. Strategic relevance on the world stage would follow.

❈   ❈

Over the next several months, we returned to Pakistan, and I deployed teams to take a deeper look at the opportunities that Matt and I had initially identified. We circulated a draft plan within the embassy that was subsequently approved early in 2010.

Under our proposed plan, TFBSO would place teams in Lahore and Karachi, with the full sponsorship of the local governorate as well as the U.S. Embassy. The Lahore team would include land-grant university agricultural experts to work with the textile sector on improving cotton yields and irrigation technology. A manufacturing team would work with textile factories to identify and introduce efficient practices to improve factory productivity and competitive positions. Finally, a textile-marketing effort would be launched to provide Pakistani textile company sales personnel with strategies for competing for American and European clothing, including how to better market to young female clothing buyers who were inundated with options for supply in the competitive global marketplace, and who were especially sensitive to negative media images of Pakistan as a hostile work environment for women.

In Karachi, we would focus on facilitating growth for existing American companies already present in Pakistan and on investor engagement to provide access to capital for Pakistani entrepreneurs.

We proposed a major effort in partnership with the U.S. Geological Survey to perform an overhead mineralogy survey along the Pakistani frontier, similar to the work that had been done in Afghanistan and shelved by USAID back in 2004. The same geological formations of the Hindu Kush that created a treasure of mineral wealth in Afghanistan did not stop at the artificial border of the Durand Line. USGS projected that similar mineral wealth existed in the northern frontier Pashtun and Baloch regions of the country. We also sought to provide engagement in the energy sector in Pakistan.

There was great sensitivity to the mineral and energy proposals in Islamabad. The Pakistanis were convinced that overhead aerial electromagnetic surveys of the country, even if limited to the tribal areas, were a backdoor attempt by the U.S. to gain greater intelligence about military assets and their location. The energy sector was a maelstrom of conflicting agendas. At the request of Raphel's team, we scaled back the first phase of the mineral sector effort to focus strictly on water-resource analysis, and particular the use of modern technology to monitor snowpack and to project water-resource availability for agricultural use.

By early in 2010, our launch plans were approved by the embassy in Islamabad and by Richard Holbrooke. By summer we would have working operations in the most important cities of Pakistan.

12.
BLACK HORROR

January in Baghdad is a beautiful time of year. The blistering heat of the summer is forgotten as temperatures drop and rains fall, washing away the layers of dust that have accumulated throughout the year. Everything is fresh, the air is cool and crisp, and the mood of the people is happiest. It is my favorite time of the year in Iraq.

I had returned to Baghdad from Washington full of enthusiasm for our mission in the new year after our successes in 2009. Our work in Afghanistan to build an economic strategy had been well received by all involved in the mission there, as well as in the corridors of power in Washington. In Iraq, our mission was running at full speed, with weekly results rolling in around the country, from factory expansion to private investments to foreign company engagement. Regina Dubey, in her newly appointed role as operations director in Iraq, had accelerated the completion of our factory restart projects. Everywhere I traveled in Iraq, we could count on a warm reception from a local community now grateful for the results of our work.

The villa/hotel compound where we hosted visitors in Iraq was now fully occupied by visiting company representatives as well as TFBSO staff. As a team, TFBSO was melding new members into a long-established Iraq crew, with the normal rough edges between the newcomers and the old guard. But these were minor issues, and part of the generally positive trend the entire organization felt regarding our mission.

The business-incubator compound we had established a year earlier in the Green Zone was now full, and many of the business representatives staying in our small hotel were repeat guests—a situation that was not part of our plan. Our goal was to provide medium-term office and living space at the incubator compound for companies once they had visited Iraq once or twice to provide a workplace giving them time to establish their own permanent operation elsewhere in the city. The hotel was for first-time visitors.

We were running out of room.

Monday, January 25, 2010, was an unusually slow day for us. The weather was clear and bright, with a high that afternoon of about 65 degrees Fahrenheit. I had been jammed in back-to-back meetings with Iraqi officials and traveling around the country for the past few days, and Monday was the first time I had had to catch my breath. That morning, Eric Clark and I had taken a run along the Tigris River, covering almost five miles and working out our constant jet lag. When I returned to the villa, I asked our drivers and security team if we could go check out some possible locations for expansion of our Green Zone incubator facilities across the river in Baghdad, outside of the Green Zone.

I frequently moved about in the city now. Streets were busy with the routines of normal life—school children, street vendors, and cars—all the daily activity one would see in any city in the region. Today, I wanted to revisit some of the large hotel complexes directly across the river from the Green Zone. The old Sheraton Hotel, the Palestine Hotel, and the Babylon Hotel were large multistory buildings along Abu Nuw'as Street, a boulevard that paralleled the river with parkland along its boundary. I wanted to check out the current state of the buildings and explore the idea of renting a few floors for expanding our incubator operation.

Matt, Eric, and I took two new members of the TFBSO team along with us who were on their first trip to Iraq and who wanted to see some of Baghdad. Elizabeth LoNigro had recently joined TFBSO as one of the new candidates provided by the White House personnel office. She had worked as a senior member of Mayor Michael Bloomberg's staff in New York City and then gone on to complete graduate education at Johns Hopkins University in international relations. Tanisha Dozier, a young White House political appointee from Chicago, had joined the Task Force only a few weeks earlier.

Our security detail was a top-notch team, composed primarily of former British SAS special forces and assembled by Tim Spicer, a long-standing advisor to the Task Force on matters of security in Iraq and a bit of a legendary figure in the world of security operations. They were low key and extremely professional with years of experience working in Iraq, including more than a year supporting TFBSO. John Chadderton, who had served as the personal security lead for Jeremy Greenstock, the former British ambassador to the United Nations, then ambassador to Iraq immediately following the invasion by U.S. forces in 2003, was the head of my security detail. The security team viewed the trip as a routine Task Force engagement in the city, no different from our near-daily engagements throughout Baghdad and every other province of the country.

Crossing the Al Jumariyah Bridge after departing the Green Zone, we turned right onto Abu Nuw'as Street, and parked our vehicles a couple of blocks north of the Palestine Hotel. We walked along the river. The parks that were crowded with families on weekends were quiet on that early Monday afternoon.

As we drove down Abu Nuw'as Street toward the Babylon Hotel, Matt and I marveled at the transformation of the area since we had first toured it with Multi-National Division–Baghdad soldiers in 2006. At that time it had been a true war zone, the streets had been empty, and buildings were in complete disrepair. The buildings still needed work, but every shop was open, and the restaurants along the river were clearly thriving. It was a great day to be in Baghdad.

We arrived at the Babylon Hotel, passed through a guard gate for vehicles manned by private security personnel, parked, and entered the hotel. It had undergone a major cleanup, and its first-floor shopping plaza was full of small stores selling clothing, souvenirs, and other wares. While Chadderton went off to see if the hotel manager could see us, we strolled from shop to shop, buying a few items. Stopping in one store, we noticed an Iraqi national soccer team jersey for sale. Eric and I each wanted one for our kids, but only one was in the correct size for Eric's young boy. He bought one, and we spoke to a young woman who managed the shop. In broken English, she told us about her business, how it was steadily improving, and how optimistic she felt about the future.

Hotel manager Basim Antoon was pleased to hear we had stopped by and told Chadderton to have us come up to his office. Leaving the shops, we passed through the main lobby of the hotel and climbed its spiraling staircase up to the second floor where the management offices were located. Several staff members greeted us, and Antoon's secretary escorted us into his office. I embraced Antoon with a customary greeting and introduced the rest of the team. We sat and talked at length.

In prior meetings, Antoon was generally a gloomy fellow when it came to discussing affairs in Baghdad. An Iraqi Christian, he lamented how many of Baghdad's Christian community had fled either to Irbil in the Kurdish north of Iraq or out of the country altogether. But today his spirits were high, and he was enthusiastic about my idea of leasing some rooms in the building for companies to use as office and living space. As we shared tea and sweets, Matt and I swapped stories with Antoon about recent struggles and how much things had improved. He was as optimistic as I had ever seen him.

We were happily conversing about business and the improvement in daily Iraqi life when suddenly we heard a sound I had not heard in a long time, the telltale deep resonant booming report of an explosion a few miles away. Matt and I were seated on a couch in Antoon's office to the right of, and perpendicular to, his large desk. Antoon was in a wingback chair facing us, with Eric Clark, Elizabeth LoNigro, and Tanisha Dozier seated in chairs to his left, facing us as well. The couch was immediately in front of a large plate glass window that formed the outside wall of Antoon's second-story office, directly overlooking Abu Nuw'as Street and the large circular driveway entrance to the hotel building. The back of the couch where Matt and I sat next to one another rested against the window. At the report of the explosion, Matt and I looked out the window and could see in the distance to the north of the hotel a cloud of smoke rising. It appeared to be a good three to four miles from us, perhaps in the Karrada neighborhood of Baghdad.

We commented to Antoon that it appeared we had spoken too soon in our statements about how normal life had become in Baghdad. But we were not at all worried at that point. Random sporadic car bombs still took place every few weeks in Baghdad, usually targeting Iraqi government or police facilities. This was no doubt such a case, or perhaps a rocket had been launched at a government building.

There was no cause for us to worry. Chadderton entered the office and informed me that we were fine and that his team was inquiring to determine what had happened, but that there was no reason to depart before finishing our discussion.

A few more minutes passed, as we were now discussing companies that were likely initial possible occupants of any space we might lease. The minor tension that had risen at the sound of the bombing in the distance had faded, and we were relaxed and discussing possibilities, when a strange sound filled the room. To my ears, it was a loud screeching noise—and my mind immediately identified it as the sound of a rocket passing close by. I turned to look out the window, and then began to turn my head back to Antoon, opening my mouth to say that I was hearing a rocket attack.

Before I could utter a sound, the world went black in a rushing roar that consumed us in a split second.

I felt my body lifted into the air, the sensation similar to the feeling of being in the ocean and caught in heavy surf with your feet lifted from under you and your body propelled forward—only at far greater velocity and force. My senses could discern no sound, no vision, other than a horrific blackness and immense rage of noise. I felt my head and body hit hard surfaces, but I felt no pain. I was strangely disassociated from the impact.

I could see nothing. My ears failed me. I could hear nothing, my head pounded, and my thoughts were incoherent. My wits were gone. I could not think. A foul stench filled the air: the unmistakable smell of smoke from cordite explosive was choking off my breath. Gasping for air, I first felt pain as my chest expanded to breathe. I was lying on top of hard irregular surfaces, pipes or boards, with sharp edges pressing against my chest.

My eyes opened, but blackness remained, and water filled my eyes and face. I reached with my hand to wipe the water away, to find it sticky and thick—not water, but blood—my own blood, pouring into my eyes. My wits started to return as I thought of my wife and my children. How badly was I hurt? Would I ever see them again?

Furniture had become sticks and pipe and broken glass and metal. Matt had been sitting next to me. *Where is he? Where is Eric? Where is Elizabeth? Where is Tanisha?* I heard the shrieking of women outside the office. Wailing of women followed. The foul smoke began to fade, and as I wiped blood from my eyes I started to see. John Chadderton called from the doorway: "Sir, please stay where you are, I promise you I will get you out of here and I will get you all to safety."

Elizabeth LoNigro came to my side as I struggled to my feet. Dazed, with a large laceration on her leg, she pulled a scarf from her neck and began to help wipe the blood from my eyes and face.

The ceiling was gone, its tiles and supports hanging randomly about us, electrical wires and the tangle of broken furniture blocking our path to any exit. I saw Eric and Matt as we moved carefully toward the door. Tanisha was up and moving as well, but Antoon was nowhere in sight.

We make our way down the spiraling grand stairwell, now wreathed in foul smoke and covered in rubble, following Chadderton and gaining a little more distance from the front of the building. Bodies were randomly scattered, some bloodied with wounds, several motionless and clearly dead. The shops that lined the front of the hotel where we had shopped minutes earlier, their windows facing the driveway, had been obliterated. The small shop where we bought the soccer jersey minutes earlier was now rubble and twisted metal. The body of the young woman lay in its midst.

The wailing of the survivors rose in volume.

Adrenaline coursed through my veins as our situation became clear. A few weeks earlier, the car bombing of an Indian government building in Kabul, Afghanistan, was immediately followed by an attacking truck full of militants who shot many of the survivors. Was such a follow-up attack now imminent? I raised this possibility to Chadderton, as he led us to the rear exit of the hotel, facing the Tigris River. The American Embassy stood across the river in the distance. Our security team formed a perimeter, their assault rifles at the ready, as we waited outside and recovered our senses. Looking at one another, we did not speak.

Sirens approached as emergency vehicles entered the hotel compound. We slowly moved as a group along the back of the hotel compound to the parking lot, where our vehicles were located and running, ready to depart as soon as we loaded up.

Everyone needed medical treatment. The concussive impact of the explosion was unimaginably violent. Had we been unconscious?

Chadderton then informed me that we could not leave. The Iraqi police had blocked every roadway as a result of the bombings, and no traffic was permitted to pass on any city streets. Until the roads were opened, we would have to stay put.

As we sat, not knowing yet what exactly had happened, we sank into shock over what we had just experienced.

After an hour had passed, Chadderton returned to the vehicle and explained what had happened. The screeching sound we had heard was not a rocket. It was the screeching of tires on an automobile loaded with explosives as it raced into the exit of the hotel driveway and rushed toward the building, flipping upside down directly beneath Antoon's office before detonating. Matt and I had been only a hundred feet away from the car bomb. Three hotels had been hit within minutes of each other, first the Sheraton as we had heard, and then the Meridian followed the Babylon.[1] It was a carefully coordinated attack that would have taken days of planning to execute. After three and a half years of work in the "red zone," during the worst of the violence the country had experienced, our luck had finally run out. We were simply in the wrong place at the wrong time.

As the second hour of waiting passed, there was no indication of how long it would be before we could leave and seek medical attention. We had attracted attention along the street, where a crowd had formed to watch the emergency crews and the aftermath of the attack, as our SUVs were sequestered in a far corner of the parking lot and our security team was maintaining an armed perimeter. We needed to get out of there.

Our security team medic continued to check vital signs for each of us, and to check our wounds. After two hours, the bleeding had mostly subsided, and Matt and I carefully returned to the rear of the hotel to find a restroom with some water to wash the caked, dried blood away from our faces, arms, and hands. Looking in a full mirror for the first time, I was shocked at how I appeared.

I told Chadderton before we exited the building that I wanted no cameras, no cell-phone photos, or pictures of any kind. The last thing we needed was photographs of my team and me covered in blood circulating on the Internet.

After two and a half hours had passed, we were finally permitted to leave. Driving south on Abu Nuw'as Street, we crossed the Jadriya Bridge near Baghdad University then quickly reentered the Green Zone, where we sped to the Combat Support Hospital.

As we entered the facility, uniformed medical personnel looked at us in shock. We looked bad—our clothing was ripped and covered in blood, and any exposed skin was covered with cuts and emerging bruises as well as larger wounds. Asking what had happened, the medical staffers were bewildered. Newly deployed, they had never heard of our mission and had no idea that there were hundreds of American civilians working throughout Iraq. They could not understand why we had been "outside the wire."

For the next several hours, wounds were x-rayed, cleaned, and stitched. We refused offers to stay overnight—our quarters weren't far away, and we just wanted to get back to our own "home" away from home. A strange sense of euphoria at having survived set in as we drove back to our compound.

✳   ✳

As we sat down that night together and the shock of the day began to affect us, we were confronted with another reality: a large South Korean business delegation led by General Chang had arrived that evening in Kuwait and was departing for Baghdad that night. We had worked hard to put their visit together and to set up a busy itinerary for them. Our security team was already en route to Baghdad Airport to pick them up. The following morning I was supposed to take them to meet with General Odierno at 0800, followed by a full day of meetings with Iraqi officials.

Sonja Stephens was a street-smart Brooklyn native who had been my first employee in the Pentagon business transformation office back in 2004. She was fluent in Korean, was traveling with the Korean delegation, and was with them in Kuwait.

She advised me that it was too late to call them off without causing a major issue in Kuwait, and we did not want news to get out that we had been in the bombing. As phones rang, I downplayed to the staff in Washington what had happened, and Eric Clark issued strict instructions to our press relations team to keep the incident out of the media.

Media attention would have done grave damage to our mission of drawing international businesses to Iraq. Our work had always been dangerous, far more dangerous in earlier years when we worked in the open during periods of violence throughout the country. The Babylon Hotel incident had been the result of our work to scope out new potential locations for operations. No international company representatives were present. It was one thing to call the Task Force a red-zone operation, a team of civilian business leaders willing to operate in harms' way. Now we were being put to the test; we had just experienced the violence that we had always said we were willing to risk. How we reacted to that violence would speak volumes about the sincerity of our mission. If we walked away, our words would have been cheap.

I informed Secretary Gates's Chief of Staff Robert Rangel back in D.C. that we were okay, and received a short note in response.

I decided to allow the Korean delegation to proceed. When the Koreans arrived late that night, they looked at us in shock, but never wavered in their intention to stay and continue their engagement and negotiations over business investments with the Iraqi government.

Matt insisted on joining me the following morning as we drove the group from Baghdad down to General Odierno's headquarters at Camp Victory. Entering his office wing at Al Faw Palace, his senior staff gaped at us. Matt and I looked like hell. By now, our head injuries included many large contusions and bruises, mine plainly evident on my shaved head. Matt's condition was worse than my own, with a large deep cut to his forehead that had required several stitches to close. We were groggy and tired, and had pounded down Advil that morning to alleviate the aching of impact. My arm throbbed, and my entire side was now turning purple from the impact of the force of the blast.

But our role was simply to introduce the Koreans and then let Odierno do his thing. As much as I just wanted to go away and find a quiet place to rest, surely I could get through that. General Chang and General Odierno had met once before in an earlier visit, and they had the affinity common to senior commanders who had seen combat. After an hour of discussion of new Korean investment proposals and of the security situation throughout the country, the delegation left as Odierno asked me to remain behind.

I sat again, as he looked at me directly and asked if I was okay.

After I assured him I would be fine once I had a few days to recover, he told me he would have to keep a closer eye on my team. I reminded him that our mission was formed with the understanding we were operating at risk. I had no intention of giving up. Odierno was a great leader, and a great man, and while our mission was not always in his natural comfort zone as a commander, he had never failed to provide support for us, or to advocate for the criticality of our work with leaders in Washington. We weren't going to let him down by walking away from our mission.

That afternoon, I escorted the delegation to a meeting with recently appointed U.S. Ambassador Christopher Hill, who was thrilled to meet with South Koreans. He was still getting to know Iraq, but as a seasoned veteran diplomat with vast experience in east Asia, he was perfect with the Korean delegation. He looked stunned at my appearance and did not know quite what to say beyond letting me know that they had been monitoring the situation remotely while we were stuck at the hotel parking lot, and to express his relief that we appeared to be all right.

Before the Korean delegation departed, major agreements were signed with the Government of Iraq to make multibillion-dollar investments in the revitalization of industrial operations in southern Iraq. Their visit was a resounding success and led to plans for an Iraqi delegation to visit Seoul to discuss economic partnership between Iraq and South Korea, an agreement that was signed several months later.

*　　*

Almost daily, somewhere in the world, bombs are detonated by zealots seeking to make some political or religious point. As citizens we have grown numb to reports of such violence, which have become lost in the endless scroll of 24/7 coverage of events large and small, the trivial and the severe. But no words can express the abject horror of being subjected to that unexpected violence. I will never hear of a bombing again without feeling a quake within, an echo of that blast that ripped through our gathering with a friend in Baghdad on a beautiful January day.

And no matter how hard I try, I will never forget meeting the optimistic young woman keeping her shop during the last minutes of her life, the images of death and broken bodies strewn around us, or the haunting song of sirens and wailing playing on and on and on.

13.

UPON FURTHER REVIEW

There had been a steady degradation in decorum among Iraqi government ministers through 2009 and early in 2010. As political parties assembled their candidate lists and campaigning began, Iraqi leaders immersed themselves in the rough-and-tumble of electoral politicking. The weekly dinners we had hosted from 2008 through 2009 in which cabinet ministers from various parties would gather at the Task Force's home in Baghdad were over. Now meetings could only take place with individual ministers, all passionately attacking the positions of their colleagues from other parties.

Elections took place in March 2010 as planned. My thought at the time was that TFBSO had a natural "end date" in Iraq corresponding to the end of the period covered by the Status of Forces Agreement signed by the Bush Administration that permitted the U.S. military to maintain its presence until the end of 2011.[1] In spite of the expected sporadic violence during the election campaign, there was every reason to expect our momentum to build again once a new government was in place.

After the ballots were counted, Ayad Allawi led a secular list of candidates that had received the largest number of seats in the Parliament. A Shiite, he was secular in his orientation to governing, and his coalition had received broad backing from Sunni leaders throughout northern and western Iraq. I was hopeful that he would establish himself as a unifying figure within Iraq. But rather than travel to southern Iraq to reach out to the supporters of secondary Shia parties and build a coalition, Allawi boarded flights to Saudi Arabia and Turkey for meetings with his campaign financiers and supporters in those countries. This had a chilling effect on public perceptions of Allawi in southern Iraq. Finishing second in the balloting, incumbent Prime Minister Nouri al-Maliki, in turn, traveled to Tehran. Each faction, rather than reach out "across the aisle" to forge unity, instead sought support from its regional backers.[2]

It is difficult, without spending extended time in southern Iraq, to understand fully the deeply ingrained siege mentality of Iraq's Shia population. For generations, they have been the subjugated class of Mesopotamia and of the Arab World. In 1916, prior to the end of World War I, but in anticipation of the fall of the Ottoman Empire, British, French, and Russian diplomats negotiated a partition of the Arab regions of Syria, Mesopotamia, and Palestine. This partition, known as the Sykes-Picot Agreement, paid little attention to the cultural or ethnic considerations of the local populations. Immediately following the end of the war, commitments were made in meetings of the newly established League of Nations promising independence to these Arab regions. France, and then Britain, soon seized direct authority over their respective allocations, drawing the borders of states such as Syria, Iraq, Jordan, Lebanon, and Palestine. Many of the ethnic and sectarian conflicts that plague the region to this day are the result of the misalignment of colonial national borders drawn by the British and French—borders that created states that separated contiguous ethnic and/or religious communities into different nations.[3]

The British established a monarchy in Iraq after the defeat of the Ottomans and placed a Sunni Hashemite king from modern-day Saudi Arabia in power in Baghdad. This was a bizarre, culturally tone-deaf decision that elevated an Arab sultan over an ancient Mesopotamian culture far removed from the culture of the Arabian peninsula. Shia Iraqis were, as a result, subjugated to lower-class status despite being a larger percentage of the Iraqi population. More recently under Saddam Hussein, the Shia were often treated with great brutality. As in other Shia populations in the Arab world, those in southern Iraq have a long memory of the support offered to Saddam Hussein by other Sunni Arab countries.[4]

It has been a colossal strategic blunder from a geopolitical perspective that Saudi Arabia and its neighboring countries on the Persian Gulf have refused to offer any developmental aid or meaningful diplomatic engagement in Iraq since 2003. By leaving a vacuum of regional engagement in Iraq, they have made it easy for Iran to gain influence among ethnic Arab Shiites. Had Saudi Arabia invested in southern Iraq after 2003 and built schools, roads, hospitals, or power plants to help their Arab brothers get on their feet, they could have set back Iranian ambitions and created a great ally.

But they did not. The hostility of Saudi Arabia to Shia-led Iraq has been continual since 2003. Presumably the presence of their own restive Shia minority makes the idea of a Shia Arab leadership in Iraq impossible for Saudi Arabia to accept.

When Ayad Allawi flew to Saudi Arabia following the 2010 elections, the die was cast. Iraq's free and aggressive media widely reported his visits. The Shia of southern Iraq were bombarded by warnings from Iranian-backed sectarian political parties and clerics that Allawi was a tool of the biased Sunni Arab world who would subjugate the Shia again, as Saddam had done, even though Allawi was himself Shia. The Shia political parties, so critical to forming a coalition with Allawi, instead backed away.

And so began the long stall that would cause 2010 to be a lost year in the development of the new Iraq.

For the Iraqi political elite, these negotiations over power and authority were not trivial. There was much to lose. Control of the Ministry of Defense and the Ministry of Interior were highly desired— and viewed with suspicion, as Saddam had abused these organizations as tools of his power. While the U.S. had rebuilt these ministries and the Iraqi military from the ground up, the fear was palpable that a leader would again turn these ministries against the Iraqi people.

Another great prize in these negotiations was the Ministry of Oil. To control the oil ministry was to control the current and future wealth of the country and to wield an incredible instrument of influence and control over Iraq's development. In 2009, after years of negotiations, the Ministry of Oil had finally signed the first agreements for the redevelopment of Iraq's largest oil fields—its "super giant" fields. These fields, each with proven reserves in excess of five billion barrels of petroleum, were offered to international oil companies for development through a competitive bidding process.

In open price competition with state-owned firms from nations seeking to secure access to reserves for future strategic energy requirements, the amount of profit for private Western companies collapsed, with the prices per barrel of increased oil production fixed at levels as low as two dollars or less. Such low prices created profit margins for American firms far, far lower than their shareholders would normally expect, causing most American companies to eventually walk away from the negotiations. It is no small irony that many of the largest oil contracts in Iraq's first bidding round signed in 2009 went to national oil companies from countries that actively opposed the American action to remove Saddam from power. But that was exactly the situation.

When the negotiations were completed, the results were sobering for Western interests. While some Western firms acquired rights to develop major fields such as the giant West Qurna and Ramallah fields of Basra, most of the largest contracts went to state-owned firms such as China National Petroleum Company, Korea Gas, Lukoil of Russia, and PETRONAS of Malaysia. Only one major American oil company was awarded a super-giant field—ExxonMobil. In spite of the hundreds of billions of dollars spent deposing Saddam and securing Iraq, American oil companies largely were closed out of the most expansive oil-development contracts ever awarded.[5]

Had the Iraqi Government been moderately more flexible in negotiations, and negotiated agreements sooner, Iraq in 2009 and 2010 could have been in the midst of an economic boom—with billions of dollars being invested in oil development and secondary and tertiary benefits of that investment accruing throughout the Iraqi economy.

That did not happen. So in 2010, as the Iraqi political system was frozen in gridlock while political parties attempted to form a governing coalition, the Iraqi economy stalled. Oil contracts signed in 2009 did not lead to immediate development of the fields, as the necessary "next-step" agreements on transport of equipment, authorization to begin specific projects, and other activities were on hold.

As the political wrangling continued, the control of oil wealth was a key element of the debate. The core of the issue was geological: the proven oil reserves of Iraq, discovered decades earlier, were almost exclusively located in the Shia and Kurdish territories of the country. The Sunni north and west of the country were largely left out. With increasing sectarian suspicions among all factions, the concern that oil wealth would be unfairly distributed to the Sunni created a great amount of distrust, complicating political negotiations.

In spite of the political uncertainties, TFBSO continued to host investors seeking to gain an early foothold in Iraq in anticipation of an inevitable oil-driven economic expansion. In the absence of a national government, we focused these investors on the investment commissions in the provinces, organizations that were responsible for promoting investment at the provincial level and that TFBSO had actively supported with technical and financial staff in most of the provincial capitals. Authorized under recently established Iraqi investment law to approve investments up to $250 million, we now began exercising the provincial commissions as progress in Baghdad ground to a halt.

As this provincial focus increased, troubling signs became clear. Most investors wanted to visit Basra. A few were interested in real estate development in the holy cities of Najaf and Karbala, where continual religious tourism drawing millions of visitors throughout the year made these cities ideal for hotel and commercial construction. Some were interested in Baghdad, given its immense population of potential consumers. But most firms were seeking to get operations established in the Kurdish north or the Shia south where the oil boom was expected shortly to get underway. Almost none were interested in the west of the country.

I grew increasingly concerned about this trend. It was not hard to envision Iraq a few years hence with a bustling economy in the Shia and Kurdish areas driven by oil field development, while the most-militant Sunni areas of the north and west fell further and further behind economically. Such a situation would create the perfect climate for civil unrest and destabilization.

A meeting with our friends at the United States Geological Survey offered a potential solution. TFBSO was serving to facilitate the reengagement of USGS in Iraq, to evaluate water resources, and to partner with the Iraqi Geological Survey on technical assessment of mineral resources. Through USGS, the Task Force was introduced to oil-industry exploration experts with decades of experience working on surveys of the fields of northern Saudi Arabia. In meetings with these experts, we were told of large geological structures that extended well into western Iraq that may hold vast reserves of petroleum. As there had never been proper seismic surveys of western Iraq, there was no way to validate these projections. A survey initiative could serve to clarify if such reserves existed or not.

We developed a proposal based on this information, calling for the allocation of funding for initial seismic survey work in Anbar Province. The goal was to determine if significant oil reserves were present. If such reserves existed, it would provide the Sunni population with equal footing economically, and reduce a great deal of the tension present in the Iraqi political system. If a survey showed that no reserves were present, then we proposed an alternative economic-development strategy focused on aggressive agricultural development and assistance in the Euphrates Valley to the Syrian border, with the hope of someday creating an economic corridor to the Mediterranean if Syria one day liberalized its political system.[6]

This proposal was written, reviewed by USGS, and then widely distributed. But the funding was denied. The U.S. was spending billions of dollars in Iraq, but the administration refused to allow any direct engagement in the oil sector. There was no way that the Minister of Oil Hussein Shahrastani would approve Iraqi funding to performing exploration in the west of Iraq in the next several years. Without it, there was no ability to draw investment.

It was one more example of the futility of American engagement in the most important sector of the Iraqi economy. Other examples abounded. Among the most frustrating was the mindless flaring of natural gas off the oil wells of southern Iraq. For decades, since the first exploratory wells had been drilled by British oil companies in the 1950s, Iraqi oil fields had flared, or burned, the associated natural gas that was present in the oil fields that would emerge when oil was pumped from the ground. This flaring, a once-common practice that has declined dramatically in the past twenty years, wastes valuable energy and releases a large amount of pollutants into the atmosphere. As the oil fields in

Basra and the surrounding provinces expanded, the number of gas flares (essentially tall pipes that release the natural gas from the wells, with fiery plumes at the top of the pipe high in the air) increased.

Flying into Basra at night for the first time in a Blackhawk helicopter in 2007, the entire horizon for mile after mile was ablaze with orange flame from the gas flares. International oil companies were eager to capture the valuable natural gas, which could be used to power electrical turbines and assist in the resolution of the embarrassing lack of electrical power throughout the country. The financial impact was compelling. Literally millions of dollars' worth of natural gas were being burned every day. But the Oil Ministry refused to award contracts in spite of multiple proposals. Only in 2011 did a contract finally get awarded, to Royal Dutch Shell, to capture flared gas for the southern oil fields.

What was little recognized throughout this period was the terrible impact that flaring of gas was having on the health of the population of southern Iraq. Southern Iraq has some of the highest incidence rates of pediatric cancer in the world, with the cancer largely attributed to the inhalation of hydrocarbon compounds released by gas flares. The Task Force lobbied continually for consideration of proposals to capture the gas, as a human health imperative, to no avail. The Bush Administration was adamant in its "hands-off" stance with regard to the oil sector. Other than legal advisors working within the State Department, and a diplomatic effort to resolve outstanding legal framework disputes over sharing of oil revenue, there was no tactical effort permitted to drive rapid development of the oil sector in Iraq.[7]

When the Obama Administration took office, we adopted a different tack. Given the administration focus on carbon-based global warming, we provided statistics showing how the flaring of gas in southern Iraq was releasing more carbon than all of the motor vehicles in New England combined. Clearly if the reduction of carbon was a priority for the new administration, the U.S. should be pressing Iraq to cap the gas flares and capture the wasted natural gas. Using the natural gas to generate electricity would gradually eliminate the widespread use of diesel generators in the country for backup power, further reducing carbon production.

Again, as in the Bush Administration, the tactical issues involving the oil and gas sector were not given any priority. While American advisors continued to lobby the Iraqi government to resolve its legal framework for hydrocarbon development, no development proposals were put forth sponsored by the U.S. government, no incentives to accelerate the capture of flared gas were put in place, nothing. For a fraction of the monthly cost of military operations and development aid consultants in Baghdad, a focused effort could have cleaned the air of southern Iraq, reduced cancer among the children, and started the process of increasing electrical generation using a cleaner source of energy than diesel. It was a form of insanity: for the fear of reinforcing widely held public opinion about why the U.S. went to war, an economic, health, and environmental catastrophe was allowed to continue for almost a decade.

*   *

For TFBSO, the good news that helped offset the frustration with the lack of progress in key ministries was the near-weekly launch of completed projects that had been funded by Congress in 2008 and 2009. With factories reopening and production lines being installed, every city we visited greeted us warmly and showed true appreciation for the work we had done to restore operations in once-idled factories. As factories were coming online, local businesses grew more active, further stimulating employment and economic activity. Investors now visiting Iraq no longer were shown scenes of empty streets and military personnel on every corner, but now saw bustling streets and reemerging commerce.

Regina Dubey performed phenomenally during 2010 to keep the industrial projects on track to completion. She also spearheaded several additional important initiatives, expanding our greenhouse distribution program in every province of Iraq, and, in a program she initiated, deployed deep-well drilling equipment to the tribal regions of far western Anbar Province, enabling water irrigation for farmers to increase dramatically agricultural production in an area of extreme arid desert. Eric Clark successfully facilitated the first Western private business investments in asphalt production and construction materials in Anbar Province by a Canadian American investment consortium led by an Iraqi American family originally from Baghdad.

In Maysan Province, Gerry Brown and a bright young team leader, Noah Buntman, led the restoration of sugar processing at the old sugar refinery near Al Amarah, the provincial capital. In spite of the mass of semiromantic literature written about the restoration of the marshes and the rebirth of "marsh Arab" culture since 2003, little had been done in Maysan Province to restore economic life to this most downtrodden region of the country. Iraq had emerged in recent years as the world's largest importer of refined sugar, in spite of the presence of ample marshland suitable for sugar cultivation. As its sugar refineries in Maysan and Mosul were state-owned, they had fallen out of use after 2003 along with almost all other Iraqi factories. Ironically, much of the sugar now imported to Iraq was being produced in a state-owned factory in Iran, fewer than 100 kilometers across the border from the idled Al Maysan sugar factory.

Brown and Buntman worked to acquire parts and equipment to restore the factory to operation. They then invited international sugar industry leaders to Iraq, to limited response. At last a Brazilian delegation visited Al Maysan to meet their Iraqi counterparts. It was another example of "business-diplomacy" on the part of TFBSO, as this represented the first meaningful business engagement between Brazil and Iraq, facilitated by an American economic-development team.

The project also served as another example of collaboration with a Provincial Reconstruction Team. Led by Anne Callaghan, the PRT facilitated the engagement by TFBSO, and later described the restarting of the factory as a highlight of the PRT engagement in Maysan, as it energized the entire community to see the factory operational again—a symbol that, after almost a decade, life was returning to normal.

Another new member of our senior leadership team finally made breakthrough headway getting technology companies engaged in Baghdad. Dr. Stanley Lumish—a seasoned executive, Bell Labs Fellow, and former colleague from my days at JDS Uniphase—now led our information technology–sector team that David Scantling had established years earlier. While simultaneously kicking off our tech-sector efforts in Afghanistan, Lumish persuaded Microsoft to establish a technical-training center and new supply relationships in Baghdad. He also, with Eric Clark, facilitated the engagement of Google in Iraq, leading to the launch of an Iraqi version of the Google search engine, google.iq. These widely publicized steps helped us further accelerate the improving perception of Iraq as a place for international business engagement, even during the postelection gap in national leadership during 2010.

That same year, the relationship with the Baghdad Embassy had not been improving for TFBSO. The supportive relationship with Ambassador Crocker had been replaced by the less-engaged Christopher Hill. The latest rotation of appointed leaders assigned to work on economic development were rigidly ideological, and now were again criticizing TFBSO initiatives—in spite of the high regard in which we were held in Washington and in all other U.S. agencies working in Iraq. On one occasion I found myself meeting with embassy staffers assigned to administer PRTs, several of whom who launched into a tirade about our work to restart state-owned industries and rehashing our apparent "socialist" leanings. I found this remarkable. Even in an Obama Administration, we were still confronting bureaucrat ideologues who had never worked in the private sector, and who were advocating shock-therapy principals of economic development. Some of these staffers had recently been criticizing Iraqi leaders over our transitional privatization effort that, while stalled over the lack of a new government, had restored normal life to the Iraqi industrial sector.

I pointed out that they might consider how completely hypocritical these criticisms appeared to Iraqis. In the face of economic hardship far-less threatening than Iraq faced every day, America had recently taken over General Motors, Chrysler, the Bank of America, AIG, and a number of other blue-chip companies, all of which were now essentially "state-owned enterprises." To criticize Iraq over its policy of careful transitional privatization when America was quick to nationalize industries to save its economy from a spike in unemployment was absurd.

It was an example of another unfortunate aspect of American foreign policy in practice. Even when an administration, regardless of the party in power, has a clear policy, there is too often little sense of alignment among the career staffers placed overseas. TFBSO had done more than anyone else to stimulate the private sector in Iraq, and had facilitated billions of dollars in contracts to international companies, and billions in foreign investment in Iraqi industry. But still, even among career foreign aid staff members, we were being painted as socialists within the State Department.

The discussion demonstrated that nothing had really changed since our first difficulties in 2006. It wasn't about "socialism," or economic points of view, or anything other than effectiveness. We were clearly and widely renowned in Iraq by 2010 for being effective and for making a difference. The people who were working within the embassy compound were seething with frustration over their inability to engage, even within the Green Zone, while we worked freely throughout the country. For that contrast, we were resented and subjected to the petty torment of bureaucratic sniping over socialism, lack of "coordination," and other inanities.

✳ ✳

As we rolled up our quarterly project reviews and I surveyed the impacts of TFBSO on Iraq since its inception, there were literally hundreds of initiatives that had been delivered to improve every province of the country. As of 2010, we had facilitated more than $5 billion in signed agreements for foreign investments in Iraqi businesses by American, European, and Asian companies. More than $5 billion more had been submitted and were now stalled in review at the national level while debate continued over a new government. More than 5,000 private Iraqi businesses had received direct stimulus from U.S. contracts since the inception of TFBSO support to Major General Darryl Scott at Joint Contracting Command. Our Procurement Assistance Center (PAC) had directly supported the transparent execution of more than $10 billion in contracts by the Iraqi government.

McKinsey & Co. studied our economic impact and the secondary and tertiary effects of the factory-restoration program, and estimated that as many as 350,000 Iraqis were now employed because of the reversal of the original policy on state-owned enterprises. Adding to the results on foreign investment, the stimulus of private Iraqi businesses using Iraqis first, as well as the agricultural-development programs including greenhouse distribution, and it was clear that TFBSO had played a major role in restoring economic activity throughout Iraq.

By the end of 2009, there was no credible argument left against our mission—and our services were in increasing demand. Now that we were underway in Pakistan, I was developing a close relationship with Richard Holbrooke, the president's Special Representative for Afghanistan and Pakistan (SRAP), who was proving to be a crucial supporter of our work in the absence of viable civilian alternatives within the State Department.

We had the right organization with the right approach at a critical moment to make a significant positive effect far beyond Iraq. If we could successfully deliver what we were capable of, the benefit to American security and the way in which our nation is perceived in the Islamic world, could be altered for the better for years to come.

As we returned home from Kabul via Dubai and were waiting at Dubai Terminal 1 for our regular flight on United Flight 977, I received a message to call my Chief of Staff Rebekka Bonner right away. It seemed we had a problem.

As part of our annual budget allocation process, like every other organization operating in the CENTCOM Area of Responsibility, we had to review our detailed program spending and projected operating costs with the U.S. Army CENTCOM (ARCENT) Comptrollers (C8) who oversee financial management.

Fundamentally this is no different than a financial review within a company, albeit with far more arcane processes and paperwork required. For more than four years, we had sent staff members to Kuwait to review our financials and to get funds transferred to our accounts for execution of our work.

As our work was well known in CENTCOM, having the direct sponsorship of the CENTCOM Commander General Petraeus, as well as the commanders for Multi-National Force–Iraq General Odierno and the commander for International Security Assistance Force–Afghanistan General McChrystal, this was mostly a formality, a healthy review of good program management and project plans by specific TFBSO program managers and administrative staff.

This time, however, something was amiss.

A financial attorney within the ARCENT Judge Advocate General organization in Kuwait had reviewed our budget documentation, as had been done for four years. As always, all was in order. But before approving it, this young attorney had fired off an e-mail to the Office of the General Counsel for Secretary Gates at the Pentagon, seeking approval.

This was unexpected and highly unusual. As our work had been underway for years and been reviewed by attorneys at ARCENT many times before, it was unusual to seek a legal review at a higher level, especially all the way to the Office of the Secretary of Defense (OSD). There are several tiers of attorneys between OSD and ARCENT lawyers deployed forward in Kuwait.

The OSD Office of General Counsel (OGC) responded to ARCENT by denying legal approval for our mission. Specifically, the lead fiscal attorney within OGC stated that our mission was a violation of the legal authorities of the Department of Defense, as it was in fact not a military mission but a foreign assistance mission, and as such should be done by the Department of State. To use funds appropriated to the Defense Department for military requirements in the CENTCOM Area of Responsibility would violate federal law. He imposed a freeze on funding for all of our activities immediately.

On hearing this news while in Dubai airport, I was livid. Secretary Gates had issued direction for our work to be expanded to Afghanistan in support of General McChrystal. General Petraeus and the U.S. Embassy in Islamabad had requested our engagement in Pakistan. The OGC had reviewed Secretary Gates's memorandum authorizing our work. How could it now be ruled a violation of Defense Department authority under the law? How was this possible?

I didn't sleep much on the fourteen-hour flight home.

Looking into this, I soon learned something else: the newly appointed lead fiscal attorney for the Department of Defense was the former General Counsel for the Coalition Provisional Authority. The former lead attorney for the CPA had, as one of his first acts in his newly appointed role, ruled our mission—which had worked for four years to clean up the economic disaster in Iraq that began under CPA—an illegal misapplication of appropriated funds.

At the moment when we were supposed to be focusing on accelerating an approved plan to build a viable economy for Afghanistan, we were suddenly consumed with legalese, with fear for personal liability risks if members of our teams were injured or worse, killed. While Holbrooke and Secretary of State Hillary Clinton were publicly emphasizing the criticality of a "civilian surge" to complement the military surge in Afghanistan, the only team actually fielding numbers of civilian experts into the country was being stalled by the former CPA lead attorney.

By the following morning, Secretary Gates demanded quick resolution of this issue by the Undersecretary of Defense for Finance, Comptroller Robert Hale, who stated he would get it resolved immediately. Sitting down with Hale, he asked that I bring him up to speed on the problem. After I finished reviewing the situation, it became clear this wouldn't be quickly resolved. Hale was taking the ruling by the fiscal attorney at face value. There was no effort to push back, to demand better legal justification. His proposed solution was to use CERP funds: "Commanders Emergency Response Program" funding appropriated for use by lower-level commanders in the field to do quick impact projects to build rapport with local leaders.[8]

CERP had a long history in the Department since the early days of the Iraq War. As it became clear that our troops needed a tool other than military operations to stabilize local communities, Congress had appropriated funds for use by local commanders in the field. Initially envisioned for use in small projects, less than $250,000, CERP appropriations had increased drastically over the years. Now exceeding $1 billion annually, the Department was undertaking larger and larger projects using CERP—to the consternation of Congress. Generally, the larger the project, the less successful the result.[9]

I asked how it was possible to use local commander funds authorized by Congress for small local projects for our mission, and how that could be viewed as more legally sound than the original approach of just using normal defense-budgeted funds for normal operations. Hale had no answer, but reassured me not to worry, that the Department would use CERP to bridge our work expenses until the fall budget could be passed, at which time Congress would be asked specifically to appropriate funding for our work.

I knew from prior hearings and briefings on the Hill that this approach was going to cause major problems.

I explained to Hale that as much as 50 percent of our total budget was to execute programs that were clearly and incontrovertibly Departmental business. Specifically, our work to automate Department payments using local private banks was clearly not foreign assistance. Our work involved in military contracting under Iraqi First and Afghan

First programs, to review contractors and ensure host-nation businesses were capable of delivering to DOD specifications were also clearly not foreign assistance programs. There were many other examples. Yet the attorneys had made a blanket ruling about our entire mission. Had the attorneys even reviewed our specific program spending?

It is an unfortunate fact of our current national security structure that the legal framework that defines the roles and responsibilities of the Departments of State and Defense is no longer relevant. In conflicts like Iraq or Afghanistan, the lines between strictly military operations or strictly foreign assistance operations are completely blurred. The entire principal of postconflict stabilization is built on the notion of seamless interplay between and among the establishment of security, the restoration of basic infrastructure and governance, and the rapid economic improvement to undermine local sympathy with violent insurgent actors.

There are literally dozens, perhaps hundreds, of activities undertaken in the field in Iraq and Afghanistan by the military that do not fit the classic definition of military operations, but are instrumental to establishing security and keeping our troops from harm.

The interpretation provided by the fiscal lawyer, however, was rigid. Citing case law from 1984, when the Department of Defense built a hospital using Defense-appropriated funds in Honduras following a disaster-relief mission, the attorneys stated that our work was strictly forbidden. The notion that three-decade-old Cold War case law would form the legal foundation for how the military applies its assets in a twenty-first-century counterinsurgency campaign was a sign of how poorly aligned our national support structure was to the needs of modern defense challenges.[10]

Had this ruling been part of a broad assessment by a newly appointed fiscal lawyer of DOD activities writ large that too closely "walked the line" between military operations and foreign assistance, it might have been understandable. But that was not the case—our mission was specifically targeted for this ruling.

That sense of being singled out for special attention was reinforced later that week. Hale called for an immediate review of our program spending to get clarity on the elements that I had explained were well within the legal authority of the Department, specifically the Afghan

First contracting program, communications sector programs, and the automated banking program.

The funding for those programs was eventually restored, but for the rest, our choice was now clear. We had to use either CERP or find Congressional relief. I was convinced that using CERP for our mission would trigger great anger in Congress, especially in the House, and that we would pay a heavy price for this down the road. To his great credit, Hale began using all means necessary to get relief from Congress. Working with the Assistant Secretary for Legislative Affairs, Liz King, Hale directly lobbied for our mission to get TFBSO legal authority into the annual defense supplemental budget submission now in final review.

Hale also made clear something very troubling. No matter what happened on the Hill, our work in Pakistan was done; we were not to return to Pakistan. I explained that this work had been initiated at the request of CENTCOM and was sponsored by the Ambassador in Islamabad, to no avail. I had just held a press conference in Lahore with the Governor of Punjab Province, Salman Taseer, announcing the launch of our programs in that critical place. Now we were being shut down before we ever got started.[11]

I was about to become what I hated most: an American who promised something big and delivered nothing, in a place that could ill-afford such mistakes.

✳   ✳

While fighting in Washington for two weeks every month to get funding to sustain our buildup of staff, my other time was spent working throughout Afghanistan, trying to get as much done as soon as possible.

As we began our efforts in Afghanistan, Matt Schoeffling had met and subsequently introduced me to a person who would rapidly accelerate our work. Milt Bearden was a living legend within the intelligence community, known for a number of remarkable career accomplishments working at the epicenter of major historical events over the past several decades. He ran the Afghanistan field operations for the Central Intelligence Agency during the famous "Charlie Wilson's War" era of the 1980s, when U.S. support to the Afghan insurgency led to eventual Soviet defeat, contributing to the end of the Cold War. He subsequently ran CIA operations in East Germany during the fall of the Iron Curtain. When it came to Afghanistan and knowledge of its tribes and regions, there was no one better able to help TFBSO than Bearden. After a few meetings, he joined our team as a senior advisor.

Bearden spent many hours with Matt and me, explaining the region, its recent history, its tribal complexity, and the current situation. It was as if we had gained access to an encyclopedia of cultural and geopolitical knowledge—knowledge that was invaluable as we considered various strategies for developing the Afghan economy. Through his work with us, many ideas were purged, and many others were refined in a way that made them not only feasible, but quickly achievable.

With the help of Bearden, and a very low-profile security team consisting of senior former Army Special Forces personnel with long experience in Afghanistan, Matt Schoeffling had established operations in Kabul, Mazar-e-Sharif, Herat, Helmand, and Jalalabad. We were in the process of getting a base set up in the city limits of Kandahar when the funding crisis erupted, putting those plans on hold—something we found very upsetting but could do nothing about.

By June, we had just fewer than 100 people in country, broken into three principal focus areas: quick-win light-industrial development and expansion projects to demonstrate immediate progress to local communities, medium-term "artisanal" mining and energy-sector development initiatives to build investor confidence in these new sectors and long-term mineral and hydrocarbon natural resource development.

In Kabul, in addition to an operational location near the headquarters of ISAF as well as the U.S. Embassy, we established a headquarters site. This location was far from the rest of the international community, in an old neighborhood surrounding the former royal palace at Darul Aman. Acquiring two adjacent houses, we outfitted them with the necessary communications gear and a very small Afghan security team. One building was set up as a guesthouse for visiting company representatives, the other for our senior leadership. In Baghdad, our guesthouse and headquarters site was a frequent location for visiting U.S., international, and Iraqi officials for meals, meetings, and ceremonies. In Kabul, we kept our profile much lower. Meetings and meals were held at local restaurants or hotels. Our operation was as low profile as it could have been, and we steadfastly refused to discuss its location with anyone, American or otherwise.

We had greater confidence in our own ability to keep ourselves safe than we were willing to place in ISAF, whose forces were largely far removed from Kabul. Our security staff struck up "quick-reaction" agreements with local American Special Forces teams operating at bases not far from our headquarters, but we were under no illusions. If our location became known to the wrong people, it would be an ideal target for Taliban attack, and there would be no reaction "quick" enough to save us. We made arrangements with our neighbors to share information about activity in the area and to provide immediate support if problems occurred. We also struck a deal with a local provider of private helicopter airlift services to extract us in the event there was an outbreak of widespread violence. Surrounded by the mountains and with a view of the regal but broken-down ruins of Darul Aman Palace, I slept better in Darul Aman than I ever did in the "safer" confines of the Green Zone in Baghdad, with its constant threat of rocket attacks.

Our operations in the other cities in Afghanistan were set up in similar fashion. Our goal was to seem unimportant, to avoid the trappings of "official" status that increased the likelihood of being targeted.

Now, however, we were strapped for talent. Our original operating plan required us to get 250 people into the country by the end of summer. We had less than half the number we needed, and with the funding crisis in Washington, we would not be able to finish building our teams until Congress passed legislation granting us a budget. Although we never hired people fast enough to satisfy my frustration with government bureaucracy, we had been ramping up a team in Afghanistan at record speed. Where the other U.S. agencies were struggling to get civilians into Afghanistan, and were largely packing the new "civilian surge" participants into stacked mobile homes jammed into the U.S. Embassy compound, we were placing talented civilians throughout the country at a rapid pace. But now our hiring was stalled.[12]

Gathering the entire organization for a meeting, I explained our situation. Every one of us would have to fill the shoes of people we had not yet hired. From me down to the security staff and cooks, if there was a mission that required manpower, we would all step up to fill the gaps.

This was especially important for our mineral-development team. The first step in this critical program was to complete field surveys of twenty high-priority mineral deposits that we had identified in partnership with the Afghan geological survey. These field surveys required expeditionary work, with helicopter transport into remote backcountry, often at altitudes far above 10,000 feet, and then trekking with heavy equipment into locations where samples could be gathered. We drilled where possible to gauge the depth of deposits, and hundreds of pounds of rock were hauled out for subsequent chemical analysis at accredited laboratories, and then returned to the Afghan Geological Survey for long-term storage.

Minister of Mines Wahidullah Shahrani and his Afghan Geological Survey team were quick to assist with manpower, but they lacked the staff to do this work as well. Our goal had been to complete the assessment of these deposits during the summer, while the weather in the high country permitted expeditions. If the work slipped into the fall, the harsh winters in the Hindu Kush would delay further work for almost a year. For now, all of TFBSO would have to fill the gap in staff; if needed, we all would become field geologists. I told the team that anyone physically able might be called on to assist in mineral survey work.

Potentially world-class deposits of copper, gold, iron, lithium, rare earths, cobalt, and chromite were sampled and analyzed through the summer months. Every member of the team, including all of our senior leadership and me, worked on these missions, carrying heavy gear into the sites along with our Afghan partners and hauling samples out. One trip involved sampling brine from a dry lake bed in the far west of Afghanistan, literally a kilometer from the Iranian border. We drilled through layers of hardened salt that had accumulated over thousands of years, to reach liquid brine where highly valuable lithium and other salts were believed to be concentrated. A Marine Special Forces team airlifted us to and from the site and provided a secure perimeter while the team collected samples. For me, the physical work was a welcome relief from the endless frustrations of Washington and the fight with lawyers over funding our mission.

We successfully set up the Afghan mission by learning from our mistakes in Iraq. Our goal was to get businesses running and to encourage private investors and corporations from outside of Afghanistan to engage in the country either as trading partners or as investors. Wherever possible, we avoided depending on the military. We were part of their mission, and seamlessly integrated into the counterinsurgency strategies of General McChrystal and his senior command, but we avoided living on military bases whenever possible. The goal was to show private companies that they could set up operations in Afghanistan themselves without needing military support. It was a lesson from Iraq we had learned well.

I also approached our relationship with the U.S. Embassy in a different manner than I had in Iraq. While the Iraq mission had been launched in the midst of great conflict between the Defense and State Departments, and our Iraq work was focused on reversing failed policies still pursued by the State Department in 2006, it had become clear that much of the later conflict with the Baghdad Embassy had resulted from a misunderstanding of our work among newly appointed staffers. To avoid this in Afghanistan, I put some of my best leaders in charge of managing the relationship, leaders with proved backgrounds in communications. Barney Gimbel, the former journalist who had a stellar background in public communication, handled the relationship with embassy staff and USAID. Eric Clark handled our relationship with ISAF. They juggled managing these large headquarters relationships with their primary responsibilities of leading major programs and projects in Afghanistan. Their success in relationship management made a big difference. In Baghdad, it seemed we were constantly dealing with conflict over nothing. There was almost no such lost time in Afghanistan. Given how short we were on people, their success in building trust with the headquarters staffs was instrumental in our early success.

We brought our first investor delegation to Afghanistan in February 2010. The invited group was chosen to make an impact, to send a message—mainly to the still-dubious Afghan government—that we were serious in this effort. I met with Afghan leaders continually who were hopeful but skeptical that anything tangible would come from our work. After eight years they had lost a lot of belief that meaningful economic support from the West would ever happen. I made clear that if they did their part and helped us execute the phased strategy we had lain out, that investment would indeed follow. Our first delegation sealed the deal. Howard Buffett, the son of Warren Buffett and future heir to the chairmanship of Berkshire Hathaway, had been introduced to General Petraeus more than a year earlier, who in turn connected him to us. In addition to his passion for farming, Buffett ran the Howard G. Buffett Foundation, which made investments in sustainable agriculture programs, primarily in African countries. He readily accepted my invitation to visit Afghanistan, asking only if he could take along his son, Howard W. Buffett, a rising leader in his own right, who at the time worked at the White House as one of the president's policy advisors.

I also invited Ian Hannam, a force-of-nature investment banker from London whom I had met years before at a ceremony in Baghdad. Hannam ran capital markets for J.P. Morgan in London. Famous for his work to finance and launch some of the world's largest mining companies, Ian was charismatic and patriotic, having served in the British Special Forces early in life. He had a passion for economic development as a way out of violence and hardship and would be a perfect messenger to reinforce our optimism with the Afghan government and business community.

Our first delegation generated excitement in Kabul. Ambassador Eikenberry took the lead in hosting the group, arranging a dinner reception and spending hours offering advice and counsel about the situation in Afghanistan. Having such a stellar group visit clearly boosted the morale at the embassy. General McChrystal greeted the team at ISAF headquarters and provided full support for several of the legs of the engagement, including airlift and security. I was amused at Ian Hannam, normally cocksure and confident, as he reverted to the persona of a young British officer in the presence of McChrystal; the four stars had clearly sapped much of his normal confident swagger.

McChrystal and his staff were also energized by this first group, who met with McChrystal's team both on arrival and at departure, reinforcing our strategy and the potential for our approach to work. Chambers of Commerce meetings in Kabul and Herat and a dedicated trip to Jalalabad were all part of the itinerary.

Any residual doubt that we were serious was now gone. Eric Clark and I began lining up additional delegations, laying out a schedule through 2010 that would steadily build momentum. Eric and Barney were also keen on using media to build awareness and support for our new mission, but I preferred to stay quiet. I could not imagine Western media viewing our work as anything other than a last-ditch attempt by the Pentagon to recast the Afghan mission as a success, and I was also convinced that media attention would cause me political problems in the administration. Through the first half of 2010, we stayed quiet and did our work.

Our efforts were energized by another addition to our leadership team. Howard W. Buffett resigned his post at the White House to join TFBSO. He had been affected greatly by his visit with his father, soon reaching out to me with an offer to help our mission. That summer, our dialogue culminated in Howard W. assuming management of our agricultural development team, including the TFBSO agricultural fieldwork of the Texas A&M Borlaug Institute led by Ed Price. He traveled throughout Afghanistan at great personal risk to his safety to accelerate our agricultural programs by forging links to the American agriculture sector as well as the Borlaug Institute.

After he joined the team, I learned that Buffett was taking far larger risks than we originally realized. Severely injured in a car accident at age eighteen, both of Buffett's legs had been reconstructed with metal rods to enable him to walk, leaving him frequently in severe pain years after the event. To travel via military airlift throughout Afghanistan was a remarkable commitment to serving his country, given his health challenges. We only learned of his injury and condition after he joined the team, when we were arranging our standard emergency procedures for medical care in the event of violence.

Price had recommended that TFBSO launch an agricultural training center in Jalalabad, Afghanistan, but that had been put on hold because of our funding restraints. Buffett pushed the proposal to the Howard G. Buffett Foundation, which stepped up with a major grant to construct a modern agricultural college in Jalalabad, including a long-term grant to the Borlaug Institute to broadly engage in development on completion.[14] TFBSO would provide direct sponsorship to this effort. Having Buffett join TFBSO also sent a jolt of energy into our efforts in Washington. It was no small thing to have someone of his stature give up a policy role at the White House to put his life on the line with TFBSO. The Pentagon bureaucracy was taken aback, and for a short time stepped up its support for efforts to find near-term solutions to our funding problems.

*   *

Some of the most effective initial business successes were driven by Rudi Shenk, the Obama campaign official whose background in business and law combined with his knowledge of the Persian language Farsi made him an invaluable team leader. Getting his Farsi comfortable with the Afghan Dari dialect, Rudi immersed himself in his program and focused on rapid expansion of indigenous industries—including everything from carpet weaving and finishing to native crafts to food processing. Within three months of his efforts, Rudi brokered the first international export agreement for Afghan raisins.

Unknown to most, for decades Afghanistan had been the global leader in raisin production, an industry that employed thousands from vineyards to processing centers to packaging operations. Since 2002, no one had done anything to revive this industry. Rudi and David Kudla assessed the state of the industry and found that the problem was simply the lack of state-of-the-art cleaning and processing operations in major raisin-growing centers. Identifying a single producer of raisins that met international standards, Rudi engaged the Food and Drug Administration to determine how to get this operation certified for export to the United States. Weeks later, Sweet Dried Fruit of Austin, Texas, signed the first agreement for import of Afghan raisins since before the Soviet invasion of 1979.[15]

Soon Rudi identified similar production opportunities for Afghan agricultural products, including saffron. The introduction of saffron farming in the far west of Afghanistan had been initiated by Afghans returning to the country after 2001. Widely claimed as a success story by international aid agencies, it actually had never received any international support, but was always on slideshows in briefings about Afghan successes in development. Saffron is extremely valuable and profitable, and Afghan saffron was of very high quality but was frequently contaminated with foreign matter and other pathogens and could not be exported. While it was being grown, there was no market access outside of Afghanistan for saffron. Consistent with other development efforts we had seen, it lacked completion.

Similar stories could be heard throughout the country. Handwoven carpets from Afghanistan are world renowned, and commanded top dollar in shops in the West. But the carpets were never sold directly to Western buyers, but instead routed through Pakistani finishing companies who received almost all of the profit for Afghan labor. Pomegranate juice cost five dollars a pint in the West, and Afghan pomegranates were the best in the world, two times the size of pomegranates grown elsewhere. But there were no juicing operations or concentrators to attack this growing global market.

Shenk identified case after case of such opportunities and launched initiatives to attack each one: opening channels to international sales wherever possible and identifying strategies and developing plans to enable production to meet international standards when needed. His work sent a message to business leaders in Afghanistan that something was changing and that, for the first time since 2002, they were going to receive overdue support for their critical contribution to the Afghan economy.

Soon after our work began delivering results, General McChrystal asked me to join him in one of his frequent meetings with Karzai. I was taken aback by this request. In Iraq, I knew every politician at every level very well, from the cabinet ministers down to the governors and mayors of just about every province. But engagement with Prime Minister Nouri al-Maliki was reserved for the Commander of Multi-National Forces–Iraq, or for the U.S. Ambassador. While Maliki knew of my work through the reports of various Iraqi cabinet ministers, I had only met him when he formally received the Korean business delegation the day after the Babylon Hotel bombing, and the Koreans had insisted that I join them.

Joining McChrystal with Karzai was illuminating on a number of levels. McChrystal had clear rapport with Karzai, his earnest style and constant effort to demonstrate respect put Karzai at ease. They were able to have very frank conversations about problems and issues, and Karzai clearly listened to McChrystal. After a period of discussion, McChrystal then described TFBSO and our work and then turned the meeting over to me.

Pulling out my maps, I proceeded to show Karzai the locations of many of the most-valuable mineral deposits in Afghanistan, potentially worth hundreds of billions of dollars. I laid out a vision of an Afghanistan where he no longer needed to ask for foreign assistance, where the government could finance its own army and security needs, and where the development of education, health, and welfare of the Afghan people would no longer depend on the charity of foreigners. It was a vision within his grasp if Afghanistan would partner with us—in security operations as General McChrystal needed, but also in ensuring transparency and modern practices in tendering and awarding contracts for mineral development.

The mineral wealth, I explained, could be Afghanistan's greatest blessing, or a terrible curse. There were plenty of examples of nation-states that had declined into violence and anarchy as a result of failures to properly develop mineral wealth. Congo came to mind. There were examples such as Chile, where development of mineral resources under responsible leadership with appropriate labor, environmental, and health regulations in place had created great wealth and benefit to society. Which way Afghanistan went would be largely up to Karzai. He had, in his newly won five-year term, the opportunity to set Afghanistan on a path to economic sovereignty. By the time his term ended, he could go down as a great figure in history, not only in Afghanistan but also in the entire region.

Karzai asked me who I thought would consume the mineral wealth as it was developed. The Afghan government had awarded the rights to develop a well-known world-class copper deposit south of Kabul to a Chinese company two years earlier, a decision that had generated a scandal involving the prior Minister of Mines, who was accused of receiving bribes during the tender process. I laid out our proposed vision, in which all of the neighboring countries, including China, India, Pakistan, and Russia, were reliant on mineral wealth from Afghanistan and the high-tech materials such as lithium and rare earths were consumed by European, Japanese, and American firms. Such a future, I explained, would give the international community and Afghanistan's neighbors a strong incentive to foster peace in his country and would discourage meddling and interference in Afghan affairs. Of course, whom Afghanistan traded with was up to Afghanistan's leaders, not Americans.[16]

Karzai grew increasingly energized as we pored over the maps, and I described what was present in the locations indicated and how we were working together with Afghans to survey the sites and gather field data that would enable companies to bid on developing the resources. McChrystal was pleased. As the meeting ended, I was pleased as well. I felt that, perhaps for the first time, we could maximize our contribution to the U.S. mission. Regardless of past issues with the Karzai government, there was an air of positive energy, and a fresh start that McChrystal had established that was full of potential.

I joined McChrystal and Eikenberry with Karzai on additional occasions in the spring, providing updates and information on all of our activities, not just on mineral development but also on all of our work across many sectors of the Afghan economy.

Darren Farber's work to deploy common contracting information systems in earlier years now paid huge dividends. As we pored over contracting data, Farber's team identified major problems in Defense contracting in Afghanistan. While the use of Afghan First as a contract policy was in place, the concentration of funds was flowing to a very small number of contractors. Fifty Afghan firms were receiving more than 90 percent of defense contracts awarded under the Afghan First program with a value of almost $1 billion per year.[17]

The political effect of this concentration of spending was clear. Local communities were resenting Afghan firms that won all of the U.S. contracts, causing bad feeling toward the U.S. mission instead of creating goodwill. Farber, working with Joint Contracting Command and ISAF economic-development staffers, ensured broader distribution of contracts, providing greater stimulus to Afghan businesses. He also moved to provide greater contract flow to Afghan companies that used indigenous labor and materials, another major change. Prior to this, many contracts went to Afghan businesses that were essentially importers of foreign goods, creating few if any Afghan jobs and providing little economic stimulus. Again, lessons learned in Iraq greatly accelerated our ability to make an impact in Afghanistan.

Kris Haag, as he had done in Iraq, leveraged the new work in contracting by Farber to launch a banking-sector development program. Within a short time, Citibank announced the establishment of formal relationships with the Afghanistan International Bank. The banking sector had grown increasingly unstable because of financial improprieties at Kabul Bank, the largest Afghan financial institution. The AIB-Citibank announcement helped calm nerves among Afghan deposit holders.[18] Using Defense contracting as an incentive, Haag's team, led by Nadia Dawood, facilitated the distribution of deposits across a number of private Afghan banks, reducing the threat of a financial crisis if Kabul Bank, as feared, went into default.

Our ability to impact Afghanistan was far faster than it was in Iraq. I continued to split two weeks a month among Iraq, Afghanistan, and, until the legal fiasco at home, Pakistan. But it was easy to get caught up in the growing momentum we had in Afghanistan. It made our funding and hiring freeze all the more frustrating. I thought about how much we could get accomplished if we could only reach our planned staffing levels. In Washington, I did everything I could to find temporary solutions, even appealing to USAID in an effort to partner for a solution, all to no avail.

14.

CHECKMATE

For the first time since 2007, I independently reengaged Capitol Hill. Thirteen times between May and October 2010 I met with committee staffers from both the Armed Services and Foreign Relations Committees in the House and in the Senate. Some of these meetings were impromptu at my request; some were formally arranged large engagements that included State Department and USAID representatives as well as dozens of staffers. Making the rounds in low-key meetings with staffers from all the armed services committees in the House and Senate, I explained our circumstances to them all.

The committee staffers were bewildered. How could work that had been formally approved by Secretary Gates be declared antideficient by a single attorney one month later? Why, after four years, including more than a year within the Obama Administration, was the Department now seeking legislative authority for our work? What had changed? As they began to connect the dots from CPA to the present, several on the staff openly speculated that this was an agenda-driven effort to shut down my mission.

Most of the Foreign Relations committee staffers were not receptive to my appeals. Showered with slideshow-deep briefings from USAID about the wonderful work underway in Afghanistan and Iraq, and never exposed to operating reality beyond slideshow visits to highly selected, Potemkin village–style projects while in heavy armor, they had no way to judge the truth of what I was saying.

June 2010 had been eventful for many reasons. That month, I left my budget fight in Washington long enough to travel to California to recruit businesses and potential business leaders to Afghanistan. As a long session with a group of executives from investment firms and import/export businesses wrapped up, my BlackBerry went off. It was Eric Clark, reporting that there was a troubling media story about to hit about General McChrystal. I asked him a few questions, but the piece wasn't available to read yet—Clark had heard from ISAF staff that it was bad. I wasn't too worried—there was always some media storm blowing through.

I was wrong.

The next day, the now-infamous *Rolling Stone* magazine piece hit the newsstands, and all hell broke loose. Reading the article, in which McChrystal allegedly had been highly critical of the Obama Administration, I feared for the worst.[1]

My fears were realized a day later, when Secretary Gates and President Obama accepted McChrystal's resignation of his command of ISAF and announced his replacement, CENTCOM Commander General Petraeus.

I hated to see McChrystal go. Anytime there is a command turnover there is a loss of momentum, and we had always experienced disruption when there were changes of command in Iraq as we realigned to a new general and his expectations. But this time, Petraeus was taking over. As he had sent us to Afghanistan in the first place, and as I had kept him up to date on our work no less than weekly since we launched the mission, we would not miss a beat. If anything, he would push us harder. That was fine with me—I needed his advocacy to get our funding fiasco resolved.

But I was deeply distraught for McChrystal. I had felt he was perfect for the job of working with President Hamid Karzai—his earnestness and supportive style was effective in persuading Karzai to make difficult decisions, and there was early clear positive momentum in Kabul in spite of disputes with Ambassador Eikenberry over the decision to increase the numbers of American troops—the so-called Afghan "surge." Petraeus in command would be different—very different. For one, he was not the General Petraeus who had taken over Iraq at the worst of the insurgency and who had had to prove himself. Now he was "General Petraeus," the man who had turned the tide in Iraq, the indispensable leader who was Commander of CENTCOM, volunteering to take a formal demotion in position to save the Afghan mission. There would be no doubt who was in charge in Afghanistan, no controversy between the civilian and military missions. His gravitas was unquestionable—he would dominate the international presence in Afghanistan.

I suspected Karzai's reaction to this would not be favorable. There had been significant controversy with the U.S. Administration over his recent reelection, but in McChrystal he had found someone within the American mission he could work with, and now that person was gone. I felt certain that Karzai would never believe this decision was based on inappropriate quotes in a rock music magazine. He would assume it was part of an overarching conspiracy to eventually remove him from power. Petraeus was going to have his hands full convincing him otherwise.

※   ※

During the transition from McChrystal to Petraeus I grew to know and depend on a great source of support and counsel, the former Afghan Finance Minister Ashraf Ghani. A fascinating character with impeccable academic credentials and a background in international development predating 2002, Ghani had a calm, patient way of explaining matters, and would sit with me for hours over tea or meals advising me on how we should develop our plans to accommodate Afghanistan's unique challenges. An ethnic Pashtun, he was particularly helpful as we worked to try to increase our engagement in the south and east of the country. He was also quick to grow frustrated with international experts holding forth on opinions of Afghanistan, his temper flaring when "one-year" diplomatic or military experts would contradict his opinions. His style and fluent English made him an easy "go-to" point of contact for constantly rotating State Department and ISAF leaders seeking Afghan leadership on issues—an over-dependence that was not always healthy for Ghani or for U.S. interests, as his opinions—while highly informed—did not always represent those of the power brokers within the Afghan leadership.

He was a student of USAID and its efforts at development, and over time had become a withering critic of its inability to deliver anything of tangible benefit relative to cost. Ghani shared an analysis with me he had performed years before, which showed that for every dollar spent by USAID on a particular program in a country, less than ten cents actually was spent in the country.[2] The rest of the ninety cents is stripped away by a set of contracted service providers, whose margins are sky-high compared to private-sector service industries. This dilemma became clear as Darren Farber began engaging with NATO contracting commands and USAID in an effort to unify the Afghan First program to represent all contracting, not just U.S. military contracts. We were stunned to learn that, with a $4 billion budget in 2010, USAID had only five "warranted" contract officers—duly certified officials legally authorized to spend U.S. government money on goods and/or services —on the ground in Afghanistan to execute this massive budget. By contrast, the Department of Defense had more than 250 contracting officers in the country, to oversee less than half of the USAID budget.

I thought about my private-sector life. In the technology sector, I had a team of more than forty supply engineers and purchasing professionals to manage spending on high-tech parts and supplies of less than $1 billion a year.

There was more to learn. USAID contracts were not at all like Defense Department or other government contracts. Instead, USAID uses a modified contract process, in which a private company is essentially handed hundreds of millions of dollars to execute a broadly defined program with more generally defined delivery objectives or milestones required to receive payment. So a USAID contract firm essentially receives a set of broad directions, for example "create economic opportunity within Helmand Province focused on the agriculture sector," and a tranche of funding. Funds are transferred prior to work beginning.[3] I thought about, in my time running business modernization, the endless Government Accountability Office reports on lack of financial accountability within the Pentagon because of the inability to automatically audit finances to the level of purchase orders for specific goods and services. Yet USAID often executed broadly defined agreements committing hundreds of millions of dollars with only general guidance about the purpose of the program. There was no way a supplier could be relied on to deliver effective results in the face of an inability by the customer (in this case USAID) to articulate reasonable expectations of delivery and performance.

Yet, with only five contract officers in Kabul, it was impossible to see how USAID could do it any other way. Contracted suppliers had the best of all possible setups: a customer giving them large amounts of money with only loosely defined products expected in return. It was no wonder that Ghani found there was little that made its way to the local communities.

✳ ✳

In the fall of 2010, JP Morgan Chase helped end the ongoing debate we had with State over the viability of Afghan mining. While we worked with the Afghan government compiling data for newly surveyed mineral deposits on our top 20 list of priority sites, Ian Hannam was pursuing an initial investment in a gold mine that had been licensed years earlier. Located in Baghlan Province in north-central Afghanistan, the gold deposit had very high-grade ore. A prominent and respected Afghan business man, Sadat Naderi, had been introduced to TFBSO by the U.S. Embassy as a potential partner for international investors. Naderi owned the license to develop the Baghlan mine. TFBSO introduced him to Hannam, who negotiated an investment to create a new Afghan mining company, the first Western investment in mining in Afghanistan in more than fifty years.

To make the investment happen, Hannam arranged for the Minister of Mines, Wahidullah Shahrani, and me to visit New York, where we were guests of JP Morgan Chase Chief Executive Jamie Dimon. Dimon was interested in the project, making clear that if the financials passed muster and if appropriate regulations and transparent practices were in place, he believed investors would definitely pursue opportunities in Afghanistan.

Hannam's investment in Naderi's Baghlan gold mine electrified our efforts and generated great excitement in Kabul, both in ISAF and in the Afghan government.[4] Like the early "ice-breaking" transactions we had completed with investors in Iraq years before, having J.P. Morgan involved in Afghan mining provided a jolt of confidence to other international companies and business leaders that Afghanistan was a serious opportunity worth consideration. Immediately, companies began seeking information about investing in Afghan mining, soliciting technical data. Our plan, drafted in collaboration with Shahrani and his staff, called for several major gold and copper deposits to be offered for public tender early in 2011. TFBSO built a world-class data center and provided state-of-the-art geological analysis tools for the Ministry of Mines and Afghan Geological Survey, training its technical staff on the use of modern software and providing its staff with a full set of the USGS data and supplemental field-survey results.[5]

As Emily Scott's team worked with the Ministry of Mines, they discovered archives filled with Soviet-era mineral surveys and assay sample results. It was a treasure trove of information, all in Russian. From the state of the archive, it was clear that the information had not been accessed since the Soviets departed twenty years earlier.

We hired Russian geologists and set to work reviewing and cataloging the archive. Alex Chaihorsky, a Russian American scientist with many years of experience working in the former Soviet Union, led this effort. Highly detailed maps and associated technical data were digitized and integrated with the USGS overhead survey results, providing in many cases validation of the overhead surveys and reducing the need for additional field sampling. This integrated data set would be moved to the new data center to be operated by the Afghans. The Afghans were initially skeptical that we would provide them with the data; they had been asking for the initial USGS data studies for years, but USAID had never provided them with the data files. As our scientists worked in partnership, they gradually began to believe we were serious about giving them everything. It was another step to enabling the Afghan government to manage its own national resources.

※　※

As the summer had turned into fall, it became clear that quick legislative relief on our budget was not forthcoming. We had reached a plateau of staff in Afghanistan at about 120 people by August, at which time several major security and life-support contracts were running out of funding.

By September, our team would start to collapse for lack of resources.

In Kabul on a monthly rotation that August, I delivered to General Petraeus a briefing laying out our original plan for staffing the Afghanistan mission, and how far from that plan we actually were. It culminated in the reality that, absent an infusion of $8 million by September 30, we would have to cease operations.

For the first time in my long relationship with Petraeus, he openly expressed his personal frustration with me. "You are the Deputy Undersecretary. You have to make Washington work. You can't expect me to manage your Washington problems on top of everything else. Throw your badge on the table if you have to. Have you seen Gates about this?"

What I could not tell him was that I had requested meetings with Gates for three months, but his Chief of Staff Robert Rangel would not put me on his calendar. Closely managed, Gates's calendar was not directly accessible to me. Without Rangel's support, I could not just walk into Gates's office. Rangel had been told to work with Comptroller Bob Hale to fix this budget problem, and my only assumption was that Rangel didn't want this aired in front of Gates again—to his way of thinking this issue was being resolved as quickly as it could be.[6]

I left ISAF Headquarters feeling like I was failing miserably. The U.S. was now spending $10 billion a month on military operations in Afghanistan, and I was in the commanding general's office telling him I couldn't handle a paltry $8 million budget gap.

Petraeus referred to my briefing slides in his weekly command videoconference with Secretary Gates the next morning. Once again, all hell broke loose at the Pentagon. In response to an apparent demand from Gates that the issue get resolved, Deputy Secretary of Defense Bill Lynn held a sudden meeting about TFBSO, the first time he had engaged in our situation at all.

Lynn's background in business consisted primarily of a role as a lobbyist for the giant defense contractor Raytheon, a point of some controversy when his nomination to serve as deputy was announced. By law, the Deputy Secretary of Defense is required to have extensive industry operations experience, a requirement that was waived by the Senate Armed Services Committee when he was appointed. Based on conversations with my colleagues in other management roles in the building, it appeared he took a much more hands-off posture to managing the day-to-day affairs of the building than had his predecessor Gordon England. Business transformation efforts invigorated by England in 2004 were slowly grinding to a halt under Lynn, with the Business Transformation Agency soon to be disbanded as a result of the absence of the necessary leadership to drive improvement.

For the first time since England had departed in January 2008, I sat in the Deputy Secretary's office, along with Robert Hale, Liz King, Robert Rangel, and several other junior staffers as well as deputy fiscal attorneys.

Lynn was impressive, grilling the fiscal attorney and quickly concluding that the argument against our work had no logical grounds at all. I wondered where he had been—and why he had not been involved earlier when it might have made a difference. After an hour of discussion, all but Rangel and Hale departed for a final discussion about what to do.

Later that day, Rangel called and apologized to me for the situation. He indicated that he had not been fully aware of how poorly crafted the OGC position was, and that had he engaged sooner and more directly, he could have prevented this from happening in the first place. He then explained that now, given that the Department had put this issue in front of Congress and asked for legislative relief, it was too late to overturn the legal opinion within the Pentagon. He stated that I would have to use CERP to keep the lights on at current staff levels until the annual Defense budget passed in the fall, at which time I should get fully authorized and could completely staff our work in Afghanistan.

We received an infusion of CERP funding in the last week of September, just in time to avoid a mission shut down. As the Fiscal Year 2011 Defense Budget bogged down in election year politics on the Hill, we ended up receiving additional infusions of CERP two more times.

Finally, in October, we received good news. Final draft legislation had been reviewed on the Hill authorizing TFBSO for 2011. Reportedly preapproved by the State Department, it was very broadly written, not even limiting us to a specific country.[7] I was surprised by this, and pleased. In a meeting with Holbrooke that September, he had indicated that he was weighing in to get us authorized for 2011, and again directly asked if I would be willing to move our mission to report directly to him. Again, I demurred, but this time I considered it far more seriously than I had in our first meeting almost a year earlier. A remarkable personality, Holbrooke was proving to be a valuable counselor and strong ally for our efforts. Perhaps we would be able to deliver what we committed to him, both in Afghanistan and in Pakistan as well.

The whole episode, however, had rattled our mission to the core. Rather than spend precious time at home recruiting more leaders to manage an expanding mission, I had spent all my time in D.C. fighting yet another war within the bureaucracy. Instead of having hundreds of civilians in Afghanistan to support the eighteen-month surge, we would not have our team until the beginning of 2011 at the earliest. That would leave us only six months of "surge window" to maximize our impact. A nation at war had allowed a key element of its strategy in Afghanistan to be derailed by a single attorney.

✳   ✳

In the fall of 2009, we had returned to Herat to launch our operations center for western Afghanistan and been invited to visit Herat University. One of our strategic advisors, Nader Uskowi, an Iranian American who had joined the Task Force at the recommendation of Milt Bearden, was eager for us to meet a group of students. Arriving at the university, I was surprised to find a large, modern, three-story academic building housing a computer science program. Matt Schoeffling, Nader Uskowi, Eric Clark, and I sat to hear presentations, and what we heard was astonishing.

Presentations were given in English by young Afghan men and women, all students at the university. Using slideshows and online demonstrations, the students presented software solutions that they had developed as part of their required projects for earning their computer science degrees. The work was first-class.

As we watched in surprise, I began to ask questions, and they began to answer. There were more than 200 graduates of the program, which had been established four years earlier. All talented programmers and graphic designers, they had learned state-of-the-art technology and were eagerly hoping to work in the IT sector. But none of them had jobs in their chosen field. As the presentations ended, we sat together and talked at length. They told stories of their participation in online chat rooms for programmers around the world, and how they would talk to software engineers about programming problems or challenges. They had learned to falsify their online identity, never saying they were from Afghanistan, because online communities would immediately dismiss them as lying—"they say there are no programmers in Afghanistan"— and cut them off.

They peppered me with questions. Prior to our arrival, they had studied our group and knew my background from Silicon Valley. "Do you think we could build an IT industry here?" "Do you think we could be like Bangalore someday?"—a reference to the center of the IT industry in India that only a decade earlier had been a nondescript small Indian city. "Can you help us find jobs?"

The University of Herat had been the beneficiary of a rare successful international development initiative, in this case led by Germany. The Technical University of Berlin had established the IT program, educating the faculty in Germany and sending them back to Herat to teach computer science to young Afghan students. The center was a remarkable example of what international development should be: an enabler for a better life.

The young graduates were like programmers I had met anywhere else in the world. Their dress was "Afghan bohemian," stylish and a little rebellious, the women covering their hair but unafraid to speak up and assert their point of view. There was an air of desperation in their pleas. They had done their part, bought into the dream, but were now stuck with no prospects. Several had started companies and were attempting to develop private-sector solutions, but had no financial capital or marketing expertise.

One young woman, in particular, stood out. Roya Mahboob was a young Afghan programmer, but her leadership skills were clear in the group meeting. She had been the champion of this program, advocating for its expansion in Kabul with the Ministry of Education. Quiet but determined, she had a fierce quality that stood out when she spoke. Now serving on the faculty of the university, she was launching a private company and was aggressively seeking to gain access to international markets.

I felt something I had not felt since years earlier, when my pockets would be stuffed with written notes from Iraqi factory workers begging for us to help give their jobs back. A sense of moral obligation to help people who were denied something they had every reason to expect given their qualifications: a job and a future. I also grew angry at our own development aid organizations and their failure to engage in supporting these people. USAID and every other alphabetical development organization in Kabul were spending staggering amounts of money on IT services from foreign IT service providers, importing workers to do what these and many other young Afghans could do.

I glanced at Uskowi, whose eyes were misting with emotion for these young people. He knew we would not able to ignore this group. He was right.

Over the coming months, we launched a full-scale engagement program to get these young people employed. Stan Lumish visited Herat and spent time gaining greater knowledge of their skills and abilities, affirming that their talent was on par with global competitors. Darren Farber linked the start-up companies to the Afghan First initiative, immediately providing an infusion of revenue for software-development support contracts at a fraction of the cost that ISAF normally paid.

The biggest thing the young companies needed was decent office space where they could work. Recalling our business-incubator concept in Baghdad, I began the work to establish a true Silicon Valley–style start-up incubator compound for Herat. Just as in the American tech sector, if we could create an environment with necessary network and computing resources that fostered a creative atmosphere and begin linking the international IT industry to this center, I was confident that the dream to become "like Bangalore" was possible.[8]

By September 2010, I was making Herat part of my monthly Afghan engagement, flying commercially from Kabul to check in on our projects and programs. We had initiated efforts in areas as diverse as carpet finishing, agricultural development, irrigation, light industry expansion for businesses in the Herat industrial park, mineral resource development, and the IT sector program with the students and start-ups at the university. The Governor of Herat, Daud Shah Saba, worked in collaboration with the Task Force across all of its efforts, providing direction and counsel that accelerated our ability to deliver outcomes quickly. An Afghan-Canadian, Saba had earned his doctorate in geology and had a special interest in our mineral programs, volunteering more than once to participate in field surveys with our geology teams.

The progressive economic mindset of Herat made it an ideal laboratory for TFBSO to demonstrate real effects on daily life. I placed Victoria McColm, who had worked with TFBSO in Iraq and had a background in business and in foreign development, in charge of daily operations in Herat after our hiring freeze had been announced.

Late in September, Matt Schoeffling, Stan Lumish, Kris Haag, Nader Uskowi, and I ended a long day of meetings by going to dinner at a local restaurant. We had grown accustomed to doing this, both in Kabul and in Herat, where our presence never generated any strange reactions. This time, we went to a popular establishment high on a nearby hillside, with a panoramic view of the city and surrounding river valley. The Afghans in the restaurant paid us no attention as we were seated at a table and ordered dinner.

Our food arrived, and we began eating, when suddenly an ear-splitting explosion filled the air with glass from the windows of the restaurant. Diving under the tables, the telltale smell of cordite explosive filled my nose as smoke blinded our vision. My ears were ringing from the deafening blast. The restaurant grew quiet. Looking at Matt and Stan and Kris, we nodded at one another and quickly got up, moving to the door. As we exited the restaurant, several Afghans called out to us as we left, seemingly pleading with us not to go.

By morning we learned that we had not been the target. Afghanistan was in the midst of campaigning for provincial elections, and there had been a heated campaign in Herat for seats in the provincial council. One of the most controversial candidates had been in the restaurant with us that night. The bomb was a homemade "flash-bang" grenade, designed to make noise, break glass, and cause disorientation, but otherwise, not injure its recipients. The politician had been the target, and the Afghans were aghast that we had been present when it happened. I received direct apologies from several local officials, who were clearly concerned that we would alter our work in Herat over the incident.

I was relieved to learn we were not the targets. We went on with our work as usual. I had been in many close calls over the years, near

misses by rockets that had rattled my ears or broken nearby windows.
I told myself it was no big deal.

But that night in Herat, my sleep was interrupted by nightmares.
Vivid images of broken bodies, blood, and cordite smoke. Wailing of
women. For several consecutive days, then on random nights thereafter,
the images of the bombing in Baghdad interrupted my sleep.

I talked with Matt about it at length. The Herat "flash-bang" had
triggered a similar effect on him.

✳   ✳

Washington again took a turn for the worse, in a number of ways. The
gap between the value that commanders placed on our mission and the
utter lack of support in official Washington was never greater. There is
no enemy in the world that can defeat the United States military, but
the Beltway bureaucracy has no trouble bringing it to its knees.

The draft legislation we reviewed that fall exceeded our best expectations, but Congress was at an impasse. There would be no Defense
Authorization Bill before the November congressional election. As I
had feared, Congress was not pleased at the decision by Comptroller
Robert Hale to use Commanders Emergency Response Program funds
to sustain TFBSO—not because they did not support our program,
but because these funds were not appropriated for this purpose. We
were summoned again to the Hill and grilled before committee staffers
demanding explanation for this misuse of funds. When the meetings
began, the Pentagon staffs representing the Finance and Legislative
Affairs organizations would, at the first pointed question, look at each
other, then look at me, leaving me to have to explain the Defense
Department position on our program and its funding.

In one meeting, involving the staff of the House Appropriations
Foreign Operations Sub-committee, Matt Schoeffling and Kris
Haag attended with me. One of the young staff members launched
into a lecture about how the Defense Department had no business
wasting money doing development work. She recited the false claims
of economic-development achievements that USAID slideshows
indicated, and then looked at us and demanded that we explain "our
value to the mission, as she did not see any value in our team at all."

On December 13, Milt Bearden called me with terrible news. Richard Holbrooke had collapsed and been hospitalized in grave condition. He had suffered an aortic rupture, and was undergoing surgery. The following morning, I was informed that he had passed.[9]

I had grown to admire Holbrooke a great deal. No one was neutral when it came to Richard Holbrooke: people either loved him or hated him. He was forceful and direct in his opinions, and it took a lot of effort to convince him of something he did not initially believe. Still, I found him a refreshing contrast to the passive-aggressive behavior of too many civilians, who would look you in the face and agree with you only to cut your legs out from under you when you turned your back. I doubt he had ever been too impressed with me personally, but he supported the hell out of our efforts. He had provided wise counsel to me and had become an advocate for our work. I would miss him.

As the shock at his sudden death set in, I also realized we had lost our only real ally at the State Department. Just days before Christmas, I was pleased when the Senate finally passed the Defense Authorization Bill into law.[10] But just before New Year's Day, I received troubling news from my long-standing legislative affairs advisor, Esther Swartz. The legislation authorizing the mission of TFBSO had changed radically in the final version passed by the Congress. We were in trouble. The Authorization Bill funded TFBSO for Fiscal Year 2011 (four months of which had already passed), but only for Afghanistan. The Pentagon was given the task to prepare a plan to transition the work of TFBSO to USAID by no later than September 30, 2011.

With that hammer stroke, I knew that our mission had effectively been killed. The draft legislation that had been reviewed and approved through endless discussion and negotiation with the interagency leadership throughout the summer had apparently been replaced, in a late-night negotiating session, by new legislation sent from the State Department. No one in the Pentagon had seen the changed legislation before it was passed. It was beautiful Washington-style bureaucratic "wet-work," a last-minute death sentence accomplished outside of formal processes or normal operating routines.

And then on January 4, 2011, I received still more bad news. Salman Taseer, the progressive governor of Punjab Province in Pakistan, was gunned down by one of his bodyguards and killed.[11] He had become embroiled in a conflict with Islamic clerics over his opposition to a broadly defined antiblasphemy law that had resulted in the imprisonment and persecution of Christians and other religious minorities. This conflict motivated his assassin, who received praise from many clerics for killing the governor. Only a few short months earlier, Taseer and I had held a joint press conference in Lahore to launch our economic-development program. Now he was gone.

Gathering the senior leadership, our first priority was to shut down our Iraq mission. I was sick thinking about it. All of the trust, all of the relationships, all of the potential, would be abandoned. The embassy in Baghdad was in the midst of its own transition, from Ambassador Christopher Hill to recently appointed Ambassador James Jeffrey. Jeffrey had served on the National Security Council during the Bush Administration, and was well known in Iraq and in the region. He had most recently served as U.S. Ambassador to Turkey. He was a good choice for the role of ambassador, but I was under no illusions that the State Department or USAID would step up to fill the gaping hole we were about to leave in Iraq. The embassy security posture was now more restrictive than it had ever been—with diplomats restricted from free movement even within the "Green Zone," in spite of widespread improvement in the security environment.

Late in January, I returned to Iraq for one last time. Traveling throughout the country, I thanked my team members who had put their lives on the line doing work no other civilians would do and saying goodbye to my Iraqi friends. It was incomprehensibly sad. And foolish. America was shutting down its only effective civilian engagement in Iraq, after spending almost a trillion dollars and the blood of almost 40,000 of its sons and daughters, with 4,487 having given the ultimate sacrifice of their lives. The cost of our operations was a tiny fraction of the budget of the ongoing military and diplomatic mission in Iraq.[12]

Our Iraqi friends could not understand why we were leaving. I explained that the role of the Defense Department was ending in Iraq, and it was time for us to go and for other U.S. agencies to take over, but I could see they didn't buy it. They knew better than anyone else the limitations that our civilian counterparts were forced to work under.

By the end of February, nine of my eleven senior team leaders had tendered their resignations. The end of the "surge" period was June 30.

That would mark the end of the eighteen months the president had given the Pentagon for the additional forces to make a difference in Afghanistan. I asked the leadership team to stay as long as they could, to try to maximize our impact by June 30 wherever possible, so we would not abandon the military mission we had pledged to support. Several of them agreed to hold on until the summer, but several others simply could not stay on for that long. Over the coming months, we lost senior leaders, and I was unable to replace them. Each who departed took years of experience operating in high-risk conflict zones, as well as established trust with Afghan counterparts, with them. Each departure had a devastating impact on our mission.

On February 22, I sent Secretary Gates a detailed memorandum outlining the declining state of our operations given the congressional decision to move our mission to USAID.[13]

Along with the memorandum, I submitted my letter of resignation from government service, effective June 30, 2011.

✳　　✳

In the spring of 2011, the Ministry of Mines began the process of tendering four major copper/gold deposits located in the provinces of Badakhshan, Ghazni, and Herat. Each had the potential to generate significant financial return to investors as well as to the Afghan government. At the end of the first phase of the tender process, forty-one international mining companies, including a dozen Western firms, submitted formal indications of interest and purchased technical details on the sites.

Kris Haag's energy team continued its initial efforts at launching the oil and gas sector in northern Afghanistan, providing support to the Ministry of Mines first public tender of an oil field in the Amu Darya Basin west of Mazar-e-Sharif known as the Kashkari Block. With wellheads still capped from Soviet-era development, TFBSO petroleum engineers opened wells and tested crude samples from throughout the field. These sample results were provided to bidders with the public tender of this first field to be awarded in August 2011.

This initial oil-field award was for a small deposit, with a proven reserve of 50 million barrels, and a potential for an additional 50 million barrels yet to be proved. The objective of awarding the Kashkari Block was to demonstrate to the international community that oil production was again viable in Afghanistan, and to begin defining processes within the Afghan government for the oversight and management of these valuable resources. Once Kashkari was successfully awarded and oil production restored, the much-larger Afghan–Tajik Basin was to be offered for tender to international companies. With reserve estimates approaching one billion barrels, the Afghan–Tajik Basin could potentially draw major multinational oil companies to Afghanistan.

It was imperative that this process be transparent, and free of any interference or undue influence from TFBSO leadership or any government leaders. Any sense that we were steering or influencing the award of development rights for Afghan oil would be devastating to our credibility with the Afghan government.

TFBSO provided financial and legal advisors, assigning them to work directly for the minister, in much the same way as Scott King's procurement support team had done in Iraq years earlier. No TFBSO leader was permitted access to the bidding process or the assessment of bids. Clear technical and financial criteria were defined in the bidding process, and the TFBSO advisors' role was to advise and consult on the structure of the bidding process. Only Afghan leaders would be permitted to participate in the review process.

Of all the work we undertook in Afghanistan, none had received greater allocation of resources than our support of the large marine effort in Helmand Province. Bill Duncan, who had successfully led many of our factory revitalization efforts in Iraq back in 2006, rejoined TFBSO in 2010, immediately deploying to the marine base in Helmand. But his efforts were often frustrated. Agricultural-development programs were stymied again by recalcitrant USAID regulations against commodity support for globally competitive crops such as cotton and wheat. The local cotton gin had been closed for years because of its ownership by the government of Afghanistan. Duncan worked to reopen the cotton gin in Lashkar Gah and to establish small enterprises focused on produce marketing as well as logistical operations.

For Helmand, however, our most important and guarded effort involved field surveys at the massive extinct volcano at Khan Neshin. Khan Neshin Mountain is a rare, massive "carbonatite" volcano formation whose emergence had rerouted the path of the Helmand River more than 60,000 years ago. Overhead surveys had indicated the presence of rare-earth elements: compounds that are widely applied in high-tech applications. Economically viable rare-earth elements in Helmand could potentially create an entire new economy, making the income from poppy cultivation and heroin production seem insignificant by comparison. Developing rare-earth mining operations would also provide a strong incentive for local tribes to disavow violence. As explained in one of several meetings with tribal leaders, you cannot sell valuable commodities on global markets if people are afraid of being killed visiting the mining site.

We were hopeful that Khan Neshin would contain a variety of rare earths known as "heavies," heavy rare-earth elements that are truly in short supply globally. The only known deposits of certain heavy rare earths are, in fact, in China. Locating a heavy rare-earth deposit in Helmand would be a major discovery.

Emily Scott and Alex Chaihorsky worked to translate and digitize former Soviet trench site maps at Khan Neshin, which served to provide guidance on where TFBSO should gather additional samples. Two missions to Khan Neshin were completed. When the data rolled in, the results were encouraging. The size of the light rare-earth element deposits were economically viable—about half the size of the major U.S. deposit at Mountain Pass, California. No heavy rare earths were identified, however. The results were published jointly with the U.S. Geological Survey in 2011.[14]

Of all the work we undertook in Helmand, the Khan Neshin opportunity was most promising to provide an economic future for that troubled river valley. We hoped that, someday, responsible development of these mineral assets would offer a decent future to the long-suffering citizens of Helmand.

At the time when we launched our Afghan mission, devoting Bill Duncan and his team to Helmand had made sense; we were ramping up our staffing and wanted to offer full support to the marines, even though aspects of the marine mission in that remote area seemed dubious during our original assessment. Bill's team was only partially established before the hiring freeze took hold. After our funding crisis ended our hiring, I regretted the decision to focus on Helmand, instead wishing we had sent the team to Kandahar. Kandahar was the center of Pashtun culture, and the key to stability in southern Afghanistan.

I visited Kandahar on several occasions, driving through the city in low-profile vehicles. It was the most dangerous city in Afghanistan by far, reminding me most of Fallujah or Ramadi in Anbar Province in Iraq back in 2006. But it also had great commercial potential. The adjacent Arghandab District was a rich agricultural zone filled with orchards and fertile land. I had plans to place a large team of business-development experts in the city itself, far from the massive locked-down military base at Kandahar airport. Provincial Governor Toryalai Wesa and local power broker and brother of Hamid Karzai, Ahmed Wali Karzai, were supportive and committed to ensuring our security. But the hiring freeze followed by the impending shutdown of our mission prevented us from ever getting anything launched in Kandahar beyond Rudi Shenk's raisin-processing center. It was a huge missed opportunity.

Our investor engagement took off in spite of our challenges. Companies from technology giant IBM to the fashion company kate spade, from Google and YouTube to Schlumberger visited and toured Afghanistan business opportunities as our guests, all initiating or proposing business-development efforts following their engagement.[15] Emaar Properties of Dubai, developer of the tallest building in the world (the Burj Khalifa) toured Kabul and Herat, with Chairman Mohamed Alabbar immediately following up with a residential development proposal for Kabul and the charitable donation of a large primary and secondary school for girls in Herat.[16] Alabbar served as a remarkable role model for the Afghan business community. A self-made entrepreneur, he rose from a childhood sharing a single room with twelve siblings to become one of the most successful property developers and influential business leaders in the world. Afghan business and government leaders were deeply moved to have him visit the country, freely traveling in areas of risk, and discussing business opportunities with them. It reinforced our model of providing access to inspiring business leaders from around the world—not just America—as a symbol of hope for troubled war-torn societies.

Of all the visits, the most remarkable was a delegation of senior executives from Google and YouTube. The group came from Google offices in Silicon Valley, Bangalore, Hong Kong, Sydney, and Tel Aviv. Touring Afghanistan, they were full of ideas and advice, and energized by the discovery of the new technology companies we introduced them to.[17] But what made the visit most compelling was a lengthy discussion with General Petraeus as they were departing the country. I sat and listened as they shared their observations of Afghanistan.

They began with facts we all knew well. Afghanistan had a literacy rate of less than 25 percent. Yet it had a mobile phone penetration rate of almost 60 percent. While most Afghans could not read, more than 80 percent had access to satellite television at home or within their communities. What this meant, from the perspective of the Google/YouTube team, was that Afghans were desperate to connect, to gain access to information from the world outside their village or home. They discussed this observation at length. Mobile communications were not cheap for impoverished Afghan citizens. What did it say for an Afghan to get a mobile phone when much more basic needs went unfilled? It could only be that connectivity was more important than other needs.

The Google executives passionately believed that access to information among all citizens was one key to stabilizing Afghanistan, and that if Afghans had access to timely information, they could eventually self-correct the problems in governance that the United States was spending billions attempting to resolve. Their advice was simple. Stop spending money on infrastructure projects the Afghans cannot sustain. Take a small percentage of all of the development dollars and enable networks for citizens to gain access to information.

At this time, Egypt was in the midst of its "Arab Spring" revolution. Members of Google's Egyptian leadership team had been actively blogging to rouse citizens to rise up in protest against the Mubarak regime. It was a heady time for Google and its YouTube subsidiary, for Facebook, and for Twitter, all of which appeared to be the tools of the masses rising up against oppression throughout the region.

They had a point.

In the spring, I presided at the opening of a state-of-the-art Information Technology Incubator facility in Herat. With five start-ups moving in at launch, the facility offered bandwidth, computer resources, and shared space for collaboration among teams. Google and IBM established operations at the center, providing legitimacy and support to the effort. We signed private contracts for support to the center for a full year, ensuring its continuity after September 30, and giving the new companies as much runway as possible to maximize their opportunity to succeed.[18]

✳   ✳

As we frantically worked to maximize our impact in Afghanistan before the mission would abruptly end in September, disturbing aspects of the international mission became clear. By now we had been working in Afghanistan for almost two years and had reached a basic level of engagement and understanding that enabled structural problems to become apparent.

In the south of Afghanistan, it was increasingly clear that the Pashtun were deeply conflicted over the U.S. mission. Widespread and pervasive corruption was endemic, and as we would talk with soldiers and marines we would often hear stories of frustration over the behavior of the local government and the security forces the U.S. was spending billions of dollars to establish on a rapid timeline. Absent local confidence and trust in the institutions we were rushing to create—almost ten years late—there was an emerging wait-and-see attitude among local business and political leaders.

As we had learned in Iraq years earlier, corruption is often a hidden vote of no confidence in the future on the part of political leaders. When there is no confidence in the future of a country, politicians take what they can get now to secure their own personal interests before the system falls apart. It seemed that this was increasingly the case in Afghanistan. The ISAF commander for anticorruption initiatives, an old friend and colleague from Iraq, Brigadier General H. R. McMaster, related disconcerting stories of graft and corruption that had been uncovered—too often directly associated with the rapid effort to build government and security institutions.[19]

The dynamics that were working to reinforce corruption went beyond a lack of confidence in the future and included internal flaws in the very structure of the new Afghan state. Afghanistan has a hyper-centralized executive branch of government—every executive role, from the national ministries down to provincial governors, mayors of municipalities, and district administrators is appointed by the president. Every financial resource at the national and local levels is allocated and administered by the Kabul government.[20]

Afghanistan's constitution was drafted following the overthrow of the Taliban regime. The motivation for the hypercentralized structure of the Afghan constitution was to discourage the reemergence of regional warlords who had subjected the country to endless conflict after the Soviet occupation ended in the early 1990s—to ensure that every element of political authority was appropriated by the central government.

When traveling throughout Afghanistan, meeting with local officials at the provincial and municipal or district levels, the frustration at slow responses to requests in Kabul was everywhere. Governors of major provinces cannot even hire basic administrative support staff without first getting approval from bureaucrats in Kabul, who often reject selected candidates for even entry-level jobs and insist on placing political patrons instead.

Spoils systems exist in any electoral democracy, providing opportunities for a newly elected executive to reward supporters with positions in a new administration. The United States is no exception—one need only consider the qualifications of some of the appointees of a newly elected American president to see that this is a characteristic of our democracy as well. But to extend national patronage to the most local level is to ensure a system of government whose executive branch places performance of duties at a distant second priority compared to distributing favors and gaining political support.

Afghanistan is plagued by ineffective local government, undermining the ability of the U.S. to wage an effective counterinsurgency campaign against the Taliban. Corruption is widespread and pervasive at every tier of the governance structure. Afghan frustration with the lack of basic local governance is the number one reason cited for supporting the Taliban—*at least Talibs can enforce the law.*

Imagine if the governor of your state, the head of your county government, and the mayor of your town were all appointed by the president of the United States. Would you feel that they governed with the consent of the local citizens, as the democratic ideals we are fighting for would presumably require? What if your only say over the officials who ruled your locality was a national election every five years marked by ballot irregularities, in which a single individual was selected to govern from a faraway city. Would you believe this governing system was accountable to the people? Or would you believe that the people were at the mercy of the system?

The inability of the Afghan government to establish credible, competent institutions formed the crux of the heated debate in Washington over the military surge in 2009 and the conflict that erupted over the merits of increasing military forces. This debate was focused on the particular behaviors of the sitting Afghan President, Hamid Karzai, and quickly devolved into a public discourse over Karzai's fitness to lead his country—humiliating Karzai on the world stage and doing great damage to his relationship with the United States.

This debate was focused on the wrong problem. No individual can lead Afghanistan effectively under the current constitutional political system. The nation is simply too culturally fractured, geographically divided, and traumatized by decades of brutality to enable a single figure to appoint every leader of consequence at every level of government while simultaneously serving as commander-in-chief of the military, appointing the justices in the national court system, engaging with the Parliament to pass laws and budgets, and all the while working with the international community to manage its donor aid and associated demands.

One man cannot know enough qualified talented people to appoint effective leaders across such a vast patronage system. All a person can do, even with the best of intentions, is appoint family members, acquaintances, and political patrons in an effort to staff the far-flung Afghan government. Replacing the man at the top will eventually lead to another cycle of crony-driven appointments—it would be the case in any society. In a broken society such as Afghanistan it is a recipe for exactly the government that exists now with too many corrupt, incompetent, and ineffective local institutions that have no trust or sense of buy-in among the people they seek to govern.

The absence of any local democratic control as prescribed by the new Afghan constitution actually ensures that the president of Afghanistan is a weak leader in the eyes of the people as well as the tribal and financial power brokers in Afghan society. It is the paradox of hypercentralized leadership in an information age. A leader is doomed to be the scapegoat for everything that goes wrong at the local, provincial, and national level in such a system, leaving him or her beholden to the unofficial tribal power structure that moves behind the scenes to undermine the leadership absent offers of additional political patronage. Distribution of power is the best antidote for this central-ization of blame—but the Afghan government is designed to centralize all power, and therefore all blame, in the office of its president.

Would-be tribal warlords as well as the Taliban have an inept government based in Kabul to point the finger at for all the problems of the people, contrasting their benevolent tribal leadership and/or Sharia law with the inability of the national government to provide even a basic rule of law and security at the local level.

It is not the person of Hamid Karzai that causes the Afghan system to fail. It is not the lack of a "Nelson Mandela" leadership figure, or a "George Washington" of Afghanistan, that prevents the Afghan government from developing competent institutions. The current constitutional framework demonstrates no faith in the people of Afghanistan, instead stripping their power to govern themselves and placing it in the hands of a faraway elected king. And so the Afghan people demonstrate no faith in their government. This problem must be resolved before Afghanistan can develop local institutions critical to long-term stability.

✳   ✳

In spite of our growing unease over the obvious structural chal-lenges in Afghan governance, we continued to build momentum for our economic-development mission—even as it was facing a sudden end only months away. We continued to push hard to accelerate progress economically—from my perspective, economic development was a foundation on which democratic institutions were completely dependent—so that any progress we could make in building economic capacity would positively affect the long-term reform of Afghan society and government.

The media engagement we had initiated paid off in generating increased interest in business in Afghanistan. The January 6, 2011, *Bloomberg BusinessWeek* cover story focused on the Task Force and its work to facilitate business development in Afghanistan. *Fortune* magazine profiled the J.P. Morgan investment in Sadat Naderi's Baghlan Gold Mine in the May issue in a multipage spread that described the TFBSO mineral development program. It was all too little, too late, to save our mission, but these high-profile business publications increased interest in the Afghan economy. TFBSO had recast the public debate in Afghanistan. Instead of talking only about violence and war, an unexpected subject was now being discussed: business.

After the launch of the IT incubator in Herat, we arranged for the leaders of several of the technology start-ups to visit Silicon Valley. After months of work to get visas and travel plans locked down, the group visited Google, IBM, and several other major technology companies who rolled out a red carpet for the guests, who also visited several large start-up incubators filled with new technology companies. *Fast Company* magazine covered the visit, which was the first such effort to introduce young Afghan tech entrepreneurs to their American counterparts.[21] Technology industry leaders began repeated visits to Afghanistan, hiring young Afghans as interns and establishing direct lines of communication with Afghan technology leaders. Atul Vashistha, the CEO of NeoIT and a leader in IT services establishment in developing countries, connected the Young President's Organization of Silicon Valley to the Afghan IT sector leaders, providing a direct line for leaders to engage with peers and mentors in the American technology sector. It was a strong beginning.

Early in spring, Task Force team leader Lee Sanderson—a passionate advocate for women's economic development and empowerment, arranged a meeting for me with the leadership of the newly established American University–Kabul. The campus was seeking financial support for the construction of a facility to house a women's studies program. After much discussion, I agreed the Task Force would fund the effort, but only if the mission of the facility was focused on women's economic development and opportunity. In May, we convinced the Defense-contracting community to allow us to award a grant enabling the construction of this remarkable facility—a symbol of sustainable empowerment that will bear dividends for many years to come.

Building on the success of the Buffett Foundation's constructing a college of agriculture in Jalalabad, TFBSO provided funds to complete the construction of a sister facility located at Herat University, again to be supported by the Borlaug Institute under a grant from the Task Force. These three educational institutions—two agricultural colleges and the women's economic-development center at AUK—would be another lasting legacy of TFBSO in Afghanistan.

It was such a waste for our mission to be fading away when we could see the impact of our work after such a relatively short amount of time.

I sent formal last-ditch proposals to Secretary Gates, Chairman Mullen, and the Joint Chiefs, as well as new CENTCOM Commander General James Mattis, and General Petraeus. I solicited their support for an effort to reestablish the Task Force, focused on restoring our work in Iraq, in Pakistan, and in Afghanistan, with State Department support and funding, a small fraction of the funds USAID was spending on consultants and advisors locked behind fortified compounds throughout the region.[22] Secretary Gates's impending departure, as well as that of Admiral Mullen, made it impossible to gain the necessary support from the State Department to make this happen.

Throughout the spring, I lobbied and pushed to have the mandate of TFBSO reinstated, to enable me to recruit new staff and restore our mission, all to no avail. With no funding and no staff, and a focus reduced only to Afghanistan for a few short months, it was impossible to resurrect the mission again.

On Friday, July 1, 2011, I packed my belongings and said my goodbyes. Even though I had provided five months' notice, the Pentagon had no one identified to take my place to wind down the mission by the end of September. I attempted to talk Kris Haag into letting me place him in charge, but he refused. He wanted to stick around long enough to get the oil sector on its feet, and then he would depart as well.

The following Tuesday, I left the Pentagon for the last time. It was one month shy of seven years since I had arrived at the Pentagon from Silicon Valley, filled with a naive, eager desire to serve my country. I had been overwhelmed with the Pentagon and its history, its gravity, its sense of mission, on that first day walking the halls, taking in the sights and sounds.

Now, as I drove away, I felt absolutely nothing for the place.

15.

FIXING THE SYSTEM

*". . . and they shall beat their swords into plowshares . . .
nation shall not lift up sword against nation, neither shall
they learn war any more." Isaiah 2:4*

*"The Prophet Muhammad (peace be upon him) was asked
what type of earning was best, and he replied: 'A man's work
with his hands and every (lawful) business transaction.'"
Al-Tirmidhi: 846*

In November 2008, Indian security forces captured a single member of the ten-person terrorist cell that had executed coordinated attacks in Mumbai on landmark hotels and tourist attractions. Later confirmed by Pakistani officials to be a Pakistani citizen and a member of the radical Islamist organization Lashkar-e-Taiba (LeT), the detainee, Mohammed Ajmal Amir Kasab, hailed from southern Punjab Province. He, along with his terrorist colleagues, received comprehensive psychological, weapons, and combat training in mountainous regions of Pakistan east of Islamabad, near the disputed region of Kashmir.

To entice Ajmal Kasab into participating, LeT offered cash compensation to his family of less than $5,000. Assuming similar compensation was offered to his colleagues, as well as another fifteen trainees who were not selected for the final mission, the cost of the labor for three days of horror in the principal city of the world's second-largest country was less than the cost of a single U.S. service member deployed to Afghanistan for two months.

Kasab was interrogated on camera by Indian police after his capture. His testimony is revealing.

"We were told that our big brother India is so rich and we are dying of poverty and hunger. My father sells daha wada [a Pakistani sweet] from a stall in Lahore and we did not even get enough food to eat from his earnings. I was promised that once they knew that I was successful in my operation, they would give 150,000 rupees [about $3,000] to my family."

"If you give me regular meals and money I will do the same for you that I did for them."

According to police accounts, when he was questioned about his knowledge of Islam, he had no knowledge at all, and could not recite a single verse from the Koran.[1]

One of the most surprising aspects of traveling in impoverished areas of the Middle East and south Asia is the ubiquitous presence of satellite dishes. Millions of poor people may live in shanties, mud huts, or rock dwellings on hillsides, but the vast majority have a small generator and a satellite dish, as well as a mobile telephone. From this link to the outside world, they are served hundreds of channels, each providing a window into a world they have never known and have little hope of entering.

The "flat world" of Thomas Friedman that Iraqi Sheikh Sabah al Khafaji was expecting to gain access to, the globalized hyperconnected economy that has lifted ancient societies into increasing levels of prosperity, remains distant for much of the Islamic world. The reasons for this are too numerous to list, ranging from poor governance to the curse of natural resources to colonial borders drawn by British and French mapmakers designed to create rifts among ethnicities and sects.

To be a young man in a deeply conservative religious society, in which marriage can only be contemplated if you have a job, is to increasingly to live without hope. The region has a massive bulge of youth with increasing numbers of jobless young people entering the workforce every year, only to find that no opportunities exist and their dreams must be delayed. These young people are bombarded daily by images on television, Web pages, and social media of long-impoverished infidel cultures in China, India, and smaller nations such as Vietnam and Bangladesh, now enjoying the fruits of prosperity.

When traveling in Iraq and Afghanistan, the most common refrain I heard from leaders in business and government was one of extreme disappointment at our failure to provide access to economic opportunity. America's legacy from past wars abides throughout the region: the apocryphal notion that we defeated Germany and Japan, only to then rebuild them into global economic powers. South Korea followed, lifted from poverty by American know-how and economic support. According to this mythology, to be defeated by America in war is to be guaranteed a quick ticket to prosperity and a coveted place in the global economy.

Historical reality tells a far less compelling story of America's postwar engagements. In postwar Europe, the Marshall Plan was only devised after three years of floundering ineptitude among new, immature European governments lacking the capacity to reconstruct their destroyed economies, compounded by American indifference after years of war. Only when starvation took hold in Germany, and Communist parties began to gain support in Western Europe and create a real threat of Soviet expansion, did the United States put forth the Marshall Plan, a financial investment program that provided capital for European governments and industries in return for meeting benchmarks in rebuilding free market economies. America did not rebuild Europe; it provided financial support and business expertise to Europe, enabling Europeans to rebuild their own countries.[2]

In Japan, General Douglas Macarthur served as the de-facto head of state for six years after receiving the surrender in Tokyo Bay in 1945, rewriting the Japanese Constitution and implementing sweeping fundamental societal and economic reforms.[3] But it was not until the 1960s that Japan's economy began to emerge as a trading partner of any significance in global markets, with prosperity to follow. Postwar Japan was an impoverished, shattered society for more than a decade before economic vitality was fully restored.[4] Yet the myth of rapid American reconstruction of the Japanese economy is widely believed among Arab populations.

South Korea experienced even greater deprivation following the Korean Conflict. The "Han River Miracle" and its associated industrialization of Korea did not begin until almost ten years after the end of hostilities in 1953, and had little to do with American support. America provided security against attack from North Korea, but the economic development of South Korea is a testament to Korean leadership and ingenuity.

It is a modern myth we cannot escape. Not that we try very hard to escape it. Most Americans believe these myths as well, having little to no understanding of the mechanics of postwar reconstruction in Europe or Asia. After the downfall of both Taliban Afghanistan and the Saddam Hussein regime in Iraq, American officials trumpeted the oncoming benefits of our occupation—the economic reconstruction of these broken societies, feeding expectations we have never met before, and are not equipped to meet today. Yet those unfulfilled—and unfulfillable—expectations, cast before youthful restless societies desperate to have their day, have created tremendous disappointment, frustration, and bitterness toward the United States.

*   *

In Iraq and Afghanistan today, America has failed to deliver on its mythology. A generation of millions of young Iraqis and Afghans have only our military occupation as a memory of America. The USAID and State Department civilians they encountered were wrapped in body armor and surrounded by armed private mercenaries, speeding through towns in armored black SUVs. It is reasonable to expect that Iraq and Afghanistan will, if their governments continue to advance in capacity and commitment to liberalization, follow the long paths of postwar European and Asian countries and emerge as economically viable members of the community of nations.

But until that day comes, we have a problem. Young frustrated Iraqis and Afghans are bombarded by messages from radical mullahs claiming that the denial of prosperity was always the design of the West, and that America is the architect of an anti-Islamic war. It only takes a tiny percentage among the millions of disaffected young people listening to this preaching to create another generation of radicals bent on vengeance against the United States.

In no country is this risk greater than in Pakistan. We have set the stage for yet more disappointment in that troubled nation, with public announcements by American officials of iconic projects and the building of infrastructure as a sign of American goodwill, embodied in the Kerry-Lugar Act. I personally committed to Pakistani business leaders our plans for TFBSO to help their businesses gain access to growth and opportunity, only to be stripped of all authority to deliver on those promises by a callous, turf-obsessed Washington bureaucracy. The messages of radicals grows louder as our drone attacks hammer away at Taliban, Al Qaeda, and other insurgent havens sponsored by Pakistan's national intelligence service, while the "carrots" strategy of Richard Holbrooke remains unfilled.

As of 2013, annual funding appropriations under the Kerry-Lugar Act have been reduced by a third, from the original $1.5 billion per year to less than $1 billion since 2010. Of these appropriated amounts, less than half is being allocated to the promised iconic projects or direct economic support of industries and agriculture. Much of the infrastructure spending is being invested in an effort to improve electricity production at power plants and dams. But as in Iraq, this investment is not sufficient to make a meaningful difference in the availability of electricity for the vast majority of Pakistani homes and businesses and therefore creates little goodwill among Pakistan's citizens.

And so America faces a conundrum. The developing nations of the Middle East and south Asia are hotbeds of radicalism, financed by America's oil dependency on Saudi Arabia and its radical Wahhabi Islamic doctrine that sparked the passions of the 9/11 attackers. These nations fall further and further behind their neighbors, who are increasingly prosperous as they connect to the global economy and liberalize their political and economic systems.

The military-industrial complex of the United States Defense Department, forewarned by President Eisenhower in 1961, has now been augmented by a "development industrial complex," a near lockdown of the majority of USAID contracts by a small number of highly connected firms that deliver too little of tangible value to local communities where funding is supposed to be targeted.[7] Study after study by the Government Accountability Office point out the futility of American foreign aid spending, yet still the budgets are passed and programs reauthorized. The reaction of the development-aid community when confronted with their failure is to point at the mammoth Defense budget: "We spend nothing compared to the Pentagon." And they are correct. But it is an irrelevant comparison.

Development aid represents about $25 billion in annual U.S. spending. While it pales compared to the $600 billion U.S. Defense Budget, it is nonetheless a staggering amount of money. It is larger than many market segments of the United States economy that attract leading blue-chip companies. American foreign aid is a market and has the same forces of entrenched players protecting their market access that plague other government budgets. But unlike transportation, healthcare, or other nondefense spending, poorly executed development aid uniquely harms national security.[8]

Development aid spending creates expectations of goodwill that, when unfilled, foster disappointment and suspicion and undermine our national interests. Failed expectations fuel the embers of disappointment and anger that radical organizations fan into flames. It is a cycle of failure that can be, and must be, reversed.

✳   ✳

After working beside this broken system for five years, in postwar countries (Iraq and Afghanistan, Sudan) impoverished developing countries (Rwanda), and a regional power sliding into poverty and instability (Pakistan), I have been frequently invited to participate in discussions among government advisors seeking solutions to our broken foreign assistance framework.

Our assistance programs generally fail to establish sustainable, economically viable outcomes at the project, program, and national levels in countries that receive assistance in the region. If America is going to spend billions of dollars on nonmilitary foreign assistance programs in the region, it should deliver results that benefit the perception the citizens of the region have of the U.S.

Our inability to provide even symbolic access to economic opportunity is crippling our image in the region. Our regional myth as the great rebuilder of postwar countries must be at least partially confirmed by operational reality if we are to build relationships with citizens in the region that defy constant radical anti-Western messages of hatred and violence. For now, we have the worst of all worlds: heavy expenditures on failed assistance programs, a complete inability to foster rapid sustainable economic development, and myth-driven high expectations generated by our very presence in the region and promises from American political leaders.

This first step toward a solution is a simple reversion to an earlier organizational structure: end Department of State management of foreign assistance.

The Foreign Service plays a vital role in the establishment of foreign policy of the United States, but its culture is and will always be diplomatic and strategic in nature. Diplomats are not implementers. The culture of diplomacy, so critical to negotiation and resolution of conflict without resorting to violence, is absolutely wrong for development program management.

The primary instrument for administration of foreign assistance, USAID, was moved under the State Department in 2005, in a misguided effort to better align its programs with security and counterterrorism policy, particularly in the Middle East and south Asia. The jury is now in on this transition. USAID remains ineffectual at its principle mission of delivering cost-effective program outcomes that advance American foreign policy in the region. From staffing to allocation of resources to the hiring of a USAID Administrator, the priority of the senior State Department leadership is the fulfillment of its primary diplomatic mission, not the successful execution of foreign assistance programs. The USAID Administrator position was left vacant for more than a year in the midst of a ramp-up of effort in Afghanistan and Pakistan, a clear example of where the priority of the State Department was focused during the change of administrations.[9]

The argument for aligning USAID under the Department of State was to ensure alignment of its programs with policy objectives.[10] But this argument could be made for any element of foreign policy, including Defense. All of our instruments of foreign engagement must be aligned to the policy objectives of an administration. Using organization structure is a poor substitute for managing the alignment of the leadership of an administration to the policy of the president. Organizational realignment is an operational decision, not a policy-alignment decision. It sets the culture and operational priority of how an organization will execute its work, how its objectives will be met, its resources allocated, and its people rewarded. A blend of strategic objectives caused by mixing disparate organizations into a single structure is crippling to improved operational capability.

Too often, the Washington solution to operational challenges within federal agencies is to consolidate failing organizations into ever-larger cabinet-level departments, where problems are subsumed into massive bureaucratic infrastructures, stifling any ability to focus on improvement and increase agility.

The Bush Administration, given its well-known struggle to create a common direction among its national-security cabinet secretaries—particularly State and Defense—compensated for the failures of the National Security Council to forge common direction by centralizing organizational alignment. In the case of USAID, this has been a distraction, reducing its ability to focus on improving its operational execution as it is further and further woven into an ill-fitting diplomatic management framework.

Establishing foreign assistance as a standing organization relieved from incompatible diplomatic management thinking is an essential first step to solving our broken foreign-assistance system.

＊　　＊

The second step is to separate economic development from foreign aid.

As we began engaging with USAID in Iraq in 2006, the relationship was initially very positive but differences between the people working in TFBSO and USAID were stark. USAID, at its heart, is a humanitarian relief organization. Helping people through the provision of emergency assistance, food, clean water, and health care, is the clear overarching culture of USAID when it is at its best. In Afghanistan, the most-effective assistance program the United States has pursued has been in rural health care. Life expectancy of Afghans has increased from forty-seven years in 2001 to more than sixty years today—a stunning improvement. This has been achieved through the provision of clean water, vaccinations for communicable diseases, and most important, pre- and postnatal health-care for infants and young mothers. It represents the best of America, and earns widespread praise and recognition among Afghan citizens. It is a program led by USAID.[11]

Young people who go to work at USAID are among the best of us all, foregoing material wealth to help serve humanity around the globe. They seek a career providing humanitarian relief for the suffering and impoverished. In an age of materialism and the pursuit of financial wealth, the few remaining USAID development workers are rare and special people indeed.

Economic development, however, is not directly a humanitarian activity. It has tremendous humanitarian benefits, but they are not the primary objective of the enterprise. Establishing businesses and free enterprise is a wholly different mindset than that of humanitarian assistance. There is a reason we have schools of business; the skills and culture associated with creating successful business enterprises are unique and do not generally overlap with the skills and aptitudes associated with providing humanitarian assistance.

Humanitarian impulses will always dominate USAID, as they should. Yet USAID has been given the task, as the principal agency assigned responsibility for foreign assistance, with managing tactical economic development in the Middle East and central Asia.

If the United States wants to "fulfill its myth" and provide tangible economic opportunity in impoverished regions of the Middle East and central Asia, it must separate the management of tactical economic development from USAID. USAID would be liberated then to rebuild the ability to do what it, historically, has done best—humanitarian assistance—freed from expectations it will never be able to fulfill, that it will build and connect troubled countries to the global economy.

The creation of an organization capable of fulfilling the economic-development mission of linking conflict-ridden countries to tactical economic opportunity must be done from scratch. There is no existing entity capable of performing this activity today within the federal government.

✳   ✳

Everyone stateside wants to keep Americans safe, which is a noble goal, but counterproductive in practice. We need to repeal the security restrictions imposed by the Crowe Commission as they are applied to foreign assistance efforts.[12] There is nothing more absurd than the sight of American civilians walking the streets in body armor and military helmets, surrounded by private security guards carrying automatic weapons, while they try to "engage" the public.

Civilian body armor is the ultimate manifestation of a failed American mission. The message we send to local citizens is that their lives are less valuable than our own: a message they quickly understand and resent. It is not possible to deliver foreign development assistance successfully outside of distributing food, water, and shelter, if an environment requires heavy armor for movement among a population. If an environment requires armored engagement, the mission is a military mission and the work should be performed by our uniformed military.

Our regional embassy compounds are equally appalling in terms of the public image they project. The prison-like architectural requirements of the Crowe Commission recommendations are now common throughout the region. We maintain large embassies with hundreds (or thousands in the case of Iraq) of employees who never leave their compounds except in armored convoys or via helicopter airlift. The paranoia and misunderstanding these large expensive missions create within a country is significant, not to mention the expense of tax dollars they represent.

A simple principal should guide our missions in the Middle East and central Asia. If a nation is too dangerous for our civilians to move among the public without a security requirement to wear body armor or travel with visibly armed security guards, then we should not have civilian development personnel in the country. If a nation is too dangerous for our embassy not to appear as a fortress with razor wire and gun placements, then we should downsize our missions to much-smaller facilities that create a lower public profile—avoiding negative public perceptions caused by massive walled forts with large numbers of mysterious personnel housed within the walls.

✳   ✳

If civilian service in the Middle East and central Asia is really a priority for us, we should add incentives for the best people to sign up and stay longer.

The current civil service deployment model for the Middle East and central Asia takes one of two forms. The first, and most common, is that of a hardship posting, a required assignment for one year that a foreign-service officer must undertake as part of post-9/11 career development. These hardship postings are typically followed by more desirable assignments in Europe, east Asia, or South America. The Middle East thus becomes a tour of duty, a necessary stepping-stone on a career path, with the assignment something to be endured until it is over. Local populations quickly pick up on the lack of enthusiasm our civilians have for working within countries in the region.[13]

The second, much rarer, model is that of the few "bureau" experts, linguists with genuine interest in the region, who take multiple assignments broken up by "breaks" of a year or more, assigned to less stressful locales. The regional-expert model is staffed by a relatively small cadre of foreign-service officers who work at senior levels within the diplomatic structure. It generally has no parallel within the USAID leadership structure. Foreign assistance leadership in countries like Iraq or Afghanistan is a pickup game of one-year rotational assignments interspersed with long-standing contractors and consultants who move from contract to contract maintaining engagement in particular countries.[14]

The lack of continuity in engagement among foreign assistance leaders working in the region is a major problem. Trust-based relationships are instrumental for effective engagement in countries throughout the region, and these can only be formed over time. The unique nature of the cultures, languages, dialects, and norms of doing business differ widely even within countries in the region. Asked how TFBSO was able to execute successfully so many initiatives, I attributed the outcomes almost entirely to the continuity of engagement of our leadership team, most of whom worked continually in the country for several years. It is a management model I learned in the private sector. Companies that expand international markets maintain continuity of engagement in the markets they seek to open, sometimes for many years. A good sales manager for an international market is irreplaceable, and is well compensated for its contributing to the financial success of the firm. Such continuity is essentially impossible to establish within the civilian agencies today.

The United States must adapt its foreign policy organizational structures to reflect the unique and dangerous circumstances we face in the Middle East and south Asia. Radical Islam is not going away, yet we insist on structurally treating our nonmilitary foreign engagement in countries in this region as if they were in Europe or South America. The United States Defense Department, with its regional combatant commands, has established overarching management structures that accommodate and facilitate region-specific engagement to ensure operational effectiveness. Our civilian agencies have no such effective, regional structure.

Our civilian agencies should create separate corps of professionals dedicated to working on the unique challenges and opportunities present in the Middle East and south Asia. Compensation and career development should be enhanced for professionals working in these regions, and the notion that assignments in these regions are "hardship" postings should be eliminated. Linguistic and cultural training must be enhanced and continual. As with the educational assistance offered to military officers, civilian professionals focused on these regions should receive increased educational and developmental opportunities to expand their knowledge.

The increased security threat that civilians in these regions would operate under would be acknowledged and compensated for, with enhanced insurance, health care, and support infrastructure similar to that offered to the uniformed military. It should be understood that the Crowe Commission security posture will not be applied, and that there is a higher risk of injury or death, as part of the "entering" employment arrangement. Rather than seek to lock our civilians behind walls and wrap them in armor, we should acknowledge and honor their service and the risks they take, and afford them the same respect we grant members of the military for risking their lives in service to the nation.

To those who would argue that it would not be possible to create such a corps of regionally focused professionals, I would offer our experiences with TFBSO as a counterargument. TFBSO fielded hundreds of experienced business professionals in some of the most violent areas of Iraq and Afghanistan with the understanding that they would work in harm's way, and would be risking their lives. I recruited volunteers with no institutional support outside of a small Pentagon office set apart from the bureaucracy. Americans in business or development stand ready to volunteer if asked, if the ability to succeed in their mission is clear, and if support for the unique needs of such positions is well established.

✳ ✳

We need to manage government contractors effectively.

The United States military has an indispensable organization established to bring engineering and construction expertise to bear in support of our national security objectives: the United States Army Corps of Engineers. Our humanitarian relief and foreign assistance effort has no such capability. The negative effects of this are clear and indisputable. For the past decade, civilian-led infrastructure development programs in the Middle East and south Asia have underwhelmed. From failures at restoring Iraqi electrical capacity to failed road and dam and infrastructure programs throughout Afghanistan to the current lack of progress in deploying Kerry-Lugar funding to build infrastructure in Pakistan, the past decade has been a continuing demonstration of inept management of large-scale public infrastructure programs.

Yet these programs continue to be trumpeted as new commitments of American goodwill to the region. As in economic development, if we insist on claiming we are going to build infrastructure in the region for sewer, water, electricity, and transportation requirements, then we had better learn how to do it, because today we cannot.

For the past ten years, the U.S. has sought to outsource this critical work, simply signing large contracts with major firms to deliver infrastructure projects. Yet every civil works project must have oversight and management by trained engineers and construction experts capable of ensuring successful delivery.

Stuart Bowen, the Special Inspector General assigned to weed out waste and fraud in Iraq reconstruction programs, has long advocated for the establishment of a civilian equivalent to the U.S. Army Corps of Engineers.[15] After ten years of futility, and no end of appropriations for infrastructure in the region in sight, it is a step that is long overdue. Just as economic development and humanitarian assistance require unique skills and aptitudes, engineering and construction require no less. If, as Secretary Clinton committed in her 2009 tour of Pakistan, the United States seeks to construct iconic public infrastructure as a gesture of goodwill, it should be willing to commit the resources necessary to direct and manage the work successfully.

✳   ✳

I often wonder how the postwar reconstruction of Iraq might have gone had we approached it differently. If the Iraqi Army had been left intact but immediately placed under American command. If the bureaucracy had been left intact, and hard-core Baathists removed through a more diligent risk assessment instead of throwing out thousands of government workers all at once, crippling the functioning of the Iraqi government for years. If the industrial base had been left operational instead of shutting it down and throwing everyone out of work because the Iraqi government owned the factories. And if America had marshaled its private-sector businesses to come to Iraq and immediately engage in commercial activity—not for money or for contracts to build things, but strictly to create business relationships and begin buying and selling goods, as Chinese and Korean firms have flooded in to do since relative peace was restored in 2008.

Iraq would have become a far less dangerous place had these steps been taken. What Iraqis were hoping for, what Afghans were hoping for, and what the youthful populations of the region are still seeking, is a connection to the same economic dynamism taking hold in China and India. Within American industry are the people capable of making those connections, yet our government leaves them sidelined while we deploy ineffective bureaucracy to critical missions.

Instead of billions upon billions of dollars spent every month on military operations, a set of tax incentives or tax credits to encourage American companies to engage immediately in commercial development in Iraq would have cost far, far less in treasure and in the lives of our men and women in uniform.

We are, per capita, among the largest consumers of oil and mineral wealth on Earth. With 5 percent of the world's population, we consume 25 percent of the world's oil.[16] Yet we discouraged active engagement of our own natural-resource companies in Iraq and Afghanistan, even though these companies would have introduced the worlds' most-advanced technologies and the most sensitive environmental and social labor practices in use anywhere in the world today. Instead, companies from China and the former Soviet Union are moving in, bringing far less socially desirable practices. What interests are served by the hostile stance we take to our own private sector? Not the interests of Iraqi or Afghan society. Not the interests of the environment. And not the interests of our own long-term security and stability.

✳   ✳

Perhaps most important, if we plan on rebuilding economies, we need more experts who have actually built or operated businesses.

One of the most common refrains I heard in Iraq in 2006 came from U.S. personnel, both civilian and military, with regard to the state of Iraqi factories: "I visited a factory the other day and it looked like a dump." We would then visit the site, and find an older but reasonable-looking industrial operation. What became clear over time was that the vast majority of Americans serving in our government have no idea what a real factory looks like. If they have an image at all, it is from futuristic motion pictures or images of computer assembly lines, as if industrial welding shops or heavy industrial plants look like high-tech clean rooms. The government mirrors our society at large: most Americans of this generation have never visited a working factory or seen an industrial operation.

This lack of familiarity with industrial operations extends to mining industries as well. Precious little new mining development takes place in the United States any more. Most of the mining experts TFBSO hired to work in Afghanistan came out of retirement, and were in their late sixties or seventies. Most Americans never hear or think much about mining any more. It is a dirty business to our "service economy" workforce.

In developing countries, however, these "dirty" industries are the industries that count. There isn't much demand for consultants, Web page designers, smartphone application programmers, or gourmet chefs in the wild areas of Afghanistan. Iraqi oil-field equipment manufacturing plants are not clean rooms. But for nations emerging from generations of conflict, the high-paying jobs these industries create form the bedrock of a middle class. The jury remains out on how long the American middle class will survive the exodus of our own manufacturing offshore—but if we seek to help get troubled countries on their feet, we must build teams of people comfortable with old-fashioned industrial operations again, from factories to mines to smelters and processors.

There are plenty of experienced people with these skills, many of them among the long-term unemployed, their expertise no longer needed in today's America for today's service-industry jobs. As with the geologists who came out of retirement to assist TFBSO with its field surveys of mineral deposits in the Hindu Kush, aging manufacturing engineers and managers who answered the call to work throughout Iraq and Afghanistan will answer it again if asked.

But someone has to ask.

✳   ✳

In 2010, TFBSO Chief of Staff Elizabeth LoNigro brought in a book for me to read. Written by Harry Bayard Price, it was entitled *The Marshall Plan and Its Meaning: An Independent and Unbiased Appraisal of the Entire Record.*[17]

It was illuminating and humbling. Most Americans know the general framework of the story. The heroic effort of giants of postwar history, including President Harry S. Truman, Averill Harriman, and of course George C. Marshall, developed a new approach to foreign policy, one that acknowledged the necessity of recreating an economically sovereign and prosperous Europe. But the details are less well known.

It was desired, within Congress as well as the Truman Administration, to "create a 'businesslike' organization designed to accomplish an emergency operation with maximum efficiency." To achieve this objective, a new federal agency was established—the Economic Cooperation Administration—which would oversee the implementation of the Marshall Plan. Acknowledging the crushing effect on innovation and agility of the stifling postwar bureaucracy, the new agency was given unprecedented administrative freedom to operate by the Congress. As Harry Bayard Price wrote, "The ECA, as a temporary agency, was given the scope and flexibility needed for a complex, hard-hitting emergency operation. Administrative limitations were held to a minimum; a number of conventional restrictions were waived."[18]

Staffed with executives from American industry, normal pay grades were exempted for the top fifty business leaders recruited to the ECA. Recognizing the inability of the State Department to administer operational activity, but wanting to enforce the alignment of ECA activities to foreign policy directives, Congress resolved the matter by requiring frequent coordination with the Secretary of State by the ECA Administrator.

The first Administrator of the ECA was appointed by president Truman in 1948. Paul G. Hoffman, the president of Studebaker Motor Company, was selected. Within months of his appointment, Hoffman had established an agile, lean organization that operated the ECA in a manner that would be familiar to a modern-day technology company.

Interviewed about his leadership style after departing the ECA in 1952, Hoffman stated, "My concept of dealing with people in an organization is to get the maximum out of each. This creates an impression of some lack of order. The smoothest machine is authoritarian, but you don't get the best out of people that way. When they are expected to think, they operate not as smoothly but much better. . . . In government there's a tendency to go on the principle: you keep out of my empire and I'll keep out of yours. I don't think we broke this down wholly in ECA, but we did to a great extent."[19]

As the Marshall Plan's financial investments in productive capacity shepherded by the ECA took hold and economic production increased throughout Europe, the ECA's success gained additional fathers in Washington. The outbreak of the Korean conflict and the fall of the Iron Curtain shifted the focus of American foreign policy from postwar economic reconstruction back to military security. The ECA was eventually subsumed by this shift and abolished in 1951 by the establishment of the Mutual Security Agency, which would be enmeshed within the bureaucratic structures of the Defense and State Departments that the ECA had been originally empowered to avoid.[20]

The circumstances that resulted in the establishment of the ECA to administer the Marshall Plan sound strangely familiar. I would go as far as to argue that Deputy Defense Secretary Gordon England, in establishing TFBSO as a business group carved away from the Pentagon and State Department bureaucracies and given broad latitude to rectify the mistakes of the early occupation of Iraq, was walking in the footsteps of Truman and Marshall and the ECA.

But the crisis that TFBSO was sent to rectify has not been subsumed, as the ECA mission was, by a change of circumstances. While many of the mistakes of the early economic decisions in Iraq were reversed through TFBSO, and Afghanistan has been shown a path to eventual economic sovereignty, the region remains far too disconnected from the global economy given how connected the region's people are in every other respect.

Early in the 1960s, President John F. Kennedy established a group of volunteers given a task with a purpose: to go into the impoverished regions of the world and offer assistance.[21] The Peace Corps was an embodiment of American goodwill, addressing the needs of its time.

Today, the developing world has moved up on the hierarchy of needs. Famine and widespread illiteracy are no longer as pervasive in the developing world. Now, the assistance that the developing world seeks is economic, in creating productive enterprises that generate employment, a tax base, and a middle class capable of sustaining democratic institutions. Perhaps it is time to create a "business corps," drawing up our unique entrepreneurial capacity to assist those less fortunate. The cost of such an effort would be low relative to the military and humanitarian missions into which we now pour billions.

If we insist on maintaining a large military presence in the Middle East and south Asia, as seems likely, and if we insist on promising to invest to improve the lives of citizens of the region, then we must create institutions capable of making improvement happen. In past times of crisis, we have taken the steps necessary to do this. As with the ECA, as with TFBSO for war-torn Iraq and Afghanistan, the United States must establish business-driven institutional capability to weave the economies of the troubled countries of the Middle East into the community of nations, and to create mutually beneficial relationships that are not based on politics or religion or security, but on commerce, ending once and for all the lie that America wishes ill on the people of the Islamic world.

EPILOGUE

I am often asked why we kept at it, in the face of all the difficulties
and impediments, across two administrations.

Those who ask never got to see the gratitude in the eyes of
soldiers and marines in the field when we showed up and stayed to
help, regardless of the success or failure of a particular effort, letting
America's finest know that there were civilians willing to risk all in
support of their mission. To work with, and learn from, great leaders
of our time, the military commanders Peter Chiarelli, George Casey,
David Petraeus, Ray Odierno, Michael Mullen, Ed Giambiastiani,
Stanley McChrystal, Lloyd Austin, John Allen, and countless others.
To work with legendary diplomats like Ryan Crocker and Richard
Holbrooke. To have the privilege of support from Deputy Secretary
of Defense Gordon England. To be carried across administrations as
different in their politics as two presidencies could be by Secretary of
Defense Robert Gates—one of few remaining statesmen of this era of
history—and to work directly for him for two years.

To work with a remarkable team of dedicated, patriotic civilian
leaders from all walks of private and public American life, all who
risked their lives, gave time from their families, and sacrificed financially, to lead hundreds of business people, agronomists, and financial
experts to assist our military and our nation in a time of need.

All of these factors were fuel that helped us persist through difficulties, but nothing inspired us to carry on as much as the impact of having factory workers, farmers, and merchants throughout Iraq and Afghanistan grasp your hand, look you in the eye, and offer their thanks for helping them regain their livelihoods and their dignity.

Visiting Iraq today, one is struck by the absence of Americans. Foreigners are everywhere now in Iraq, not only in the long-stable Kurdistan region, but also in the south of the country, where an economic boom is underway. Foreign commercial activity has grown from $3 billion in 2008 to more than $50 billion projected in 2012. Many of the companies TFBSO led to Iraq from Korea, Japan, and Europe have thrived. American companies like General Electric and Boeing continue to build on their businesses established with TFBSO support. But you do not see Americans on the streets of Iraq. The oil industry lies sequestered in secure compounds far-removed from the population centers of southern Iraq.

Our massive embassy and our regional consulates remain locked down, and our civilian personnel continue to be required to wear armor and travel with heavily armed guards in armored convoys when they travel at all. Chinese, Russian, Korean, and European businessmen are everywhere. Americans are absent.

Iraq, in a newly emerging regional configuration, takes on an incredible importance to the stability and security of the Middle East. There are two possible outcomes. Iraq may become a fault line of ongoing conflict between the worlds of Sunni and Shia Islam, subject to endless acts of terror and violence as regional powers interfere among Iraq's sects and ethnicities to gain advantage in their ancient struggle.

I believe that a more hopeful outcome is an Iraq that buffers these two worlds: an economic power with an educated workforce and relatively evolved democratic institutions that diffuse power between strong provinces and a weaker central government. There are many challenges that remain before Iraq can assume this role, but existential threats were faced and overcome once before in 2006–07 when Al Qaeda and Shia militias were in control of vast areas of the country only to face rejection by the Iraqi people. Iraq today has a large, well-trained military, including special forces adept in counterterrorism operations. Its oil production is expanding, with the country now second only to Saudi Arabia in its oil exports among OPEC countries. Sporadic violence, protests, and spectacular attacks will remain unfortunate facts of Iraqi life as another national election approaches in 2014, but I believe that Iraq will pull through.

There are many who would argue that I am being, as always, too optimistic.

Effective American engagement is a key element of Iraq's future, and on this front recent developments are not encouraging. As expected, the last U.S. military forces withdrew from Iraq on December 31, 2011, under the terms of the Status of Forces Agreement negotiated by the Bush Administration and the Government of Iraq in 2008. Much public effort was made to negotiate a new agreement allowing U.S. presence in Iraq beyond 2011, but neither Iraqi President Nouri al-Maliki nor President Obama succeeded in efforts to extend American military engagement.

Visitors to Iraq today will notice that everyday Iraqi citizens find our withdrawal bewildering. In their experience the U.S. had expended massive cost and treasure in their country, and while there remains great resentment among elements of the Iraqi population—particularly Sunnis—at the American invasion and subsequent problematic occupation, they cannot fathom why we walked away. On the one hand, Iraqi nationalism makes our departure a cause for pride. On the other, there is a sense of uneasiness and dread about our absence; the nation still lacks full confidence in its institutions and its security given the instability in the region.

Several prominent Iraqi politicians have expressed frustration to me at how the process of negotiating an extension of our military engagement played out. Too often, they complain, senior U.S. officials landed in Baghdad and held press conferences complaining about the lack of progress on a new agreement and publicly warned Iraqi leaders that the U.S. was serious about departing. Such public displays made it extremely difficult for Iraqi politicians to then advocate for an extension of the military presence. Doing so would make them look as if they were kowtowing to the Americans, an act of political suicide in Iraq. It would have been much better, according to these leaders, for the U.S. to have kept the negotiations private and worked behind the scenes instead of publicly demanding progress.

It is hard to say if a different approach would have mattered given the fragmented nature of Iraq's electorate today, and the fragility of the governing coalition Maliki barely holds together.

But it is clear that the United States has lost a great deal of influence in the country at an extremely inopportune time, when the role of Iraq in regional stability may become critical. The American vacuum is not going unfilled. Iranian influence in Baghdad grows ever stronger, and if/when Syria falls, Iran will redouble its efforts to exert influence in Baghdad after losing its ally in Damascus.

It is an ironic state of affairs. In spite of the difficulties and challenges for both America and Iraq during the eight years of American military engagement, Iraqis still long for the America of the movies— fast cars, the best technology, the best know-how. They wanted our private sector, and instead got our bureaucracy. The most popular cars among Iraqi youth today are American muscle cars—Dodge Challengers, Chevy Camaros, Ford Mustangs, mostly bought elsewhere in the region and imported to Iraq. Enterprising Iraqi vendors drive to Amman, Jordan, every other day, bringing back trunkloads of Big Macs and KFC fried chicken to sell to Iraqis craving Americana. A day-old Big Mac sells for $8 on the streets of Baghdad. But as of 2013 not a single iconic American franchise is present in Iraq outside of the Kurdistan region.

Ongoing conflict among neighbors seeking to advance their own security interests makes it harder to be optimistic about Afghanistan in the near term. But the development of Afghanistan's natural resources, and the potential that this development has created for the country to stand on its own feet economically, moves forward. International interest in developing Afghanistan's mineral resources continues to grow. Recently a conflict erupted in the Afghan Parliament regarding newly proposed legislation to further encourage international development of the mining sector. Many Afghans view the new legislation as being too favorable to private interests: a healthy public debate arose over an issue that is entirely new to Afghanistan.

The delay in passing new mining legislation caused a minor uproar in the international community. The entire foreign-aid and military-funding transition strategy for Afghanistan is based on projected growth in revenue from mining. The TFBSO mining program, greeted with derision by the Washington foreign aid bureaucracy when it was publicly launched in 2010, became the basis of the entire transition strategy for Afghanistan. It is a remarkable shift from the original discussions of fruit shipments to India as the only economic engine for impoverished Afghanistan.

As feared, the State Department leaders that had accomplished the last-minute legislation change to move TFBSO to USAID by September 2011 suddenly refused to take responsibility for the mission, insisting that the Pentagon keep the mission alive another year. ISAF commanders were adamant that the work had to continue. So against the warnings of the risks of extending the work given the loss of leadership, the mission was sustained beyond 2011 to focus on wrapping up projects in Afghanistan only. The organization was moved four levels down into the Pentagon civilian bureaucracy, and moved out of the Pentagon into an obscure remote facility in Arlington, Virginia. All of the senior sponsorship and exemption from bureaucracy that had made the program succeed was now removed.

In 2012, five of the remaining TFBSO personnel were killed in Afghanistan, and another died of substance abuse. In the previous five years, with hundreds of employees working outside the wire in Iraq, Afghanistan, and Pakistan as well as African countries, we had lost one team member to a rocket attack on the Green Zone in Baghdad. In only one year, absent seasoned experienced leaders accustomed to working in conflict zones, six people died. It was a predictable and heartbreaking outcome.

In spite of this, several programs maintained momentum and delivered promised results. Kris Haag stayed on to ensure his petroleum-resource development program, including the first private investments in oil fields in northern Afghanistan, was completed. Lee Sanderson remained to ensure that key programs in carpet processing and marketing, food processing, and most important, the new women's economic center at American University Kabul were completed. The remaining Afghan projects will be slowly wrapped up in 2013, with the last remnant of TFBSO to depart with U.S. forces early in 2014.

The completion of projects already launched by TFBSO in Afghanistan is a small comfort compared to the original expansive vision in the TFBSO economic-development strategy for that troubled country. In Iraq, since TFBSO suddenly departed in January 2011, momentum for the privatization of state industry has stalled. Several solicitations for private investment in state companies have been issued by the Iraqi government since 2010, to little interest among international investors skeptical of Iraq in the absence of effective American engagement. The Iraqi economy is thriving in the oil-rich south and Kurdish north, driven by foreign investment and burgeoning private-sector development. As feared, however, the Sunni regions of western Iraq are falling behind economically. This is a dangerous development given the collapse of Syria and the corresponding reemergence of Al Qaeda radicals moving freely across the vast desert border separating Syria and Iraq—and the very situation TFBSO warned against in 2009.

In Pakistan, the historic election of a new prime minister and a peaceful transition of civilian administrations was followed by further economic decline, destabilizing the new administration of Nawaz Sharif. Economic revitalization is a stated objective of every political faction in Pakistan, yet no tactical progress is being made. Increasing radicalization of disaffected Pakistani young people will be the result.

Among the "Arab Spring" nations that have overthrown their leadership and elected Islamist-leaning governments, the number-one priority stated by their new leaders is economic development. Our civilian institutions are not situated to assist with this priority—creating a tremendous missed opportunity for our country to build lasting mutually beneficial relationships that can, over time, reduce the flames of anti-Americanism.

Weeks before I departed the government I was sitting with John Hamre, former Deputy Secretary of Defense under the Clinton Administration and now President and Chief Executive of the Center for Strategic and International Studies (CSIS), lamenting the impending demise of TFBSO. Hamre was as wise as always. "Our foreign aid system is a lumbering dinosaur," he said. "You guys were like a furry little mammal running around that the dinosaur could not stomp on, but after five years finally they got you."

I liked this metaphor a lot. The idea of us scurrying around the legs of the frustrated lumbering brontosaurus of the Washington bureaucracy was amusingly descriptive. And with the metaphor came cause for optimism.

The furry little agile mammals eventually prevailed as the dinosaurs became extinct.

One can always hope.

ACKNOWLEDGMENTS

During my government service, and especially during the years working with the military in active combat missions, business colleagues often asked what it was like to work with the military. What it was like to work inside the Pentagon. And what it was like to work with the federal bureaucracy. This book is my best effort to answer their questions. In writing this I had two overarching objectives. The first was to be accessible to readers from walks of life that are not continually exposed to the Washington, D.C., Beltway workings and machinations of government, but are nonetheless bombarded with what passes for news coverage in our constant flow of 24/7 information. I hope that the businessman, the pragmatic, centrist, average American, and the idealistic young person who seeks to serve will find useful insights into the challenges facing our country in the world today. The second was to create a sense of the possible, to provide a hopeful vision for effectively engaging the world, at a time when it is easy to despair about the state of our government and its ability to respond effectively to the challenges of the day.

The reader will judge if I've succeeded or failed in this effort, and if I've fallen short of the goal the failure is strictly my own. I have been fortunate to call on many participants in the Task Force mission to review and provide clarity on the stories and recollections within the book. Any omissions, misrepresentations, or other mistakes that may have slipped through those reviews are also my own as well.

I wish to thank the many advisors and counselors who patiently helped me along the way in Washington, a list not limited to but including Howard G. Buffett, Tom Donohue, Milt Bearden, Fareed Zakaria, Mary Boies, Malcolm Gladwell, Paul Gebhardt, Meghan O'Sullivan, John Hamre, Jerry Jones, Newt Gingrich, William Cohen, Ed Straw, J. B. Burns, David Berteau, Clare Lockhart, Nancy Spruill, Regina Meiners, Harlan Ullman, Ryan McCarthy, Jacques Gansler, Margaret Myers, Paul Strassmann, Mark Cramer, Bob Kimmitt, Peter Pace, Thomas Barnett, Arnold Punaro, Dave Pauling, Matthias Mittman, Bill Strong, Philip Grone, Chris Barlow, Bill Greenwalt, Diedre Lee, Chris Ruth, Mark Kryzsko, Cheryl Irwin, and especially my current business partner Tom Pritzker.

In addition to the senior commanders who sponsored our overall mission and who are described within the book, I also owe a debt of gratitude to the countless commanders and flag officers whose subordinate commands worked with TFBSO during the duration of its mission. I especially want to thank H. R. McMaster, Michael Meese, Dave Reist, Richard Zilmer, Vince Brooks, Frank Wiercinski, Larry Nicholson, Ed Cardon, Frank Helmick, Rick Lynch, Bill Caldwell, John Allen, Mark Hertling, Graeme Lamb, Bill Rollo, and Jonathan Shaw. Their patience with my early lack of knowledge and understanding of military matters seemed infinite, and their support was instrumental to the positive impacts of TFBSO in their areas of responsibility. Their leadership during the darkest days of violence in Iraq was an inspiration to all of us.

Prior to joining the government, I was fortunate to benefit from the influence and involvement of several mentors in my career. Many of the lessons applied successfully in the mission of the Task Force resulted from what I learned from these wise individuals over the years, specifically Jozef Straus, Syrus Madavi, Tony Muller, Mike Phillips, Scott Parker, Kevin Kennedy, Keith Powell, Tom Dorval, David Rice, Louis Clement, Javad Taheri, Jye-Chyi Lu, Marty Wortman, and Ralph Disney.

In preparing this manuscript, I benefited from the advice of many, but especially Laura O'Dell, Barney Gimbel, Jennifer Hager, Mark Perry, Gerry Brown, Dick Keil, Scott Lycan, Juli Branson, and most of all, my wife Cindy Brinkley. Four years after being told she had a year or two left to live, the indomitable Beth Law has kept her rare form of lung cancer at bay, providing inspiration to all of us. Her reviews and editing were a great help to this project. My editor, Eric Nelson, was remarkable in his continued support, and especially in applying both axe and scalpel as needed. Thanks to all of them for making this project possible.

Most of this manuscript was written during two lengthy sessions in Hatteras Village, North Carolina, during the fall and winter of 2011–12. Thanks to the restaurant and shop owners who made me so welcome during the cold quiet months in that beautiful setting.

Finally, and most important, I want to acknowledge the bedrock that helped me through five remarkable years filled with both hardship and reward. The book is dedicated to my wife, Cindy, and our children, Jack and Lindsey, who sacrificed two weeks a month of normalcy for five years while Dad worked in harm's way. Cindy persevered through the ups and downs of government service one step removed, delaying her own career so I could serve for two years, only to see that turn into a seven-year odyssey. Without their prayers, those of my parents Bill and Sherry Brinkley, and my pastor Scott Lycan, I could never have endured the challenges that the mission created.

Over the five-year life of the Task Force for Business and Stability Operations as a viable instrument of policy, more than 800 remarkable individuals served in some capacity or another, in Iraq, Afghanistan, Pakistan, Sudan, and Rwanda. Every accomplishment of the team members was a result of their dedication to the unorthodox mission and its ever-present risk of violence. I've attempted to highlight as many of the principal contributors to the mission as my editors would allow, but far too many are unmentioned in the text, each with unique experiences and contributions that cannot be captured in a project of this scale. The following appendices provide a partial list of the principle contributors to the Task Force mission, as well as a short description of many of the projects completed in Iraq and Afghanistan. To those individuals listed, and to the many others not shown, our country owes an enduring debt of gratitude.

—**Paul Brinkley,**
August 2013

APPENDIX A
PRINCIPAL CONTRIBUTORS, 2006–2011
(LISTED ALPHABETICALLY)

Wendy Acho
Chris Abbott
Jared Abraham
David Adams
Scott Adamson
Candice Adkins
Mark Ajamian
Samir Al-Azawi
Omar Al-Bakry
Kazhaw Al-Khaffaf
Mustafa Al-Qassab
Mohammed Al-Qisweeny
Firas Al-Rikaby
Sarmed Al-Yassin
Layth Albayaty
Pakeza Alexander
Kamal Allami
Winston Allen
Ahmad Almashat
Lance Alred
Saud Amer
David Amoroso
Alton Anderson
Derek Anderson
Jason Anderson
Carter Andress
Jennifer Anthis

Ahmed Araji
Alan Armstrong
Mark Asher
Rahmat Attaie
Alberto Aviles
Raed Aweina
Steve Bacot
Greg Badavas
George Bagous
Christopher Bailey
Tucker Bailey
Mark Baird
Chris Barlow
Brian Barnes
Brent Barnhill
James Bartolino
Raving Barwari
Milt Bearden
David Beine
Wayne Belcher
Lamonica Bell
David Bethany
David Bernier
Hussain Bdawi
David Bibby
David Blocker
Bryan Bloom

Nate Boaz

Chris Bobbitt

Rebecca Bonner

Brandon Boughen

Noureddine Boulouha

Jim Bowen

Sean Brazier

Gary Briers

Gerry Brown

Harry Bucknall

Howard W. Buffett

Noah Buntman

Laura Burlingame

Lalena Burns

Peter Buttigieg

Joe Bylebyl

Paul Cal

James Cannia

Diana Carey

Ellen Carey

Charles Cato

John Chadderton

Alex Chaihorsky

Albert Chang

Ladonna Choate

Ty Christian

Grace Chung

Anne Clark

Eric Clark

Gregory Clark

Tommy Clarkson

Keith Cole

John Coleman

Andy Connelly

Stacy Cook

Glenn Corliss

Robert Courson

Tommy Crangle

James Crock

James Crowther

Gene Culbertson

Corey Cunningham

Blaze Currie

William Damschen

Nick Daniel

Robert Daniels

Rick Daugherty

Beau Davis

Dick Davis

Joan Davis

Marilyn Davison

Ahmed Dawood

Nadia Dawood

Jeremy Dawson

Cynthia Dearin

Garfield De La Mothe

Nattalie De La Mothe

Jeff DePasquale

Chris Derbyshire

Mike Deville

John DeVine

Dan Digilio

Karwan Dizeyee

Jeff Doebrich

Ken Dorph

John Dowdy

Tanisha Dozier

Mackenzie Drescher

William Drewery

Regina Dubey

Justin Lee Dudley

Bill Duncan

Daniel Dunn

Brian Dunne

Jeffrey East

Laura Eavenes

Richard Elder

Jonathan Elist

Pam Elliott

Seth Engler

Cathryn English

Drew Erdmann

Muhannad Eshaiker

Shannon Espersen

Marie Esposito

Alexandra Etheridge

Dennis Evans

Nate Evans

Ahmed Abbas Fadhel

Darren Farber

Hassan Fatah

Sam Feagley

Gregory Fernette

Danielle Ferry

Ronald Fetherson

Stephen Finkel

Gina Fiore
Guy Fipps
Mercedes Fitchett
Heather Fitzgerald
Grace Fontana
Richard Ford
Marilyn Forney
Laura Foster
Bill Frank
David Frank
Benjamin Freedman
Rolanda Freeman-Ard
Bob Fulgenzi
Marion Garcia
Rebecca Garcia
Terry Garman
Steve Geary
James Gilbertson
Barney Gimbel
Laura Gladden
Matthew Glanville
William Glascoe
Jonathan Glueck
Jonathan Godbout
Matthew Gold
Trace Gorsline
Vanessa Grant
Laura Grazier
Yolanda Greene
Brian Gregory
Steven Gregory
Andrew Grosz
Susana C. Guajardo
Kyle Guinivan
Jorge Gumucio
Jose Guterriez
Barry Haack
Kris Haag
Andy Haeuptle
Tina Hager
Muhannad Haimour
Pendry Haines
Andy Hale
Stephen Halpern
Braxton Hamilton
John Hamerlinck
Vaughn Hammond
Chris Hampton

Ebti Hana
Lucas Hanback
John Hargreaves
Charlotte Harold
Moncef Harrabi
Ryan Harrell
Scott Harrington
Adam Hasiba
Monty Hayes
Tim Hayes
Kurt Heinselman
Joe Henley
Connor Herr
Robert Hill
Jan Lam Ho
Merritt Hodgdon
Deborah Hoepfer
Jeff Holcomb
Robert Hollis
George Holloway
Tory Holmes
Zaheer Hooda
Richard Hopkins
Drew Horan
Forrest Horton
Robert Horton
Stephen Houghton
Karen Hubbard
Barrett Hunter
Tom Hunter
Michael Hurley
Griffin Huschke
Julian Iddon
Ray Ishaq
Omar Ismail
Jennifer Jacobs
David Jacobson
Wail Jamil
Norton Joerg
Robert John "RJ"
Angelia Johnson
Jeff Johnson
Kirk Johnson
Martina Johnson
Scott Johnson
Christopher Johnstone
Beth Jones
Elizabeth Jones

Hope Jones
Jerry Jones
Velma Jones
Christopher Kaighen
Robert Kalacinski
Latif Karimi
Mark Keeley
John Kenney
Timothy Kenyon
Brendan Kereiakes
Lothar Kerscher
Craig Kessler
Robert Key
Ahmad Khan
Murad Khan
Derrick Kiker
Tom Kimberly
Dustin Kinder
Joeseph King
Mark King
Scott King
Steven Kirby
Kristin Kirkwood
Evan Kohn
Scott Koster
Christopher Koym
Julius Krein
Kobie Kruger
Dave Kudla
Nick Kunesh
Cynthia Kurkowski
Spencer Kympton
Lyle LaCroix
Francois Laflamme
Keith Lamore
Paul Lamothe
Eric Lampe
Dahlia Lamy
John Lane
Beth Law
Todd LeBlanc
Steve Lepse
Suzanne Lesko
Steve Levine
Mark Linsmeier
Steve Lipscomb
Elizabeth LoNigro
Julie Lopez

Jacques Loubser
Bob Love
Ginger Lucas
Marc Luley
Stan Lumish
Jerry Lundquist
Justin Lyon
John Lyons
Leah Mach
Sam Madison-Jammal
Beth Martella
Ken Mason
Dosi Massimilliano
Ajay Mathur
Assad Mattin
Cecil Mauricio
Earl Maynard
Creed McCaslin
Robin McCauley
Rich McClellan
Victoria McColm
Andrew McConnell
Beth McGrath
Bill McGregor
Trent McKnight
Jeff McKone
Elizabeth McNally
Maroun Medlej
Jack Medlin
Ward Melhuish
Scot Merrihew
Mark Metzelaar
Robert Miller
Mark Minukas
Robert Mishev
Clarissa Mitchell
Thomas Modly
John Montecucco
Robert Moore
John Morris
Bart Morrison
Mark Morse
Youssef Mourad
William Moyer
Rasha Nadeem
Al Nelson
Kenneth Nelson
Claudia Nettle

David Newsome
Quan Nguyen
Kreg Nichols
Terese Novak
John Nyre
Brendan O'Donoghue
Feras Obald
Amina Osmani
Douglas Ott
Andrew Otwell
Andy Owings
Bulent Ozozan
Carlos Pair
Benjamin Parham
Mary Beth Parisi
Dhee Patel
Larry Paukert
Miguel Payan
William Payne
Wayne Pearce
Corbin Peck
Eric Perkins
Jon Peters
Jonathan Peters
Allison Phillips
James Phinney
Darryl Piasecki
Jay Pili
Evin Planto
Paul Porter
Rich Poulson
Joe Power
Ed Price
Hemin Qazi
David Quarles
Larry Quinn
Christine Rafiekian
Steve Rahola
Jessica Rancourt
Alexandra Raphel
Raad Rasool
Kallee Ray
Brenda Reckart
Homer Register
Kirk Reickhoff
Karine Renaud
Jorge Restrepo
Matthew Reynolds

Neal Rigby
Ken Rikihana
Richard Ringrose
Will Rivers
David Robinson
Michael Rogosin
Larry Rohrwasser
Bruce Roll
Steve Rooney
Mahdi Sajjad
Stephen Saletta
Lisa Sanchez
Lee Sanderson
Jeremy Sartain
David Scantling
Tim Scarborough
Suzanne Schaffrath
John Schenk
Mike Schier
Verne Schneider
Matthew Schoeffling
Dave Schory
George Schutter
Darryl Scott
Emily Scott
Tim Seibel
Campbell Shannon
Alec Shapiro
Andrew Shaver
Robert Shaw
Rudi Shenk
Joe Shields
Ronald Shimkowski
Glen Shinn
Christian Shomber
Jack Shoykhet
Jon Shumard
Nikki Simmons
Francis Skrobiszewski
E. Terrence Sloneck
Lamar Small
Bob Smith
Mark Smith
Tom Snyder
Bob Speer
Alberta Stadtler
Sara Steele
Sonja Stephens

William Stetner
James Stevenson
Christopher Stewart
Marc Stewart
Dan Stock
Jacqueline Stokes
Jason Stokes
John Stoner
Todd Stratton
Justin Strickland
Ryan Sturgill
Nate Sung
Esther Swartz
Mike Switzer
Shawn Syed
Richard Szuminsky
Ronda Taggart
Brian Tauke
Richard Thoburn
Alan Thomas
David Thurmond
Francis Tisak
Lana Toma
Malcolm Topping
Gil Trill
Patrick Truxes
Rob Turner
Harlan Ullman
Tony Uzzetta
Lida Vail
Keith Van Leeuwen
Estelle Van Niekerk
Mark Vargas
Andrew Varrow
Greg Vaughn
James Venable
Courtney Vicario
John Villar
Elias Voces
Emily Walker
Mark Walker
Xiao Wang
Steve Warthman
Nick Waugh
Brooke Weddle
Walter Welch
Eileen Welker
Mackenzie Wells

Heather Werner
John Wetzel
Jennifer White
Giles Whiting
Stephanie Wilcox
Calvin Wilhelm
Katiri Willaum
John Williams
Lloyd Williams
Colby Winegar
Shawn Winn
John Wirt
Dennis Wisnosky
Kevin Woelflein
Eva Wohn
Gary Wolfe
Eric Wood
Molly Wood
Kat Woolford
James Wright
Lee Yarberry

APPENDIX B
MAJOR PROJECT DESCRIPTIONS:
IRAQ AND AFGHANISTAN, 2006–2011

Geography	Sector	Description
National	Agriculture	Acquired and distributed more than 1,200 industrial greenhouses across 11 provinces, enabling the establishment of more than 400 new produce cultivation businesses.
National	Agriculture	Provided engine parts for an existing fleet of idled helicopters used to spray date crops throughout Iraq, resulting in a 50 percent increase in date production in two years.
National	Agriculture	Established a collaborative partnership with the Department of Agriculture to enable rapid deployment of U.S. land-grant faculty throughout Iraq as a part of TFBSO.
National	Banking	Developed and implemented scalable national infrastructure for electronic funds transfer for Iraqi banks, enabling SWIFT transactions and the establishment of correspondent banking relationships with international banks and deployment of electronic payment systems and card services throughout Iraq.
National	Banking	Established a shared service consortium, AMWAL, providing common electronic-banking transaction-processing for Iraqi banks.
National	Banking	Deployed hundreds of point-of-sale devices across Iraq in retail establishments, restaurants, and hotels, enabling the use of card-based electronic payment throughout the country.

National	Banking	Provided direct support and financial analysis to the Central Bank of Iraq in collaboration with the Department of Treasury.
National	Banking	Collaborated with the Department of Treasury to establish links to threaten finance prevention capabilities for electronic payment infrastructure.
National	Banking	Facilitated the introduction of Export Import Bank of the United States to Iraq, culminating in the opening of EXIM Bank financing for Iraq, opening export markets for American-made products.
National	Banking	Facilitated the introduction of Overseas Private Investment Corporation (OPIC) to Iraq, culminating in the financing of real estate projects throughout Iraq.
National	Corp. Development	Facilitated engagement in Iraq by Abu Dhabi Investment Council, a sovereign wealth fund, culminating in investments in Iraqi oil-field services.
National	Corp. Development	Facilitated engagement and a successful bid by Boeing Corporation for $3B contract for 737 and 787 aircraft, including a training facility at Baghdad International Airport.
National	Corp. Development	Facilitated engagement and a successful bid by Bombardier for $1B contract for Canadian Regional Jets by Iraqi Airways.
National	Corp. Development	Facilitated engagement by Cisco Systems in Iraq, resulting in the establishment of sales channels and a reseller network.
National	Corp. Development	Facilitated engagement by Corinthian Capital of Los Angeles, culminating in investments in fiber-optic network links to Iraq from Saudi Arabia as well as in Gryphon Air.
National	Corp. Development	Facilitated engagement and a successful bid by General Electric for a $4B contract for large-scale electricity generation turbines to add 10 gigawatts of generation capacity to the national network.
National	Corp. Development	Facilitated engagement by Hyatt Hotels, culminating in the submission of a proposal to renovate and operate the historic al Rashid Hotel in Baghdad.
National	Corp. Development	Facilitated engagement by Morgan Stanley in Iraq, resulting in a discussion of future establishment of investment-banking relationships and petrochemical trading in Iraq.
National	Corp. Development	Facilitated engagement by Navistar, culminating in proposals to sell and service military vehicles for the Ministry of Defense.
National	Corp. Development	Facilitated engagement by Northern Gulf Partners, a New York investment fund, culminating in investments in Iraqi oil-field services, real estate development, and construction.

National	Education	Provided direct support and funding for more than 40 Iraqi students to enroll in American land-grant universities for graduate education in agriculture.
National	Natural Resources	Facilitated the reintroduction of the United States Geological Survey to Iraq, funding water resource analysis and mineral assessment projects in collaboration with the Iraqi Geological Survey (GEOSURV).
National	Private-Sector Development	Established a comprehensive training and education program for management teams at state-owned enterprises in for-profit operation, marketing, sales, and investment analysis. More than 300 business leaders in major industrial operations from across the country completed this training.
National	Procurement Assistance	Established a procurement assistance help-desk that serviced more than 200 provincial requests for assistance, enabling the execution of $1.8 billion in provincial contracts.
National	Procurement Assistance	Provided direct procurement assistance and "side-by-side" support to ten Iraqi ministries through the Procurement Assistance Center.
Anbar	Agriculture	Developed, installed, and tested a new poultry disease testing unit at Anbar University.
Anbar	Agriculture	Developed a new academic curriculum for Anbar University College of Agriculture.
Anbar	Agriculture	Established a cooperative for potato cultivation and processing in Al Qaim.
Anbar	Agriculture	Acquired a feed milling system for poultry farming cooperative in Anbar.
Anbar	Agriculture	Developed a crop rotation system aligned to local water, soil, and weather for feedstock production.
Anbar	Agriculture	Developed an irrigation program for Western Anbar, providing a deep water drilling platform, pivot irrigation systems, and associated installation and technical support.
Anbar	Corp. Development	Facilitated the first foreign investment in Anbar by a Canadian investment firm for prefab housing.
Anbar	Corp. Development	Facilitated the development of an Iraqi water bottling company using existing U.S. water purification facilities.
Anbar	Corp. Development	Facilitated foreign investment proposals for oil exploration in Anbar.
Anbar	Corp. Development	Facilitated a foreign investment proposal for development of New Ramadi City.
Anbar	Corp. Development	Facilitated the engagement of SEAF program development in Ramadi in 2008–09.

Anbar	Education	Arranged engagement of agriculture faculty from U.S. land-grant universities including Kansas State, Oklahoma State, Penn State, Texas A&M, and Mississippi State to develop cooperative relationships with Anbar University.
Anbar	Foreign Direct Investment	Facilitated $80M of private investment in the Fallujah Cement Company.
Anbar	Foreign Direct Investment	Facilitated $100M of private investment in the Al Qaim Cement Company.
Anbar	Foreign Direct Investment	Facilitated $200M of private investment in the Kubaysa Cement Company.
Anbar	Industrial Capacity Restoration	Provided spare parts and cleanup enabling the restart of the Fallujah Cement Company.
Anbar	Industrial Capacity Restoration	Restored production operations at the State Company for Ceramics–Ramadi, providing training, marketing support, spare parts, and equipment repair.
Anbar	Private-Sector Development	Facilitated the award of 1,318 contracts valued at more than $350 million to Anbar-based private companies through the Iraqi First program.
Anbar	Procurement Assistance	Provided procurement assistance to the Anbar government for 24 water resource projects totaling $10.6 million.
Anbar	Procurement Assistance	Provided procurement assistance to the Anbar government for a $1.8 million acquisition and establishment of a blood bank.
Anbar	Procurement Assistance	Provided procurement assistance for the acquisition of 31 municipal ambulances.
Anbar	Procurement Assistance	Provided procurement assistance for acquisition of dental equipment for clinics throughout Anbar.
Anbar	Procurement Assistance	Provided procurement assistance in the execution of $5 million to enable health services at the Health Center in Al Sagra Nahia.
Babil	Agriculture	Provided training in poultry farming and irrigation to more than 500 farmers, young people, and university employees.
Babil	Agriculture	Developed a 4H-style poultry raising project for 350 young people in Babil.
Babil	Agriculture	In support of the Al Hillah Agricultural Association, developed and implemented a pilot drip irrigation program to demonstrate yield improvement and water resource conservation.
Babil	Agriculture	Prepared detailed economic analyses for 14 crop varieties, enabling effective business planning by farmers and provincial agriculture officials in Babil.

Babil	Agriculture	Funded the establishment of an agricultural marketplace enabling more efficient trade and commerce for locally grown commodities.
Babil	Agriculture	Trained 137 farmers and agricultural leaders in design and operation of wind-powered irrigation and pumping systems.
Babil	Agriculture	Provided poultry nutrition workshops and training to coalition and local leaders in north Babil Province.
Babil	Agriculture	Facilitated the establishment of the Babil Provincial Agricultural Advisory Committee.
Babil	Corp. Development	Facilitated a multimillion dollar acquisition of Iraqi-assembled trucks by the major regional logistics firm, Agility Logistics.
Babil	Corp. Development	Facilitated engagement in Iraq by Case New Holland, culminating in assembly and partial production of farm tractors at restored factory operations in Iskandiriyah.
Babil	Corp. Development	Facilitated engagement and proposal by Massey Ferguson to assemble and market farm tractors in Iraq.
Babil	Corp. Development	Facilitated engagement and proposal by Oshkosh to assemble and support large trucks and military vehicles in support of Iraqi government institutions, culminating in a contract award in 2009.
Babil	Corp. Development	Facilitated the reestablishment of a commercial relationship and truck assembly operations with Scania at restored factory operations in Iskandiriyah in 2008.
Babil	Education	Developed cooperative scientific programs and exchange relationships between U.S. land-grant universities and the University of Babil via hosted engagements in 2008–09.
Babil	Industrial Capacity Restoration	Established assembly operations for Valmont Pivot Irrigation Systems at restored factory operations in Iskandiriyah.
Babil	Industrial Capacity Restoration	Established manufacturing operations for production of industrial-scale greenhouses at restored factory operations in Iskandiriyah.
Babil	Industrial Capacity Restoration	Established assembly operations for industrial trucks, off-road vehicles, and motor vehicles at restored industrial operations in Iskandiriyah.
Babil	Industrial Capacity Restoration	Facilitated establishment of containerized-housing unit (house trailer) construction operations at restored factory operations in Iskandiriyah.
Babil	Industrial Capacity Restoration	Established commercial relationships and a proposal for truck assembly operations by Daimler Benz at restored factory operations in Iskandiriyah.

Babil	Industrial Capacity Restoration	Facilitated the placement of orders for carpet production for international retail outlets at the State Company for Handwoven Carpets in Al Hillah.
Babil	Private-Sector Development	Enabled the award of 461 contracts at a value of $53 million to private companies in Babil Province through the Iraqi First program.
Babil	Procurement Assistance	Provided procurement assistance for contracts exceeding $50 million for municipal improvements in Al Hillah city center.
Babil	Procurement Assistance	Provided procurement assistance for acquisition and installation of lighting on the main road from Al Hillah to Karbala, a major route for religious pilgrims.
Baghdad	Banking	Enabled widespread deployment of point-of-sale devices and automated-payment infrastructure throughout Baghdad.
Baghdad	Banking	Enabled the migration to electronic payment for U.S. government contracted services, moving more than $650 million from cash to electronic payment in 2009.
Baghdad	Corp. Development	Established international business incubator facilities in Baghdad providing temporary office, network, and life support services for foreign company engagement.
Baghdad	Corp. Development	Facilitated the entry of Honeywell in Iraq, culminating in its establishment of operations in Baghdad and Basra.
Baghdad	Corp. Development	Facilitated the reentry of Daimler Benz to Iraq, in collaboration with the German embassy, culminating in the establishment of corporate offices in Baghdad and a national dealership network.
Baghdad	Corp. Development	Facilitated the development of an Iraqi bottled water company in Baghdad using existing U.S.-owned water purification facilities.
Baghdad	Corp. Development	Facilitated the entry of Caterpillar to the Iraq market, culminating in the establishment of generator sales and service operations throughout Iraq.
Baghdad	Corp. Development	Facilitated the entry of Cummins Diesel to the Iraq market, culminating in the establishment of generator sales and service operations throughout Iraq.
Baghdad	Corp. Development	Assisted Groupo Cadini, an Italian clothing retailer, in establishing retail outlets in Baghdad and initial supply relationships with Iraqi clothing factories.
Baghdad	Corp. Development	Facilitated engagement by TerraBuilt, a company that provides ecologically sustainable construction technology, culminating in proposals for construction projects in the Baghdad region.

Baghdad	Corp. Development	Facilitated engagement of more than 60 multinational companies in Iraq from TFBSO base of operations in Baghdad, more than half of which engaged in follow-up business activity.
Baghdad	Corp. Development	Facilitated engagement by Agilent Technologies in Iraq, exploring sales opportunities for instrumentation and test equipment with Iraqi ministries and academic institutions.
Baghdad	Corp. Development	Facilitated the establishment of a corporate office for Eaton Corporation in Baghdad, enabling Iraqi contract awards for electrical equipment.
Baghdad	Corp. Development	Facilitated real estate development proposals for development of hotel and retail properties in central Baghdad.
Baghdad	Corp. Development	Enabled Finmeccanica of Italy to establish corporate offices in Baghdad to pursue contracts with Government of Iraq.
Baghdad	Corp. Development	Provided support to Gryphon Air in launching commercial service from Kuwait to Baghdad, enabling normal business engagement by multinational companies.
Baghdad	Corp. Development	Facilitated the establishment of General Motors MAC Iraq repair operations in 2007–08 near Baghdad International Airport.
Baghdad	Corp. Development	Facilitated the establishment of a generator repair and distribution facility by Caterpillar near Baghdad International Airport in 2008.
Baghdad	Corp. Development	Facilitated the official entry of Microsoft to Iraq, culminating in the establishment of business operations and a training center for Iraqi technologists.
Baghdad	Corp. Development	Facilitated the entry of Google into the Iraq market, culminating in the establishment of the google.iq search engine.
Baghdad	Corp. Development	Facilitated the engagement of Skylink USA with the Ministry of Transportation, enabling the eventual expansion of operations at Baghdad airport.
Baghdad	Corp. Development	Facilitated the development of a proposal for a five-star hotel property by Summit Global Group of the United States, culminating in award of investment license and initiation of construction.
Baghdad	Education	Developed cooperative scientific programs and exchange relationships between U.S. land-grant universities and Baghdad University.
Baghdad	Foreign Direct Investment	Provided direct support to the establishment and development of the Iraqi National Investment Commission, enabling $800 million in new business licensing and investment by 2009.

Baghdad	Industrial Capacity Restoration	Restored carpet-weaving operations at the State Company for Handwoven Carpets, by establishing commercial relationships with U.S. and UK retailers ABC Carpet & Home and Harrods of London.
Baghdad	Industrial Capacity Restoration	Constructed a new facility for the State Company for Dairy Production at Abu Ghraib.
Baghdad	Industrial Capacity Restoration	Facilitated the expansion of production in excess of 100 percent for woven blankets at the State Company for Wool.
Baghdad	Industrial Capacity Restoration	Facilitated increased production of leather goods by more than 1,000 hides per day at the State Company for Leather Goods.
Baghdad	Industrial Capacity Restoration	Restored production operations at the Nassr State Company for Mechanical Industries in Taji, providing market demand access, spare parts, and training.
Baghdad	Industrial Capacity Restoration	Acquired computer-aided design equipment, modern software training, production equipment, and welding equipment enabling restoration of operations at the Heavy Equipment and Engineering State Company in Baghdad.
Baghdad	Industrial Capacity Restoration	Enabled the award of 7,901 contracts at a value of $1.8 billion to private Baghdad companies through the Iraqi First program.
Baghdad	Procurement Assistance	Provided procurement assistance to more than 80 percent of acquisitions, worth almost $2 billion, by the Baghdad Provincial government in 2008–09.
Basra	Agriculture	Facilitated training and education in wind-powered drip irrigation technology to Basra farmers, university faculty, and provincial agriculture officials.
Basra	Agriculture	Repaired a large-scale water pump system providing water to thousands of acres of farms and livestock cultivation ranges.
Basra	Agriculture	Facilitated the formation and establishment of the Basra Provincial Agriculture Advisory Committee.
Basra	Agriculture	Proposed and facilitated the establishment of two mobile veterinary clinics, enabling farmers in marsh areas to treat livestock.
Basra	Agriculture	Provided funding and support to refurbish facilities and expand the University of Basra tissue culture lab.
Basra	Agriculture	Provided funding and support for equipping University of Basra soil- and water-testing labs.
Basra	Banking	Enabled migration from cash payment to electronic payment of $94.5 million to Basra-based private companies in 2009.

Basra	Corp. Development	Facilitated engagement by AI Development in assessment of and proposal for industrial and real estate development opportunities in Basra.
Basra	Corp. Development	Facilitated engagement by ArcelorMittal in Basra, culminating in a $3B proposal to establish a major steel production operation at the site of the State Company for Iron and Steel.
Basra	Corp. Development	Facilitated engagement by East Pacific Capital, culminating in proposals to build international hotels at Baghdad and Basra International Airports.
Basra	Corp. Development	Facilitated the entry of Japanese International Cooperative Agency into Iraq, enabling the execution of $5 billion in Japanese soft loan commitments for Iraq reconstruction.
Basra	Corp. Development	Facilitated the reentry of Mitsubishi Heavy Industries into Iraq, culminating in proposals for oil and gas contracts in southern Iraq.
Basra	Corp. Development	Facilitated the entry of Nippon Koei for execution of Japanese soft loan projects based at the port of Umm Qasr.
Basra	Corp. Development	Facilitated the introduction of date-ethanol technology to Iraq, including linkage to Iraqi date companies culminating in a take-or-pay agreement with an international energy-trading company.
Basra	Corp. Development	Facilitated the entry of STX heavy industries into Iraq for an initial proposal to restore steel production, culminating in more than $10 billion in reconstruction contracts to date.
Basra	Foreign Direct Investment	Enabled a MOU for $3 billion redevelopment of the Basra Iron and Steel Company by a Korean consortium.
Basra	Foreign Direct Investment	Enabled an agreement for a Korean consortium to invest $3 billion in a petrochemical facility in Basra.
Basra	Health/ Procurement Assistance	Provided procurement assistance for technical equipment contracts in Basra for the Ministry of Health.
Basra	Health/ Procurement Assistance	Provided direct procurement assistance to enable service and medical specialist contracts for the Basra Children's Hospital.
Basra	Health/ Procurement Assistance	Provided procurement assistance for contracts in excess of $60 million for Basra infrastructure projects.
Basra	Industrial Capacity Restoration	Provided a generator for the Umm Qasr hospital, enabling health-care services for the community and employees of the Port of Umm Qasr.

Basra	Industrial Capacity Restoration	Facilitated increased production at Umm Qasr Cement through the provision of spare parts and equipment upgrades.
Basra	Industrial Capacity Restoration	Restored production at Basra Petrochemical Company through the provision of new equipment and spare parts.
Basra	Industrial Capacity Restoration	Restored production at Ibn Majid Heavy Industries through the provision of equipment, spare parts, and training in computer-aided design technology.
Basra	Industrial Capacity Restoration	Constructed local open air market facilities in Hayyaniyah neighborhood, enabling expanded access for local merchants.
Basra	Private-Sector Development	Enabled the award of 770 U.S. contracts valued at $381 million to private Basra-based companies through the Iraqi First program.
Dhi Qar	Agriculture	Developed a model farm project for Dhi Qar providing equipment and training to develop wheat irrigation practices using leading agricultural techniques.
Dhi Qar	Agriculture	Facilitated the establishment of agricultural associations enabling information sharing and equipment access for the Dhi Qar farm community.
Dhi Qar	Agriculture	Facilitated the establishment of the Dhi Qar Provincial Agricultural Advisory Committee.
Dhi Qar	Banking	Enabled migration from cash payments, allowing $39M in electronic payments to Dhi Qar vendors in 2009.
Dhi Qar	Private-Sector Development	Facilitated the award of 41 contracts worth $5 million to private Dhi Qar companies via the Iraqi First program.
Dhi Qar	Procurement Assistance	Provided direct procurement assistance for acquisition of a $19 million sewer network in Dhi Qar.
Dhi Qar	Procurement Assistance	Provided direct procurement assistance for $13.5 million in local community contracts.
Dhi Qar	Procurement Assistance	Provided procurement assistance for critical city infrastructure contracts in excess of $75 million.
Diyala	Agriculture	Provided support to expand production and packaging-operations improvements at the Zuhairat Date Processing Cooperative in Diyala.
Diyala	Agriculture	Provided a pivot irrigation system demonstration project at the Diyala Agriculture Extension Farm in 2009.
Diyala	Agriculture	Developed a 40-acre demonstration site for drip irrigation and the use of plastic mulch for vegetable cultivation, a key to water conservation initiatives.

Diyala	Agriculture	Installed ten drip irrigation systems with the Diyala Agriculture Association in 2009.
Diyala	Agriculture	Implemented a 15-acre pivot irrigation system in collaboration with the Diyala Agricultural Association.
Diyala	Industrial Capacity Restoration	Restored production at Diyala Electric company, providing equipment and training and communications infrastructure for the production of electrical transformers.
Diyala	Industrial Capacity Restoration	Provided equipment enabling restoration and expansion of production at Khalis Medicinal Alcohol company.
Diyala	Private-Sector Development	Enabled the award of 293 contracts worth $65 million to private Diyala-based businesses through the Iraqi First program.
Diyala	Procurement Assistance	Provided procurement assistance for $1.7M in road and public works projects by the Diyala provincial government.
Dohuk	Private-Sector Development	Enabled the award of 45 contracts worth $3 million to Dohuk private companies through the Iraqi First program.
Irbil	Agriculture	Facilitated U.S.-based investment in a tomato cannery operation in northern Irbil Province.
Irbil	Corp. Development	Facilitated engagement by Cummins Diesel, culminating in a dealership establishment in Irbil.
Irbil	Corp. Development	Facilitated engagement by Suzer Group of Istanbul, investor in the Coca-Cola bottling plant in Irbil.
Irbil	Foreign Direct Investment	Provided direct support to the Kurdistan Regional Government for investor engagement, facilitating four major business and investment delegations to Irbil from 2007 to 2009.
Irbil	Private-Sector Development	Enabled the award of 113 contracts worth $9 million to Irbil-based private companies via the Iraqi First program.
Irbil	Procurement Assistance	Provided direct procurement assistance to the KRG Ministry of Transportation for review of operations contracts.
Karbala	Agriculture	Provided textbooks and revised academic curricula for the College of Agriculture at Karbala University.
Karbala	Agriculture	Provided training and education in wind-driven irrigation technology for Karbala farmers and agricultural officials.
Karbala	Foreign Direct Investment	Facilitated foreign investment of $120M in the Karbala Cement Company.
Karbala	Industrial Capacity Restoration	Restored production operations at Al Furat Chemical Company, providing spare parts, equipment repair, and power generation equipment.

Karbala	Private-Sector Development	Enabled the award of 8 contracts totaling $3.2 million to Karbala-based private companies via the Iraqi First program.
Karbala	Procurement Assistance	Provided support and assistance in review of proposals for the future Mid-Euphrates Airport.
Karbala	Procurement Assistance	Provided direct procurement assistance for $10.6 million in contracts for education and infrastructure projects in Karbala.
Kirkuk	Agriculture	Provided education and demonstration of modern agricultural irrigation and cultivation techniques for farmers and officials in Kirkuk.
Kirkuk	Agriculture	Developed and implemented a sheep pasture demonstration program in Kirkuk.
Kirkuk	Agriculture	Provided four-row planter equipment to Kirkuk provincial agriculture officials enabling the demonstration of improved grain-planting techniques.
Kirkuk	Agriculture	Provided education and demonstrations of no-till and dry land wheat cultivation methods in collaboration with the U.S. Provincial Reconstruction Team.
Kirkuk	Agriculture	Provided a proposal for an integrated model grain-farming operation in collaboration with the Kirkuk Provincial Reconstruction Team.
Kirkuk	Banking	Enabled migration from cash payment to electronic payment in the amount of $4.5 million to Kirkuk private companies in 2009.
Kirkuk	Foreign Direct Investment	Facilitated foreign investment of $150 million in Kirkuk Cement Company.
Kirkuk	Procurement Assistance	Provided direct procurement assistance for $15 million in provincial contracts for health care and water infrastructure in Kirkuk.
Kirkuk	Procurement Assistance	Facilitated the improvement in provincial budget execution in Kirkuk from 43 percent in 2007 to 81 percent in 2009.
Maysan	Industrial Capacity Restoration	Restored cultivation of sugar in the marshes of Maysan Province, providing $1.4 million in equipment and training.
Maysan	Industrial Capacity Restoration	Restored production at Maysan Sugar Company, providing packaging equipment suitable for local market requirements.
Maysan	Industrial Capacity Restoration	Provided agricultural assistance in tissue culture analysis for sugar varieties and new plant strains.

Maysan	Industrial Capacity Restoration	Created a large-scale sugar industry restoration program for Maysan Province, facilitating engagement from U.S. and Brazilian industry and academic experts in Al Amarah, in collaboration with the U.S. Provincial Reconstruction Team.
Maysan	Industrial Capacity Restoration	Facilitated a visit to Brazil for the Maysan Sugar Management Team to learn best practices for sugar cultivation and processing.
Maysan	Private-Sector Development	Enabled the award of 9 contracts totaling $3.2 million to Maysan-based private companies under the Iraqi First program.
Muthanna	Agriculture	Established new academic curriculum at the Muthanna School of Agriculture
Muthanna	Education	Provided university-level textbooks and course materials for the Muthanna School of Agriculture.
Muthanna	Private-Sector Development	Awarded 10 contracts valued at $1.1 million to private companies in Muthanna under the Iraqi First program.
Muthanna	Procurement Assistance	Provided procurement assistance for $9.4M in contracts for educational housing and local infrastructure in Muthanna.
Muthanna	Procurement Assistance	Enabled an increase in budget execution in Muthanna from 51 percent in 2007 to 82 percent in 2009.
Najaf	Corp. Development	Facilitated engagement by UK-based ArmourShield to develop manufacturing capacity in Najaf.
Najaf	Industrial Capacity Restoration	Enabled increase in garment production through provision of modern design and cutting equipment at the Najaf Company for Ready-Made Clothing.
Najaf	Industrial Capacity Restoration	Enabled the first export agreements for Najaf-produced clothing to international retailers.
Najaf	Private-Sector Development	Enabled the award of 20 contracts valued at $4 million for Najaf private companies via the Iraqi First program.
Najaf	Procurement Assistance	Provided procurement assistance for $43.8 million in infrastructure and public facility projects in Najaf.
Nineveh	Agriculture	Provided no-till seed drills to provincial extension services for rental to local wheat farmers, improving yields by 30 percent where applied, and reducing water consumption and soil loss.
Nineveh	Agriculture	Acquired 20 tractors and drills for the Al Qosh Farmer's Association in Nineveh for use in no-till wheat-farming operations.

Nineveh	Agriculture	Provided direct procurement assistance of 36 greenhouses with heating and irrigation capabilities, establishing a revolving fund using revenues from cultivation businesses to fund additional greenhouses.
Nineveh	Agriculture	Provided training in small-scale agriculture business development to former insurgents.
Nineveh	Banking	Enabled migration to electronic payment, moving $29M in cash payments to electronic banking in Ninewa Province in 209.
Nineveh	Foreign Direct Investment	Facilitated foreign investment of $120 million in Sinjar Cement Company.
Nineveh	Industrial Capacity Restoration	Acquired dairy production equipment enabling the expansion of Ninewa Dairy operations to new markets.
Nineveh	Industrial Capacity Restoration	Provided raw materials and market analysis for the restoration of production at Ninewa Furniture Company.
Nineveh	Industrial Capacity Restoration	Provided equipment enabling the establishment of cancer and asthma therapy production operations at Ninewa Pharmaceutical Company.
Nineveh	Industrial Capacity Restoration	Restored production at Mosul Clothing Factory, providing equipment and raw materials.
Nineveh	Industrial Capacity Restoration	Restored production operations at Mosul Textile Factory, providing equipment and raw materials.
Nineveh	Private-Sector Development	Enabled the award of 881 contracts valued at $132 million to private companies in Ninewa Province via the Iraqi First program.
Nineveh	Procurement Assistance	Provided direct procurement assistance for a $32 million contract for a new highway interchange, removing significant transportation bottleneck in Ninewa Province.
Nineveh	Procurement Assistance	Provided direct procurement assistance for a $50 million multiyear acquisition upgrading electrical grid links to the national electrical system.
Nineveh	Procurement Assistance	Provided direct procurement assistance for a $25 million contract for a polio victim hospital.
Nineveh	Procurement Assistance	Provided direct procurement assistance for $25 million in contracts for new housing developments.
Nineveh	Procurement Assistance	Enabled an increase in budget execution in Ninewa from 9 percent in 2007 to 55 percent in 2009.
Qadisiyah	Agriculture	Facilitated the establishment of the Qadisiyah Provincial Agriculture Advisory Committee

Qadisiyah	Banking	Enabled migration from cash payment to electronic payment in the amount of $7.5 million to Qadisiyah-based companies in 2009.
Qadisiyah	Industrial Capacity Restoration	Restored production at the Diwaniyah Tire Company, providing equipment and a boiler required to restart tire-manufacturing lines.
Qadisiyah	Private-Sector Development	Enabled the award of 345 contracts valued at $24 million to private companies in Qadisiyah via the Iraqi First program.
Qadisiyah	Procurement Assistance	Provided procurement assistance for $15.1 million in contracts for water treatment systems in Qadisiyah.
Qadisiyah	Procurement Assistance	Enabled an increase in budget execution from 44 percent in 2007 to 98 percent in 2009.
Salah ad Din	Industrial Capacity Restoration	Restored production at the Baiji Northern Fertilizer Company, providing parts and equipment enabling urea-production operations.
Salah ad Din	Industrial Capacity Restoration	Restored production at the Tikrit Flour Mill, enabling processing of the local wheat harvest in 2007 as an element of local counterinsurgency.
Salah ad Din	Agriculture	Provided education and training in no-till wheat cultivation to local farmers and agriculture officials, improving soil quality and enabling water conservation.
Salah ad Din	Banking	Enabled migration from cash payment to electronic payment in the amount of $99 million to Salah ad Din private companies in 2009.
Salah ad Din	Foreign Direct Investment	Facilitated $180 million in foreign investment by Marubeni of Japan in the Baiji Northern Fertilizer Company.
Salah ad Din	Private-Sector Development	Enabled 687 contracts worth $4 million to Salah ad Din private companies via the Iraqi First program.
Salah ad Din	Procurement Assistance	Provided direct procurement assistance and training to Salah ad Din provincial leaders.
Salah ad Din	Procurement Assistance	Provided direct procurement assistance for $3.5 million in water infrastructure and medical equipment for hospitals in Salah ad Din.
Salah ad Din	Procurement Assistance	Enabled an increase in budget execution from 33 percent in 2007 to 43 percent in 2009.
Suleymania	Banking	Worked directly with Asiacell of Suleymaniyah to facilitate the rollout of mobile-banking capability throughout Iraq.
Suleymania	Education	Facilitated the establishment of scientific exchange relationships and cooperative technology sharing with American land-grant universities and the University of Suleymania.

Suleymania	Private-Sector Development	Enabled the award of 29 individual contracts valued at $33 million to private companies based in Suleymania via the Iraqi First program.
Wasit	Agriculture	Facilitated the establishment of the Wasit Agricultural Advisory Committee.
Wasit	Industrial Capacity Restoration	Restored production at State Company for Textiles, providing raw material enabling direct revenue generation.
Wasit	Private-Sector Development	Enabled 379 contracts valued at $129 million to private companies in Wasit via the Iraqi First program.
Wasit	Procurement Assistance	Provided direct assistance to contract execution for bridge construction in Al Kut, valued at $13.3 million.
Wasit	Procurement Assistance	Provided direct assistance to contract execution for infrastructure construction in Wasit, valued at $8 million.

Afghanistan

National	Afghan First	Performed analysis of U.S. military contracting, defining a strategy for broader distribution of contract awards across eligible private Afghan companies, in conjunction with Joint Contracting Command.
National	Afghan First	Created and launched Afghanfirst.org, the only trilingual Web site providing online contract proposal solicitation for Afghan businesses.
National	Afghan First	Established automated financial transaction execution for U.S. contracts, enabling traceability of $10 billion in finances, reducing opportunities for terrorist threat financing.
National	Afghan First	Established an interagency database crossing Departments of Defense, State, and USAID, providing online visibility to more than $24 billion in spending since 2010 to track the impact on Afghan economic development.
National	Afghan First	Eliminated manual procurement system and associated manual reporting through collaboration with the Office of Management & Budget, reducing nonvalue-added workload on contracting officers and enabling improved performance of contract execution and oversight.
National	Afghan First	Introduced and implemented a comprehensive contractor past-performance assessment system for all U.S. and NATO contractors, enabling effective identification of high-performing Afghan firms.
National	Afghan First	Established electronic data interface support teams to accelerate migration from cash payments to electronic payments for contractors.

National	Afghan First	Enabled a streamlined Electronic Funds Transfer vendor-registration process in support of private Afghan banks and accelerating adoption of modern banking practices by Afghan companies.
National	Afghan First	Created and deployed the "Host Nation Wealth Effect" tracking system to broaden distribution of U.S. and NATO contracts to a larger number of Afghan companies.
National	Afghan First	Assessed more than 1,700 Afghan companies receiving contracts from U.S. and NATO commands, disqualifying more than 280 vendors since 2010.
National	Agriculture	Established a training and education program to revitalize and modernize grape cultivation throughout Afghanistan.
National	Banking	Established a certified group of 9 Afghan private banks capable of modern electronic transaction processing and regulatory compliance, migrating U.S. contract payments to these qualified institutions.
National	Banking	Established an Electronic Funds Transfer (EFT) Assistance Center to facilitate the adoption of electronic payments to Afghan companies, strengthening the private banking system and reducing terrorist threat financing.
National	Banking	Facilitated the establishment of a correspondent banking relationship between Citibank and Afghan International Bank.
National	Natural Resources	Financed, established, and implemented a nationwide mineral assessment program in collaboration with United States Geological Survey, compiling overhead surveys, Soviet-era fieldwork and mapping, and a newly performed field sampling initiative for high-priority mineral deposits located throughout Afghanistan.
National	Natural Resources	Launched international mining industry engagement in collaboration with Afghan Ministry of Mines. Hosted 16 international mining firms to visit Afghanistan for high-level meetings as well as reviews of geology and field surveys for high-priority mineral-deposit development.
National	Natural Resources/ Afghan First	Organized Afghan Vendor Day events in Kabul, hosting international companies to meet with Afghan companies, forming relationships and opportunities for business development and expansion.
National	Banking	Provided direct support and equipment enabling the establishment of more than 200 EFT-enabled banking locations throughout Afghanistan in three years, from a base of fewer than 30 locations in 2009.

National	Natural Resources	Provided direct support to the Afghan Ministry of Mines for the public tender of 4 major mineral deposits, including iron, gold, and copper. Provided a team of analysts to support transparent execution of the tender and bid assessment process.
National	Private-Sector Development	Facilitated the introduction of Google/YouTube to Afghanistan, culminating in the establishment of google.af.
National	Private-Sector Development	Facilitated engagement by Case New Holland to assess market opportunities and potential future production operations for farm equipment.
National	Private-Sector Development	Facilitated engagement by leading fashion company kate spade new york, culminating in the market establishment for Afghan cashmere products and handmade fashions produced at Turquoise Mountain Arts craft training center.
National	Private-Sector Development	Established an investment and business development program, facilitating engagement by multinational companies including IBM, Google/YouTube, Citibank, Hyatt, J.P. Morgan, Sweet Dried Fruit, kate spade new york, Morgan Stanley, Schlumberger, Chevron, ExxonMobil, among other multinational firms.
National	Natural Resources	Facilitated investment led by J.P. Morgan to develop and expand the Baghlan Gold Mine.
Baghlan	Natural Resources	Performed analysis of clay and gypsum deposits to verify quality for compliant cement production in Baghlan Province.
Baghlan	Natural Resources	Performed analysis of cement quality from production operations in Baghlan Province, objective was to verify suitability for large-scale construction projects.
Balkh	Natural Resources	Performed field assessment, sample collection, and associated laboratory analysis of copper deposits in Balkh Province.
Balkh	Indigenous Industries	Established and constructed a modern handwoven carpet cutting, washing, and finishing facility in Mazar-e-Sharif, providing Afghan carpet producers with direct access to foreign markets and eliminating dependence on Pakistani middlemen.
Bamyan	Natural Resources	Provided direct support to the Ministry of Mines for public tender and transparent assessment of bids for development of the major iron-ore deposit in Haji Gak, culminating in tender award to an Indian firm.
Daykundi	Natural Resources	Performed field assessment, sample collection, and associated laboratory analysis of tin and tungsten deposits in Daykundi Province.

Farah	Natural Resources	Performed field assessment, sample collection, and validated presence of an industrial-scale deposit of lithium in Farah Province.
Farah	Natural Resources	Performed field assessment, sample collection, and laboratory analysis confirming presence of industrial-scale tin reserves in Farah Province.
Ghazni	Natural Resources	Performed field assessment, sample collection, and laboratory analysis confirming presence of $30 billion of porphyric gold/copper deposits in Zarkashan in Ghazni Province.
Ghazni	Natural Resources	Performed field assessment, sample collection, and laboratory analysis confirming presence of industrial-scale lithium reserves in Ghazni.
Ghor	Natural Resources	Performed field analysis, sample collection, and laboratory analysis validating presence of industrial-scale mercury deposits in Ghor Province.
Ghor	Natural Resources	Performed analysis confirming presence of industrial-scale lead and zinc deposits in Ghor Province.
Helmand	Agriculture	Established a cold storage facility for improved market access for fruit and vegetable farmers in Gheresk.
Helmand	Agriculture	Established a produce-sorting operation with transshipment capability to cold storage facility, enabling improved market access for farmers in Marjah.
Helmand	Agriculture	Restored production at an idled cotton gin through the provision of spare parts, enabling market access for cotton farmers in Helmand Province.
Helmand	Industrial Development	Established a motorcycle repair operation and vocational education center for young people in Now Zad in Helmand Province.
Helmand	Natural Resources	Performed field surveys, sample collection, and laboratory analysis validating the presence of viable lithium reserves in Helmand Province.
Helmand	Natural Resources	Performed field surveys, sample collection, and associated laboratory analysis validating the presence of large-scale industrial deposits of light rare-earth elements at Khan Neshin Mountain in Helmand Province.
Helmand	Natural Resources	Performed field surveys, sample collection, and associated laboratory analysis validating the presence of viable deposits of travertine, and porphyric gold-copper deposit in Chaigai Hills of Helmand Province.
Herat	Agriculture	Completed the construction of modern facility housing at the College of Agriculture at Herat University.

Herat	Agriculture	Provided an academic exchange, training, and support to faculty at the College of Agriculture at Herat University.
Herat	Agriculture	Developed a strategy for poultry industry development including hatchery, feed mill, and production centers.
Herat	Agriculture	Acquired and installed two center-pivot irrigation systems as model projects for water conservation and cooperative extension in conjunction with the Buffett Foundation and Borlaug Institute.
Herat	Corp. Development	Established a modern business incubator facility for high-tech companies in Herat Province, leveraging the presence of IT College at Herat University, as well as support from Google and IBM.
Herat	Corp. Development	Enabled the launch and initial expansion of 6 information technology start-up companies in Herat.
Herat	Industrial Development	Developed a comprehensive economic-development strategy for Herat Province in collaboration with city and provincial leaders, leveraging the local resource and human capital advantages as well as geographical location. This strategy was adopted and ratified by provincial and municipal governments as a roadmap for future development.
Herat	Industrial Development	Established two women-owned and -organized cooperatives for production, marketing, and distribution of canned and processed agricultural products.
Herat	Natural Resources	Performed field surveys, sample collection, and associated laboratory analysis validating the presence of copper reserves valued at $29 billion in Dusar-Shaida.
Herat	Natural Resources	Performed field surveys, sample collection, and associated laboratory analysis verifying quality of barkum and limestone deposits in Herat.
Kabul	Agriculture	Performed an analysis of raisin production, linking an existing ISO-compliant raisin company to the international market, restoring an export market for the once globally dominant raisin industry in Afghanistan.
Kabul	Banking	Provided direct support to the banking sector, in collaboration with Department of Treasury and Department of State, during the Kabul Bank crisis.
Kabul	Corp. Development	Provided a grant enabling the construction of a center for women's economic development at the American University of Kabul.
Kabul	Indigenous Industries	Facilitated a joint venture with Sweet Dried Fruit and Tabasom, enabling dried fruit export to U.S. markets.
Kabul	Natural Resources	Provided training and equipment to the Afghan Geological Survey, enabling expanded performance of field surveys and analysis of Afghan mineral wealth.

Kabul	Natural Resources	Constructed and established a world-class data center and mineral analysis systems for the Afghan Geological Survey, providing access to all overhead surveys, translation of former-Soviet field analyses, and sample survey results for deposits throughout Afghanistan.
Kandahar	Agriculture	Developed a plan and launched a project enabling modern raisin-processing and -packaging in Kandahar, with a goal of enabling expanded export market access.
Kandahar	Agriculture	Provided training and educational support to raisin growers throughout southern Afghanistan to improve packaging and hygiene of raisin-processing operations.
Kunar	Natural Resources	Developed artisinal chromite-mining business operations in Kunar Province in collaboration with U.S. Special Forces and local Afghan leaders.
Kunduz	Natural Resources	Performed field surveys, sample collection, and associated laboratory analysis for celestite production in Kunduz Province.
Logar	Natural Resources	Performed field surveys, sample collection, and associated laboratory analysis validating the presence of a "sister" world-class copper deposit at North Aynak, adjacent to an existing copper deposit under development by a Chinese mining interest.
Mazar-i-Sharif	Energy	Constructed and established a facility near Mazar-i-Sharif for compressed natural gas production, creating a market for local natural gas resources.
Mazar-i-Sharif	Energy	Coordinated and partially financed the repair of a gas pipeline from Sheberghan to Mazar-i-Sharif enabling the restart of an existing idled fertilizer factory capacity, providing a key resource for local agriculture.
Mazar-i-Sharif	Energy	Converted several hundred vehicles to compressed natural gas fuel from gasoline, kick-starting a market for use of indigenous fuel resources with a goal of reduced dependence on imported energy.
Nangahar	Agriculture	Facilitated a grant to establish a new College of Agriculture including a state-of-the-art facility at Nangahar University in Jalalabad by the Buffett Foundation with support of the Borlaug Institute.
Nimruz	Natural Resources	Performed field surveys, sample collection, and associated laboratory analysis validating the presence of an industrial-grade lithium deposit in Nimruz Province.
North	Energy	Performed an analysis of oil resources at capped wellheads in Amu Darya Basin, validating existing reserve estimates. Opened wells to production, with shipment of oil to refining operations near Mazar-i-Sharif, rebuilding confidence that oil production is viable in the northern region and facilitating successful oil-sector development.

North	Energy	Provided direct support to the Ministry of Mines for the successful tender of Kashkari Block in the Amu Darya Basin, resulting in the first international development of oil resources since 2001.
North	Energy	Provided direct support to the Ministry of Mines tender for oil concessions for reserves estimated to approach 1 billion barrels.
North	Energy	Performed seismic-imaging surveys for oil deposits in northern Afghanistan, developing clarity on the scale of reserves in support of future tender proposals.
Nuristan	Natural Resources	Performed field surveys, sample collection, and associated laboratory analysis of pegmatite deposits in Nuristan Province.
Panjshir	Natural Resources	Performed analysis of known world-class deposits of emerald, silver, and iron ore in the Panjshir Valley, quantifying scale and grade in support of future development.
Parwan	Energy	Defined and implemented a program to establish local electricity production and sustainment for micro-hydro generators used in remote local villages for electricity access.
Parwan	Energy	Re-established the failed micro-hydro electricity-generation projects by deploying prepaid meters to remote local communities, generating revenue to finance the maintenance of generator systems.
Patika	Natural Resources	Performed field surveys, sample collection, and associated laboratory analysis of gold deposits at Katawas in Patika Province.
Sar-i-Pul	Energy	Restored oil production at Angot Oil field, reopening capped wells and generating the first Afghan oil production since 2001.
Takhar	Natural Resources	Performed field surveys, sample collection, and associated laboratory analysis, validating a potential for evaporite deposits containing minerals used in fertilizers in Takhar Province.
Takhar	Natural Resources	Performed field surveys, sample collection, and associated laboratory analysis validating the scale of gold deposits in Takhar.
Zabul	Natural Resources	Performed field surveys, sample collection, and associated laboratory analysis validating the scale of gold and copper reserves at Kundalan.
Zabul	Natural Resources	Performed field surveys, sample collection, and associated laboratory analysis for copper and gold deposits in Zabul.

NOTES

CHAPTER 1

1. JDS Uniphase Fourth Quarter and Fiscal Year Ending 2002 Financial Results, June 30, 2002.
2. DOD Policy Memorandum, "Employment of Highly Qualified Experts," Office of the Undersecretary of Defense for Personnel & Readiness, David W. Chu, February 27, 2004.
3. Scale reference on size of department of defense business operations.
4. DOD Acquisition and Logistics Excellence Week Kickoff—Bureaucracy to Battlefield, Remarks as Delivered by Secretary of Defense Donald H. Rumsfeld, The Pentagon, Monday, September 10, 2001.
5. Undersecretary of Defense–Comptroller Dov Zakheim Briefing on the DoD Financial Management Program, Hearing before the Subcommittee on Readiness and Management Support of the Committee on Armed Services, United States Senate, 107th Congress, March 6, 2002.
6. BMMP Restructuring Proposal Briefing to the Undersecretary of Defense–Acquisition, Technology, & Logistics, United States Department of Defense, November 2004.
7. United States Government Accountability Office, Report to Congressional Committees, DOD Business Systems Modernization: Progress in Establishing Corporate Management Controls Needs to Be Replicated Within Military Departments, May 2008.
8. Paul McCloskey, "Business Transformation Is Turning Heads," *Federal Computer Week*, March 26, 2006.

9. Hearing before the Subcommittee on Government Management, Finance, and Accountability of the Committee on Government Reform, House of Representatives, 109th Congress, June 8, 2005.

10. Hearing before the Subcommittee on Readiness and Management of the Committee on Armed Services United States Senate, One Hundred Ninth Congress, November 9, 2005.

11. Ronald Wilson Reagan National Defense Authorization Act for Fiscal 2005, United States Congress, Public Law 108-375, October 24, 2004.

CHAPTER 2

1. "Defense Visitor Opens Tarmiya Qada Building," Armed Forces Press Service, DVIDS, June 2, 2006.

2. Thomas L. Friedman, *The World Is Flat, A Brief History of the 21st Century* (New York: Macmillan, April 2005).

3. State Department Office of Inspector General Report No. ISP-IQO-0557, Review of Staffing at U.S. Embassy Baghdad, March 2005.

4. Milton Friedman, *Capitalism and Freedom* (Chicago: University of Chicago Press, 1962).

5. Naomi Klein, *The Shock Doctrine: The Rise of Disaster Capitalism* (New York: Henry Holt & Co., April, 2010).

6. Policy on Acquisition of Host Nation Produced Goods & Services, General George Casey, Commander, Multi-National Forces–Iraq and Major General Darryl Scott, Commander, Joint Contracting Command–Iraq and Afghanistan, May, 2006.

7. National Infrastructure Protection Plan–Defense Industrial Base Sector, Department of Homeland Security Report, 2009.

8. Millennium Challenge Corporation, www.mcc.gov.

9. "Accelerating Reconstruction and Stability Operations in Iraq," Memorandum from Deputy Secretary of Defense Gordon England, Department of Defense, June 2006.

10. Rajiv Chandrasekaran, *Imperial Life in the Emerald City: Inside Iraq's Green Zone* (New York: Alfred A. Knopf, 2006).

11. United Nations Security Council Resoluton 1483, Establishment of Development Fund for Iraq, May 2003.

12. Coalition Provisional Authority Order Number 30, Reform of Salaries and Employment Conditions of State Employees, September 8, 2003.

13. Coalition Provisional Authority Order Number 12, Trade Liberalization Policy, June 8, 2003.

14. The Marshall Plan, A Handbook of the Economic Cooperation Administration, 1950.

15. "Hard Lessons, the Iraq Reconstruction Experience," Report of the Special Inspector General for Iraq Reconstruction, January, 2009.

16. Ibid.

17. "Rebuilding Iraq 'Will Cost $55Bn,'" BBC News, October 3, 2003

18. "Bechtel Leaves Iraq After 52 Deaths in Three Years," Fox News, November 2, 2006.

19. Thomas E. Ricks, *Fiasco: The American Military Adventure in Iraq* (New York: Penguin Press, 2007).

20. "United States Government Operations in Iraq," National Security Presidential Directive, May 11, 2004.

21. "Management of Interagency Efforts Concerning Reconstruction and Stabilization," National Security Presidential Directive/NSPD 44, December 7, 2005.

22. "Report of the Accountability Review Boards on the Embassy Bombings in Nairobi and Dar es Salaam on August 7, 1998," Crowe Commission Report, United States Department of State, January, 1999.

23. Chandrasekaran, *Imperial Life in the Emerald City.*

CHAPTER 3

1. Fragmentary Order, Commander Multi-National Corps–Iraq, July, 2006.

2. Vali Nasr, *The Shia Revival: How Conflicts Within Islam Will Shape the Future* (New York: W.W. Norton & Co., April 2007).

3. Heinz Halm, *The Shiites: A Short History* (Princeton: Markus Wiener Publishers, 2007).

4. "A Push for More Power at Iraqi Plant," *Washington Post,* August 25, 2004.

5. "Report of the Tikrit Provincial Reconstruction Team—Baiji Fertilizer Plant," December, 2006.

6. *United States Code,* Title 10, Section 2533a.

7. "Policy for Acquisition of Uniforms for Iraqi Security Forces," Department of Defense, Office of Procurement and Acquisition Policy, 2006.

8. Michael R. Gordon and Bernard E. Trainor, *The Endgame: The Inside Story of the Struggle for Iraq, from George W. Bush to Barack Obama* (New York: Pantheon Books, 2012).

9. "Baghdad Factory Reopens, Four Years After Invasion," ABC News, January 31, 2007.

10. "Occupying Iraq, A History of the Coalition Provisional Authority," RAND Corporation, 2009.

CHAPTER 4

1. Task Force for Business and Stability Operations Memorandum, March 11, 2007.
2. "To Stem Violence, U.S. Aims to Create Jobs," *Washington Post*, December 12, 2006.
3. The Iraq Study Group Report, United States Institute for Peace, 2007.
4. "Robert Gates Confirmed as Secretary of Defense," Associated Press, December 6, 2006.
5. Media Roundtable, Lieutenant General Peter Chiarelli, "Update on Operations in Iraq," Combined Press Information Center, Baghdad, Iraq, December 12, 2006.
6. Leon Hesser, *The Man Who Fed the World: Nobel Peace Prize Laureate Norman Borlaug and His Battle to End World Hunger* (Dallas, Tex: Durban House Pub. Co., 2006).
7. Letter from Minister of Agriculture, Government of Iraq, to Dr. Ed Price, March 2007.
8. *U.S. Agency for International Development, Employment Participation and Unemployment in Iraq* (Washington, D.C.: Government Printing Office), May 2007.
9. Fareed Zakaria, "A Surge that Might Work," *Newsweek*, March 4, 2007.
10. Rudy Giuliani and Newt Gingrich, "Getting Iraq to Work," *Wall Street Journal*, January 12, 2007.
11. John Birkeland, "Doing Good While Doing Well: The Unheralded Success of American Enterprise Funds," *Foreign Affairs*, September/October 2001.
12. Quarterly Report and Semi-Annual Report to the United States Congress of the Special Inspector General for Iraq Reconstruction, July 30, 2007.
13. John Warner National Defense Authorization Act for Fiscal Year 2007, Public Law 109-364, 109th Congress.

CHAPTER 5

1. Stabilizing and Rebuilding Iraq: Conditions in Iraq Are Conducive to Fraud, Waste, and Abuse, Government Accountability Office GAO-07-525T, April 23, 2007.
2. Susan Ross-Ackerman, *Corruption and Government: Causes, Consequences, and Reform* (New York: Cambridge University Press, 1999.
3. "Stabilizing and Rebuilding Iraq: U.S. Ministry Capacity Development Efforts Need an Overall Integrated Strategy to Guide Efforts and Manage Risk," United States Government Accountability Office, GAO-08-117,

October 2007.

4. 2007 National Budget for the Republic of Iraq, Iraq Ministry of Finance, 2007.

CHAPTER 6

1. "Ambassador Crocker Visits Baqubah," American Forces Press Service, August 30, 2007.
2. "Economic Task Force Works to Move Iraq from Front Pages to Business Pages," American Forces Press Service, September 4, 2007.
3. "U.S. Falters in Bid to Boost Iraq Business," *Washington Post*, August 24, 2007.
4. "Pazyryk Carpet, New Insights." Wolfgang Klose, 2008.
5. Vali Nasr, *The Shia Revival: How Conflicts Within Islam Will Shape the Future* (New York: Norton, 2006).
6. "Grant Thorton LLP Report on Property Valuation Methodology for Baghdad Commercial Development," Task Force for Business and Stability Operations, 2008.
7. "Provincial Reconstruction Teams in Iraq," United States Institute for Peace Special Report, March 2007.
8. "Provincial Reconstruction Teams: Building Iraqi Capacity and Accelerating the Transition to Iraqi Self-Reliance," State Department Fact Sheet, January 11, 2007.

CHAPTER 7

1. Hisane Misaki, "Japan in Iraq—Goodbye Troops, Hello Aid," *Asia Times*, July 26, 2006.
2. "As British Leave, Basra Deteriorates," *Washington Post*, August 7, 2007.
3. "Summary of the Second Iraq-Japan Economic Forum, Baghdad Iraq," Joint Press Release, December 20, 2009.
4. "Daimler Benz Announces Truck Assembly Operation in Iraq," German Embassy Press Release, 2008.
5. "Germany and Iraq Sign Investment Accord," Reuters, July 23, 2008.
6. Frank Ledwidge, *Losing Small Wars: British Military Failure in Iraq and Afghanistan* (New Haven: Yale University Press, 2011).
7. Ibid.
8. "The Endgame," Michael Gordon and Bernard Trainor, Knopf Doubleday, September, 2012.
9. Gordon and Trainor, *The Endgame*.
10. Thomas Pritzker, William Strong, and Steve Wilson, "Investment

Opportunities in Iraq," *Chicago Tribune,* September 9, 2008.

11. "OFW Killed in Iraq Died a Hero," *Migrante,* Manila, June 9, 2008.

12. "Organic Cotton Facts," Organic Trade Association, June 2010.

13. Amendment to Public Law 99-349 (Bumpers Amendment), 1986.

14. Report of the Borlaug Institute to the Task Force for Business and Stability Operations in Iraq by Region and Province, 2009.

15. National Defense Authorization Act for Fiscal Year 2008, Public Law 110-181, January 28, 2008.

16. Halm, *The Shiites.*

17. Ullrich Fichtner, "Paul Brinkley's War—Pacifying Iraq With the Weapons of Capitalism," *Der Spiegel,* April 22, 2009.

CHAPTER 8

1. "Google's Iraq Tour of Duty" Fast Company, October 27, 2010.

2. "GE Inks Iraq Power Deal Worth $3B," *Huffington Post,* December 16, 2008

3. "Honeywell Expands into Iraq," Honeywell Corporate Press Release, *Business Newswire,* October 5, 2010.

4. "5.5B Airline Deal With Boeing Boosts Iraq," *Washington Times,* May 26, 2008.

5. "EXIM Bank Opens for Short-Term and Medium-Term Financing in Iraq," Export Import Bank Office of Communications, July 22, 2010.

6. "USGS Activities in Support of Economic Development and Stabilization in the Natural Resource Sectors of Iraq," USGS Report, 2009.

7. "Continuation of Task Force for Business and Stability Operations in Iraq," Department of Defense Memorandum OSD 02903-09, Secretary of Defense Robert M. Gates, March 11, 2009.

8. "CSC Expands Electronic Banking Services Into Iraq—Offers MasterCard Products," CSC-SAL Press Release, January 4, 2009.

9. "STX Heavy to Build $3B Plant in Iraq," Kim Hyun-cheoi, KITA, February 5, 2010.

10. "Agreement Between the United States of America and the Republic of Iraq on the Withdrawal of United States Forces from Iraq and the Organization of Their Activities during Their Temporary Presence in Iraq," US-Iraq Status of Force Agreement, 2008.

11. Steven Lee Myers, "Iraq—Open For Business," *New York Times,* October 21, 2009.

CHAPTER 9

1. Letter to Deputy Secretary of Defense William Lynn from U.S. Special Envoy to Sudan Jonathan S. Gration, September 25, 2009.
2. Letter to Deputy Secretary of Defense William Lynn from Commander, United States Africa Command, October 15, 2009.

CHAPTER 10

1. "Want to Save Iraq? Invest," *Newsweek,* December 30, 2008.
2. Preliminary Non-Fuel Mineral Resource Assessment of Afghanistan 2007, United States Geological Survey, 2007.
3. International Monetary Fund Nominal GDP Per Capita—Afghanistan, 2009.
4. McKinsey & Co., Study on Foreign Aid to Afghanistan as Percentage of Nominal GDP, 2009.
5. McKinsey & Co., Study on USAID Spending in Afghanistan 2002-2008, 2009.
6. Ibid.
7. Task Force for Business and Stability Operations—Analysis of DOD Contracting In Afghanistan, 2002–2009. February 2010.
8. Summaries of Important Areas for Mineral Investment and Production Opportunities of Nonfuel Minerals in Afghanistan, United States Geological Survey and Task Force for Business and Stability Operations, 2011.
9. "Continuation of Task Force for Business and Stability Operations," Secretary of Defense Robert M. Gates, Department of Defense Memorandum #OSD 03356-10, March 25, 2010.

CHAPTER 11

1. Farzana Shaikh, *Making Sense of Pakistan* (New York: Columbia University Press, 2009).
2. "Election 2008 Results," Associated Press of Pakistan, February 2008.
3. Enhanced Partnership With Pakistan Act of 2009, Public Law 117-73.
4. Ahsan Abdullah, "An Analysis of BT Cotton Cultivation in Punjab, Pakistan Using the Agriculture Decision Support System (ADSS)," *AgBioForum,* 13, no. 6 (2010).

CHAPTER 12

1. "Lethal Blasts in Baghdad Target Hotel Compounds," *Washington Post,* January 26, 2010.

CHAPTER 13

1. "Agreement Between the United States of America and the Republic of Iraq on the Withdrawal of United States Forces from Iraq and the Organization of Their Activities during Their Temporary Presence in Iraq," US-Iraq Status of Force Agreement, 2008.
2. "The 2010 Iraqi Parliamentary Elections," *New York Times,* March 28, 2010.
3. William R. Polk, *Understanding Iraq: The Whole Sweep of Iraqi History, from Genghis Khan's Mongols to the Ottoman Turks to the British Mandate to the American Occupation* (New York: HarperCollins, 2005).
9. Nasr, *The Shia Revival.*
4. "No Boon for U.S. Firms in Iraq Oil Deal Auction," Reuters, December 12, 2009.
5. "Proposal For Seismic Surveys in Anbar Province," Task Force for Business and Stability Operations, 2009.
6. "As Iraq's Oil Boom Progresses, So Does Gas Flaring," *National Geographic,* September 25, 2012.
7. "Lessons Learned on the Department of Defense's Commander's Emergency Response Program in Iraq," Report of the Special Inspector General for Iraq Reconstruction, January 2012.
8. Ibid.
9. Department of Defense Office of General Counsel Memorandum— Funding for Task Force for Business and Stability Operations Violates Title X, *United States Code,* June 2010.
10. "PAK-U.S. Envoys Ready to Increase Economic Ties," Governor's House Press Conference, Lahore Pakistan, May 4, 2010.
11. "Civilian Surge Plan for Afghanistan Hits a Snag," NPR, September 19, 2009.
12. "Investor Delegation Visits Kabul," Armed Forces Press Services, 2009.
13. Two Americans Launch Idea After Viewing Afghan Farms—Howard G. Buffett Foundation and Agrilife lead $1.5M Project," AgriLife Today, Texas A&M University, July 2010.
14. "Sweet Dried Fruit Signs Agreement to Import Afghan Raisins," Task Force for Business and Stability Operations Release, 2009.
15. Afghanistan Economic Development—Task Force for Business and Stability Operations Briefing to Afghan President Hamid Karzai, 2010.
16. Task Force for Business and Stability Operations—Analysis of DOD Contracting in Afghanistan 2002–2009, February 2010.
17. "Citi and Afghanistan International Bank Enter into Banking Agreement," *PR Newswire,* October 18, 2010.

CHAPTER 14

1. "The Runaway General," *Rolling Stone,* June 22, 2010.
2. Ashraf Ghani and Clare Lockhart, *Fixing Failed States: A Framework for Rebuilding a Fractured World* (Oxford and New York: Oxford University Press, 2008).
3. Ibid.
4. "JP Morgan's Hunt for Afghan Gold," *Fortune,* May 2011.
5. "Afghan Mineral Resources Laid Bare," *Earth,* December 29, 2011.
6. Briefing to Commander International Security Assistance Force Afghanistan, Task Force for Business and Stability Operations, August 2010.
7. Draft Language for National Defense Authorization Act—TFBSO Funding, September 2010.
8. "TFBSO Launches First Ever IT Incubator in Afghanistan—IBM and Google Assisting Department of Defense Venture," *PR Newswire,* May 25, 2011.
9. "Richard C. Holbrooke, Giant of Diplomacy, Dead at 69," *New York Times,* December 13, 2010.
10. Ike Skelton National Defense Authorization Act of 2011, Public Law 111-383, January 7, 2011.
11. "Salman Taseer, Punjab Governor, Shot Dead in Islamabad," *New York Times,* January 4, 2011.
12. Comments Commemorating Shut Down of TFBSO Iraq Mission, Paul A. Brinkley, January 2011.
13. "Status of Task Force for Business and Stability Operations," Memorandum to Secretary of Defense Robert M. Gates, Paul A. Brinkley, February 14, 2011.
14. Robert Tucker, Harvey Belkin, Klaus Schulz, Stephen Peters, Forrest Horton, Kim Buttleman, and Emily Scott, "A Major Light Rare-Earth Element (LREE) Resource in the Khanneshin Carbonatite Complex, Southern Afghanistan," *Journal of Economic Geology,* 107, no. 2 (April 2012).
15. Jason Kelly, "Afghanistan: Land of War and Opportunity," *Bloomberg Businessweek,* January 6, 2011.
16. "The Master Builder of the Middle East," *Bloomberg Businessweek,* July 1, 2007.
17. E. B. Boyd, "Google, IBM, YouTube, and Kabul?: Pentagon Hosts Afghan Tech Entrepreneurs in the US," *Fast Company,* June 20, 2011.
18. "TFBSO Launches First Ever IT Incubator in Afghanistan—IBM and

Google Assisting Department of Defense Venture," *PR Newswire,* May 25, 2011.

19. "McMaster: Afghan Anti-corruption Drive Is Working," *Washington Post,* January 1, 2012.

20. Constitution of Afghanistan, January 26, 2004.

21. E. B. Boyd, "Google, IBM, YouTube, and Kabul? Pentagon Hosts Afghan Tech Entrepreneurs in the US," *Fast Company,* June 20, 2011.

22. "Status of the Task Force for Business and Stability Operations," Memorandum to the Joint Chiefs of Staff, Paul A. Brinkley, April 28, 2011.

CHAPTER 15

1. "Mumbai Terrorist Wanted to Kill and Die and Become Famous," ABC News, December 3, 2008.

2. "The Marshall Plan and the Future of US-European Relations," German Information Center, New York.

3. William Manchester, *American Caesar: Douglas Macarthur 1880–1964* (New York: Back Bay Books, 2008).

4. Ian Buruma, *Inventing Japan: 1853–1964* (New York: Modern Library, 2003).

5. "The New Korea: An Inside Look at South Korea's Economic Rise," Myung Oak Kim and Sam Jaffe, AMACOM, 2010.

6. Inspectors General of the Departments of State, Defense, and USAID, "Quarterly Progress and Oversight Report on the Civilian Assistance Program in Pakistan," March 31, 2013.

7. "GAO Report Suggests that USAID Remains More of a Contracting Agency Than an Operational Agency," Center for Economic and Policy Research, November 21, 2011.

8. "USAID Chief Chosen," *New York Times,* November 10, 2009.

9. Robert McMahon, "Q&A: Transforming U.S. Foreign Aid," *New York Times,* March 17, 2006.

10. "Afghanistan Life Expectancy Rising as Healthcare Improves, Survey Shows," Associated Press, November 30, 2011.

11. "Report of the Accountability Review Boards on the Embassy Bombings in Nairobi and Dar es Salaam on August 7, 1998," Crowe Commission Report, United States Department of State, January, 1999.

12. Stephen Barr, "At Foreign Service, Road to the Top Will Run Through Hardship Posts," *Washington Post,* December 10, 2004.

13. Nancy Dammann, *My 17 Years With USAID: The Good and the Bad*

(Coral Springs, Fla: Llumina Press, 2004).

14. "Hard Lessons, the Iraq Reconstruction Experience," Report of the Special Inspector General for Iraq Reconstruction, January, 2009.

15. United States Per Capita Consumption of Petroleum, United States Department of Energy, 2012.

16. Harry Bayard Price, *The Marshall Plan & Its Meaning* (Ithaca, N.Y.: Cornell University Press, 1955).

17. Ibid.

18. Ibid.

19. Ibid.

20. Ibid.

21. Executive Order 10924: Establishment of the Peace Corps, 1961.

INDEX

ABC Carpet and Home, 134–136
Abu Dhabi, 139
Abu Ghraib (town), 133
Abu Ghraib prisoner-abuse scandal, 28, 59
accusations of wrongdoing, 120–123,
    125–126, 130–131, 171–172
Adelphi Capital, 96
Adnan Palace, 129
Afghan First program, 266–268, 278,
    284–285, 291, 360–361
Afghanistan, 156, 177, 207–229, 231, 264,
    265, 282–293, 324
    agricultural development, 213–214,
        215–216, 223, 228, 273, 274–276,
        297, 299, 305–306
    banking sector, 278–279
    business delegation visits, 272–274,
        299–300
    corruption, 277, 301–304
    drug trade, 213–214, 215, 221
    foreign aid, failures of, 215–216,
        217–218, 221–224, 284–285, 309,
        319
    future outlook, 330–331
    Gross Domestic Product, 221, 227
    initial visit to, 14–16
    intranational trade, 225–226, 228
    lessons from Iraq applied to, 272, 278
    major project descriptions, 360–367
    military contracts, 68, 224–225, 278, 284

    mining industry, 198, 199, 210–211,
        216, 227–229, 271, 277–278,
        285–286, 292, 296, 297–298, 305,
        321–322, 330–331
    oil industry, 227–228, 296–297,
        320–321, 331
    Provincial Reconstruction Teams, 144
    security, 214–215, 218, 224, 270
    Soviet occupation, 14, 218, 268–269
    "surge" in, 265–266, 270, 282, 303
    Task Force budget crisis, 199, 264–268,
        270–271, 286–289, 294
    Task Force mission shutdown, 299, 301,
        306, 331–332
    Task Force operational location, 269–270
    technology sector, 289–291, 299–301,
        305
    USAID, 210–211, 215–216, 217–218,
        223–224, 272, 284–285, 286, 291,
        297, 314–315
    youth, 310–311
    See also ISAF; Karzai, Hamid; specific city;
        province
Afghanistan International Bank, 278–279
Afghan–Tajik Basin, 297
AFRICOM, 201–205
Agricultural Bank, 118
agricultural development
    Afghanistan, 213–214, 215–216,
        223, 228, 273, 274–276, 297, 299,

305–306
Africa, 197, 202
  Iraq, 66–67, 93–95, 109–111, 159–164,
    176, 196, 260
  major project descriptions, 345–367
  Pakistan, 235, 236, 237, 240
  See also Borlaug Institute
AIG, 262
airlines, 138
Ajmal Amir Kasab, Mohammed, 307–308
Alabbar, Mohamed, 299
Al Amarah, Iraq, 261
Al Anbar. *See* Anbar Province, Iraq
Al Araji, Sami, 70–71, 184
Al Faw Palace, 31, 34, 61, 83–84, 249
Allawi, Ayad, 253–254, 255
Allen, John, 28
Al-Maliki, Nouri. *See* Maliki, Nouri al-
Al Maysan sugar factory, 261
Al Qaeda, 26–28, 35, 59–60, 74, 99, 108,
    132, 212, 311, 328, 332
Al Qaim, Iraq, 102, 157, 180
Al Qaim Phosphates, 180
Al Rashid Hotel, 155
"American Dream," 3
American elections, 105, 164–165,
    175–179, 181–182
American Express, 184
American public opinion, 109, 168,
    181–182
American reconstruction, myth of, 309–310,
    312–313, 315
American University Kabul, 305, 331
Amman, Jordan meetings, 26–28
AMWAL, 184–185
Anbar Province, Iraq, 26–28, 29–30, 36, 61,
    74–76, 94, 95, 96, 157, 162, 172–174,
    180, 183, 258, 260, 347–348
Antoon, Basim, 244–245, 246, 247
"Arab Spring," 300, 332
Araji, Ahmed, 163
Araji, Sami al, 70–71, 184
ArcelorMittal, 156, 185–187
ARCENT (U.S. Army CENTCOM),
    264–265
Arellano, Bambi, 143
Assad, Shay, 68
Austin, Lloyd, 154–155, 176
Austrian Airways, 138

Baathists, 111–112
  See also de-Baathification of government

Baban, Ali, 196
Babil Province, Iraq, 36–43, 94, 95, 102,
    162, 348–350
Babylon Hotel bombing, 198, 241–251
Badr organization, 157
Baghdad, Iraq, 32, 99, 137–138
  Babylon Hotel bombing, 198, 241–251
  development projects, 81–82, 102,
    132–134, 138–141, 149–150, 155,
    162, 176, 182, 195, 257, 261–262,
    350–352
  "Restoring Law" (Fardh al Qanoon)
    campaign, 131–134
  Sadrist Party, 139, 153–154
  security collapse of 2005–06, 61, 83
  See also Camp Victory; Green Zone
Baghdad Province, Iraq, 36, 94, 95
Baghdad Security Plan, 131
Baghlan Province, Afghanistan, 285–286,
    305, 362
Bagram Air Base, 14
Baiji Fertilizer, 66–67, 96, 127, 180
Bailey, Tucker, 192
Baird, Mark, 128, 141, 154, 158, 180, 210
Baldridge, William, 118–119
banking-sector development, 116–117,
    118–119, 133, 141, 155, 184–185,
    278–279, 345–367
Bank of America, 262
Baqubah, Iraq, 99–100
Basra, Iraq, 139, 148–149, 150–156, 162,
    185–187, 192, 217–218, 219, 256, 257,
    258–259, 352–354
Basra Iron & Steel State Company, 151,
    185–187
Basra Province, Iraq, 150–151, 162
Bearden, Milt, 268–269, 289, 294
Bechtel, 57–58
Bedouin culture, 28
Berkshire Hathaway, 273
Berkson, Brad, 11–12, 13, 14, 21, 178
Berry Amendment, 68
Bloomberg, Michael, 242
Bloomberg Businessweek, 304–305
blue-chip companies, 238, 262, 312
BMMP (Business Management
    Modernization Program), 19–21, 87
body armor, 33, 137–138, 316
Boeing, 49, 182, 328
bombing in Herat restaurant, 292–293
bombing of Babylon Hotel, 198, 241–251
bombings of embassies in Kenya and

Tanzania, 59–60
Bonner, Rebekka, 264
Borlaug, Norman, 93
Borlaug Institute, 93–95, 97, 176, 209, 274, 306
Bowen, Stuart, 73, 105, 319–320
Brazil, 261
Bremer, L. Paul, 44
Brinkley, Cindy, 14, 126
British military forces, 148, 151–153, 213, 243
Brooks, Vince, 131–132
Brown, Gerry, 115–116, 135, 179–180, 183–184, 189, 200, 261
BTA (Business Transformation Agency), 23–28, 47, 49–50, 89–90, 137, 288
budget execution assistance, 113–115, 133, 142–146, 263
budget funding crisis, 199, 264–268, 270–271, 281–282, 286–289, 293–294
Buffett, Howard G., 199, 273
Buffett, Howard W., 273, 274–275
Buffett, Warren, 273
Bumpers Amendment, 160–161
Buntman, Noah, 261
bus factory, 35–43, 63
Bush, George H. W., 89
Bush, George W., 158, 166–169, 197
Bush Administration, 3, 18–24, 59, 73, 87, 89–90, 166–169, 175–176, 178, 179, 182, 183, 197, 202, 253, 259–260, 295, 314, 329
"business corps," 324–325
business delegation visits
    Afghanistan, 199, 272–274, 299–300
    Iraq, 96–101, 108–109, 149, 181–182, 185–187, 192, 248–250, 261–262
business incubators, 183–184, 241–242, 291–292, 300–301, 305
Business Management Modernization Program (BMMP), 19–21, 87
business training for factory managers, 141–142
Business Transformation Agency (BTA), 23–28, 47, 49–50, 89–90, 137, 288

Callaghan, Anne, 261
Camp Bastion, 213
Camp Fallujah, 29–30, 74
Camp Leatherneck, 213
Camp Pendleton, 24–25
Camp Taqqadim, 28–29

Camp Victory, 31–36, 43, 61, 78, 87–88, 95, 96, 100, 105, 181, 249–250
carpet production, 134–136, 193, 276, 331
"carrot and stick" strategy, 233, 311
Case New Holland (CNH), 110–111, 163, 191
Casey, George, 26, 33, 34, 61–62, 86, 90, 91–93, 94, 96, 98
cash-based system, 118–119, 184–185
Caterpillar, 96, 111
cell phones, 154, 220, 300, 308
cement production, 102, 117, 157, 180, 225
CENTCOM, 174–175, 178, 209, 264, 265, 268, 282–283, 306
Center, Will, 233, 235, 237
Center for a New American Security (CNAS), 179
Center for Strategic and International Studies (CSIS), 155, 332–333
Central Intelligence Agency, 89, 268–269
ceramics production, 74–76, 172–174
ceremonial check presentations, 127
CERP (Commanders Emergency Response Program), 266, 268, 288, 293
CFS Industries, 156
Chadderton, John, 243, 245, 246–247
Chaihorsky, Alex, 286, 298
Chandrasekaran, Rajiv, 56
Chang, Kyung-Soon, 185, 186, 248, 249
Chang, Sunyoung, 185–187
Charge of the Knights (Saulat al Fursan), 153–155
"Charlie Wilson's War," 268–269
"check" ceremonies, 127
Chiarelli, Peter, 33–36, 42–43, 45, 48, 62–63, 90, 91–93, 94, 102, 123, 155
Chicago Tribune, 156
Chile, 46
China National Petroleum Company, 256
Chinese investment, 227, 256, 277, 320, 321
Christian community, 244, 295
Chrysler, 262
Chu, David, 13
CHUs (containerized housing units), 78, 102, 110
Cisco Systems, 238
Citibank, 278–279
civilian body armor, 33, 137–138, 316
civilian service deployment model, 44, 224, 225, 317–319

civilian surge, 265–266, 270

Clark, Eric, 182, 187, 242, 244, 246, 248, 260, 261–262, 272, 273–274, 282, 289

Clinton, Hillary, 190, 234, 239, 265–266, 320

clothing factories, 63–65, 67–68, 102–103, 159–161, 299

CNAS (Center for a New American Security), 179

CNH (Case New Holland), 110–111, 163, 191

Coalition Provisional Authority (CPA), 43, 44, 46–47, 49, 51, 53–60, 66, 67, 68–69, 77, 78–79, 86, 112, 116, 143, 157, 265–266, 281

Code of Conduct violations, 120

Cold War, 2, 267, 269

colonialism, 63, 254

Commanders Emergency Response Program (CERP), 266, 268, 288, 293

Commerce Department, 150, 189–190, 233

commercial air service, 138

Congress
    Defense Department reporting to, 18, 19, 26, 86
    "highly qualified expert" hiring policy, 13
    Iraq Study Group, 88–89
    Task Force appropriations, 104–105, 162–163
    Task Force budget crisis, 281–282, 288–289, 293–294

containerized housing units (CHUs), 78, 102, 110

"contingency contracting," 25–26

contract management, 25–26, 47, 68, 77–78, 86, 208–209, 224–225, 278, 284–285, 319–320

contractors, 44, 85, 223, 317–318

contributors list, 339–344

copper mining, 210–211, 227, 228–229, 286, 296

corruption, 111–112, 113, 114, 118, 151–152, 232, 277, 301–304

COSIT, 101–102

cotton production, 133, 159–161, 215, 237, 240, 297

Council on Foreign Relations, 155

counterinsurgency strategies, 34–35, 47, 61–62, 92, 94, 105, 131–134, 105, 166, 214, 267, 272

CPA. See Coalition Provisional Authority

CPA Order, 12, 55

Crocker, Ryan, 104–105, 108, 127, 129, 142, 154, 175, 180–181, 182, 262

Crowe, William, 59

Crowe Commission, 59–60, 316, 318

CSIS (Center for Strategic and International Studies), 155, 332–333

C-SPAN, 129

Cummins Diesel, 96, 111

Daimler Benz, 116, 149–150, 183, 191

dairy operations, 133

Dawa Party, 139, 140

Dawood, Nadia, 279

de-Baathification, 53–54, 56, 57, 113, 320

Defense Authorization Bill, 293–294

Defense Business Board, 22, 122

Defense Department
    budget, 17, 20, 104–105, 312
    business operations, 16–17
    Congress, reporting to, 18, 19, 26, 86
    decentralized management structure, 17–18, 20
    financial reporting, 19–21
    legal framework/role and responsibility, 267
    modernization initiatives, 18–24, 87, 89–90
    recruitment of Paul Brinkley, 11–14
    workforce inventives, 18
    See also specific leader; organization

Defense Policy shop, 51

Delawari, Noor, 212–213

Department of Defense. See Defense Department

Department of State. See State Department

Deputy Secretary of Defense. See England, Gordon; Lynn, Bill; Wolfowitz, Paul

development aid. See foreign aid

Development Fund for Iraq (DFI), 54–55, 116–117

"development industrial complex," 311–312

Devine, John, 210–211, 216

DFI (Development Fund for Iraq), 54–55, 116–117

Dhi Qar Province, Iraq, 162, 354

Dimon, Jamie, 285–286

diplomacy versus development, 313, 314

Diyala Electric factory, 127, 180

Diyala Province, Iraq, 99–100, 161, 162, 354–355

Donohue, Rory, 215–216

Donohue, Thomas, Jr. 96, 192

Donohue, Thomas Sr., 72–73, 96
dot-com bubble, 9–10
Doura neighborhood, 132
Dowdy, John, 53, 63, 64, 69, 71–72, 141, 200, 208, 209
Dozier, Tanisha, 242, 244, 246
drone attacks, 235, 311
drug trade, 213–214, 215, 221
Dubey, Regina, 173–174, 184, 195, 200, 221, 241, 260
"duck and cover" bunkers, 83
Duncan, Bill, 85, 115–116, 130, 297, 298–299

Earl, Robert, 49, 50, 121, 166
Eastern European model, 45–46, 67, 104
Eaton Corporation, 183
Economic Cooperation Administration (ECA), 322–324
economic development. *See* foreign aid; Task Force for Business and Stability Operations; USAID
economic prosperity, access to, 2–5, 107–108, 231–232, 235, 307–313, 320
economic shock therapy, 45–46, 54–56, 67, 262
Edelman, Eric, 50–51
educational initiatives, 305–306, 331, 348
Eikenberry, Karl, 209, 212, 220–221, 273, 278, 282
elections. *See* American elections; Iraq
electricity, 55, 66, 78–79, 100, 157, 182, 259, 260, 311
electronic financial transactions, 118–119, 133, 184–185
Emaar Properties, 299
England, Gordon, 23, 48–49, 50, 52, 61, 62, 72, 73, 86, 101, 121, 122–123, 125, 129, 130–131, 147, 158, 166, 167, 168, 169, 174–175, 178, 196, 197, 288, 324
"enterprise zones," 235
Etihad Airways, 138
Euphrates River, 29, 163
Export-Import Bank, 182
ExxonMobil, 256

Facebook, 300
factories, 321
    assessments of, 48, 53, 63–68, 73–79, 192
    "big check" ceremonies, 127
    business training for managers, 141–142
    financial account seizures, 54–55, 116–117
    job restoration, 129–130, 263
    pre-/post-Saddam economy, 54–56, 82
    sectarian patterns, 78–79
    self-confidence, 82–83
    shock therapy, 45–46, 54–56, 67, 262
    state-owned enterprises, restarting of, 45–47, 49, 63–70, 116–117, 157, 167–168, 180, 262
    "top ten" list of, 85, 103, 129
    See also business delegation visits; *specific industry*
failure, cycle of, 312
Fallujah, Iraq, 27, 74
Fallujah Cement, 180
false accusations, 120–123, 125–126, 130–131, 171–172
Farber, Darren, 78, 118–119, 141, 204, 208–209, 224–225, 278, 284–285, 291
Fardh al Qanoon ("Restoring Law"), 131–134
farming. *See* agricultural development
Fast Company magazine, 305
fatalistic attitude, 154
fertilizer production, 66–67, 127, 156, 180
Fiat, 110
Fil, Joseph, 96, 132
financial crisis of 2008, 156
financial infrastructure. *See* banking-sector development
financial return on investment, 107
First Marine Expeditionary Force (I-MEF), 24–30, 47, 61, 96
Fisher, David, 89
"flash-bang" grenades, 292–293
flat organizational structure, 180
Flournoy, Michele, 179
food processing, 96, 97, 216–217, 228, 331
Foreign Agricultural Service, 161–162
foreign aid
    budgets, 311–312
    Cold War origins of, 2
    versus economic development, 314–315
    failures of, 2–4, 215–216, 217–218, 221–224, 284–285, 311–312, 319–320
    organizational structure, 313–314
    solutions for fixing, 313–325
    See also USAID
Foreign Corrupt Practices Act, 112
foreign service deployment model, 44, 224,

225, 317–319

Fortune magazine, 305

Forward Operating Base Kalsu, 36–37, 48

free market policies, 46, 55, 67, 82, 116, 309

free trade zones, 235

Friedman, Milton, 46

Friedman, Thomas J., 40, 63, 308

funding crisis, 199, 264–268, 270–271, 281–282, 286–289, 293–294

garment manufacturing, 63–65, 67–68, 102–103, 159–161, 299

gas flares, 195, 258–260

Gates, Robert, 4, 89, 123, 125, 158, 167, 168, 169, 177–178, 183, 189, 197, 221, 229, 249, 264–265, 266, 281, 287–288, 296, 306, 327

Geary, Steve, 115–116, 130

General Dynamics, 21

General Electric, 17, 57–58, 182, 183, 328

General Motors, 17, 262

German investment, 149–150, 290

See also specific company

Ghani, Ashraf, 210, 283–284, 285

Gibson, Jay, 178

Gimbel, Barney, 200, 272, 274

Gingrich, Newt, 104

glass manufacturing, 74–76

global financial crisis of 2008, 156

GOCO (government-owned-contractor-operated) facilities, 49

gold mining, 210–211, 227, 228, 285–286, 296, 305

goodwill, 60, 110, 127, 217–218, 311–312, 319–320, 324

Google, 182, 261–262, 299–301, 305

Government Accountability Office (GAO), 23–24, 284, 312

government-owned-contractor-operated (GOCO) facilities, 49

Grant Thornton LLP, 114–115, 157, 209–210

Gration, Scott, 202, 204

greenhouse program, 163–164, 191, 196, 260

Greenstock, Jeremy, 243

Green Zone
  bureaucratic "beast," 84–85, 137
  containerized housing units (CHUs), 78
  hotel investment projects, 138–141
  Iraq Reconstruction Management Office, 43–46
  restrictive security policies, 45, 60, 84–85, 95, 143, 144, 295
  rocket attacks, 83–84, 131, 153–154, 158–159, 331
  Task Force facilities, 128, 131, 134, 180–181, 183–184, 241–242
  USAID budget execution training, 113–114, 143

Groundworks International, 154

Gryphon Air, 138

Gulf Air, 138

Gulf War I, 135, 152

Haag, Kris, 29, 44, 48, 52, 77–78, 118–119, 141, 179, 180, 184–185, 208, 221, 278–279, 292, 293, 296, 306, 331

Hadley, Stephen, 167

Hale, Robert, 266–268, 287, 288, 293

Hamre, John, 332–333

Hannam, Ian, 273, 285–286

"Han River Miracle," 186, 310

hardship postings, 317, 318

Hariri, Fawzi, 117, 129, 156, 157, 184

Harriman, Averill, 322

Harrods of London, 135

Head, Graham, 134, 135

Heavy Engineering and Equipment Supply Company (HEESCO), 132

Helmand Province, Afghanistan, 198, 213–216, 269, 297–299, 363

Herat, Afghanistan, 216–218, 269, 273, 289–293, 299, 300–301, 305, 306, 363–364

Herat University, 289–291, 306

heroin production, 213–214, 215, 221

Hewlett-Packard, 29

"highly qualified expert" hiring policy, 13

Hill, Christopher, 250, 262, 295

Hillah, Iraq, 102

hiring freeze, 199, 270–271, 292, 298–299

Hoffman, Paul G., 323

Holbrooke, Richard, 232–233, 240, 264, 265–266, 294, 311

Holmes, Greg, 154

Holmes, Zoraida, 154

Honeywell, 182

hotel investment projects, 138–141, 155, 257

Howard G. Buffett Foundation, 273, 274, 305–306

humanitarian aid, 2, 62, 314–315

Humvees, 37–38, 65
Hussein, Saddam, 31, 32, 34, 54, 92,
    134–135, 152, 254, 255
Hyatt Hotels, 155
Hyundai Heavy Industries, 185

IBM, 12, 182, 238, 299, 301, 305
IEDs (improvised explosive devices), 37,
    65, 74
I-MEF (First Marine Expeditionary Force),
    24–30, 47, 61, 96
Immeldt, Jeffrey, 182
Imperial Life in the Emerald City
    (Chandrasekaran), 56
incubator compounds, 183–184, 241–242,
    291–292, 300–301, 305
India, terrorist attacks in, 231, 233,
    238–239, 307–308
industrial operations. *See* factories; mining
information technology. *See* technology
    sector
infrastructure programs, failure of, 56–58,
    223, 319–322
Institute for Defense and Business, 192
insurgents. *See* terrorists and insurgents
International Security Assistance Force. *See*
    ISAF
International Steel Group, 156
Internet bubble, 9–10
intranational trade, 225–226, 228
investigations into wrongdoing, 120–123,
    125–126, 130–131, 171–172
Iran, 28, 63, 64, 139, 140, 157, 164, 217,
    255, 330
Iran-Iraq War, 116, 134, 152
Iraq
    Al Qaeda, 26–28, 35, 74, 99, 108, 132,
        212, 328, 332
    budget execution assistance, 113–115,
        133, 142–146, 263
    business delegation visits, 96–101,
        108–109, 149, 181–182, 185–187,
        192, 248–250, 261–262
    corruption, 111–112, 113, 114
    de-Baathification of government, 53–54,
        56, 57, 113, 320
    elections of 2010, 190, 253–254, 255,
        256
    failed public infrastructure programs,
        56–58, 319–320
    future outlook, 328–331, 332
    intracountry trade relationships, 77

major project descriptions, 345–360
military surge, 105, 131–134, 144, 166,
    265–266, 295–296
military withdrawal, 177, 188–189, 253,
    329–330
post-Saddam reconstruction, 56–58
pre-/post-Saddam economy, 53–56, 82
unemployment, 101–102
See also Green Zone; Hussein, Saddam;
    terrorists and insurgents; *specific city;
    industry; province*
Iraqi Army, 53, 57, 68, 102, 131, 153–155,
    320
Iraqi First program, 26, 47, 67–68, 117,
    118, 133, 141, 184–185, 266
Iraqi Geological Survey, 183, 258
Iraq Reconstruction Management Office.
    See IRMO
Iraq Relief and Reconstruction Fund
    (IRRF), 56–58
Iraq Study Group, 88–89
Irbil, Kurdistan, 96, 141, 244, 355
IRMO (Iraq Reconstruction Management
    Office), 43–47, 48, 59, 67, 68–70,
    84–85, 95, 142–143, 190
IRRF (Iraq Relief and Reconstruction
    Fund), 56–58
ISAF (International Security Assistance
    Force), 175, 199, 212, 218, 264, 265,
    269, 270, 272, 273, 278, 282, 283–284,
    285, 287, 301, 330–331
ISCI (Islamic Supreme Counsel of Iraq),
    139, 140
Iskandiriyah, Iraq, 36–43, 44, 46–47, 53,
    61, 63, 78, 96, 102, 110–111, 115–116,
    130, 149–150, 163, 191
Islam, 304
    Al Qaeda, 28
    "Arab Spring," 332
    Pakistan, 231–233, 235, 239, 295,
        307–308
    radicalization of youth, 231–232,
        307–312
    See also Shia; Sunni
Islamabad, Pakistan, 138–139, 233,
    234–235, 236, 237, 240
Islamic Dawa Party, 139, 140
Islamic *madrassas,* 231
Islamic Supreme Counsel of Iraq (ISCI),
    139, 140
IT. *See* technology sector

Jabr, Bayan, 116, 117, 129
Jaish al Mahdi militia, 83–84, 139, 153–155
Jalalabad, Afghanistan, 269, 274, 305–306
Jamali, Rafique, 234
Japan, 147–149, 150, 309
J.C. Penney, 159
JDS Uniphase, 9–12, 23, 42, 85, 90, 261
Jeffrey, James, 295
jet lag, 65, 84, 87, 91, 101, 165, 242
JGC, 148
jihad, 231
job restoration, 129–130, 263
job rotation, 224, 225, 317–319
Joint Contracting Command, 31, 48,
    136–137, 208–209, 263, 278
Joint Special Operations Command, 212
Joint Visitors Bureau Hotel, 31, 87–88, 96
Jonas, Tina, 50
Jones, Hope, 189
Jones, James, 190
Jones, Jerry, 94, 178, 200
J.P. Morgan, 118, 273, 285–286, 305

Kabul, Afghanistan, 199, 212–213,
    218–220, 223–224, 269–270, 273, 277,
    331, 364–365
Kabul Bank, 279
Kagame, Paul, 203, 204
Kandahar, Afghanistan, 269, 299, 365
Karachi, Pakistan, 238–239, 240
Karbala, Iraq, 157, 163–164, 257, 355–356
Karzai, Ahmed Wali, 299
Karzai, Hamid, 222, 276–278, 282–283,
    299, 303–304
Kashkari Block, 296–297
kate spade new york, 299
Kennedy, John F., 324
Kennedy, Kevin, 23
Kenney, James, 159
Kerry-Lugar Act, 233, 311, 319
Khadimiyah, Iraq, 133, 135–136
Khafaji, Sabah al, 39–43, 63, 78, 191
Khalilzad, Zalmay, 68–69, 84, 127, 144,
    208
Khan Neshin Mountain, 198, 297–298
Kian, Bijan, 182
Kicklighter, Claude "Mick," 51, 130–131
kidnappings, 143
Kimmitt, Mark, 178
Kimmitt, Robert, 119
King, Liz, 268, 288
King, Scott, 114–115, 140, 142, 157, 189,

195, 200, 208, 209–210, 297
Kirkuk Province, Iraq, 161, 356
Korea Gas, 256
Korean War, 186, 310, 323
Krieg, Ken, 50, 51–52, 130, 172
Kudla, David, 115–116, 200
Kunesh, Nicholas, 147–148, 149
Kurdistan, 96, 101, 113, 135, 136, 141,
    172–173, 183, 185–187, 193, 244, 257,
    328, 332, 355

Lahore, Pakistan, 200, 235–238, 239–240
land-grant universities, 93–94, 97, 161–162,
    202, 239–240
Lashkar-e-Taiba (LeT), 307–308
Lashkar Gah, Afghanistan, 213, 215–216,
    297
Law, Beth, 127–128, 137, 158, 179,
    187–188
Law, Steve, 128, 188
League of Nations, 254
Legislative Affairs Office, 104, 268, 293,
    294
Lehman Brothers failure, 156
LG Corp., 185
loan programs, 117, 147–149, 150
Locke, Gary, 190
Lockheed Martin, 49
LoNigro, Elizabeth, 242, 244, 246, 322
Lopez, Julie, 210
Love, Bob, 23, 25–27, 28–29, 44, 52, 61,
    72, 78, 81–82, 84, 97, 98, 105, 127, 137,
    141, 158, 192, 197, 200, 201, 204–205
LS Industries, 185
Lukoil, 256
Lumish, Stan, 182, 261, 291, 292
Lundquist, Jerry, 141
Lute, Douglas, 157–158
Lynn, Bill, 287–288
Lyons, John, 200

MacArthur, Douglas, 309
madrassas, 231
Mahboob, Roya, 290–291
Maliki, Nouri al-, 113, 129, 139, 140, 254,
    276–278, 329–330
Mandviwalla, Saleem, 200, 234, 235
Mansour neighborhood, 143
Marmon Group, 155
Marriott, William, 138–139
Marriott Corporation, 138–139, 203
Marshall, George C., 322

Marshall Plan, 56, 309, 322–324
Marshall Plan and Its Meaning, The (Price), 322–324
"marsh Arab" culture, 139–140, 261
MasterCard, 184
Mattis, James, 306
Maysan Province, Iraq, 261, 356–357
Mazar e Sharif, Afghanistan, 218, 269, 296, 365
MCC, 227
McCain, John, 176
McChrystal, Stanley, 212, 220–221, 264, 265, 272, 273, 276–278, 282
McColm, Victoria, 292
McDonnell Douglas, 85
McFarland, Sean, 28
McGrath, Elizabeth, 89–90
McKinsey & Co., 14, 53, 71–72, 85, 141–142, 209, 263
McMaster, H. R., 301
McSherry, Rod, 162
Meals-Ready-to-Eat (MREs), 65
media. *See* news media
Medlin, Jack, 199, 210–211, 216
Meese, Michael, 98–99
Microsoft, 182, 261
military surge
  Afghanistan, 282, 303
  Iraq, 105, 131–134, 144, 166, 265–266, 295–296
military withdrawal from Iraq, 177, 188–189, 253, 329–330
Millennium Challenge Corporation, 50
Miller, Bob, 199
mining industry
  Afghanistan, 198, 199, 210–211, 216, 227–229, 271, 277–278, 285–286, 292, 296, 297–298, 305, 321–322, 330–331
  Iraq, 183, 258
  Pakistan, 240
"Miracle on the Han River," 186, 310
Mississippi State University, 162
Mitsubishi Heavy Industries, 100, 148
Mittal, Aditya, 156
MNCI (Multi-National Corps–Iraq), 33–36, 62, 72, 85, 91–93, 98, 127, 154–155, 165, 176, 192
MNFB (Multi-National Force–Baghdad), 96, 131–132
MNFI (Multi-National Force–Iraq), 26, 31–33, 43, 47, 49, 61–62, 67–68, 72, 84–85, 91–93, 98, 127, 165, 174–175, 176, 184, 264
mobile telephones, 154, 220, 300, 308
Modly, Tom, 21–22, 23, 24, 48, 49–50, 52, 74–76, 87, 89–90, 126, 178, 184, 200, 208
Moore, Thomas "Tango," 92, 98
Morgan Stanley, 155
Mosul, Iraq, 93, 162, 261
MREs (Meals-Ready-to-Eat), 65
Mullen, Michael, 158, 221, 306
Mumbai terrorist attacks, 231, 233, 238–239, 307–308
Musharraf, Pervez, 232
M.W. Kellogg & Co., 66
myth of American reconstruction, 309–310, 312–313, 315

Naderi, Sadat, 285–286, 305
Nagl, John, 179
Najaf, Iraq, 63–65, 67–68, 102–103, 162, 257, 357
Najaf Province, Iraq, 64, 162
Nassr industrial operations, 96, 102
Natale, Ronald, 188
National Defense Authorization Act of 2005, 24
National Investment Commission (NIC), 139, 140, 183–184
nationalism, 30, 329
National Security Council, 157–158, 295, 314
National Security Presidential Directives (NSPDs), 59
nation building, 142
NATO forces, 212, 218, 232, 284
natural gas, 66, 203, 258–260
NBC News, 102–103
Negroponte, John, 147
Neller, Robert, 29
NeoIT, 305
news media, 207, 234
  Afghanistan, 274, 304–305
  General McChrystal interview, 282
  negative focus, 30, 71, 105, 112, 129
  Task Force mission, 90, 102–104, 122, 125, 129, 156, 248–249, 304–305
Newsweek magazine, 103–104, 207
NIC (National Investment Commission), 139, 140, 183–184
Nicholson, Lawrence, 213
9/11 terrorist attacks, 19, 311

Nippon Koei, 148
Northern Fertilizer Company, 66–67
Northrup Grumman, 49
NSPDs (National Security Presidential Directives), 59

Obama Administration, 175–179, 181–182, 202, 232, 259–260, 262–263, 281, 282, 329–330
Odierno, Raymond, 92, 96, 97, 131, 154, 176, 178, 182, 192, 248, 249–250, 264
Office of the General Counsel (OGC), 264–265, 288
Office of the Secretary of Defense (OSD), 17, 22, 23, 50, 265
oil and gas industry
    Afghanistan, 227–228, 296–297, 320–321, 331
    Iraq, 57, 73, 111, 151, 163, 192, 195, 255–260, 320–321, 322, 328–329, 332
    See also gas flares
oil-based command societies, 111
Oklahoma State, 162
Operation Enduring Freedom, 229
Operation Iraqi Freedom, 229
opium production, 213–214, 215, 221
organic cotton, 159–161
OSD (Office of the Secretary of Defense), 17, 22, 23, 50, 265
O'Sullivan, Meghan, 157–158
Othman, Sadi, 102–103
Oval Office briefing, 166–169, 197
Overseas Private Investment Corporation (OPIC), 141

PAC (Procurement Assistance Center), 114–115, 142–144, 263
Pair, Carlos "Butch," 137, 165, 183
Pakistan, 200, 231–240, 263–264, 265
    failed public infrastructure programs, 319, 321
    future outlook, 332
    Hillary Clinton tour, 234, 239, 320
    radical elements, 138–139, 231–233, 235, 238–239, 294–295, 307–308, 311, 332
    Task Force shutdown, 268
Pakistan People's Party, 232
Palestine Hotel, 242, 243
Panjshir Valley, 218, 366
Parwan Province, Afghanistan, 218, 366

patronage systems, 302, 303
Pazyryk carpets, 136
Peace Corps, 324
Pearl, Daniel, 238
pediatric cancer, 195, 259, 260
Penn State, 162
Pentagon. *See* Defense Department
Perkins, David, 176
Petraeus, David H., 158, 306
    Afghanistan, 174–175, 199, 207–208, 209, 264, 273, 282–283, 287, 300
    Iraq, 93, 94, 98–99, 102–103, 105, 126, 129, 131, 138, 159, 166, 173, 174–175, 178, 182
    leadership style, 175
    Pakistan, 232, 265
petrochemical industry, 73, 151
PETRONAS, 256
phosphate production, 102, 180
Pinochet, Augusto, 46
Pohong Iron & Steel (POSCO), 185–187
political parties, 139, 253–254
pomegranates, 276
poppy trade, 213–214, 215, 221
potato seed episode, 94–95, 98
Pottery Barn Rule, 3
Powell, Bill, 192
Powell, Colin, 3
PPAT (Provincial Procurement Assistance Teams), 142, 144, 145–146
Price, Ed, 94, 95, 200, 209, 210, 215–216, 274
Price, Harry Bayard, 322–324
PricewaterhouseCoopers, 184
Pritzker, Tom, 155–156
private security forces, 57–58, 60, 215, 316
privatization of state-owned enterprises, 49, 117, 157, 180, 262
Proctor & Gamble, 238
Procurement Assistance Center (PAC), 114–115, 142–144, 263
project descriptions list, 345–367
Provincial Procurement Assistance Teams (PPAT), 142, 144, 145–146
Provincial Reconstruction Teams (PRTs), 137–138, 144–146, 162, 261, 262
public infrastructure programs, 56–58, 223, 319–322
Punjab Province, Pakistan, 235, 268, 294–295, 307–308
pyramid organizational structure, 165, 180

Qadir, Abdul, 129
Qom, Iran, 63, 64
Qubaysah, Iraq, 157
"quick-reaction" agreements, 270

Rafidain Bank, 117, 118
Rahimi, Asif, 212–213
raisin production, 275, 299
Ramadi, Iraq, 30, 74–76, 162, 172–174
Ramadi Ceramics, 172–174
Rangel, Robert, 177–178, 249, 287, 288
Raphel, Robin, 233–234, 240
rare-earth mining, 211, 228, 298
Rashid Bank, 118
Raytheon, 287
Reagan, Ronald, 1
"red zone," 137–138, 247, 249
regional-expert model, 317–319
Reist, David, 25, 26–28, 29, 61
religion. *See* Islam; Shia; Sunni
Republican Palace, 131, 143, 154, 159, 194
"Restoring Law" (Fardh al Qanoon),
    131–134
Ridha, Ahmed, 139, 140
Ringrose, Richard, 135–136
rocket attacks, 83–84, 131, 151–152,
    153–154, 158–159, 331
Rolling Stone magazine, 282
Rotana Hotel, 139–141
Royal Dutch Shell, 258–259
Rumsfeld, Donald, 18–19, 87–88, 89
Rwanda, 203

Saba, Daud Shah, 291–292
Sabah al Khafaji, 39–43, 63, 78, 308
Sadr, Moqtada al, 139
Sadr City neighborhood, 83–84, 139,
    153–154
Sadrist Party, 139–140, 153–155
saffron farming, 275–276
Saguid, Dionasis "JoJo," 158–159
Salah ad-Din Province, Iraq, 32–33, 92,
    162, 359
Salih, Barham, 112–113
Saloom, Joseph, 44
Samora, Joseph, 110
Sanderson, Lee, 184, 305, 331
satellite television, 2, 231–232, 300, 308
Saudi Arabia, 231, 254, 255, 329
Saulat al Fursan (Charge of the Knights),
    153–155
Scania trucks, 39, 191

Scantling, David, 29, 44, 52, 100, 141, 200,
    261
Schlumberger, 299
Schmidt, Joachim, 149
Schoeffling, Matthew, 129, 137, 148–149,
    155, 179, 180, 185–187, 188, 200, 208,
    209, 221, 236, 239, 242, 243, 244, 246,
    247, 249, 268–269, 289, 292, 293
Schwartz, Todd, 98, 104–105
Scott, Darryl, 26, 31, 43, 46–47, 48,
    53, 67–68, 69, 72, 78, 117, 118–119,
    136–137, 263
Scott, Emily, 198, 286, 298
SDL Incorporated, 9
Secretary of Defense. *See* Gates, Robert;
    Rumsfeld, Donald
sectarian tensions, 28, 30, 36, 78–79, 113,
    254–255, 257, 328, 332
security collapse of 2005–06, 36, 61, 83,
    112, 151–152
security restrictions
    Afghanistan, 214–215, 218, 224, 270
    civilian body armor, 33, 137–138, 316
    Green Zone, 45, 60, 84–85, 95, 143,
        144, 295
    reforms proposed for, 316, 318–319
    State Department, 45, 59–60, 67, 84–85,
        95, 143, 144–145, 295, 310
    Sudan, 204
seed potato shortage, 94–95, 98
Senior Executive Service (SES) Association,
    13
September 11, 2001, 19, 311
Shabibi, Sinan, 196
Shahrani, Wahidullah, 212–213, 271,
    285–286
Shahrastani, Hussein, 258
Sharia law, 28, 304
Sharif, Nawaz, 332
Shenk, Rudi, 275–276, 299
Sheraton Hotel, 155, 242, 247
Shia, 32
    factories, 78–79
    holy cities, 63–64, 163–164, 257
    militias, 35, 63, 83–84, 108, 148,
        151–155, 157, 328
    oil resources, 257–258
    political parties, 139–140, 253–254, 255
    siege mentality, 254–255
    tensions with Sunni, 28, 30, 36, 78–79,
        113, 254–255, 257, 328, 332
    trade relationships with Sunni, 77

shock therapy, 45–46, 54–56, 67, 262
Silicon Valley, 10, 305
Silk Road, 226
Sistani, Ayatollah Ali, 63, 64
Snyder, Tom, 52, 63, 128, 154
soccer ball manufacturing, 81–82, 102, 168–169
socialism, 45–46, 67, 69, 167, 218, 262–263
Society for World Interbank Financial Telecommunication (SWIFT) transactions, 119
soft loan funding, 147–149, 150
"soft objectives," 234
soft power efforts, 92
sour gas, 66
Southern Fertilizer Company, 66
South Korea, 185–187, 248–250, 276, 310, 320
South Sudan, 197, 202
Soviet occupation, 14, 218, 268–269
Special Representative for Afghanistan and Pakistan (SRAP), 264
Spicer, Tim, 243
spoils systems, 302, 303
SRAP (Special Representative for Afghanistan and Pakistan), 264
start-up incubators, 183–184, 241–242, 291–292, 300–301, 305
State Company for Automotive Industries, 191
State Company for Hand Woven Carpet, 135–136
State Company for Mechanical Industries, 110–111
State Company for Ready-Made Clothing, 63–64
State Department, 98, 127, 180–181, 323
　Afghanistan, 209, 212, 220–221, 270, 272, 283–284, 285
　Africa, 202, 203–204, 205
　anticorruption efforts, 112
　Bumpers Amendment, 160–161
　business expertise, lack of, 44, 262, 321
　CPA transfer to, 51, 59
　humanitarian relief, 62, 314–315
　ideological views on development, 262–263
　organizational realignment, need for, 267, 313–314
　procurement assistance, 113–114, 142–146
　restrictive security policies, 45, 59–60, 67, 84–85, 95, 143, 144–145, 295, 310, 316
　Task Force budget crisis, 265, 281–282, 289, 294
　Task Force shutdown, 295, 306, 331
　Washington, D.C. conference, 189–190
　See also Crocker, Ryan; Eikenberry, Karl; Hill, Christopher; Holbrooke, Richard; IRMO; Khalilzad, Zalmay; Provincial Reconstruction Teams; USAID
state-owned enterprises, 42, 45–47, 49, 54–55, 63–70, 101–102, 116–117, 157, 167–168, 180, 215, 262
Status of Forces Agreement, 188–189, 253, 329
Steele, Sara, 184, 195
steel industry, 132, 151, 156, 163, 185–187
Stephens, Sonja, 158, 189, 248
Stoner, John, 141–142, 200
Strong, Bill, 155, 156
Studebaker Motor Company, 323
STX, 186
Sudan, 202, 204
sugar processing, 261
Sunni, 32, 139, 254, 329
　Al Qaeda, support for, 26–28, 132
　Amman, Jordan meetings, 26–28
　elections of 2010, 253–254, 255
　factories, 78–79
　oil resources, 257–258
　rocket attacks, 83
　tensions with Shia, 28, 30, 36, 78–79, 113, 254–255, 257, 328, 332
　trade relationships with Shia, 77
　Triangle of Death, 36, 95
Sunni Awakening, 28
supply chain management, 10, 11–12, 17
surge. *See* civilian surge; military surge
Swartz, Esther, 104, 179, 294
SWIFT (Society for World Interbank Financial Telecommunication) transactions, 119
Sykes-Picot Agreement, 254
Symington, Stu, 203
Syria, 74, 102, 254, 258, 330, 332

Taji, Iraq, 96, 102
Taliban, 213, 214, 232, 270, 302, 304, 311
Tareen, Shaukat, 234
tariff policies, 55, 82, 116, 164
Tarmiyah, Iraq, 32–33, 191

Taseer, Salman, 200, 235, 268, 294–295
Task Force for Business and Stability
Operations (TFBSO), 52–53
"big check" ceremonies, 127
budget execution assistance, 113–115,
133, 142–146, 263
budget funding crisis, 199, 264–268,
270–271, 281–282, 286–289,
293–294
business-incubator compounds, 183–184,
241–242, 291–292, 300–301, 305
business training for factory managers,
141–142
congressional appropriations for,
104–105, 162–163
continuity of engagement, 317–319
economic effectiveness, 263
establishment, 48–52
factory assessments, 48, 53, 63–68,
73–79, 192
"feeding the bureaucratic beast," 84–85,
137
foreign investments results, 263
Green Zone facilities, 128, 131, 134,
180–181, 183–184, 241–242
investigation of wrongdoing by, 120–123,
125–126, 130–131, 171–172
IRMO hostility, 43–47, 48, 68–70,
84–85, 95, 142
job restoration, 129–130, 263
legislative roadblocks to restarting
factories, 68, 86–87, 160–161
major project descriptions, 345–367
personnel management, 85–86, 87
shut down of missions, 200, 268, 294,
295–296, 299, 306, 331–332
staff at Republican Palace, 194
state-owned enterprises, restarting of,
45–47, 49, 63–70, 116–117, 157,
167–168, 180, 262
"top ten" list of factories, 85, 103, 129
working in harm's way, 62, 91, 318–319
See also business delegation visits; *specific
geographical location; industry*
Technical University of Berlin, 290
technology sector, 182, 261–262, 289–291,
299–301, 305
terrorists and insurgents
Babylon Hotel bombing, 198, 241–251
economic motives, 34–35, 53, 231–232,
307–313, 332
financial transactions, 119

Green Zone rocket attacks, 83–84, 131,
153–154, 158–159, 331
Herat restaurant bombing, 292–293
IEDs, 37, 65, 74
Kenya and Tanzania embassy bombings,
59–60
Pakistan, 138–139, 231–233, 235,
238–239, 294–295, 307–308, 311,
332
Salah ad-Din Province, 32
security collapse of 2005–06, 36, 61, 83,
112, 151–152
Shia militias, 35, 63, 83–84, 108, 148,
151–155, 157, 328
Triangle of Death, 36, 95
See also Al Qaeda; counterinsurgency
strategies
Texas A&M University, 89, 93, 162, 274
textiles, 63–65, 67–68, 102–103, 133,
159–161, 203, 215, 235, 236, 237, 240
See also carpet production
TFBSO. *See* Task Force for Business and
Stability Operations
Tigris River, 32, 60, 132
Tikrit, Iraq, 32
tractor assembly, 109–111, 163, 191
Trade Bank of Iraq, 118
trade policies, 55, 82, 116, 164
trade relationships, 77, 225–226, 228
trailers. *See* containerized housing units
(CHUs)
travertine, 216
Treanor, Mark, 99
Treasury Department, 118–119, 142
Triangle of Death, 36, 95
Triton Containers, 155
truck-assembly operations, 116, 149–150,
191
Truman, Harry S., 322–324
Twitter, 300

UAE (United Arab Emirates), 180–181, 182
Uhrig, Scott, 11
Umm Qasr, Iraq, 148, 150–151
unemployment, 101–102
Uniform Code of Military Justice, 120
United Arab Emirates (UAE), 180–181, 182
United Nations sanctions, 54, 55, 77,
109–110
United States Institute for Peace, 89
universities, 289–291, 305–306
See also land-grant universities

University of Idaho, 163
University of Juba, 202
University of Maryland, 162
USAID (U.S. Agency for International
  Development)
  Afghanistan, 210–211, 215–216,
    217–218, 223–224, 272, 284–285,
    286, 291, 297, 314–315
  Africa, 202, 203–204
  agricultural development, 95, 160–161,
    176, 215–216, 223, 297
  budget execution training, 113–114, 143
  contract system, 284–285, 311–312
  humanitarian relief, 62, 314–315
  Pakistan, 234, 240
  post-Saddam reconstruction, 56–57
  private investment fund request, 104–105
  reforms proposed for, 313–315
  restrictive security policies, 143, 204,
    295, 310
  Task Force budget crisis, 281–282,
    293–294, 306
  Task Force mission moved to, 294,
    295–296, 331–332
U.S. Army CENTCOM (ARCENT),
  264–265
U.S. Army Corps of Engineers, 32, 56–57,
  105, 133, 319
U.S. Chamber of Commerce, 72–73, 96,
  97–98, 122
U.S. Commerce Department, 150,
  189–190, 233
U.S. Department of Agriculture (USDA),
  160–162, 176
U.S. embassies. *See* State Department
U.S. Food and Drug Administration, 275
U.S. Geological Survey (USGS), 182–183,
  199, 210–211, 227, 237, 240, 257–258,
  286, 298
Uskowi, Nader, 289, 291, 292

Vashistha, Atul, 305
Vicario, Courtney, 204
Virginia Tech, 162, 202
Visa, 184

Wachovia Corporation, 99
Wall Street Journal, 104
Ward, William "Kip," 204
Warfighter Support Office, 23, 25
Washington, D.C. conference of 2009,
  189–190

Wasit Province, Iraq, 162, 360
Werner, Llewelyn, 188
Wesa, Toryalai, 299
whistleblower protection, 122
Wilson, Steve, 156
Winn, Shawn, 82
Wolfowitz, Paul, 22
Women for Women, 184
women's business development, 184, 240,
  305, 331
World Bank, 56, 101
World Is Flat, The (Friedman), 40, 63, 308
Wynne, Mike, 21, 50, 51, 137

youth, 3, 35, 231–232, 235, 307–312, 320,
  330, 332
YouTube, 299–300

Zakaria, Fareed, 103–104, 207
Zakheim, Dov, 19
"zero tariff" regime, 55, 82, 116
Zilmer, Richard, 25, 26, 29, 96
Zubai, Hoshyar, 129

PAUL A. BRINKLEY

served five years as Deputy Under Secretary of Defense and
director of the Task Force for Business and Stability Operations,
charged with revitalizing the economies of Iraq and Afghanistan. He
is the recipient of the Joint Distinguished Civilian Service Medal
and the Secretary of Defense–Defense of Freedom Medal. Currently,
Brinkley is President and CEO of North America Western Asia
Holdings. He has published articles in *Newsweek* and *Military Review*
and has been profiled in *Businessweek, Fortune, New York Times,
Washington Post, Der Spiegel,* and *The Economist.*